Andrew Bender

# Amsterdam

## The Top Five

**1 Albert Cuypmarkt**
Sample the wares at Amsterdam's
biggest street market (p113)
**2 Rijksmuseum**
See what made the Dutch masters
(p110)
**3 Canals**
Explore the city from a different
perspective (p56)
**4 The Dam**
Visit the always-buzzing heart of
the country (p58)
**5 Red Light District**
Take a walk on the wild side (p61)

# The Author

## ANDREW BENDER

Born in New England and schooled in Philadelphia, Andy has lived in Tokyo, France and, now, Los Angeles, but he's considered Amsterdam his spiritual home since he first swapped biking at the beach for biking the canals. Yet another Lonely Planet author with an MBA, he did what every MBA secretly wants to do – get out of the business world and see the real world. His travel writing has appeared in the *Los Angeles Times*, *Travel & Leisure*, *Fortune*, *Men's Journal* and in-flight magazines as well as Lonely Planet guides in Europe and Asia. When not on the road he still bikes at the beach, consults on cross-cultural communication, sees friends and family as often as he can, obsesses over Japanese and Korean food, enjoys the occasional margarita (Herradura, fresh lime juice, no salt) and schemes over ways to spoil his nieces and nephews.

## PHOTOGRAPHER
### RICHARD NEBESKÝ

Richard was not born with a camera in his hand; but, not long after, his father, an avid photo enthusiast, gave him his first happy snap unit. Ever since then, camera was always by his side while skiing, cycling or researching Lonely Planet travel guidebooks around the globe. Work for various magazines, travel guide book publishers and plenty of social photography followed.

# Contents

**Published by Lonely Planet Publications Pty Ltd**
ABN 36 005 607 983

**Australia** Head Office, Locked Bag 1, Footscray,
Victoria 3011, ☎ 03 8379 8000, fax 03 8379 8111,
talk2us@lonelyplanet.com.au

**USA** 150 Linden St, Oakland, CA 94607,
☎ 510 893 8555, toll free 800 275 8555,
fax 510 893 8572, info@lonelyplanet.com

**UK** 72–82 Rosebery Ave, Clerkenwell, London,
EC1R 4RW, ☎ 020 7841 9000, fax 020 7841 9001,
go@lonelyplanet.co.uk

**France** 1 rue du Dahomey, 75011 Paris,
☎ 01 55 25 33 00, fax 01 55 25 33 01,
bip@lonelyplanet.fr, www.lonelyplanet.fr

# Introducing Amsterdam

**We know what you're thinking: Amsterdam is where people go to smoke dope. You're grinning, aren't you? We want you to. Or maybe you're thinking that Amsterdam is where hookers tempt from red-lit windows, where magic mushrooms are sold as freely as green beans, or where gays and lesbians can enjoy wedded bliss. It's all true. Yet none of it is the reason we love this city.**

Actually, we take that back. We love it for all those reasons, even if we don't necessarily partake. We love it because Amsterdam is the most tolerant and, by many measures, the freest city we know.

Some would argue that too much freedom isn't good, but here's where Amsterdam makes sense: it recognises that freedom's fraternal twin is responsibility - the responsibility not to harm or inconvenience others and to afford others the same freedoms you have.

Being on the water – indeed being *of* the water – Amsterdam has always had to look outwards. Its traders brought silks from Japan, porcelain from China, tea from Ceylon, coffee and cocoa, objects once foreign, now everyday. With new goods came new people – Jews, Huguenots, Indonesians – and new words, ways and foods.

With no royalty or church calling the shots as in other European countries, trade, industry and populism came to rule. What's more, a can-do spirit led to a breezy confidence. Need more land? Go make some!

There are barely 750,000 residents, yet nobody would say it's not a world leader.

Amsterdam's also a place of clever beauty. Without a single internationally known building, it has looks that make Paris, London and even Venice jealous. A stroll along the western canals, through the lanes of the Jordaan or beneath the greenery of the Plantage can lead straight into a trance. The

## Lowdown

**Population** 735,000 (plus an estimated 20,000 unregistered)
**Bicycles** 600,000 (estimated)
**Time Zone** Western European (GMT+1hr)
**Windmills** 6
**Canals** 165
**Houseboats** 2500
**Three-star double hotel room around** €125
**Cup of coffee** €1.75
**Glass of Heineken** €2.50
**Tram ticket** €1.60
**Bicycle rental (day)** €7
**Van Gogh Museum admission** €9
**Basic grade marijuana in a 'coffeeshop'** €4
**'Oral favours' in the Red Light District** €30
**No-no** Walking in the bike path. What are you, suicidal?

interplay of water and steeple, streetside and tree, window and bridge and brick and roofline and sky is mesmerising.

One other element completes the picture, though it's as hard to define as it is to pronounce. It's called *gezelligheid*, translating somewhere between conviviality, friendliness, snugness, taking an interest, and wanting-to-be-around-others-but-not-so-much-that-you-make-a-pain-out-of-yourself.

But Amsterdam is about more than an attitude or a building or an object. It's about a moment: sipping a perfectly poured beer in a centuries-old 'brown café', biking with the wind against your pores and the cobblestones beneath your feet, losing yourself within Van Gogh's brushstrokes, cosying in a park, meditating on a bell gable, savouring the *gehakt* at a sandwich shop or a tomato basil chocolate bonbon, laughing at a drag queen or, better, laughing with her.

We love Amsterdam because it sweats the big stuff and doesn't worry about the small stuff. We love it because we've never had a bad time there. We love it because we don't know of a more relaxing city in Northern Europe. But most of all we love it because while other places preach tolerance, in Amsterdam it's a way of life.

## ANDY'S TOP AMSTERDAM DAY

Wake up late. If I'm lucky it will be to the sound of the bells at the Westerkerk.

Shower, don't shave, hop on the junky-but-trusty bike and head to a café in the Jordaan for breakfast with a friend. A market morning along Westerstraat or the Noordermarkt dovetails beautifully with a ride down the Prinsengracht and browsing in the Negen Straatjes. From there it's a short jump to Dam Square to see what's on at the Nieuwe Kerk. Lunch: roasted whatever-looks-good, over rice, in Chinatown.

If we're feeling ambitious, we might continue on to see the latest building in the Eastern Docklands, but more likely we'll bike back through the city centre, past the fancy cars and fancy shoppers of Nieuwe Spiegelstraat and PC Hooftstraat, to spend a relaxing afternoon in the Vondelpark: a concert or people watching at the Round Blue Teahouse.

By dinnertime, it's back to the Jordaan to try the newest, the trendiest, the most sociable restaurant, topped off by a beer with perfect two fingers of foam at a canalside café table. The sun dims, boats hum, and the bells of the Westerkerk still chime.

### My Essential Amsterdam

- **Red Light District** (p61) At once blissfully tawdry and achingly beautiful, especially (both) at night
- **Negen Straatjes** (p84) 'Nine alleys' packed with boutiques, dining and cafes, separated by stately canals
- **Van Gogh Museum** (p111) For the beauty and the pathos. Ordinarily I'd include the Rijksmuseum and the Stedelijk, but they're due to be closed for a while
- **Albert Cuypmarkt** (p113) Where the diversity of the city comes together
- **Canal Boat Ride** (p56) To put it all in perspective

# City Life

# City Life

## AMSTERDAM TODAY

Spokes.

It's hard to imagine Amsterdam without them.

We *could* talk about the spokes on bicycles, unavoidable on the city's streets – as you'll see from the moment you set foot there. We could even say that, from the air, the city resembles a tyre, with its lovely canals encircling the centre and the radial canals its spokes.

But we like the implication that spokes lead to a hub, and that's the way we think of this city: a gathering place, the world's original melting pot. Immigration of Jews and Huguenots from the middle of the last millennium gave way to more recent immigration of Indonesians, Surinamese and Turks, just to name a few. Amsterdam is also a legendary venue for culture vultures and hearty partiers. It all means that there's something for everyone, a place where – we hope – you may find something you didn't know you liked.

Customers enjoying an outdoor café

## CITY CALENDAR

There's no bad time to visit Amsterdam. Queen's Day on 30 April is celebrated with the biggest street party in the country, and is an unforgettable experience. In warm weather, the folk of this exciting city take to the streets and canalsides, and even restaurants with drop-dead interiors might move their seating outdoors. Summer abounds with open-air concerts, theatre and festivals, often free. Culture vultures might aim for the Holland Festival in June or the Uitmarkt at the end of August, or the quirky Parade in July. A few of the events listed here are out of town but are worth the trip. Amsterdam RAI convention centre (www.rai.nl) also hosts shows throughout the year: arts, boats, film and horse-jumping events among them. Where no contact info is given, contact the VVV (Vereniging voor Vreemdelingenverkeer, tourist information) for further information.

See the Directory chapter (p251) for a list of public holidays – when the city has a tendency to shut down.

## January

### ELFSTEDENTOCHT (ELEVEN CITIES' JOURNEY)

If it has been cold enough for long enough, this gruelling skating marathon through the countryside of Friesland attracts thousands of participants. Years may pass before conditions are right, but when they are it provides great relief from January's cold, dull, dark days.

### Top Five Quirky Holidays & Events

- Elfstedentocht (above)
- Stille Omgang (opposite)
- Gay Pride Canal Parade (p10)
- Arrival of Sinterklaas (p11)
- Cannabis Cup (p11)

## Hot Conversation Topics

Say you're enjoying a beer with friends at a café overlooking a canal. What are you likely to hear?

- 'It took me forever to park my bike!'
- 'What are you getting Jakob and Pieter as a wedding gift?'
- 'I hear Marieke is going to take a loss on her flat.'
  'Well, of course, she bought it in 2001!'
- 'Where's the afterparty?'
- 'They're saying the new metro line will open 2011. I wonder what they'll be saying in 2013!'
- 'Did you see the police raid at that club on Rembrandtplein on Saturday night?'
- 'Who wants to go to Schiphol to see the exhibit from the Rijksmuseum?'
- 'I hope my bike is still there.'

# February

## CARNAVAL

A Catholic tradition, best enjoyed in the cities of southern Holland (especially Maastricht), that shows Amsterdammers also know how to don silly costumes and party for Carnaval.

## COMMEMORATION OF THE FEBRUARY STRIKE

Held on 25 February, wreaths are laid at the Dockworker monument (p99), in the former Jewish quarter, in memory of the anti-Nazi general strike in 1941.

# March

## STILLE OMGANG (SILENT PROCESSION)

Held on the Sunday closest to 15 March, Catholics walk along the Holy Way (the current Heiligeweg is a remnant) to commemorate the 1345 Miracle of Amsterdam (see p75).

# April

## NATIONAL MUSEUM WEEKEND

Usually held on the second weekend of April, there is free entry to all museums (it's extremely crowded).

## KONINGINNEDAG (QUEEN'S DAY)

If you could visit Amsterdam at any time, this is it. Held on 30 April, there's a free market throughout the city (anyone can sell anything they like, kids love it), street parties, live music, dense crowds and lots of beer – it's a collective madhouse. The whole country under the age of 30 visits Amsterdam, while all of Amsterdam over the age of 30 escapes. See also the boxed text on p15.

# May

## REMEMBRANCE DAY

Held on 4 May for the victims of WWII, Queen Beatrix lays a wreath at the Nationaal Monument on The Dam (p59) and the city observes two minutes' silence at 8pm; making noise then is thoughtless in the extreme.

## LIBERATION DAY

To mark the end of German occupation in 1945, it is commemorated with street parties, a free market and live music on 5 May. The Vondelpark (p112) is a good place to be.

## LUILAK ('LAZY-BONES')

In the early hours on the Saturday before Whit Sunday, children go around ringing door bells, making noise and waking people up. Luilak is a remnant of a pre-Christian festival celebrating the awakening of spring.

## NATIONAL CYCLING DAY

Held on the Second Saturday of the month, National Cycling Day includes family cycling trips along special routes.

## NATIONAL WINDMILL DAY

Also held on the second Saturday of May, windmills unfurl their sails and are open to the public.

## DRUM RHYTHM FESTIVAL

Held mid-month, you can relish avant-garde dance as well as soul and funk on Java Eiland in the Eastern Harbour region.

## OPEN GARDEN DAYS

Held mid-month, this is a chance to see some of the private gardens behind canal houses.

## PINKPOP
www.pinkpop.nl

This three-day outdoor rock festival, held around Pentecost (May/June) near Landgraaf in the southeast, has in the past featured performers including Moby and the Cardigans.

## CANAL RUN

Held at the end of the month or early June, this event consists of 5km, 9km and 18km runs along canals.

# June
## OVER HET IJ FESTIVAL
www.overhetij.nl in Dutch

From June or July, big performing-arts events (dance, theatre, music) take place around the former NDSM (Nederlandsche Doken Scheeps-bouwmaatschappij) shipyards north of the IJ. It's often exciting and always interesting.

## HOLLAND FESTIVAL
www.holndfstvl.nl

For all of June the country's biggest music, drama and dance extravaganza centres on Amsterdam. Highbrow and pretentious meets lowbrow and silly.

## ROOTS MUSIC FESTIVAL

This is a week-long festival of world music and culture held in late June at various locations throughout the city.

## PARKPOP
www.parkpop.nl in Dutch

On the last Sunday of the month, Europe's largest, free rock festival is held in the Zuiderpark in The Hague. Some 350,000 people attend annually.

## INTERNATIONAL THEATRE SCHOOL FESTIVAL

Held at the end of the month; Dutch and international theatre schools strut their stuff.

# July
## NORTH SEA JAZZ FESTIVAL
www.northseajazz.nl

The world's largest indoor jazz festival is held mid-month in the Netherlands Congress Centre in The Hague – pretty much any name you've heard of has performed here. Many musicians visit Amsterdam as well.

## JULIDANS
Dance Festival at venues citywide.

# August
## CANAL PARADE

Held on the first Saturday, this is the only water-borne, gay-pride parade in the world.

## PARADE
www.mobilearts.nl

For the first two weeks of the month, this Carnavalesque outdoor theatre festival, held in the Martin Luther King Park, provides unforgettable ambience.

## DANCE VALLEY
www.dancevalley.nl

Held mid-month, tens of thousands fill a valley outside of town to groove to loads of DJs.

## GRACHTENFESTIVAL (CANAL FESTIVAL)
www.grachtenfestival.nl

In the second half of the month this is a five-day music festival (mainly classical), around the canal belt. It features the Prinsengracht Concert from barges in front of the Pulitzer Hotel.

## HARTJESDAG ZEEDIJK

Held on the third Monday and the weekend leading up to it, this festival, dating back to medieval times, showcases street theatre and includes a parade and music along Zeedijk and Nieuwmarkt square.

## UITMARKT

For the last weekend of the month, local troupes and orchestras present their coming repertoires free of charge throughout the city. A bit like Koninginnedag (p9) but much more easy-going.

# September
## BLOEMENCORSO (FLOWER PARADE)

On the first Saturday of the month, a spectacular procession of floats wends its way from Aalsmeer in the morning to The Dam.

## JORDAAN FESTIVAL
☎ 624 69 08

Held during the second week, this street festival promotes merriment and entertainment in a 'typically Amsterdam' neighbourhood.

## Sinterklaas

Every year on 6 December the Dutch celebrate Sinterklaas in honour of St Nicholas (Klaas is a nickname for Nicholas, or Nicolaas in Dutch). Historically the bishop of Myra in western Turkey around AD 345, St Nicholas is the patron saint of children, sailors, merchants, pawnbrokers – and Amsterdam.

In mid- to late November, the white-bearded saint, dressed as a bishop with mitre and staff, arrives in Amsterdam by ship from 'Spain' and enters the city on a horse to receive the city keys from the mayor. He is accompanied by a host of mischievous servants called *Zwarte Pieten* (Black Peters), Dutch helpers in blackface (or politically correct blue- or greenface) who throw sweets around and carry sacks in which to take naughty children away. Well-behaved children get presents in a shoe that they've placed by the fireplace with a carrot for the saint's horse (he stays on the roof while a Black Peter climbs down the chimney).

On the evening of 5 December people give one another anonymous and creatively wrapped gifts accompanied by funny/perceptive poems about the recipient written by Sinterklaas. The gift itself matters less than the wrapping (the greater the surprise the better) and poetry (the more the person is put on the spot the better).

The North American Santa Claus evolved from the Sinterklaas celebrations at the Dutch settlement of New Amsterdam (which eventually evolved into New York).

### MONUMENTENDAG
☎ 552 48 88; www.bmz.amsterdam.nl
Registered historical buildings have open days on the second weekend of the month.

### CHINATOWN FESTIVAL
☎ 642 23 99
The Chinese community celebrates on Nieuwmarkt square mid-month.

### DAM TOT DAM LOOP
www.damloop.nl
This is a 16km road footrace between the Dam in Amsterdam and the Dam in Zaandam.

## October
### AMSTERDAM MARATHON
www.amsterdammarathon.nl
Held mid-month, thousands of runners loop through the city, starting and finishing at the Olympic Stadium. A variety of races take place.

## November
### SINTERKLAAS ARRIVES
The children's saint arrives by ship (see boxed text, above).

### CANNABIS CUP
www.hightimes.com
This marijuana festival, held during the last half of month, is hosted by *High Times* magazine. Awards are for best grass, biggest spliff etc; there is also hemp expo and fashion show.

### ZEEDIJK JAZZ & BLUES FESTIVAL
Amsterdam's biggest jazz festival, on the last weekend of the month, sees hundreds of jazz and blues acts out on the street and in the pubs along Zeedijk, free of charge.

## December
### SINTERKLAAS
Officially 6 December but the main focus is gift-giving on the evening of 5 December, in honour of St Nicholas (see boxed text, above).

### CHRISTMAS
Celebrated on 25 and 26 December, but religious families mark Christmas Eve on 24 December with Bible readings and carols.

### NEW YEAR'S EVE
You'll see wild parties everywhere; the drunken revelry includes fireworks and often injuries.

# CULTURE
## IDENTITY
It's almost a cliche to say that the Dutch are passionately liberal and believe that people should be free to do whatever they want as long as it doesn't inconvenience others; yet it's largely true. The most outrageous conduct in public might go without comment, hence the Dutch saying: Act normal, that's crazy enough. It's hard to appreciate it until you've been here.

Still, Amsterdammers also have a moralistic streak (coming from the Calvinist tradition) and a tendency to wag the finger in disapproval. Nonsmokers who wince at people smoking nearby might well be told they're making smokers feel uncomfortable. And raising a criticism over job professionalism or an overcharge on a bill may result in a very frosty reception. This manner may seem blunt or even arrogant to foreigners, but the impulse comes from the desire to be direct and honest. However, these attitudes are slowly fading, particularly in the younger generation.

Perhaps because their country is so crowded, Amsterdammers tend to be reserved with strangers. The Dutch treasure their privacy because it is a rare commodity. Yet they're far from antisocial – their inbred *gezelligheid* (see boxed text, below) will come out at the drop of a hat. Expect chummy moments at the supermarket.

Amsterdammers love to complain about their city and their 'irrelevant' country, always with a glint of humour. One of our earliest Amsterdam memories is of a grandmother and her grandson of perhaps eight years old, doubled over with laughter over a postcard in a shop: a pile of dog mess on an Amsterdam sidewalk (an ever-present problem) topped with a little Dutch flag like on a cupcake. Any city that can laugh at itself over that deserves our vote.

## The Polder Model

Not unlike the Japanese, by virtue of their close proximity, the Dutch have been forced to get along. The phenomenon of *verzuiling* (pillarisation; p21) allowed different ideologies their place in society so long as they maintained the status quo by compromise.

This social and cultural segmentation has left a culture of tolerance, and willingness to take one's time if it makes things work fairly. Much like the Japanese process of consensus-building, the Dutch will deliberate endlessly before they issue a planning permit or form a government – the 'polder model' of involving everybody who may have a legitimate say. Everyone is expected to have an opinion and to voice it.

### That's *Gezellig*

This particularly Dutch personality trait is one of the best reasons to visit Amsterdam. It's variously translated as snug, friendly, cosy, informal, companionable and convivial, but *gezelligheid* (the state of being *gezellig*) is something easier experienced than defined. To wit (with apologies to Dean Martin, one of our heroes, and fans of *That's Amore*):

When you hang out all day
in an old brown café, that's *gezellig*.
Sit and gab with your friends
and the fun never ends, that's *gezellig*.

You can sing (ting-a-ling-a-ling, ting-a-ling-a-ling)
riding on your canal boat,
While you sway (tippy-tippy-tay, tippy-tippy-tay)
from the beer someone else brought.

Take your grill to the street,
bring your couch for a seat, that's *gezellig*.
Or go chat on the porch
in your old undershirts. Suits us fine.

When you live at close range
but are never heard screaming or yelling,
It's no scam, sir or ma'am,
back in old Amsterdam that's *gezellig*.

## Sex & Drugs

Subjects such as sex are discussed openly (one newspaper recently examined puberty by showing photographs of the development of both male and female genitalia), and you might overhear a pub chat where Jan tells all details of making whoopee. The Dutch parliament even held a debate on whether to ban a TV show called 'How to Screw' (but decided not to ban it). Promiscuity, however, is the furthest thing from Dutch minds. When you don't have to sneak it, it loses its mystique.

That said, prostitution is famously legal, as is marijuana. It all comes from the ever-practical Dutch world view that these things are not going to go away so you might as well have some control over them. This doesn't mean that every Amsterdammer tokes up or that local males pay for their jollies; on the contrary, only about 5% of business in the Red Light District comes from Dutch customers (Brits comprise about 40%). Across the Netherlands, the same 5% figure also applies to pot smokers, less than in France where drug policy is much stricter. Locals leave these vices to slackers and tourists.

This world view also applies to diseases like AIDS. Amsterdam has an active education programme for at-risk groups, and it was one of the pioneers of a needle-exchange program for drug addicts.

## Dutch Obsessions

Dutch people have a great love of detail. Statistics on the most trivial subjects make the paper (eg the number of applications for dog licences, incidence of rubbish being put out early), and somewhere down the line it feeds mountains of bureaucracy. That said, when the system breaks down the Dutch are happy to improvise. There's a strong legacy of pragmatism from juggling the interests of religion and trade.

There's also a keen interest in all things foreign, perhaps from the historical need of the Dutch to understand the world for their very survival. The Dutch are inveterate travellers and the media are full of phrases in English.

Last but not least, the Dutch are famously thrifty with their money – and they often don't know what to think of this. In one breath they might joke about how copper wire was invented by two Dutchmen (they were fighting over a penny, neither one would let go, and they stretched it), and in the next tell you that they don't like being called cheap. Many complain vehemently that when prices were converted from the guilder to the euro in 2002, shopkeepers took the opportunity to raise prices rather than do a strict conversion (complaints we've also heard, by the way, in other euro-zone countries).

## Ethnic Makeup

Amsterdam has a long tradition of welcoming immigrants and integrating them into society (p42), and that tradition continues. Out of approximately 735,000 people (plus an estimated 20,000 unregistered residents), about 47% are ethnic minorities. The most recent wave of immigration goes back to the 1960s, when 'guest labourers' from Morocco and Turkey performed jobs spurned by the Dutch. In the mid-1970s, the granting of independence to the Dutch colony of Suriname in South America saw a large influx of Surinamese, who now compose the majority of the city's 10% Black population.

The vast majority of these immigrants live in the city's outskirts, such as the communities of Bijlmer and the Old West in particular, as well as the (now gentrifying) neighbourhood of de Pijp. Housing is cheaper in these areas.

Foreign residents from Western countries include some 19,000 Germans, 7500 Britons, 3700 Americans and 1000 Aussies. Thousands of (temporary) expatriates are not included in these figures.

The past few years have witnessed a significant shift to the right in the Netherlands (see p20). It's no police state (this is Holland), but the sudden rise of politician Pim Fortuyn on a platform perceived unfriendly to immigrants (and his assassination) made many Dutch consider whether immigrants are upholding the polder model or trying to force the traditions of their home countries onto the Netherlands.

Controls on immigration have been tightened in recent years, yet more than 5% of the population still doesn't have Dutch nationality. The gates haven't been slammed shut, but admission is now restricted to a few narrow categories – eg people whose presence serves

### Demographic Snapshot

- Population between ages 20 and 40: 40%
- Single households: 54%
- Households of couples without children: 20%
- Households of couples with children: 15%
- Single parent households: 9%
- Ethnic minorities: 47%
- Primary school children with non-Dutch backgrounds: 60%
- Ethnic Surinamese: 72,000
- Ethnic Moroccans: 59,000
- Ethnic Turks: 36,000
- Ethnic Indonesians: 24,000

the 'national interest' or those with compelling humanitarian reasons for getting a residence permit. For prospective immigrants from developing countries, the Netherlands is no longer an easy option.

## LIFESTYLE

Joop, 37, lives in de Pijp, an up-and-coming neighbourhood south of the central city. To reach his flat, you have to walk up two typically narrow flights of stairs – uneven steps that force you to look down as you tread. Technically it's a one-bedroom flat with living room, dining room (bonus!), bedroom, decent-sized kitchen and back balcony (another bonus!), but Joop has turned the flat's large closet into a bedroom and uses the windowed bedroom as an office. Although the building is prewar, inside, the flat is clean and comfortable. Sleekly modern furnishings offset the antique timber flooring (he has excellent taste).

Even though Joop can be out of work for long periods (he's in the performing arts), he can afford this place because it's social housing for which he pays €486 per month. Whereas in other countries social housing carries a stigma, in Amsterdam some 56% of the population lives in it – the waiting list can be five years.

Joop likes to go out – for lunch in a café in the neighbourhood, a performance night with his 'husband' (they haven't married, though technically they could – they've only been together six months, so why rush into things?). He loves the city, he says, because there's something cultural to do any night of the week, especially in summer.

## Women

Dutch women attained the right to vote in 1919 and by the 1970s abortion on demand was paid for by the national health service. Dutch women are remarkably confident; on a social level, equality is taken for granted and women are almost as likely as men to initiate social/romantic contact. It's still a different story in the workplace – relatively few women are employed full-time and fewer still hold positions in senior management.

The feminist movement is less politicised than elsewhere and certainly more laid-back. Efforts focus on practical solutions such as cultural centres, bicycle-repair shops run by and for women, or support systems to help women set up businesses.

## FASHION

Although Amsterdam has some interesting designers, we'll admit that it's not the first city you think of when you think fashion. Probably some of that has to do with the traditional Dutch aversion to showiness (although it's wise to dress up for a nice dinner out). We also suspect that it has something to do with the fact that it's hard to ride a bicycle while wearing one's finest, especially if it's likely to rain.

That said, office workers, particularly in banking and finance, do dress smartly for work. International designers can be found at the higher-end department stores and on the PC Hooftstraat, the city's fanciest shopping street.

## Gay & Lesbian Amsterdam

Partisan estimates put the proportion of gay and lesbian people in Amsterdam at 20% to 30%. This is probably an exaggeration, but Amsterdam is certainly one of the gay capitals of Europe. Mainstream attitudes have always been reasonably tolerant, but the last decade has seen considerable advance in the gay-rights movement, making it illegal to discriminate against job seekers on the basis of sexual orientation and, in a landmark move in 2001, the Netherlands became the first country to legalise same-sex marriages (Belgium and Canada now grant the same right). Gays and lesbians also have the right to adopt children, although this is restricted to Dutch children out of fear that international adoption agencies might discontinue cooperation.

As further measures of the level of acceptance, the police advertise in the gay media for applicants and homosexuals are admitted to the armed forces on an equal footing. And in this city of commerce, locals recognise the importance of lesbian and gay travellers to the economy – the Gay Games (the Olympics of the lesbian and gay world) took place here in 1998.

In general, gay and lesbian venues are open and welcoming. There are more than 100 bars and nightclubs, gay hotels, bookshops, sport clubs, choirs, archives etc, and a wide range of support organisations. However, Amsterdam's well-developed scene isn't typical of the country as a whole. Rotterdam is an exception, as are the university towns.

The centrepiece of Amsterdam's Gay Pride festival is the Canal Parade (p10), which takes place on the first Saturday in August. Dozens of (literal) floats make their way around the Prinsengracht as hundreds of thousands of spectators of all stripes look on. The days around the parade are marked by sport and culture programmes and lots of parties.

Another big party is Koninginnedag (Queen's Day; p9) on 30 April. Queen Beatrix and Princess Máxima, the Argentine wife of Crown Prince Willem-Alexander, are very popular among the gay community.

Even the club world is turning around. For years, it wasn't a matter of dressing up or dressing down; it was pretty much styleless. That's begun to change, and club doormen are beginning to be more selective. There are quite a number of shops around town catering to club-goers, some of them as fun as the clubs themselves.

# SPORT

## Football (Soccer)

The Dutch are pretty low-key when it comes to national pride, except when it comes to football. It's the Dutch national game, which is no surprise in the land of past masters Johan Cruyff and Ruud Gullit. Passions for football run so high it's almost scary. The National Football Association counts a million members, and every weekend teams, both professional and amateur, hit pitches across the country.

The national football team competes in virtually every World Cup. The Eindhoven-based PSV (Philips Sport Vereniging) coach Guus Hiddink led the South Korean team to the quarter-finals in the 2002 World Cup, and still enjoys a status akin to sainthood in that country.

Amsterdam's team, Ajax (say *ah*-yahks), plays in the hi-tech Amsterdam ArenA. Hooliganism is not unheard of, but the ArenA has a modern, hi-tech police force, and if you're sitting in the seats (as opposed to standing in the standing sections) you're unlikely to notice crowd trouble.

## Football (American)

The same arena is home to the Amsterdam Admirals (American) football team, which plays in the spring (complete with cheerleaders!) in the six-team National Football League Europe.

## Tennis

Tennis has been swarmingly popular since Richard Krajicek fell to his knees after clinching the 1996 Wimbledon final. The national tennis club is the country's second-largest sporting club after football, and many people book time on courts in all-weather sports halls.

## Dos & Don'ts

- The accepted greeting is a handshake – firm but not bone-crushing. Cheek-kissing (three pecks, right-left-right) is common between men and women (and between women and between gay men) who know one another socially.
- The typically pragmatic convention for queuing is to take a numbered ticket from a dispenser and await your turn. Always check whether there's a dispenser if you're in a post office, government office, bakery, at a delicatessen counter in a supermarket etc.
- If you're invited home for dinner, bring something for the host: a bunch of flowers or a plant, a bottle of wine, or some good cake or pastries. It's polite to arrive five to 15 minutes late (never early), but business meetings start on time.
- Dress standards are casual (most concerts, most restaurants) or smart casual (theatre, opera, upmarket restaurants and some business dealings); and slightly formal (most business dealings) or quite formal (bankers).
- A special note for drug tourists: it is 'not done' to smoke dope in public. At 'coffeeshops' it's OK and in some other situations too, but even the hippest locals detest foreigners who think they can just toke anywhere. The same applies to drinking out on the street.

Krajicek has hung up his racket but there's fresh blood on the circuit, like Sjeng Schalken and Martin Verkerk, a finalist at the 2003 French Open (see p188 for tennis centres).

## Skating

Ice skating is as Dutch as croquettes, and thousands hit the ice when the country's lakes and ditches freeze over. The Netherlands has dozens of ice rinks with Olympic-sized tracks with areas for hockey and figure skating. Amsterdam's main ice rink was named for Jaap Eden, a legend around 1900. The hero of the hour is Jochem Uytdehaage, celebrated for netting two Olympic gold medals in Salt Lake City in 2002.

## Cycling

To say that Amsterdammers are avid cyclists is a bit of an understatement. There are some 400km of bike paths in the city alone, and even if these are not used competitively virtually every Amsterdammer can relate to the sport. The five-day Tour de Nederland speeds through the city at the end of August.

## Other Sports

Sports tend to rise and fall with the fate of Dutch athletes. The Dutch volleyball team, for example, won Olympic gold in 2000, and darts has gained an enthusiastic following after the victories of Raymond van Barneveld, three times world champion. (Despite this you're not likely to find too many bars with *dartbanen* in the city. If you wander into a place with a 'tandarts' sign out front, you'll find yourself in a dentist's office!). The Netherlands has long had the world's foremost water polo league.

Amsterdam also has many opportunities for swimming (some in some lovely old facilities) and, despite the confined spaces, golf.

*Cycling Eastern Islands (p105)*

# MEDIA

## Newspapers & Magazines

There are 32 daily newspapers in the Netherlands, but the biggest by far is the Amsterdam-based *De Telegraaf*, an untidy, right-wing daily with sensationalist news but good finance coverage. The populist *Volkskrant* is a one-time Catholic daily with leftish leanings in its political and economic news. The highly regarded *NRC Handelsblad*, a merger of two elitist papers from Rotterdam and Amsterdam, sets the country's journalistic standards. The *Allgemeen Dagblad* is down-to-earth but too thin to plumb the depths. Many Amsterdammers swear by *Het Parool* for the lowdown on the capital's culture and politics. The *Financieële Dagblad* is the country's leading daily for financial and business news. Many commuters pick up copies of the free *Metro* or *Spits* from train-station racks.

English-speakers can easily find European editions of the *Economist, Newsweek* and *Time*, as well as most of the major international newspapers. The main British newspapers are available the same day, while the *International Herald Tribune* has fairly late news. Some English-language magazines cater to expats, including *Roundabout*, with mainstream entertainment listings, and *Expats Magazine*, which serves up lifestyle, arts and how-to content to the foreign business community.

## TV & Radio

The public broadcast umbrella organisation is NOS (Nederlandse Omroep Stichting; www.nos.nl in Dutch), which has three channels of documentary and current-affairs programming. Many commercial stations offer a bland diet of movies, talk shows and pseudo-investigative series, but there's also Dutch-language MTV. The wide availability of foreign channels – BBC, CNN, Germany's ARD and Belgium's Canvas, among others – offers some alternatives.

RTL 4 (www.rtl4.nl in Dutch) is a commercial broadcaster with daily news, while sister RTL5 also has financial news via its unit RTLZ. SBS6 offers the late-night 'Hart van Nederland' (Heart of the Netherlands) show with a brief news bulletin and emotional tales of Dutch home life and current events. Foreign programmes are traditionally broadcast in their original version with subtitles.

The best-known commercial radio stations are Noordzee FM (100.7 FM), Radio 538 (102 FM) and Sky Radio (101.2 FM). RTL has its own frequencies as well alongside Radios 1 through 4 from NOS. All broadcast half-hourly news reports (in Dutch), with Europop and chat sandwiched in between.

Dutch television doesn't travel well, with the notable exception of reality-series formats by Endemol of Hilversum, about 20km out of town. Big Brother was swiftly copied in the UK, Germany and the USA – and has now spread to territories as diverse as Brazil, Mexico and Africa. Endemol is also behind such international hits as Fear Factor and Star Academy.

---

### *What*-ball?

Above all else, **korfball** is very Dutch. It dates back to 1903, when an Amsterdam schoolteacher sought to devise a sport that boys and girls could play together on equal footing, encouraging those Dutch values of teamwork and cooperation. Furthermore, *korf* means 'basket', and since there was already a 'basketball' the legendary Dutch spirit of compromise prevailed and the name was kept as is.

In action, korfball looks like the child of a ménage á trois between basketball, volleyball and netball. Briefly, a korfball team (four men and four women on a 40mx20m court) tries to sink a ball into a basket 3.5m off the ground. But unlike basketball, there's no running with the ball, and it's impossible for the team to feed the ball again and again to one player to shoot. Players cannot hinder members of the opposite sex and must work together in order to score.

There are korfball associations in many European countries, including in several UK cities. If you'd like to learn more, visit www.korfballnet.com. In Amsterdam, contact **Amsterdam Sport Council** ( ☎ 552 24 90) or try **SVK Groen-Wit** ( ☎ 646 15 15; Kinderdijkstraat 29).

## Dutch Language Courses

Standard courses take months and intensive courses last several weeks. Make inquiries well in advance.

**Amsterdam Summer University** ( ☎ 620 02 25; www.amsu.edu; Keizersgracht 324, 1016 EZ Amsterdam) Conducts all of its courses and workshops in English (apart from its Dutch-language training). Subjects focus on arts and sciences, as befits the traditions of the Felix Meritis building that houses it.

**British Language Training Centre** ( ☎ 622 36 34; www.bltc.nl; Nieuwezijds Voorburgwal 328E, 1012 RW Amsterdam) Offers Dutch and English courses and has a good reputation.

**Tropeninstituut** (Royal Institute for the Tropics, Language Training Department; ☎ 568 85 59; www.kit.nl; Postbus 95001, 1090 HA Amsterdam) Has intensive language courses with a large component of 'cultural training', aimed specifically at foreigners moving to the Netherlands. It's fairly expensive but very effective.

**Volksuniversiteit Amsterdam** ( ☎ 626 16 26; www.volksuniversiteitamsterdam.nl in Dutch; Rapenburgerstraat 73, 1011 VK Amsterdam) Offers a range of well-regarded day and evening courses that don't cost a fortune.

# LANGUAGE

Dutch is a member of the Germanic language family, which includes, among others, English, the Nordic languages and, of course, German. It is said that Germanic tribes wandered the area now known as the Netherlands hundreds of years before Christ and from about the year AD 700 Dutch began to take on its own identity. In the Golden Age, Dutch was the language of trade, and theatre companies from the Low Countries toured throughout Europe.

Today it is called, officially, *Algemeen Nederlands* (common Dutch). Dutch and Flemish (spoken in Belgium) are essentially two dialects of the same language. The worldwide Dutch language community also includes Afrikaans, spoken in South Africa. Many experts reckon that Dutch is the major language closest to English (Frisian is actually closer, but the Frisian language community is tiny!). That said, the casual English speaker is unlikely to recognise much similarity, thanks to Dutch pronunciation. It's riddled with guttural sounds: 'g' and 'ch' are throat-clearers, and the Dutch tend to roll their 'r's and super-aspirate their 'h's.

Dutch resembles English in one important aspect: it absorbs words from other languages. For example, the Amsterdam dialect is full of adopted Yiddish words from its immigrant Jewish community.

If you've studied German you'll be able to take a good stab at written Dutch, despite differences in the spelling. Spoken Dutch can be another matter – its pronunciation can be confounding.

That probably won't matter much to you as a visitor, as almost every Amsterdammer from age eight onwards seems to speak English very well. In fact, visitors will rarely have the opportunity to practise Dutch: some chalk it up to showing off, others to a Dutch familiarity with the difficulties of being a traveller, but more than likely they'll speak in English because it's the most practical way to communicate. When you come from a tiny country with a long history of trade, you learn to adapt or wither.

Nevertheless, a few words in Dutch are always appreciated, especially the phrase *Spreekt u Engels?* (Do you speak English?) with elderly people. Foreigners who have settled in the Netherlands report that speaking Dutch, while hardly compulsory, warms their Dutch friends and colleagues.

For a brief guide to Dutch and some useful words and phrases, see the Language chapter (p257) at the back of this book. For more extensive coverage of the language, pick up Lonely Planet's *Western Europe phrasebook*.

# ECONOMY & COSTS

Until about 30 years ago Amsterdam was the industrial centre of the Netherlands, a role it had played since the industrial revolution. In the 1960s and 1970s, however, congestion and environmental constraints forced many industries to move elsewhere in the country.

Meanwhile, low-wage competitors in Asia killed off the huge shipbuilding industry and its many support industries. The city has, however, bounced back, reinventing its historical role as a centre of trade, finance and services.

## MAIN INDUSTRIES

The main economic activities in the Greater Amsterdam area can now be divided into four categories employing roughly equal numbers of people: manufacturing and crafts; commerce, tourism and finance; administration; and science and arts. Tourism generates a turnover of €900 million a year and employs 6% of the workforce.

Amsterdam's harbour is the fifth-largest in Europe (nearby Rotterdam's is the first), and Schiphol airport is the third-largest in terms of freight and fourth-largest in terms of passengers. Less well known is that the Dutch control about 45% of European road freight; many of these trucking companies are based in Amsterdam.

Many multinationals have established their European headquarters and distribution centres in office complexes west, south and southeast of the city, drawn by a highly skilled, multilingual workforce and easy-going tax laws. It seems only natural for the city that gave the world its first conglomerates, the storied East India and West India companies (p46).

### How Much?

- Tip in a public toilet: €0.50
- Loaf of packaged *boerenbrood* (farmer bread) at Albert Heijn supermarket: €0.74
- *Kroket* sandwich at van Dobben: €2
- One hour of parking: €3
- Coffee and apple pie with whipped cream at Villa Zeezicht: €5.55
- Strippenkaart (strip-card for public transit): €6.20
- Cinema ticket (varies by time and location): €7.50
- Dutch-English dictionary: €7.50
- Bicycle lock: €10
- Train ticket to Rotterdam: €11
- *Rijsttafel* dinner at Tujuh Maret Indonesian restaurant: €23.50

## RECENT DEVELOPMENTS

Throughout the 1990s and the beginning of this century, the Dutch economy was the miracle of Europe, with consistent growth while other European economies poked along and even lost ground. Today's Netherlands is noticeably more affluent than a decade ago, even if the Dutch don't flaunt the fact that they now earn more per capita than the Germans.

However, the global recession of the early 21st century has hit. Whereas the last decade saw an escalation in real estate prices, as we went to press 'Te Koop' (for sale) signs abounded, especially for top-end housing in the canal belt. That said, spending for luxury items, especially furniture and interior décor, is jogging along.

## COSTS

For the traveller, Amsterdam is squarely in the middle range of northern European cities in terms of costs. On the culinary front, lunch will set you back between €5 and €10, with dinner about double that at a regular restaurant, though the city is not lacking for luxury options.

With rare exceptions, decent hotel rooms are not cheap. Rack rates are about €100 to €125 for a mid-range room. That said, if you shop around you can usually find excellent specials at some top hotels. You'll find a list of websites to try in the Sleeping chapter (p212).

One thing to avoid: taxis. Fares vary

### Did You Know?

Although the Netherlands introduced the euro along with 10 other European nations in 2002, many average Dutch people still calculate large-ticket items (eg real estate) in terms of the retired currency, the guilder, then convert to euros.

but are generally €2.90 at the drop and another €1.80 per kilometre, and fares mount quickly!

# GOVERNMENT & POLITICS

## LOCAL GOVERNMENT

Amsterdam is run by a mayor (Job Cohen) and a 45-member city council elected to four-year terms by the city's 15 boroughs. The current city council, in place until 2006, is one-third Social Democrats, another third Liberals and Greens and the rest a variety of parties. The council meets every three weeks (on Wednesday) in the afternoon and evening and starts each session with a one-hour public 'question time'.

Each of the boroughs has its own 'neighbourhood council' responsible for the day-to-day running of the district. In these councils, Amsterdam is as active and participatory as the polder model would suggest. District councils hear local concerns and are responsible for implementing block-to-block changes: installing new bike racks, cleaning up dog mess etc.

Amsterdam is also the sort of place where locals create informal councils to solve problems of mutual concern even without any government input (see Night Mayors, p168).

## NATIONAL POLITICS

Although Amsterdam is the nation's 'capital', the functions of government are actually 60km away in Den Haag (The Hague; p233). More than that, many Amsterdammers have begun to feel isolated from the rest of the country, which they see as swinging to the right politically. It's caused hand-wringing over the potential loss of the city's legendary freedoms. At the time of writing, the Dutch hospitality industry and Dutch health ministry were in a heated debate over the potential ban on smoking in bars, cafés and restaurants. The health minister was pushing to have it start on 1 January 2006. However, that could all change by the time you read this. It would hardly be the first time.

On top of that, much of Europe views the Netherlands as a bête noir whose lax policies on drugs and what-not are corrupting the youth of other nations (many Dutch retort, not without reason, that the Netherlands' own drug-abuse rates are among Europe's lowest and it's the other nations that should get their own houses in order!). A percentage of Amsterdammers see their city in particular being used as a scapegoat. Whereas police might have

---

### Fortuyn's Legacy

In the Netherlands, social justice, prosperity and consensus politics used to be regarded as inseparable bedfellows. But the status quo took a severe beating when Pim Fortuyn (pronounced 'fore-*town*') arrived on the scene in 2002.

During his five-month career as a politician, the ex-university professor rebuked the traditional parties for being lax on crime, for letting too many immigrants into the country, and for allowing them to stay without learning the language or integrating. Fortuyn declared that the Netherlands was 'full' and that the government should put the needs of mainstream Dutch people first.

Fortuyn's solution? Do away with back-room politics and elect a government led by business people and visionaries. After years of glacial government (where political plans were checked and rechecked incessantly), Fortuyn's dynamism struck a chord across Dutch society.

Thousands of white, low-income earners in Rotterdam and other cities rallied round the gay, dandyish Pim. For a few fleeting months he was feted as the next prime minister, even though his opponents accused him of pursuing right-wing, racist policies like those of France's Jean-Marie Le Pen.

With just days to go before the general election in May 2002, the charismatic Fortuyn was assassinated by an animal-rights activist. The news sent a seismic jolt through the country. Riots erupted in front of parliament, and for a brief instant the threat of anarchy hung in the air.

The Lijst Pim Fortuyn (LPF) party was included in the next coalition, but there was no single figure to unite his followers. Bickering among the LPF's top ministers brought down the coalition in just 87 days. In the January 2003 general election, voters all but deserted the LPF and returned to the traditional parties.

So what remains of his legacy? Most Dutch agree a social rethink was overdue, but some fear Fortuyn opened a Pandora's box of racism and intolerance. Before we start talking about the closing of a society, however, it's worth recalling that the Dutch have a centuries-old tradition of welcoming newcomers from around the globe.

## Polders & Piles

*Amsterdam, that big city, is built on piles*
*And if that city were to fall over, who would pay for it?*
– Dutch Nursery Rhyme

Amsterdam sits on a mixture of spongy peat and clay resting on a stable layer of sand more than 12m down. The first wooden houses were simply placed on top of the peat and occasionally had to be raised as they sank.

When heavier brick and stone replaced wood, engineers perfected the art of driving wooden piles down to the sand layer, sawing off the protruding ends to equal height and erecting buildings on top of the stable foundation – there are 13,659 piles under the palace on The Dam alone! Even today, you'll also notice that the city's grandest churches have wooden roofs, rather than the heavier stone ones you find in other countries.

So long as the piles were completely submerged in ground water and air couldn't get to them, they wouldn't rot, but ground-water levels varied a bit and problems were unavoidable. Also, less-scrupulous builders didn't always use enough piles, drive them deeply enough or worry about piles that snapped in the process, and many old buildings show signs of unequal subsidence – very expensive to fix. Since WWII, concrete piles have been used: they cannot rot and can be driven deeper – 20m, into the second sand layer, or even 60m, into the third.

There's a deep parallel to Dutch social life here. The traditional social order was called *verzuiling*, or pillarisation. Each persuasion (religious, business interest, political, etc) had a pillar that supported the status quo even if it meant 'agreeing to disagree'. It also meant that each group could live more or less independently of, but in harmony with, the others. This practical set-up began to crumble by the 1960s when old divisions became largely irrelevant. One more recent example of the Polder Model in action: an arrangement by which, for much of the last two decades, in exchange for unions agreeing to minimise salary increases, employers would create more jobs, and the government would chip in with tax breaks and incentives.

Pillarisation is regarded as outdated now, but its influence can still be seen in the media, education and even sports. It also left Amsterdam with its strong legacy of tolerance.

once turned a blind eye to infractions in venues like clubs, there's now far more scrutiny than before. Even Amsterdammers who'd never think of stepping foot into a wild party or 'coffeeshop' find some of the new developments excessive.

# ENVIRONMENT

Much of the land around Amsterdam is polder, land that used to be at the bottom of lakes or the sea. It was reclaimed by building dykes across sea inlets and rivers and pumping the water out with windmills (later with steam and diesel pumps). While other nations were busy colonising other territories, the Dutch just went out and built them!

Polders were created on a massive scale: in the 20th century, huge portions of the former Zuiderzee (now the IJsselmeer, a lake closed off from the sea by a dyke) were surrounded by dykes and the water was pumped out to create vast swathes of flat and fertile agricultural land – the complete province of Flevoland, northeast of Amsterdam, was reclaimed from the sea.

## GREEN AMSTERDAM

The city centre is both very green and very much not. The central streets of Damrak, Rokin and Spuistraat, for example, feel like brick jungles, but virtually any canal is a lush green belt. Otherwise, if you're looking for greenery, look out the back window: many homes in the canal belt back onto gardens or courtyards.

If you're looking to let loose, your best bet is the large open field of Museumplein (p111), or the lovely Vondelpark (p112) nearby, both just south of the city centre. A further short ride away is the Amsterdamse Bos (p115). Don't neglect the large and lovely Artis Zoo (p102), the city's first park, in the Plantage district.

*Red Light District (p61)*

## Recycling & Waste

The Netherlands is famous for being forward-thinking with recycling, but if you're walking around looking for a place to recycle your half-litre water bottle you'll be looking for a long time. There are recycling bins for *papier* (paper) and *glas* (glass), but the rest goes into the bin conveniently marked 'rest'. Same goes for metal cans, although larger bottles are sold with a deposit of €0.25 (bottles don't need to be returned to the shop where you bought them). In an effort to cut down on waste, most supermarkets do not give away bags, though you're free to bring your own. Otherwise, bags can be purchased for €0.10.

In residential neighbourhoods, new garbage receptacles are built right into the sidewalk – a truck comes along, the receptacles rise out of the ground and are replaced.

There's a similarly nifty system for *urinoirs*, whose numbers seem to multiply in warm weather. These tall plastic stands look like the letter 'x' from the top, and in each of the four corners is a hole for your 'water' (face inward, not outward, please!). When they get full a truck comes and replaces them. Simple, very practical and a lot cheaper than paying €0.50 to use a public toilet somewhere (although there's no place to wash one's hands). The only drawback: no version for women.

## URBAN PLANNING & DEVELOPMENT

'Finding rented accommodation in Amsterdam sometimes seems an impossible task', reads the city's own website. 'Generally speaking you should expect a waiting time of over five years.' Daunting, isn't it?

Free marketeers would say that the current situation is the result of social policy that encouraged low-income housing for much of the postwar period. A mere 15% of city real estate is owner-occupied, the rest being rentals. Rents are strictly controlled, unless the property is so upmarket that it jumps the hurdle into a higher-end 'free-market' category. Other strict controls include the number of rooms a household may occupy.

The cost of real estate has skyrocketed in the past decade, and buying an apartment is out of reach for most Amsterdammers. Although prices have begun to fall, the going rate within the canal belt is about €4500 per square metre, which puts a modest one-bedroom apartment at €250,000-plus; a two-bedroom apartment in the suburbs starts at €200,000.

There remains a considerable housing shortage in town which is being alleviated by new construction in the Eastern Docklands district (p107), with some adventurous new designs that are setting standards.

# Arts

# ARTS

Amsterdam has long been an international centre of the arts thanks to its tolerant, cosmopolitan and democratic spirit. For much of its history, it lacked a royal court and wealthy Church – the usual art patrons elsewhere in Europe – but the large middle class more than compensated. Amsterdam achieved international renown in painting and architecture, and the current music scene is second to none.

## VISUAL ARTS

Sure, everyone goes to Amsterdam to see the paintings by the Dutch Masters, as well they should, but you'd be doing yourself a disservice to see nothing but that. The city's vibrant arts scene boasts a number of galleries housing contemporary paintings, photography and multimedia; while shows vary in topic and interest, there's no doubt that they're alluring.

## DUTCH PAINTING

With a lineup that includes Rembrandt, Frans Hals and Jan Vermeer, the Dutch Masters are, arguably, the best-known painters ever to come out of northern Europe. To understand them, though, requires a bit of history. It starts at a time when Italy was the centre of the art world and many early painters would go there to study.

### Flemish & Dutch Schools

Prior to the late 16th century, art in the Low Countries centered on the southern provinces (present-day Belgium), particularly the Flemish cities of Ghent, Bruges and Antwerp. Paintings of the Flemish School featured biblical and allegorical subject matter popular with patrons of the day (the Church, the court and to a lesser extent the nobility).

**Top Five Museums**

- CoBrA Museum (p116)
- FOAM Photography Museum (p93)
- Museum Het Rembrandthuis (p97)
- Van Gogh Museum (p111)
- Museum Van Loon (p94)

Famous names include Jan van Eyck (d 1441), the founder of the Flemish School, who perfected the technique of oil painting; Rogier van der Weyden (1400–64), whose religious portraits showed the personalities of his subjects; and Hieronymus (also known as Jeroen) Bosch (1450–1516), with macabre allegorical paintings full of religious topics. Pieter Breugel the Elder (1525–69) used Flemish landscapes and peasant life in his allegorical scenes.

In the northern Low Countries (present-day Netherlands), artists began to develop a style of their own. Although the artists of the day never achieved the recognition of their Flemish counterparts, the Dutch School, as it came to be called, was known for favouring realism over allegory. Haarlem (p229) was the centre of this movement, with artists like Jan Mostaert (1475–1555), Lucas van Leyden (1494–1533) and Jan van Scorel (1494–1562). Painters in the city of Utrecht were famous for using chiaroscuro (deep contrast of light and shade), a technique associated with the Italian master Caravaggio.

**Top Five Galleries**

- De Appel (p91)
- Herman Brood Galerie (p158)
- Netherlands Media Art Institute (p85)
- Reflex Modern Art Gallery (p206)
- SMART Project Space (p164)

# Golden Age (17th Century)

With the Spanish expelled from the Low Countries, the character of the art market changed. There was no Church to buy artworks and no court to speak of, so art became a business, and artists had to survive in a free market. In place of Church and court was a new, bourgeois society of merchants, artisans and shopkeepers who didn't mind spending 'reasonable' money to brighten up their houses and workplaces. The key: they had to be pictures the buyers could relate to.

Painters became entrepreneurs in their own right, churning out banal works, copies and masterpieces in factory-like studios. Paintings became mass products, sold at markets alongside furniture and chickens. Soon the wealthiest households were covered in paintings from top to bottom. Foreign visitors commented that even bakeries and butcher shops seemed to have a painting or two on the wall.

Most painters specialised in one of these genres, but Rembrandt van Rijn (1606–69; see boxed text, p26) defied such easy classification. The greatest and most versatile of 17th-century artists, he excelled in all these categories. Sometimes he was centuries ahead of his time, as with the emotive brush strokes of his later works.

Another great painter of this period, Frans Hals (1581/85–1666), was born in Antwerp but lived in Haarlem. He devoted most of his career to portraits, dabbling in occasional genre scenes with dramatic chiaroscuro. His ability to render the expressions of his subjects was equal to that of Rembrandt, though he didn't explore their characters as much. Both masters used the same expressive, unpolished brush strokes and seemed to develop from a bright exuberance in their early careers to a darker, more solemn approach later on. His work was also admired by the 19th-century impressionists. In fact, Hals' *The Merry Drinker* (1630) in the Rijksmuseum's collection, with its bold brush strokes, could almost have been painted by an impressionist.

Hals also specialised in beautiful group portraits in which the groups almost looked natural, unlike the rigid lineups produced by lesser contemporaries – though he wasn't as cavalier as Rembrandt in subordinating faces to the composition. A good example is the pair of paintings known collectively as *The Regents & the Regentesses of the Old Men's Alms House* (1664) in the Frans Hals Museum (p229) in Haarlem. He lived in that almshouse, which is now the museum.

The grand trio of 17th-century masters is completed by Johannes Vermeer (also known as Jan Vermeer, say '*fehr-mehr*'; 1632–75) of Delft. He produced only 35 meticulously crafted paintings in his career and died poor with 10 children – his baker accepted two paintings from his wife as payment for a debt of more than 600 guilders. Yet Vermeer mastered genre painting like no other artist. Other paintings include historical/biblical scenes in his earlier career, his famous *View of Delft* (1661) in the Mauritshuis in Den Haag (p233), and some tender portraits of unknown women, such as the stunningly beautiful *Girl with a Pearl Earring* (1666), also in the Mauritshuis.

His work is known for serene light pouring through tall windows. The calm, spiritual effect is enhanced by dark blues, deep reds, warm yellows and supremely balanced composition. Good examples include Rijksmuseum's *The Kitchen Maid* (also known as *The Milkmaid*, 1658) and *Woman in Blue Reading a Letter* (1664), or, for his use of perspective, *The Love Letter* (1670). *The Little Street* (1658) in the Rijksmuseum's collection is Vermeer's only street scene.

## Painting Styles from the Golden Age

**Religious art** Unlike in the earlier Flemish school, which favoured allegory, Dutch School art had to be 'historically correct', in line with the Calvinist emphasis on 'true' events as described in the Bible. The same could be said for Greek or Roman historical scenes.

**Portraiture** A smash hit in this society of middle-class upstarts – group portraits did exceedingly well. Group portraits also had the advantage of costing less per head!

**Maritime scenes and cityscapes** Sold well to the government.

**Landscapes** Winter scenes and still lifes (also of priceless, exotic flowers and delicious meals), found in many living rooms.

**Genre painting** Depicted domestic life or daily life outside.

## Rembrandt: Lauded, Reviled, Genius

The 17th century's greatest artist, Rembrandt van Rijn (1606–69) grew up a miller's son in Leiden but became an accomplished painter by his early twenties.

In 1631 he came to Amsterdam to run the painting studio of the wealthy art dealer Hendrick van Uylenburgh. Portraits were the studio's cash cow, and Rembrandt and his staff (or 'pupils') churned out scores of them, including group portraits such as The Anatomy Lesson of Dr Tulp (1632). In 1634 he married Van Uylenburgh's niece Saskia, who often modelled for him.

Rembrandt fell out with his boss, but his wife's capital helped him buy the sumptuous house next door to Van Uylenburgh's studio (the current **Museum Het Rembrandthuis** p97). There Rembrandt set up his own studio, with staff who worked in a warehouse in the Jordaan. These were happy years: his paintings were a success and his studio became the largest in Holland, though his gruff manner and open agnosticism didn't win him dinner-party invitations from the elite.

Rembrandt became one of the city's main art collectors and often sketched and painted for himself, urging staff to do likewise. Residents of the surrounding Jewish quarter provided perfect material for his dramatic biblical scenes.

In 1642, a year after the birth of their son Titus, Saskia died and business went downhill. Although Rembrandt's majestic group portrait The Nightwatch (1642) was hailed by art critics (it's now the Rijksmuseum's prize exhibit), some of the influential people he depicted were not pleased. Each subject had paid 100 guilders, and some were unhappy at being pushed to the background. In response, Rembrandt told them where they could push the painting – suddenly he received far fewer orders.

Rembrandt began an affair with his son's governess but kicked her out a few years later when he fell for the new maid, Hendrickje Stoffels, who bore him a daughter, Cornelia. The public didn't take kindly to the man's lifestyle and his spiralling debts, and in 1656 he went bankrupt. His house and rich art collection were sold and he moved to the Rozengracht in the Jordaan.

No longer the darling of the wealthy, Rembrandt continued to paint, draw and etch – his etchings on display in the Rembrandthuis are some of the finest ever produced. He also received the occasional commission, including the monumental Conspiracy of Claudius Civilis (1661) for the City Hall, although authorities disliked it and had it removed. In 1662 he completed the Staalmeesters (the 'Syndics') for the drapers' guild and ensured that everybody remained clearly visible, though it ended up being his last group portrait.

The works of his later period show that Rembrandt had lost none of his touch. No longer constrained by the wishes of clients, he enjoyed new-found freedom; his works became more unconventional yet showed an ever-stronger empathy with their subject matter, as for instance in A Couple: The Jewish Bride (1665). The many portraits of Titus and Hendrickje, and his ever gloomier self-portraits, are among the most stirring in the history of art.

A plague epidemic in 1663–64 killed one in seven Amsterdammers, including Hendrickje. Titus died in 1668, aged 27 and just married, and Rembrandt died a year later, a broken man.

Around the middle of the century, the stern focus on mood and subtle play of light began to make way for the splendour of the baroque. Jacob van Ruysdael (c1628–82) went for dramatic skies and Aelbert Cuyp (1620–91) for Italianate landscapes. Ruysdael's pupil Meindert Hobbema preferred less heroic and more playful bucolic scenes full of pretty detail. You'll notice that all of these men have streets named after them in the Old South.

The genre paintings of Jan Steen (1626–79) show the almost frivolous aspect of baroque. Steen was also a tavern-keeper, and his depictions of domestic chaos led to the Dutch expression 'a Jan Steen household'. A good example is the animated revelry of The Merry Family (1668) in the Rijksmuseum's collection: it shows adults having a good time around the dinner table, oblivious to the children in the foreground pouring themselves a drink.

## 18th & 19th Centuries

The Golden Age of Dutch painting ended almost as suddenly as it began, when the French invaded the Low Countries in 1672. The economy collapsed and took with it the market for paintings. Painters who stayed in business concentrated on 'safe' works that repeated earlier successes. In the 18th century they copied French styles, pandering to the awe for anything French.

The results were competent but not ground-breaking. Cornelis Troost (1697–1750) was one of the best genre painters, sometimes compared to Hogarth for introducing humour into his pastels of domestic revelry.

Gerard de Lairesse (1640–1711) and Jacob de Wit (1695–1754) specialised in decorating the walls and ceilings of buildings – De Wit's trompe l'oeil decorations in the current Theatermuseum (p82) and Bijbels Museum (p83) are worth seeing.

The late 18th century and most of the 19th century produced little of note, save for the landscapes and seascapes of Johan Barthold Jongkind (1819–91) and the gritty, almost photographic Amsterdam scenes of George Hendrik Breitner (1857–1923). They appear to have inspired French impressionists, many of whom visited Amsterdam.

Jongkind and Breitner reinvented 17th-century realism and influenced the Hague School of the last decades of the 19th century. Painters such as Hendrik Mesdag (1831–1915), Jozef Israels (1824–1911) and the three Maris brothers (Jacob, Matthijs and Willem) created landscapes, seascapes and genre works, including the impressive *Panorama Mesdag* (1881), a gigantic, 360–degree painting of the seaside town of Scheveningen viewed from a dune.

Without a doubt, the greatest 19th-century Dutch painter was Vincent van Gogh (1853–90), whose convulsive patterns and furious colours were in a world of their own and still defy comfortable categorisation. A post-impressionist? A forerunner of expressionism? For more about his life and works, see the Van Gogh Museum (p111).

# De Stijl

In his early career, Piet Mondriaan (1872–1944) – he dropped the second 'a' in his name when he moved to Paris in 1910 – painted in the Hague School tradition, but after flirting with Cubism he began painting in bold rectangular patterns, using only the three primary colours (yellow, blue and red) set against the three neutrals (white, grey and black). He named this style 'neo-plasticism' and viewed it as an undistorted expression of reality in pure form and pure colour. His *Composition in Red, Black, Blue, Yellow & Grey* (1920), in the Stedelijk Museum's collection, is an elaborate example. Mondriaan's later works were more stark (or 'pure') and became dynamic again when he moved to New York in 1940. The world's largest collection of his paintings resides in the Gemeentemuseum (Municipal Museum, p234) of his native Den Haag.

Mondriaan was one of the leading exponents of De Stijl (The Style), a Dutch design movement that aimed to harmonise all the arts by bringing artistic expressions back to their essence. Its advocate was the magazine of the same name, first published in 1917 by Theo van Doesburg (1883–1931). Van Doesburg produced works similar to Mondriaan's, though he dispensed with the thick, black lines and later tilted his rectangles at 45 degrees, departures serious enough for Mondriaan to call off the friendship.

Throughout the 1920s and 1930s, De Stijl also attracted sculptors, poets, architects and designers. One of these was Gerrit Rietveld (1888–1964), designer of the Van Gogh Museum and several other buildings but best known internationally for his furniture, such as the Mondriaanesque *Red Blue Chair* (1918) and his range of uncomfortable zigzag chairs that, viewed side-on, are simply a 'Z' with a backrest.

*Rijksmuseum (p110)*

## Two Doors Close (Temporarily), Another One Opens

Two of the city's top museums are being renovated and may be closed when you visit.

The **Rijksmuseum** (p110), one of the leading tourist attractions in the Netherlands for its collections of Dutch Masters, will close until 2008 for renovations both planned (general upgrade) and unplanned (discovery of asbestos). Although the main building will be closed, the **Philips Wing** in the rear will have some 50 works on display at any one time. The Rijksmuseum's most-famous possession, Rembrandt's *The Nightwatch*, will be among them, as will several Vermeers and a selection of Delftware. The Rijksmuseum is due to have touring exhibits throughout the Netherlands during this time. Visit the website www.rijksmuseum.nl for details.

The nearby **Stedelijk Museum** (p111; contemporary art, mostly 20th century) will close for renovations until 2007. Until then, part of its collection will be shown over three floors of the old postal building just east of Centraal Station on Ooosterdokseiland.

Meanwhile, the Russians are coming! The State Hermitage Museum of St Petersburg is opening a branch along the Amstel in the converted almshouse known as the **Amstelhof** (p92). At the time of writing, the first stage, the Neerlandia building, was slated to open early in 2004. Small but fine exhibits include Greek Gold and treasures of Nicholas and Alexandra. The Amstelhof is due for completion in 2007 bringing the total gallery space to 4000 sq m.

One of the most remarkable graphic artists of the 20th century was Maurits Cornelis Escher (1902–72). His drawings, lithos and woodcuts of blatantly impossible images continue to fascinate mathematicians and hang on college dorm walls everywhere: a waterfall feeds itself; people go up and down a staircase that ends where it starts; a pair of hands draw each other.

## CoBrA Movement

After WWII, artists rebelled against artistic conventions and vented their rage in abstract expressionism. In Amsterdam, Karel Appel (1921–) and Constant (Constant Nieuwenhuis, 1920–) drew on styles pioneered by Paul Klee and Joan Miró, and exploited bright colours and 'uncorrupted' children's art to produce lively works that leapt off the canvas. In Paris in 1945 they met up with the Dane Asger Jorn (1914–73) and the Belgian Corneille (Cornelis van Beverloo, 1922–), and together with several other artists and writers formed a group known as CoBrA (COpenhagen, BRussels, Amsterdam). It's been called the last great avant-garde movement.

Their first major exhibition, in the Stedelijk Museum in 1949, aroused a storm of protest ('My child paints like that too'). Still, the CoBrA artists exerted a strong influence in their respective countries even after they disbanded in 1951. The CoBrA Museum (p116) in Amstelveen displays a good range of their works, including colourful ceramics.

## Current

Marlene Dumas (1953–), a native of South Africa and now resident of Amsterdam, achieved fame in the 1980s and is now best known for her drawings and paintings of the human figure – instead of using live models, she relies on images from the mass media for her subjects. Amsterdam-based painter Peter Klashorst (1957–) specialises in portraits and nudes in bright colours. He was imprisoned in Africa for painting nude women and was also the subject of a reality television show.

In the world of sculpture, Rotterdam-based Joep van Lieshout (1963–), through his company, Atelier Van Lieshout, is known for furniture, mobile-home units, model farms, even a self-contained replica village. If you don't catch his work in an exhibition, you can view his Mediamatic Supermarket, an aluminium clad, curved box of an addition to the Spar Market near the southern entrance to the IJ Tunnel. Hans van Houwelingen (1957–) is especially known for creating art in public spaces.

Contemporary Dutch designers who are finding an international following include Amsterdam's own Marcel Wanders (for chairs of knotted rope), and Rotterdam's Hella Jongerius (for hand-embroidered ceramics – yes, ceramics).

## Photography & New Media

Photographer Rineke Dijkstra (1959–) creates unflinching head-on portraits, both analytical and empathetic, of common people like soldiers carrying rifles and folks in bathing suits on the beach.

Amsterdam-based Aernout Mik (1962–) has exhibited in Europe and North America with film installations known for their combining studies in group dynamics with a sculptor's sense of space. Marijke van Warmerdam (1959–; based in Amsterdam and New York) creates absurdist loops of everyday life in repeating sequences – eg the Japanese technique of bowing.

# MUSIC

The dour church elders who once dismissed music as frivolous began to allow organ music in churches in the 17th century – it kept people out of pubs. With the possible exception of Jan Pieterszoon Sweelinck (1562–1621), an organ player in the Oude Kerk with an international reputation as a composer and a strong following in Germany, Amsterdam contributed relatively little to the world's music scene of that era.

Today, however, the world's top acts appear regularly and local musicians excel in (modern) classical music, jazz and techno/dance. In summer, free jazz, classical and world-music performances are staged in the Vondelpark (p112), and free lunchtime concerts are held at various venues throughout the year. The Uitmarkt (p10) festival at the end of August also provides lots of free music. For more about music venues, see the Entertainment chapter (p154), and check the free entertainment paper *Uitkrant* for details.

## CLASSICAL

The Netherlands has orchestras in cities throughout the country, but Amsterdam's Concertgebouw Orkest (Royal Concertgebouw Orchestra) towers over them all. It frequently performs abroad, matching works by famous composers with little-known gems of the modern era. Since the late 1980s, the director has been Riccardo Chailly; Mariss Jansons (whose long list of credentials includes the Pittsburgh Symphony) is set to take over in September 2004.

If pianist Ronald Brautigam is on the bill you'll be guaranteed a top-flight performance. Violinist/violist Isabelle van Keulen also brings in the crowds – she has also founded her own chamber music festival in Delft. Cellists of note (so to speak) are Quirine Viersen and fiery Pieter Wispelwey.

Young pianist Wibi Soerjadi (1970–) is one of the country's most successful classical musicians. He specialises in romantic works – and being handsome. Elderly ladies swoon over his Javanese-prince looks and his penchant for driving his Ferrari fast.

Soprano Charlotte Margiono is known for her interpretations of *Le Nozze de Figaro* and *The Magic Flute*. Mezzo-soprano Jard van Nes has a giant reputation for her solo parts in Mahler's symphonies.

For 'old music', you can't go past the Combattimento Consort Amsterdam (Bach, Vivaldi and Händel; venues vary). The Amsterdam Baroque Orchestra, conducted by Ton Koopman, tours worldwide but, when home, can often be seen at the **Concertgebouw** (p110). Koopman also conducts the Radio Chamber Orchestra, along with Frans Brüggen, best known for his work with the Orchestra of the 18th century. Performances by the Radio Philharmonic Orchestra are often recorded for radio and TV.

The Nederlandse Opera is based in the **Stopera** (p98; officially called the Muziektheater), where it stages world-class performances, though occasionally experimental fare stirs up controversy.

## MODERN CLASSICAL & EXPERIMENTAL

The IJsbreker (p162) is the usual venue for this type of music, which seems to thrive in Amsterdam. Dutch modern composers include Michel van der Aa, Louis Andriessen, Theo

Loevendie, Klaas de Vries and the late Ton de Leeuw. Worthwhile performers include The Trio, Asko Ensemble, Nieuw Ensemble, the Mondriaan Kwartet and Schönberg Ensemble.

The IJsbreker is due to move into a new building, projected early 2005.

## JAZZ

The distinction between modern classical and improvised music can be vague. Jazz band leaders such as Willem Breuker and Willem van Manen of the Contraband have a decades-long reputation for straddling the two genres.

Recently, the Dutch jazz scene has become more mainstream with gifted young chanteuses such as Fleurine and especially Suriname-born Denise Jannah, widely recognised as the country's best jazz singer. The latter is the first singer from Suriname to be signed to the legendary Blue Note label. Her repertoire consists of American standards but she adds elements of Surinamese music on stage.

Belting out a tune

Astrid Seriese and Carmen Gomez operate in the crossover field, where jazz verges on, or blends with, pop. Father and daughter Hans and Candy Dulfer, tenor and alto saxophonists respectively, are a bit more daring. Dad, in particular, constantly extends his musical boundaries by experimenting with sampling techniques drawn from the hip-hop genre. Candy is better known internationally, thanks to her performances with Prince, Van Morrison, Dave Stewart, Pink Floyd and Maceo Parker, among others.

Trumpeter and Jordaan native Saskia Laroo mixes jazz with dance but is also respected in more traditional circles. Other leading instrumental jazz players include pianist and Thelonius Monk Award–winning Michiel Borstlap and bass player Hein van de Geyn. Borstlap has also plunged into dance music – his recent (triple) CD, *Gramercy Park*, features house DJ Ronald Molendijk along with traditional jazz tracks and even classical music.

An effervescent soloist on flute is Peter Guidi, who set up the jazz programme at the Muziekschool Amsterdam and leads its Jazzmania big band.

The city's most important jazz venue is Bimhuis (p181) on Oude Schans. In 2005 it is due to move into the same building as De IJsbreker. For the biggest party with the biggest names in jazz, check out the North Sea Jazz Festival (p10), near Den Haag, every summer.

## POP & DANCE

Amsterdam is the pop capital of the Netherlands, and bands and DJs are attracted to the city like moths to a flame. If successful they usually jump on a plane to London or LA, as the Dutch themselves lament.

In the 1960s, though, the country's pop centre was The Hague. Even if the self-proclaimed 'Dutch invasion' seems a stretch, Shocking Blue hit No 1 in the USA with 'Venus', and Golden Earring (still going strong for over 40 years) had a string of hits and successful international tours; their album *Eight Miles High* went gold in the US. Famous Amsterdam bands in the 1960s were the Outsiders – a wild band whose lead singer, Wally Tax, was reputed to be the man with the longest hair in the country – and the Hunters, an instrumental guitar group that included Jan Akkerman. Akkerman later achieved international fame in the progressive rock band Focus (featuring Thijs van Leer as chief yodeler) and was proclaimed the best guitarist in the world in 1973.

Also in the '70s, Herman Brood burst onto the scene with His *Wild Romance* and became a real-life druggy rock star (see p158).

In the late 1970s the squatter movement spawned a lively punk music scene, followed by New Wave. In the mid-1980s Amsterdam was a centre for guitar-driven rock bands like Claw Boys Claw. Most lyrics were in English, but the pop group Doe Maar broke through in Dutch, inspiring scores of bands such as Tröckener Kecks.

Around this time Amsterdam also evolved into a capital of club music, with its spiritual base at the überclub Roxy (unfortunately it later burnt to a crisp). Music evolved from house to techno to R&B. Perhaps the best-known Dutch dance variant of house was 'gabber', a style which was popularised by acts like Charly Lownoise & Mental Theo in which the number of beats per minute and the noise of buzzing synthesizers went beyond belief.

The hip grooves of Candy Dulfer (opposite) and the hip-hoppy Urban Dance Squad made America's Top 20 during the decade. Bettie Serveert (Betty serves), a nod to Dutch tennis player Betty Stöve, grew into one of the biggest bands on the club circuit. Amsterdam also boasts a vital hip-hop scene, spearheaded by the Dutch-rapping Osdorp Posse.

In 2001 a moody Herman Brood flung himself from the roof of the Amsterdam Hilton, triggering a run on his records and paintings. After his death, the remake *My Way* became Brood's first (and last) No 1 hit in the Netherlands.

The pop scene has gone underground for the time being, but there's some interesting stuff going on in the clubs – check the reggae of Beef or The Amsterdam Klezmer Band. K-Otic is a preppy vocals-and-guitar outfit created in a star-making stunt organised by several record companies.

Raves are organised at venues throughout town. The Dutch have a major presence in the world DJ rankings, most of them big-room clubhouse and trance artists that have appeared in the US and Britain. Tiësto is the undisputed trancemeister, and other big names include Armin van Buuren, Laidback Luke and Ferry Corsten.

Pop festivals come out of the woodwork in the warmer months: Pinkpop (p10) in Landgraaf, Parkpop (p10) in Den Haag and Dynamo Open Air at Neunen. Dance Valley (p10) near Haarlem pulls more than 100 bands and a sleepless crowd of near-Woodstock proportions. Lowlands is a mega alt-music fest for happy campers held near Six Flags in Flevoland.

# WORLD MUSIC

Cosmopolitan Amsterdam offers a wealth of world music. Suriname-born Ronald Snijders, a top jazz flautist, often participates in world-music projects. Another jazz flautist heading towards 'world' is the eternal Chris Hinze, for instance with his album *Tibet Impressions*, though most of his repertoire falls in the New Age category.

Fra-Fra-Sound plays 'paramaribop', a unique mixture of traditional Surinamese *kaseko* and jazz (the moniker is a contraction of Paramaribo, the capital of Suriname, and bebop), but the bulk of world repertoire from Amsterdam is Latin, ranging from Cuban salsa to Dominican merengue and Argentinian tango. Try the following bands to get a taste of the local world scene: Nueva Manteca (salsa), Sexteto Canyengue (tango) and Eric Vaarzon Morel (flamenco).

An interesting 'Amsterdam-Brazilian' band is Zuco 103, which combines bossa nova and samba with DJ rubs on the turntable. It has strong ties with the equally eclectic New Cool Collective, a 22-member big band that blends jazz with drum n' bass.

For more information about any of these artists and gigs at Melkweg (especially), Paradiso, Akhnaton and Latin bars, see the excellent monthly salsa magazine called *Oye Listen* (€3, published in Dutch and Spanish), available in world music shops such as Concerto (p204).

The New Cool Collective is a big band with vocals that serves up a groovy cocktail of Latin, jazz, New Age and sixties go-go – they're often at Panama (p169).

The Amsterdam Roots Festival of world music is organised at different locations every year in June, centred on the Oosterpark – check the Uitburo, the VVV, or www.amsterdamroots.nl. The theatre of the Tropenmuseum (p108) often hosts non-Western music concerts.

# LITERATURE

Dutch literature has long been neglected by the English-speaking world. However, since 1991 the Dutch Literary Production & Translation Fund has been propagating Dutch literature abroad, and the efforts have begun to pay off. Many titles now appearing in English were already bestsellers in German and other languages.

In the Middle Ages Dutch literature stuck to epic tales of chivalry and allegories. But that changed in the 16th century with Erasmus, a leading Dutch humanist who wrote a satire on the church and society called *Praise of Folly*.

Golden Age literary lights included Spinoza, an Amsterdam Jew who wrote deep philosophical treatises. Spinoza rejected the concept of free will, contending that humans acted purely out of self-preservation. Mind and body were made of the same stuff he alternately called God and Nature, which got him into all kinds of trouble.

The Dutch Shakespeare, Joost van den Vondel, is heavy going in his tragedy *Gijsbrecht van Aemstel* (1637, available in translation). It describes the agony of the local count who went into exile. Vondel's best tragedy, *Lucifer* (1654), has also been translated. Other big authors of this period, Bredero (comedies) and Hooft (poems, plays, history, philosophy), have yet to appear in English.

The most interesting 19th-century author was Eduard Douwes Dekker, a colonial administrator and Amsterdam native who wrote under the pseudonym Multatuli (Latin for 'I have suffered greatly'; p77). His *Max Havelaar: or the Coffee Auctions of the Dutch Trading Company* (1860) exposed colonial narrowmindedness in the dealings of a self-righteous coffee merchant. It shocked Dutch society and led to a review of the 'culture system' in the East Indies (the forced production of tropical crops for export). The Hague author Louis Couperus (*The Hidden Force*, 1900) explored the mystery of the East Indies from the colonialist's perspective.

The WWII occupation was a traumatic period that spawned many insightful works, including *The Diary of Anne Frank* (p80). Hillesum's *Etty: An Interrupted Life* is in a similar vein but more mature. Marga Minco (*The Fall*, *An Empty House*, *Bitter Herbs*) explores the war years from the perspective of a Jewish woman who

> ## Did You Know?
>
> American author John Irving (*The World According to Garp*, *The Cider House Rules*) set his novel *A Widow for One Year* in Amsterdam's Red Light District, and Irvine Welsh (*Trainspotting*, *Porno*) wrote *The Acid House*, a short-story collection about Amsterdam's drug underworld.

survived. A brilliant, more-recent novel that deals with the war years is Tessa de Loo's *The Twins* (1993, English translation 2001), about separated twins who grow up on different sides of the fence.

Amsterdam author Harry Mulisch focuses on Dutch apathy during WWII (*The Last Call* and *The Assault*, which was made into an Oscar-winning film), but he has written much else that doesn't involve the war. In his *The Discovery of Heaven*, two friends find they were conceived on the same day, and share love, hate and women on an extraordinary quest that takes them to St Peter's gate. Gerard Reve's *Parents Worry* is a historical novel about a day in the ravaged life of a poet looking for truth and a way out.

Jan Wolkers shocked Dutch readers in the 1960s with his provocatively misogynist but powerful *Turkish Delight*, made into a (Dutch) film by Paul Verhoeven starring Rutger Hauer. Xaviera Hollander (Vera de Vries) shocked the USA with an account of her call-girl experiences in *The Happy Hooker*.

Simon Carmiggelt (*A Dutchman's Slight Adventures*, *I'm Just Kidding*) wrote amusing vignettes of the Pijp neighbourhood life in his column in the newspaper *Het Parool*. Nicolas Freeling (1927–2003, *A Long Silence*, *Love in Amsterdam*, *Because of the Cats*) created the BBC's Van der Valk detective series. Jan-Willem van der Wetering (*Hard Rain*) is another author of off-beat detective stories.

Cees Nooteboom (*A Song of Truth and Semblance*, *In the Dutch Mountains*) is accessible and amusing. For more substance, read *The Virtuoso* by Margriet de Moor, a novel about a mother, daughter and piano (*not* set in New Zealand); or *A Heart of Stone* by Renate

Dorrestein, the Dutch Fay Weldon. *In Babylon* by Marcel Möring is the perfect novel, a sort of *Arabian Nights* where people tell each other stories. Arthur Japin's *The Two Hearts of Kwasi Boachi* is a true account of two African princes who were dragged off to Holland in 1837 but failed to fit in.

Lieve Joris, an Amsterdam-based Flemish author, writes about cultures in transition in Africa, the Middle East and Eastern Europe. Her *Gates of Damascus*, about daily life in Syria, has been published in the Lonely Planet Journeys series, as has *Mali Blues*, an account of her quest to know a Mali musician. Another book in this series is *The Rainbird: A Central African Journey* by Jan Brokken, a highly regarded novelist, travel narrator and literary journalist. It's a fascinating account of white explorers, missionaries, slavers and adventurers who traipsed through the jungles of Gabon.

# THEATRE

The city has a rich theatrical tradition dating back to medieval times. In the Golden Age, when Dutch was the language of trade, local companies toured the theatres of Europe with Vondel's tragedies, Bredero's comedies and Hooft's verses. They're still performed locally in more modern renditions.

Theatre was immensely popular with all levels of society, for many reasons, not least of which because plays were often performed outdoors. Towards the end of the 19th century, however, it had become snobbish, with little room for development.

This attitude persisted until the late 1960s, when disgruntled actors began to throw tomatoes at their older colleagues and engage the audience in discussions about the essence of theatre. Avant-garde theatre companies such as Mickery and Shaffy made Amsterdam a centre for experimental theatre, and many smaller companies sprang up in the 1970s and 1980s.

Most of these have now merged or disappeared, but survivors and newcomers still stage excellent productions – visual feasts with striking sets, lighting and creative costumes. The language barrier can be an issue, depending on the production.

When it's not touring abroad, De Dogtroep stages fancy and unpredictable 'happenings' in quirky venues like the passenger ship terminal. Each show is supported by flashy multimedia effects and technical gadgetry, with every set specially developed by a team of designers and painters. A spin-off, Warner & Consorten stages dialogue-free shows that inject humour into everyday situations and objects, while music is generated with weird materials.

Cosmic (p184) deserves special mention for productions reflecting the city's multicultural communities (Surinamese, Indonesian, etc). The comedy scene is led by English-language outfits like Boom Chicago (p184).

English-language companies often visit Amsterdam, especially in summer – check the *Uitkrant* or ask at the Uitburo. Glitzy large-budget musicals in the *Chicago* and *Abba* mould have won over audiences in recent years – typically they play to full houses in the Koninklijke Theater Carré (p185) or other large venues.

The Dutch also produce some of the world's best youth theatre, and don't forget the Marionettentheater (p184), where marionettes perform opera.

The Holland Festival (p10), Over Het IJ (p10) and the Uitmarkt (p10) are big theatre events. Also worth catching is the International Theatre School Festival (p10) at the end of June, in the theatres around Nes (Frascati, Brakke Grond etc).

# DANCE

Amsterdam's National Ballet (www.het-nationale-ballet.nl) performs mainly classical ballets but also presents 20th-century works by Dutch choreographers such as Rudi van Dantzig and Toer van Schayk. The Ballet has helped launch careers of promising dancemasters such as John Wisman and Ted Brandsen (who is now the artistic director).

The Netherlands is also a world leader in modern dance. The troupe of the Nederlands Dans Theater in Den Haag leaps and pirouettes to international audiences. There are also many smaller modern dance companies such as Introdans, which can truly be described as poetry in motion. Amsterdam's Julidans festival in July brings dancers together from all over the world.

## De Tango

Tango has caught on around the Netherlands since Argentinian-born crown princess Máxima Zorreguieta married into the Dutch royal family. While it hasn't risen to the level of craze in Amsterdam, many dance schools now offer salsa and tango classes along with hip-hop and ballroom moves.

# CINEMA

Dutch films haven't exactly set the world on fire, though this has more to do with the language barrier and funding problems in a modest distribution area than with lack of talent. The Dutch film industry produces about 20 films annually, often in association with other countries. Private funding is increasing as government funding has been scaled back in recent years.

One of the most important Dutch directors of all time was Joris Ivens (1898–1989), who made award-winning documentaries about social and political issues: the Spanish Civil War; impoverished Belgian miners; Vietnam. He was also an accomplished visual artist: *Rain* (1929), a 15-minute impression of a rain shower in Amsterdam, took four months to shoot.

Directors, actors and cinematographers who've made the jump to English have often done quite well for themselves in Hollywood. Paul Verhoeven (*Robocop, Total Recall, Basic Instinct, Starship Troopers*) is perhaps the best-known Dutch director, though he was also behind the disastrous *Showgirls*. Jan de Bont directed the box-office hits *Speed* and *Twister*, and the 2003 film *Lara Croft: Tomb Raider*.

Marleen Gorris directed *Antonia's Line*, which won the Oscar for best foreign film in 1996. She has since gone on to work with Vanessa Redgrave (Virginia Woolf's *Mrs Dalloway*) and Shirley Maclaine, Jennifer Coolidge and Julia Stiles in *Carolina*. George Sluizer *(The Vanishing)*, Dick Maas (the *Flodder* series, *Amsterdamned, Down*) and Fons Rademakers *(The Assault)* have also made names internationally, even if they are not household names.

Mike van Diem is a new-generation director with success abroad – his *Karakter* won the Oscar for best foreign film in 1998. His cameraman, Rogier Stoffers, went on to make a name for himself in Hollywood (he also shot *John Q* and *School of Rock*).

Among Dutch actors, Rutger Hauer began his acting career at home as the lead in Paul Verhoeven's *Turks Fruit* (Turkish Delight, an Oscar nominee for best foreign film in the early 1970s), but has since gained glory in Hollywood with convincing bad-guy performances in disturbing films such as *The Hitcher* and *Blade Runner*. These days he works consistently, even if not in starring roles. Jeroen Krabbé also became a well-paid Hollywood actor (*The Fugitive, The Living Daylights, Prince of Tides*) and has now turned to directing, including *Left Luggage* starring Isabella Rosselini.

One of the most hilarious films featuring Amsterdam is French director Jacques Tati's classic *Traffic* (1971), which follows Monsieur Hulot as he bumbles his way through the car show in the RAI exhibition buildings. Bert Haanstra, a leading Dutch documentary maker, codirected the Amsterdam scenes.

Movies screened in the Netherlands are rarely ever dubbed but instead subtitled – as any film purist will tell you they should be.

The Filmmuseum (p112) in the Vondelpark is the national museum on this subject and occasionally screens interesting films from its huge archive. As we went to press, the Filmmuseum held daily screenings at the Bellevue/Calypso complex just off Leidseplein.

Several film festivals are held every year throughout the Netherlands, including the Rotterdam International Film Festival in February, Utrecht's Netherlands Film Festival in September, and Amsterdam's International Documentary Film Festival, held in December.

# Architecture

# Architecture

Amsterdam is an architectural marvel, with no fewer than 7000 registered historical buildings. Yet only a few buildings impress with size or scale. Rather, the city's beauty lies in the countless private dwellings, especially within the canal belt – each one, it seems, stands out in its own way. No other city in Europe has such a wealth of residential architecture.

Amsterdam was largely built by citizens and businesses, not by the government, although the government has traditionally provided land, determined sizes for housing plots and enforced what are often-stringent building standards. Even today, authorities tend to give architects more leeway than they're used to elsewhere, ensuring that Amsterdam remains at the architectural cutting edge – all the more remarkable considering the limited space.

## MIDDLE AGES

The city's oldest surviving building is the Gothic Oude Kerk (Old Church; p61), which dates from the early 14th century. The second-oldest is the late-Gothic Nieuwe Kerk (New Church; p59) from the early 15th century. In both these churches, note the timber vaulting (the marshy ground precluded the use of heavy stone) and the use of brick rather than stone in the walls. Stone was both heavy and scarce, yet there was plenty of clay and sand to produce bricks. Also note how the interior focus has shifted from the (Catholic) choir and altar to the (Protestant) pulpit.

The earliest houses were made of timber and clay with thatched roofs. Fires in the 15th century burnt down much of the city centre, and timber side walls gave way to brick; in the 16th century the thatched roofs were replaced by tiles. Timber was still used for façades and gables into the 17th century, but eventually brick and sandstone triumphed here too. Only two houses have survived with timber façades: Begijnhof 34 (mid-15th century) and Zeedijk 1 (mid-16th century). Timber, however, remained an essential building material for floor beams and roof frames.

## DUTCH RENAISSANCE

From the middle of the 16th century the Italian Renaissance began to filter to the Netherlands, and architects here developed a unique style with rich ornamentation that merged classical and traditional elements. In the facades they used mock columns (pilasters) and replaced the traditional spout gables with step gables richly decorated with sculptures, columns and obelisks. The playful interaction of red (sometimes orange) brick and horizontal bands of white or yellow sandstone was based on mathematical formulas and designed to please the eye.

The city carpenter Hendrick Staets (who planned the canal belt), the city bricklayer Cornelis Danckerts and the city sculptor Hendrick de Keyser (1565–1621) were jointly responsible for municipal buildings. It was De Keyser who perfected Dutch-Renaissance architecture. His elegant Bartolotti House (p83; Herengracht 170–172) is one of the finest examples of his work. He also designed the Zuiderkerk (p99) and the Westerkerk (p83), in which he retained Gothic elements. He set a new direction in Dutch Protestant church building with the Noorderkerk (p86), laid out like a Greek cross with the pulpit in the centre.

### Top Five Notable Buildings

- Oude Kerk (p61)
- Royal Palace (p60)
- Museum van Loon (p94)
- Beurs van Berlage (p58)
- Het Schip (p88)

## Gables, Hoists & Houses that Tip

One of the hallmarks of Amsterdam architecture is the gables (frontpieces at roof level) that adorn houses along the city's canals. They're cheery and fun, and when you get a bunch of them in a row the play of geometry can be dramatic.

The gables not only hid the roof from public view but also helped to identify the house until the French-led government introduced house numbers in 1795 (though the current system of odd and even numbers dates from 1875). The more ornate the gable, the easier it was to recognise. Other distinguishing features included facade decorations, signs or wall tablets (cartouches).

There are four main types of gables. The simple spout gable, with diagonal outline and semicircular windows or shutters, mimicked the earliest wooden gables and was used mainly for warehouses from the 1580s to the early 1700s. The step gable was a late-Gothic design favoured by Dutch-Renaissance architects from 1580 to 1660. The neck gable, also known as the bottle gable because it resembled a bottle spout, was introduced in the 1640s and proved the most durable, featuring occasionally in designs through the early 19th century; some neck gables also incorporated a step. The bell gable first appeared in the 1660s and became popular in the 18th century.

Many houses built from the 18th century onwards no longer had gables but straight, horizontal cornices that were richly decorated, often with pseudo-balustrades. These cornices could be quite long if the roofline ran parallel to the street.

Many canal houses look as if they're tipping forward. Rest assured, they're not about to collapse on you; rather, they were designed that way. Given the narrowness of the houses (and particularly, their staircases, as anyone who's ever been inside one can attest) owners needed a way to move large goods and furniture inside directly from the outside. The solution: a hoist built into the gable or cornice, so that objects could be lifted up and in through (removable) windows. The houses tip so that the goods won't bump into them. Clever, elegant, still in use and very cool to watch (we hope you catch one in action). A few houses have huge hoist-wheels in the attic with a rope and hook that run through the hoist beam. Almost all others, even those built today, have a beam with a hook for a hoist block.

The forward lean is also said to make houses seem larger. For certain, it makes it easier to admire the facade and gable from the street – a fortunate coincidence for everyone.

# DUTCH CLASSICISM

During the Golden Age of the 17th century, architects such as Jacob van Campen (1595–1657), and Philips Vingboons (1607–78) and his brother Justus adhered more strictly to Greek and Roman classical design and dropped many of De Keyser's playful decorations. Influenced by Italian architects such as Palladio and Scamozzi, they made facades resemble temples and pilasters look like columns. To accentuate the vertical lines, they changed the step gable to a neck gable with decorative scrolls, topped to imitate a temple roof. Soft red brick was made more durable with brown paint. Van Campen's city hall (now Royal Palace, p60) on the Dam is the most impressive example of this style.

The Vingboons brothers specialised in residential architecture in the western canal belt, including the current Bijbels Museum (p83; Herengracht 364–370) and the White House (now Theatermuseum, p82), or the fine example at Keizersgracht 319.

Later in the 17th century, external decorations made way for sumptuous interiors, while exterior faux columns became less ornamental or disappeared altogether. Justus Vingboons' Trippenhuis (p66; Kloveniersburgwal 29) is a good example. This was also the period of the southern canal belt, when wealthy Amsterdammers often bought two adjoining plots and built houses five windows wide instead of the usual three.

Adriaan Dortsman (1625–82) was perhaps the most representative architect of this austere classicist style. His designs include the Round Lutheran Church (p77) and the current Museum Van Loon (p94; Keizersgracht 672–674). A mathematician by training, he favoured a stark, geometrical simplicity – preferably with flat, sandstone facades – that enhanced the grandeur of his buildings.

# 18TH-CENTURY 'LOUIS STYLES'

The wealthy class now began to enjoy the fortunes amassed by their merchant predecessors. Many turned to banking and finance and conducted their business from the comfort of opulent

## Hofjes

*Hofjes* are a unique and beautiful relic of the Middle Ages. First laid out as monasteries, eventually they took on broader roles for hospitals and inns, or as refuges for orphans, widows and the elderly. Today they're leafy courtyards enclosed by rows of sweet little homes.

Amsterdam contains many *hofjes*, particularly in the Jordaan district (p85), but except for the **Begijnhof** (p75) in the Medieval Centre, they are closed to the public. If you'd like to see a number of *hofjes* in one place, take a quick train ride to Haarlem (p229).

homes. Traders no longer stored goods in the attic but in warehouses elsewhere.

The preoccupation with all things French provided fertile ground for Huguenot refugees, such as Daniel Marot (1661–1752) and his assistants Jean and Anthony Coulon, who introduced French interior design with matching exteriors. Interiors were bathed in light thanks to stuccoed ceilings and tall sash windows (a French innovation), and everything from staircases to furniture was designed in harmony. Elegant bell gables, although first introduced around 1660, became commonplace at this time. Many architects did away with gables altogether in favour of richly decorated horizontal cornices.

The Louis XIV style, with its dignified symmetry and facades decorated with statuary and leaves, dominated until about 1750. Beginning around 1740 the Louis XV style brought asymmetrical rococo shapes resembling rocks and waves. Pilasters or pillars made a comeback around 1770 with Louis XVI designs. You can see this in the Felix Meritis building (p86; Keizersgracht 324). Designed by Jacob Otten Husly (1738–97), it has enormous Corinthian half-columns. The Maagdenhuis (p78) on the Spui, designed by city architect Abraham van der Hart (1747–1820), is a much more sober interpretation of the new classicism.

# 19TH-CENTURY NEOSTYLES

Architecture stagnated in the first half of the 19th century as Amsterdam's economy struggled after the Napoleonic era. Safe neoclassicism held sway until the 1860s, when architects here and elsewhere in Europe began to rediscover other styles of the past.

The latter half of the century was dominated by neo-Gothic, harking back to the grand Gothic cathedrals in which no design element was superfluous, and neo-Renaissance, which brought De Keyser's Dutch-Renaissance architecture back into the limelight. Neo-Gothic suited the boom in Catholic church building now that Catholics were free to build new churches; residential architects focused on neo-Renaissance.

One of the leading architects of this period was Pierre Cuypers (1827–1921), who built several neo-Gothic churches but often merged the two styles, as can be seen in his Centraal Station (p57) and Rijksmuseum (p110) – both have Gothic structures and Dutch-Renaissance brickwork. Another fine example of this mixture is CH Peters' general post office, now the Magna Plaza (p77). Alfred Tepe's Krijtberg (p78) is more clearly Gothic (but note the use of

## Taking a NAP

Everyone has heard that Amsterdam (and indeed more than half the Netherlands) lies a couple of metres below sea level, but few people ask the question: which sea level? In fact, sea level varies around the globe and even around the Netherlands. The average level of the former Zuiderzee, in the lee of Holland, was slightly lower than that of the North Sea along Holland's exposed west coast.

A display in the Stopera, in the arcade between the Muziektheater and City Hall, shows the ins and outs of Normaal Amsterdams Peil (NAP; Normal Amsterdam Level), established in the 17th century as the average high-water mark of the Zuiderzee. This still forms the zero reference for elevation anywhere in the country and is also used in Germany and several other European countries.

Water in the canals is kept at 40cm below NAP and many parts of the city lie lower still. Water columns represent different sea levels, as well as the highest level of disastrous floods in 1953 (4.55m above NAP). Pamphlets explain the details.

brick), while the former milk factory (p91) designed by Eduard Cuypers (Pierre's nephew) sits firmly in the Dutch-Renaissance tradition.

Other architects were more eclectic and also incorporated medieval Dutch and German designs in a very personal way. Good examples are Isaac Gosschalk's houses at Reguliersgracht 57–59 and 63, and AC Bleijs' PC Hooft store (p92), now a 'smart-drug' shop on the corner of Keizersgracht and Leidsestraat. AL van Gendt's Concertgebouw (p110) is obviously neoclassical, but its interplay of red brick and white sandstone is Dutch Renaissance.

Art Nouveau became popular across Europe around the turn of the century, incorporating steel and glass with curvilinear designs resembling plants. In Amsterdam, Art Nouveau showed up mainly in shop fronts but little else (The Hague has far more Art Nouveau architecture). There are, however, a few fine examples, such as the Greenpeace headquarters (p82), the Crowne Plaza American Hotel (p92), and the riotous Tuschinskitheater (p183).

# BERLAGE & THE AMSTERDAM SCHOOL

The neo-styles and their reliance on the past were criticised by Hendrik Petrus Berlage (1856–1934), the father of modern Dutch architecture. Instead of expensive construction and excessive decoration, he favoured simplicity and rational use of materials. Beurs van Berlage (Bourse, or Stock Exchange; p58) displayed his ideals to the full. He cooperated with sculptors, painters and tilers to ensure ornamentation was integrated into the overall design in a supportive role, rather than being tacked on as an embellishment to hide the structure.

Berlage's residential architecture approached a block of buildings as a whole, not as a collection of individual houses. In this he influenced the young architects of what became known as the Amsterdam School, though they rejected his stark rationalism and preferred more creative designs. Leading exponents of this style were Michel de Klerk (1884–1923), Piet Kramer (1881–1961) and Johan van der Mey (1878–1949). The latter heralded the Amsterdam School in his Scheepvaarthuis (p97) at Prins Hendrikkade.

It was in this school that the humble brick housing block became sculpture, with curved corners, oddly placed windows and ornamental, rocket-shaped towers. Their housing estates, such as De Klerk's Het Schip (p88) in the Haarlem Quarter and Kramer's Cooperatiehof (p114) in the Pijp neighbourhood, have been described as fairytale fortresses rendered in a Dutch version of Art Deco. However, this 'form over function' ethic meant that their designs were not always fantastic to live in, with small windows and inefficient use of space. Kitchens were tiny because residents were supposed to eat in a proper dining room; windows were set high because residents weren't supposed to look out but read a book; and so forth.

Many architects of this school worked for the city council and designed the buildings of the ambitious 'Plan South', a large-scale expansion project mapped out by Berlage, with good-quality housing, wide boulevards and cosy squares. Subsidised housing corporations provided the funding here and elsewhere in the 1920s, a period of frantic residential building activity beyond the canal belt. This close cooperation between housing corporations, city planners and council architects made the Amsterdam School more than just an architectural movement: it was a complete philosophy of city planning.

*View from top floor of Magna Plaza (p77)*

# FUNCTIONALISM

While Amsterdam School–type buildings were being erected, a new generation of architects began to rebel against the school's impractical, expensive structures. Influenced by the Bauhaus School in Germany, Frank Lloyd Wright and Le Corbusier, they formed 'de 8' in 1927.

Architects such as Ben Merkelbach and Gerrit Rietveld believed that form should follow function and sang the praises of steel, glass and concrete. Buildings should be spacious, practical structures with plenty of sunlight, not masses of art made in brick to glorify architects.

The Committee of Aesthetics Control didn't agree, however, and kept the functionalists out of the canal belt, relegating them to new estates on the outskirts of the city – although Rietveld built his glass gallery (Keizersgracht 455) on top of Metz & Co department store (p91).

Functionalism finally came to the fore after WWII and put its stamp on new suburbs west and south of the city, thanks to the General Extension Plan that had been adopted in 1935 but interrupted by the war. The acute housing shortage meant that these suburbs were built on a larger scale than originally planned, yet they still weren't sufficient. The Bijlmermeer southeast of the city was added in the 1960s and 1970s. By this time, however, there was increasing resistance to such large-scale housing estates.

In the inner city the emphasis shifted towards urban renewal, particularly in areas that had to be rebuilt with the construction of the metro line. Architects followed examples set by Aldo van Eyck and his student Theo Bosch. Van Eyck's designs included the Moederhuis (Plantage Middenlaan 33); Bosch's included the Pentagon (p98) housing complex on the corner of St Antoniesbreestraat and Zwanenburgwal. Opinions are still mixed, however, with critics dismissing such designs as 'parasite architecture' – modern housing projects that look out of place against 17th- and 18th-century surroundings.

# THE PRESENT

Suburbs have been built on a more human scale since the 1970s, with low- and medium-rise apartments integrated with shops, schools and offices. Strict functionalism has also made way for more imaginative designs, such as A Alberts and M van Huut's ING Bank (1987) in the Bijlmermeer, an S-shaped complex of linked towers.

Most recent development has been in the northeast of town, starting with the Entrepotdok just north of the Plantage. This mid-80s redo of some 84 large 18th- and early-19th-century warehouses created mostly apartments, with studios and limited commercial space. Although the interior of the building was gutted to let in light for living space, the designers used existing facades and timber flooring.

Anyone interested in the cutting edge of Amsterdam architecture should head to the Eastern Docklands. This shipping warehouse area sat abandoned for decades until the city decided to add housing. The hulking apartment complexes don't feel like anything else you've seen in Amsterdam, but they certainly make a statement. Barcelonaplein, on KNSM Eiland, was designed by the Belgian architect Bruno Albert and features an iron 'fence' that completes a circular courtyard. The 'Whale' (2000; p108) is a mammoth apartment building named for its sloping shape that's open at the top and bottom.

Those with a serious interest in contemporary work in town should visit ARCAM (Stichting Architectuur Centrum Amsterdam; p105), or at least its website www.arcam.nl to find out the latest.

*Gabled houses in the Jordaan (p85)*

# History

# History

## THE RECENT PAST

Given Amsterdam's colourful history, the city today seems rather calm. Gone are the strict Calvinists, the seafarers trading all around the known world, and the rabble-rousers of the 1960s, but vestiges of that past remain.

Today the city still concentrates on commerce, but rather than expanding globally, it's expanding locally. Actually, the catchphrase is *inbreiding* (inspansion) – the harbour has begun to revive with petrochemical industries and container transshipment, and Schiphol airport is running out of space. New office towers are arising southeast, south and west of the city around a ring freeway. A second metro line is under construction from Amsterdam North to the city's World Trade Centre, though many locals think it a waste of time and money.

Yet the widespread recession which began in 2001 has suppressed real-estate prices, lowered tourism and made funding for the arts scarce. Whereas once the Dutch economy was the envy of a Europe in recession, as we went to press the prognosis for recovery was unclear.

Socially, too, change may be afoot. Much of Europe views the Netherlands, and Amsterdam in particular, as a corrupting influence, and the country as a whole is swinging rightward. The past year has seen noticeably more pressure on the city's nightlife in the form of police raids, and only late in 2003 did the government indefinitely postpone the implementation of a California/New York–style nationwide ban on all indoor smoking (including coffeeshops) that was due to take effect.

## FROM THE BEGINNING

Most of the region that later became known as Holland (in the west of the present-day Netherlands) started out as a land of lakes, swamps and spongy peat at or below sea level; its contours shifted with fierce autumn storms and floods. This was certainly the case where the Amstel River emptied into the IJ (pronounced 'eye'), an arm of the shallow Zuiderzee or 'Southern Sea'. The oldest archaeological finds here – coins and a few artefacts – date from Roman times, when the IJ lay along the northern border of the Roman Empire; there is no evidence of settlement then.

Isolated farming communities gradually tamed the marshlands with ditches and dykes. Between 1150 and 1300 the south bank of the IJ was dyked from the Zuiderzee westwards to Haarlem, and dams were built across rivers with locks to let water out and boats in. Around 1200, a fishing community known as Aemstelredamme – 'dam built across the Amstel' – sat at what is now the square known as the Dam. Under the count of Holland, local inhabitants created a network of work-and-maintenance groups

| TIMELINE | c 1150 | 1275 | 1345 |
| --- | --- | --- | --- |
| | Dams were built to retain the IJ between the Zuiderzee and Haarlem | The Count of Holland grants freedom from tolls to residents along the Amstel. This is credited as the founding of the city. | Miracle of Amsterdam |

and pooled their resources – a precursor to today's 'Polder Model' of public decision-making (p12).

On 27 October 1275 the count of Holland granted toll freedom to those who lived around the Amstel dam, freeing locals from paying tolls to sail through the locks and bridges of Holland. This event is reckoned as the official founding of Amsterdam.

# EARLY TRADE

Agriculture was difficult in this marshland, so fishing remained an important activity, but it was trade that provided the greatest growth. While other powerful Dutch cities concentrated on overland trade with Flanders and northern Italy, Amsterdam focused on maritime trade in the North and Baltic Seas, then dominated by the Hanseatic League (a group of powerful trading cities in present-day Germany, including Hamburg, Lübeck and Rostock).

Amsterdam's wharves churned out *cogs* – broad-beamed 100-tonne capacity merchant ships (five times the size of their predecessors) – revolutionising maritime trade and enabling the city to play a key role in the transit trade between Hanseatic cities and southern Europe.

Instead of joining the League, Amsterdam's *vrijbuiters* (booty-chasers) sailed straight to the Baltic, with cloth and salt to exchange for grain and timber. By the late 1400s, 60% of ships sailing to and from the Baltic Sea were from Holland, and the vast majority had Amsterdam as their base.

The original harbour in Damrak and Rokin had been extended into the IJ along what's now Centraal Station. Canals were cut to cater for merchant warehouses in the present-day Medieval Centre. A fire in 1452 destroyed three-quarters of the city, including most of the wooden buildings, but it was soon rebuilt in brick.

In Amsterdam, skippers, sailors, merchants, artisans and opportunists from the Low Countries (roughly the present-day Netherlands, Belgium and Luxembourg) gained their livelihood through contact with the outside world. With no tradition of Church-sanctioned feudal relationships, no distinction between nobility and serfs, and little taxation, individualism and protocapitalism took hold.

Amsterdam also became a city of religious pilgrimage: in 1345 a dying man regurgitated the Host (communion wafer), which was thrown in the fire but did not burn. A miracle was proclaimed and soon the city boasted some 20 monasteries. In 1489 Holy Roman Emperor Maximilian recovered from an illness here and showed his gratitude by allowing the city to use the imperial crown on its documents, buildings and ships.

# INDEPENDENT REPUBLIC

The Protestant Reformation was more than religious. It was a struggle for power between the 'new money', an emerging class of merchants and artisans, and the 'old money', land-owning, aristocratic order sanctioned by the established 'Catholic' Church.

## Coat of Arms

Amsterdam's coat of arms consists of three St Andrew's crosses arranged vertically – a wonderfully simple design that is found on everything from VVV tourist brochures to the thousands of brown bollards or 'penises' (so-called *Amsterdammertjes*) that keep cars from veering off the streets or parking where they shouldn't. Its origins are unclear, though the St Andrew's Cross was a popular symbol in this part of the world before Amsterdam existed. It is also said that the three crosses represented protection from fire, flood and plague.

| 1380 | 1452 | 1566 | 1578 |
|---|---|---|---|
| Canals of the present-day Medieval Centre are dug; population 10,000 | Fire destroys three-quarters of the city; brick buildings replace wooden ones | Nobles petition Spanish ruler not to introduce Spanish Inquisition; he refuses, touching off war of independence | Amsterdam captured by Calvinists; Dutch Republic declared a year later |

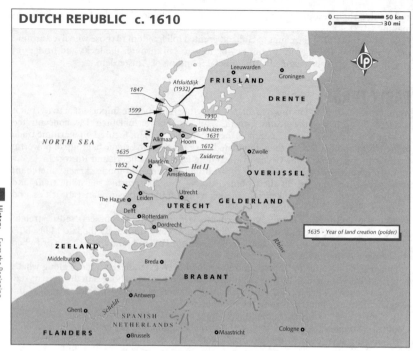

## DUTCH REPUBLIC c. 1610

*1635 - Year of land creation (polder)*

The form of Protestantism that took hold in the Low Countries was the most radically moralistic stream of Calvinism. It stressed the might of God and treated humans as sinful creatures whose duty in life was sobriety and hard work. It scorned church hierarchy and based religious experience on local communities led by lay elders.

Calvinism was integral to the struggle for independence from the fanatically Catholic Philip II of Spain, who had acquired the Low Countries. In 1566, when a coalition of Catholic and Calvinist nobles petitioned Philip not to introduce the Spanish Inquisition in the Low Countries, Philip refused; the resulting war of independence lasted more than 80 years.

Fanatical Calvinist brigands, wearing the disparaging nickname *geuzen* (beggars) as a badge of honour, roamed from city to city, murdering priests, nuns and Catholic sympathisers and smashing 'papist idolatry' in the churches. Some took to the water and harassed Spanish and other Catholic ships. Amsterdam was caught in the middle: its ruling merchants were pragmatic Catholics, but its merchants had adopted Calvinism along with most of the population, who resented heavy Spanish taxation. In 1578 the *geuzen* captured Amsterdam in a bloodless coup, the so-called Alteration. In one of the most salient restrictions at home, Catholics were forced to worship in clandestine churches (see Museum Amstelkring, p63).

With mighty Amsterdam now on their side, the seven northern provinces formed the Union of Utrecht and declared themselves to be an independent republic. The union was led by a *stadholder* (chief magistrate), William the Silent of the House of Orange, who

| c 1600 | 1618 | 1602 | 1650 |
|---|---|---|---|
| Dutch ships have a virtual monopoly on North Sea fishing; population 50,000 | World's first regular newspaper is printed in Amsterdam | Founding of United East India Company | Half of all ships sailing between Europe and Asia are Dutch; population 150,000 |

## 17TH-CENTURY AMSTERDAM

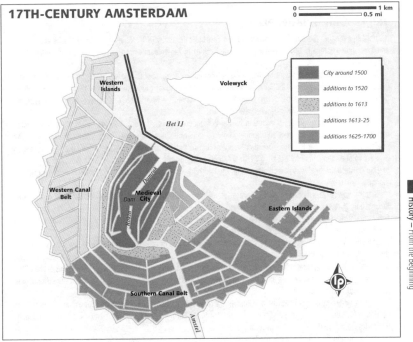

City around 1500
additions to 1520
additions to 1613
additions 1613-25
additions 1625-1700

Western Islands
Volewyck
Het IJ
Damrak
Western Canal Belt
Medieval City
Dam
Eastern Islands
Western Canal Belt
Southern Canal Belt
Amstel

History – From the Beginning

was the forefather of today's royal family (he was dubbed 'the Silent' because he wisely refused to enter into any religious debate). Their parliament, the Estates General, sat in The Hague. The Seven United Provinces (the republic's official name) soon became known to the outside world as the Dutch Republic – or simply 'Holland' because of that province's dominance. Within Holland, Amsterdam towered over all the other cities put together.

# GOLDEN AGE (1580–1700)

The city kept expanding. In the 1580s land was reclaimed from the IJ and Amstel to create the current Nieuwmarkt neighbourhood. Two decades later, work began on the canal belt that more than tripled the area of the city.

By 1600, Dutch ships dominated seaborne trade between England, France, Spain and the Baltic, and had a virtual monopoly on North Sea fishing and Arctic whaling. Jewish refugees taught Dutch mariners about trade routes, giving rise to the legendary United East India and West India Companies (see boxed text p46).

Amsterdam's fortunes continued to rise when Antwerp, its major trading rival in the Low Countries, was retaken by the Spaniards. Half the population fled, and merchants, skippers and artisans flocked to Amsterdam with trade contacts and silk and printing industries – the world's first regular newspaper, full of trade news from around Europe, was printed in Amsterdam in 1618.

| 1672 | 1688 | 1700 | 1794 |
|---|---|---|---|
| Louis XIV of France occupies parts of the Low Countries | William III of Orange marries Mary Stuart of England. England and the Netherlands join forces to defeat France. | Population 220,000 | French troops re-invade the Low Countries |

45

# The First Multinationals

It's hard to overstate the role played by the United East India Company (VOC; Vereenigde Oost-Indische Compagnie) and West India Company (WIC; West-Indische Compagnie) in Amsterdam's economic – and indeed diplomatic – history.

More than just traders, these companies were authorised to negotiate with rulers overseas on behalf of the Dutch Republic, to pursue trade opportunities as they saw fit, build forts and raise local militias. More than 1000 shareholders back home – merchants, artisans, clergy, shopkeepers, even servants – contributed capital, spreading risk and reaping rewards through generous dividends when risks paid off.

The VOC began in response to exclusion by the Portuguese from trade routes to the Orient. Some Amsterdam merchants sent a ship to break the Portuguese hold in 1595 and ships from other Dutch cities soon followed. The result: chaos. The counter-balance: 'Chambers' representing six Dutch cities came together to form the VOC, supervised by a group of 17 directors (the Heeren XVII, or '17 Gentlemen') on behalf of shareholders. Such was their importance that an Amsterdam canal was named after them, the Herengracht. The VOC was granted a Dutch government trading monopoly in 1602.

Batavia, now Jakarta, became the VOC's hub; a second hub opened on the island of Dejima, off Nagasaki, and became Japan's only gateway to European trade. Elaborate, often multilateral, trades involved Japan, Formosa (now Taiwan), China and Ceylon (now Sri Lanka), with goods including silks, spices, silver, gold, textiles, copper and, later, coffee and tea. Eventually, some 15 fleets of 65 ships plied the waters; the VOC was disbanded in 1795.

The WIC, meanwhile, consisted of five 'chambers' supervised by 19 directors (the Heeren XIX). Its ventures headed to the New World, establishing trade ports and colonies in New Netherland (now New York City and parts of neighbouring US states), the Netherlands Antilles, Suriname, Recife (Brazil) and Ghana. Piracy was also one of the aims of the WIC – the unlucky victims were largely Spanish ships. Its chief trade was in furs (from North America), sugar cane (from South America) and slaves (from Africa).

In 1674, under pressure from British and Portuguese competition, the WIC folded officially but was reconstituted and continued to operate slave routes and colonies in the Antilles in Suriname until 1791, when it closed down for good. Its territories were placed under Dutch-government control.

Next time you think some of our modern-day multinationals are seeking world domination, remember in whose footsteps they're following.

Amsterdam also welcomed persecuted Jews from Portugal and Spain, Germans provided a ready source of sailors and labourers, a new wave of Jews came from Central and Eastern Europe, as did enterprising, persecuted Huguenots from France. Amsterdam had become a cosmopolitan city, where money reigned supreme.

By around 1620, Dutch traders had rounded the tip of South America, naming it Cape Horn (after the city of Hoorn north of Amsterdam), expelled the Portuguese from the Moluccas (also known as the Spice Islands in present-day Indonesia), and established outposts in the Pacific and Americas. By 1641 the Dutch had taken control of Formosa (Taiwan) and received sole trading rights to Japan. In 1652, Dutch sailors captured the Cape of Good Hope (South Africa); they booted the Portuguese out of Ceylon (Sri Lanka) soon after. They also explored the coastlines of New Zealand (named after the Dutch province of Zeeland) and New Holland (now Australia) but found nothing of value there.

Around 1650 the Dutch had more seagoing merchant vessels than England and France combined. Half of all ships sailing between Europe and Asia belonged to the Dutch; the exotic products traded eventually became commodities (coffee, tea, spices, tobacco, cotton, silk, porcelain). Dutch freight was unrivalled thanks to cheap Baltic hemp and timber, Europe's largest shipbuilding industry, abundant investment capital, and low wages. Yet most wealth of Amsterdam proper was still generated by fishing and European trade.

| 1810 | 1813–14 | 1839 | 1887 |
|------|---------|------|------|
| The Netherlands is annexed into the French Empire | The French are overthrown; William I installed as king of the Netherlands | Railway connects Amsterdam and Haarlem | Catholic churches allowed to reopen |

In 1651, England passed the first of several Navigation Acts that posed a serious threat to Dutch trade, leading to several inconclusive naval wars; the Dutch lost New Amsterdam. Louis XIV of France took the opportunity to occupy much of the Low Countries two decades later.

The Dutch rallied behind their stadholder, William III of Orange, who repelled the French with the help of Austria, Spain and Brandenburg (Prussia). A consummate politician, William then supported Protestant factions in England against their Catholic King James II. In 1688 William invaded England, where he and his wife, Mary Stuart (James II's Protestant daughter), were proclaimed king and queen.

# WEALTHY DECLINE (1700–1814)

The Dutch Republic didn't have the military resources to continue fighting France and England head-on, but it had Amsterdam's money to buy them off and ensure freedom of the seas.

As more and more money went to this cause, Amsterdam went from a place where everything (profitable) was possible, to a lethargic community where wealth-creation was a matter of interest rates. Gone were the daring sea voyages; achievements in art, science and technology; the innovations of government and finance. Harbours such as London and Hamburg became powerful rivals.

The decline in trade brought poverty, and exceptionally cold winters hampered transport and led to serious food shortages. The winters of 1740 and 1763 were so severe that some residents froze to death.

Amsterdam's support of the American War of Independence (1776) resulted in a British blockade of the Dutch coast followed by British conquests of Dutch trading posts around the world, eventually forcing the closure of the West India and East India Companies.

In 1794, French revolutionary troops invaded the Low Countries, eventually installing a Batavian Republic, transforming the fragmented 'united provinces' into a centralised state with Amsterdam as its capital.

In 1806 this republic became a monarchy when Napoleon nominated his brother Louis Napoleon as king, and in 1808 the grand city hall on the Dam, symbol of the wealth and power of the merchant Republic, became his palace. Two years later Napoleon dismissed his brother and annexed the Netherlands into the French Empire.

Britain responded by blockading the Continent and occupying the Dutch colonies. Amsterdam's trade and fishing industry came to a complete halt. Dutch society turned to agriculture and Amsterdam became a local market town.

After Napoleon's defeat in 1813, William VI of Orange was crowned Dutch king William I in the Nieuwe Kerk in 1814. Louis Napoleon's palace became the new king's palace and has remained with the House of Orange ever since. The Britons returned the Dutch East Indies but kept the Cape of Good Hope and Ceylon. Amsterdam's seaborne economy recovered only slowly; Britain now dominated the seas.

# NEW INFRASTRUCTURE (1814–1918)

Amsterdam in the first half of the 19th century was a lethargic place. Its harbour had been neglected, and the sand banks in the IJ, which were always an obstacle in the past, proved too great a barrier for modern ships. Rotterdam was set to become the country's premier port.

Things began to look up again as the country's first railway, between Amsterdam and Haarlem, opened in 1839. Trade with the East Indies was now the backbone of Amsterdam's economy, and a canal, eventually extended to the Rhine, allowed the city to benefit from the industrial revolution at home and in Germany.

| 1889 | 1900 | 1920 | 1928 |
|------|------|------|------|
| Centraal Station opens | Population 500,000 | KLM becomes the world's first regular air service | Amsterdam hosts Olympic Games; population tops 700,000 |

*Royal Palace, The Dam (p58)*

The harbour was expanded to the east. The diamond industry boomed after the discovery of diamonds in South Africa. Amsterdam again attracted immigrants, and its population doubled in the second half of the 19th century. Speculators hastily erected new housing beyond the canal belt – dreary, shoddily built tenement blocks.

By 1887, restrictions imposed on Catholics in the Alteration were lifted, and Catholic churches were allowed to open again officially.

In 1889 the massive Centraal Station was built on a series of artificial islands in the IJ. Commentators saw this as the symbolic severing of Amsterdam's historical ties with the sea. Toward the end of the 19th century some of the city's major waterways and smaller canals were filled in, both for hygienic reasons (such as several cholera epidemics) and to create roads.

The Netherlands remained neutral in WWI, but Amsterdam's trade with the East Indies suffered from naval blockades. There were riots over food shortages. An attempt to extend the socialist revolutions to the Netherlands was quickly put down by loyalist troops.

## BOOM & DEPRESSION (1918–40)

After the war Amsterdam remained the country's industrial centre. The Dutch Shipbuilding Company still operated the world's second-largest wharf and helped carry an extensive steel and diesel-motor industry. The harbour handled tropical produce that was processed locally (tobacco into cigars, cocoa into chocolate etc) Amsterdam is still the world's main distribution centre for cocoa.

The 1920s were boom years. In 1920 KLM (Koninklijke Luchtvaart Maatschappij; Royal Aviation Company) began the world's first regular air service, between Amsterdam and London, from an airstrip south of the city, and bought many of its planes from Anthony Fokker's aircraft factory north of the IJ. There were two huge breweries, a sizable clothing industry, and even a local car factory. The city hosted the Olympic Games in 1928.

| 1940 | 1941 |
|---|---|
| Germany invades the Netherlands | Dockworkers protest treatment of Jewish compatriots |

By then the city had begun expanding north of the IJ, with housing projects for harbour workers and dockers in the new suburb of Amsterdam North. Then it expanded southwards, filling in the area between the Amstel and what was to become the Olympic Stadium.

The world depression in the 1930s hit Amsterdam hard. Unemployment rose to 25%. Labour party members, who dominated the city council, resigned in protest at public-service salary cuts, and the conservative, spend-nothing national government of Hendrik Colijn (the Herbert Hoover of the Netherlands) had free reign.

Public-works projects did little to defuse mounting tensions between socialists, communists and the small but vocal party of Dutch fascists. The city received some 25,000 Jewish refugees from Germany, although a shamefully large number were turned back at the border because of the Netherlands' neutrality policy.

## WWII (1940–45)

The Netherlands tried to remain neutral in WWII, but Germany invaded in May 1940; for the first time in almost 400 years Amsterdammers experienced war first-hand. Few wanted to believe that things would turn nasty (the Germans trumpeted that the Dutch were part of the 'Aryan brotherhood'). However, in February 1941 Amsterdam's working class protested restrictions placed on their Jewish compatriots in a general strike led by dockworkers. By then it was already too late. Only one in every 16 of Amsterdam's 90,000 Jews survived the war (one in seven in the Netherlands), the highest proportion of Jews murdered anywhere in Western Europe.

The resistance movement, set up by an unlikely alliance of Calvinists and Communists, only became large-scale when the increasingly desperate Germans began to round up able-bodied men to work in Germany.

During the 'Hunger Winter' of 1944 to 1945, the Allies had liberated the south of the country but were checked at Arnhem, and concentrated again on their push into Germany, thus managing to isolate the northwest and Amsterdam. Coal shipments ceased, many men aged between 17 and 50 had gone into hiding or worked in Germany, public utilities halted, and the Germans began to plunder anything that could assist their war effort. Dark, freezing Amsterdam suffered severe famine and thousands died. Canadian troops finally liberated the city in May 1945, at the very end of the war in Europe.

*Jewish menorah*

## POSTWAR GROWTH (1945–62)

The city's growth resumed after the war, with US aid (through the Marshall Plan). Newly discovered fields of natural gas compensated for the loss of the East Indies, which became independent

| 1945 | 1965 |
| --- | --- |
| The Netherlands are liberated | Arrests of Provos on the Spui |

Indonesia after a four-year fight. The focus of the harbour moved westwards, towards the widened North Sea Canal. The long-awaited Amsterdam-Rhine Canal opened in 1952.

Massive apartment blocks arose in areas annexed west of the city to meet the continued demand for housing, made more acute by the demographic shift away from extended families. The massive Bijlmermeer housing project (now called the Bijlmer) southeast of the city, begun in the mid-1960s and finished in the 1970s, was built in a similar vein.

In 1948 Queen Wilhelmina resigned in favour of her daughter Juliana.

## CULTURAL REVOLUTION (1962–82)

Over the previous 80 years, Dutch society had become characterised by *verzuiling* (pillarisation), a social order in which each religion and/or political persuasion achieved the right to do its own thing, with its own institutions. Each persuasion represented a pillar that supported the status quo in a general 'agreement to disagree'. In the 1960s the old divisions were increasingly irrelevant, and the pillars came tumbling down.

Amsterdam became Europe's 'Magic Centre', an exciting place where anything was possible. The late 1960s saw an influx of hippies smoking dope on the Dam, unrolling sleeping bags in Vondelpark and tripping in the nightlife hot spots. At the universities, students demanded a greater say and, in 1969, occupied the administrative centre of the University of Amsterdam. The women's movement began a campaign that fuelled the abortion debate throughout the 1970s.

In the early 1970s a fierce conflict developed between city planners and disaffected Amsterdammers over a proposed metro line through the Nieuwmarkt neighbourhood. Technology did not yet allow tunnelling through swampy ground and a large portion of the derelict district had to be razed. The inhabitants became squatters and turned the area into a fortress. The district was eventually cleared with much violence on 'Blue Monday',

*Vondelpark (p112)*

| 1975 | 1975 |
|---|---|
| Violence erupts over squatting in the Nieuwmarkt neighbourhood | The Netherlands decriminalises marijuana; Suriname becomes an independent country |

## THE PROTESTING PROVOS

Mixing street theatre and serial anarchy, a movement called the Provos set the tone for Amsterdam in the days of the Magic Centre.

In 1962, window-cleaner and self-professed sorcerer Robert Jasper Grootveld began to deface cigarette billboards with a huge letter 'K' (for *kanker*, cancer) to protest rampant, addictive commercialism. At get-togethers in his garage, he dressed as a medicine man, chanted anti-smoking mantras (under the influence of pot) and attracted other bizarre types: the poet Johnny van Doorn, also known as Johnny the Selfkicker, known for frenzied, stream-of-consciousness recitals; Bart Huges, who drilled a hole in his forehead (a 'third eye' to attain permanently expanded consciousness); and Rob Stolk, a working-class printer whose streetwise tactics helped the get-togethers become 'happenings'.

In summer 1965, happenings on the Spui attracted thousands, and were eventually disbanded by police using batons and arbitrary arrests. Eyewitness accounts characterised it as police brutality against kids having fun, and soon the whole country was engaged in heated debate.

In 1965 to 1966, the Provos proposed a series of environmental 'White Plans', most famously a fleet of white bicycles to be provided free by the city. Provos were also behind the protests at the 1966 wedding of then-Princess Beatrix and the congenial German diplomat Claus von Amsberg, who had been a member of the Hitler Youth. Despite massive security, a live chicken was hurled at the royal coach, smoke bombs ignited along the procession route, and bystanders chanted 'my bicycle back' – a reference to the many bikes commandeered by German soldiers. Naturally, it was all carried live on TV.

As much as anything, it was the Provos' own success that eventually did them in: society began to adopt their goals. Nowadays, even Queen Beatrix is passionately environmentalist.

24 March 1975. Some 30 people, mostly policemen, were injured; surprisingly, no-one was killed. The episode became a watershed; subsequently the council set about renovating inner-city neighbourhoods for new housing. Nieuwmarkt was rebuilt with affordable council houses. The metro opened in 1980.

Still, families kept moving to the suburbs, the city became dominated by small households with modest means, and housing needs outstripped the council's ability to provide. A housing shortage fuelled speculation. Free-market rents – and purchase prices – shot out of reach of the average citizen. The waiting period for a council apartment was up to five years.

Many young people turned to squatting in buildings left empty by (assumed) speculators. Legislation made eviction difficult, giving rise to *knokploegen*, 'fighting groups' of tracksuited heavies sent by owners to evict squatters by force. These new squatters, however, were prepared to defend themselves with barricades and a well-organised support network.

A few months after a particularly emphatic battle with authorities, squatters took to the streets on the occasion of the coronation of Queen Beatrix. In Amsterdam's largest-ever rioting, tear gas filled the air, and the term 'proletarian shopping' (ie looting) entered the national lexicon.

'Ordinary' Amsterdammers, initially sympathetic towards the housing shortage, became fed up with squatters jumping the queue and the violent riots. By the mid-1980s the movement had little or no outside support and was all but dead. Squatting still takes place now, but the rules are clear and the mood is far less confrontational.

# NEW CONSENSUS (1982–2000)

Twenty years after the cultural revolution began, a new consensus, epitomised by the amiable mayor, Ed van Thijn, emphasised decentralised government. Neighbourhood councils were established toward a livable city integrating work, schools and shops within walking or cycling distance; decreased traffic; renovation rather than demolition; friendly

| 1980 | 2003 |
|---|---|
| Squatters disrupt celebrations for the coronation of Queen Beatrix, 30 April | Her Royal Highness Catharina-Amalia Beatrix Carmen Victoria, second in line to the throne, is born on 7 December. |

neighbourhood police; a practical, nonmoralistic approach towards drugs; and legal recognition of homosexual couples. Social-housing construction peaked, with 40,000 affordable apartments easing the plight of 100,000 house-hunters.

A combined city hall and opera house opened in 1986 on Waterlooplein, although opinions remain divided on its architectural success. Today it's known as the Stopera – a contraction of *stadhuis* (city hall) and opera, or of 'Stop the Opera', depending on your perspective.

By the early 1990s, families and small manufacturers, which dominated innercity neighbourhoods in the early 1960s, had been replaced by professionals and a service industry of pubs, 'coffeeshops', restaurants and hotels. The ethnic make-up had changed too, with non-Dutch nationalities comprising 45% of the population. The city's success in attracting large foreign businesses resulted in an influx of higher-income expatriates.

# Districts

# Districts

Amsterdam may have a wild reputation, but it's also one of Europe's most beautiful capitals. Add in some of the world's great cultural treasures, as well as sights that are quirky, gorgeous or just plain fun, and you've got a dream destination. And while other cities are grandiose and monumental, Amsterdam is intimate and accessible: you can walk across the city centre in about half an hour, and getting around on a bike is a snap.

One of our favourite ways to see the city is just to wander – the urge will be irresistible along some canals. That's how we've found some of our favourite places. No doubt you, too, will find some favourites this way, and begin to understand what keeps drawing people back.

## ITINERARIES

### One Day

My goodness, but you're ambitious. Start (early, to beat the crowds) at the **Anne Frank Huis** (p80), followed by a trip across town to the **Van Gogh Museum** (p111) not long after it opens. **CoBrA Café** (p150) on Museumplein is a convenient lunch spot. From there you can browse **Nieuwe Spiegelstraat** (antiques row, p91) and the department stores on **Kalverstraat** (p75) en route to the **Amsterdams Historisch Museum** (p75). After all this seriousness, you'll feel like a break, and you can find it at the **Red Light District** (p61). Since you've only got one night in town, dine at Amsterdam's most renowned Dutch restaurant, **d'Vijff Vlieghen** (p135).

### Three Days

Take in the one-day itinerary, but allow yourself time to pause, elongate and explore. For example:

After the Anne Frank Huis, browse the shops of the **Negen Straatjes** (p84) and even stay there for lunch.

Near the Van Gogh Museum, also take in the Dutch masters in the Philips Gallery of the **Rijksmuseum** (p110), catch a free concert at the **Concertgebouw** (p110) or take the tour at **Coster Diamonds** (p199). Afterwards, stop for cake or quiche at **Tarte van m'n Tante** (p152) at the edge of De Pijp, then plunge into the diversity of the **Albert Cuypmarket** (p113). Stop for gelato at **Peppino's** (p152), look cool at **Madam Jeannette** (p151) or stay for dinner at modern Moroccan **Mamouche** (p151). Afterwards, go see something jazzy or ethnic at **De Badcuyp** (p182).

Be sure to leave a morning to stroll the **Begijnhof** (p75) – the nearly adjacent Amsterdams Historisch Museum makes a nice follow-up. To keep your mood mellow, see what's showing at the **Nieuwe Kerk** (p59) or feel regal at the **Royal Palace** (p60) next door. Dine at art-nouveau **Belhamel** (p139) or, if you're feeling rowdier, **de Blaffende Vis** (p142). Cap your stay with a pils at the canalside brown café **'t Smalle** (p157).

### One Week

In addition to the above, don't miss Jewish Amsterdam (p97): the **Jewish Historical Museum** (p99), a kosher lunch at **Pinto** (p137) and a visit to the **Portuguese-Israelite Synagogue** (p100). At night, follow that ancient Jewish ritual of

# A Medley of Museums

Whether its modern art or art about cats, stately homes or tropical cultures, stories of historical tragedy or miracles of modern science, Amsterdam offers a range of museums for any taste (visit the websites www.hollandmuseums.nl and www.amsterdammuseums.nl).

Most of the leading museums in town display captions in English. If captions are in Dutch only, you can usually get an English-language brochure (often free) or borrow a binder explaining the sights. Many museums have pleasant cafés (sometimes even restaurants) with gardens or courtyards – good places to relax and read up on the items on display.

Weekends tend to be the busiest times, along with Wednesday afternoons when many primary schools have the afternoon off and children are herded into museums. Many museums are closed on Mondays.

Important note: two of the city's major museums will have reduced exhibitions for the next several years: the Rijksmuseum and the Stedelijk Museum. The Rijksmuseum will have one gallery open to exhibit some of its greatest hits, and will have a travelling exhibition of its collection around the country. The Stedelijk Museum will be rehoused in an old postal high-rise near Centraal Station until 2007 (p106). Parts of the Jewish Historical Museum are also due to be closed for renovation until September 2004.

A handful of museums offer free entry, but most charge admission. Adult admissions run from about €2.50 to €9, which is pretty reasonable by the standards of world capitals; special exhibitions may cost extra. Discounts are frequently available for those aged over 65 or under 18, for students (rare) and holders of other types of cards and passes.

One worthwhile card is the **Museumkaart** (Museum Card; ☎ 0900-404 09 10, €0.45 per minute; over/under 26 €25/12.50 plus €4.95 fee for first-time registrants, photo required), which gives you free (mostly) or discounted (occasionally) admission to several hundred museums around the country for a year. It's valid for most museums in Amsterdam including the major ones, although not the Anne Frank Huis or the Royal Palace. After five or six museums the card will have paid for itself. Inquire at participating museums.

If you are making just one quick trip to Amsterdam, you might consider the **Amsterdam Pass** (24/48/72 hrs €26/36/46). It includes many of the same museums as the Museumkaart, a free canal cruise, discounts at a number of shops and attractions and a transit pass good for anywhere the GVB goes. The latter can come in handy: although Amsterdam is not an enormous city, a half-hour walk between museums can certainly eat into your limited time. The Amsterdam Pass is available at VVV locations or via www.simplyamsterdam.com.

The **Museum Boat** (p244; www.lovers.nl; €14.25) is also worth considering for the discounts offered with its day card.

Chinese food, either on the Zeedijk (followed by karaoke at **Casablanca**, p181) or aboard the floating **Sea Palace restaurant** (p149).

Hop on your bike and head toward the IJ and a ferry to the **Eastern Docklands** (p107) to explore some of Europe's most intriguing new architecture, and stop at **Gare de l'Est** for dinner (p149) – it's different every night.

Take a day in the Plantage, visit the sobering memorial at **Hollandsche Schouwburg** (p102) and feel uplifted at the **Verzetsmuseum** (p103); **Plancius** (p149) next door makes an excellent lunch stop. Then head north via the **Entrepotdok** (p104); to be entertained by retired engineers (really) at the technology museum **EnergeticA** (p104). Dine at historic **Koffiehaus van den Volksbond** (p149) or snappy **A Tavola** (p148).

Wrap up your stay with a visit to the seashore: the **Nederlands Scheepvaartmuseum** (p105) or, for a swan song, do a swan dive at **Bungy Jump Center Amsterdam** (p187).

# Bike Tours

## MIKE'S BIKE TOURS

☎ 622 79 70; www.mikesbikeamsterdam.com; meet at entrance B of Rijksmuseum, Stadhouderskade 42; per person €22; ⏲ 12.30pm Mar-Apr & Sep-Nov, 11.30am & 4pm May-Aug

Readers have written to us in praise of Mike's four-hour tours, which take you both around the centre of town and into the countryside (where you can see windmills, cheese farms and so on). Guides are well known for their insider information about the city. You may well find yourself at a pub when the tour's over.

## YELLOW BIKE TOURS

☎ 620 69 40; www.yellowbike.nl; Nieuwzijds Kolk 29; city/countryside tour per person €17/22; ⏲ city tour 9.30am & 1pm, countryside tour 11am, all tours Apr-1 Nov

Yellow Bike has been doing this for well over a decade, so they've got it down pat. Choose from a three-hour city tour or a six-hour countryside tour. These tours are a little less youth-oriented than Mike's are. Tours depart from their office.

# Gay-themed Tours

## GAY HISTORY WALKING TOUR

☎ 672 39 93; www.fantasycity.org; meet at Pink Point; per person €18; ⏱ 1pm most Sats mid-May–Aug

This two-hour tour traces the history of two 18th-century Amsterdammers sentenced to death for gay sex – my, how things have changed. It includes the Royal Palace, site of the executions.

## THE REALLY QUEER GRAND TOUR

☎ 672 39 93; www.fantasycity.org; meet at Casa Maria, Warmoesstraat 60; per person €38; ⏱ noon Tue & Fri Jun-Aug

A four-hour tour covering the Red Light District, gay leather area, bars, coffee shops, secret alleys and lots more. We don't know how they cram it all in. This tour includes a Canal Bus pass (€15 value) that's valid until noon the next day.

# Boat Tours

The companies mentioned here offer a variety of boat tours, from hour-long excursions on the inner canals to far-flung tours of architecture on the Eastern Docklands, jazz cruises, dinner cruises and candlelight cruises. Details are constantly being revised, so check websites or phone for details. Some cruises are included in the Amsterdam Pass.

Some of the more well-established players are: **Canal Bus** ( ☎ 6239886; www.canal.nl; Weteringschans 26); **Holland International** ( ☎ 622 77 88; www.thatsholland.com; Prins Hendrikkade 33a); **Reederij Lovers** ( ☎ 530 10 90; www .lovers.nl; Prins Hendrikkade 25-27); and **Reederij Noord-Zuid** ( ☎ 679 13 70; www.canal -cruises.nl; Stadhouderskade 25).

# House Tour

## URBAN HOME AND GARDEN TOURS

☎ 688 12 43; www.uhgt.nl; tours per person including lunch €37.50; ⏱ 10.15am Mon & Fri, 11.15am Sat

These well-regarded tours look at Amsterdam dwellings from the perspective of home, garden, even gable. Visits include 18th-century, 19th-century and contemporary homes.

## RED LIGHT DISTRICT TOUR

☎ 624 57 20 or VVV offices; www.robvanhulst.nl; Zeedijk 34; per person € 15; ⏱ 6pm Fri & Sat

Under the auspices of the VVV, this tour lasts about two hours. Knowledgeable guides cheerfully cover all you need to know about prostitution and drug use, and a visit to the Erotic Museum is included. Rob van Hulst Productions also organises private tours.

# MEDIEVAL CENTRE

*Eating p135; Shopping p192; Sleeping p213*

## Orientation

The city within the canal belt is referred to as Amsterdam Centrum. One of the charms of this part of town is that its history is still so evident in its layout. Damrak, the Dam and Rokin, which run down the middle of the old medieval core, used to form the final stretch of the Amstel River. The city arose around a dam built across the Amstel at what is now the Dam. The east bank was called Oude Zijde (Old Side), the west bank Nieuwe Zijde (New Side).

The marshy environment required drainage canals to create reasonably solid land. Eventually the Oude Zijde was bordered by the Kloveniersburgwal and Geldersekade, and the Nieuwe Zijde by the Singel (Moat), which marked the extents of

## Transport

Tram lines 1, 2, 4, 5, 9, 13, 16, 17, 24 and 25 all terminate at Centraal Station and run down either Damrak/Rokin or Nieuwezijds Voorburgwal. Metro station Nieuwmarkt is just on the eastern edge of the centre.

## Top Five Medieval Centre

- Feel positively regal inside the lavishly decorated salons of the **Royal Palace** (p60).
- Take in the latest exhibit or concert at **Nieuwe Kerk** (p59), which doubles as the coronation church of Dutch royalty.
- Explore the edgy, the tawdry, the sexy and the silly in the **Red Light District** (p61).
- Spend part of a quiet morning at the **Begijnhof** (p75) or go for Sunday services at its churches.
- Steep yourself in city history at the well-done **Amsterdams Historisch Museum** (p75).

the medieval city. In the late 1400s and early 1500s this modest area received a city wall, with fortified gates at strategic points.

A century later the feudal wall that cost so much to build was torn down again as the city spilled into the surrounding marshes; though some of the old fortified gates remain today. Towards the end of the 16th century, habitable islands were built to the east. These form the current Nieuwmarkt neighbourhood (p95), which lies east of the square of the same name.

Finally, in the 17th century, an enormous urban construction project resulted in the semicircular canal belt, enclosed by the Lijnbaansgracht and the zigzag Buitensingel (outer moat) now known as the Singelgracht.

# CENTRAAL STATION AREA

Most travellers start their visit to Amsterdam at this 1889 station, so we shall too.

### CENTRAAL STATION  Map pp278-9

The building occupies an important place in architectural history: it's a Dutch-Renaissance edifice with Gothic additions, built to a design by Pierre Cuypers and AL van Gendt. Cuypers also designed the Rijksmuseum (p110); both have a central section flanked by square towers with wings on either side. Also note the intricate gilded façade. Van Gendt, meanwhile, was no slouch either, having designed the Concertgebouw (p110). Visitors familiar with Japan may also notice a resemblance to Tokyo station (1914) – that's how far this building's influence spread!

The site for the station was hotly debated at the time. Most council members favoured a station at Leidseplein or in the rapidly expanding southern suburbs, but the national government went for the current site, on three artificial islands in the IJ. This cut the city off from its harbour, though the focus of the harbour had already shifted eastwards and would later move well to the west.

You can exit Centraal Station at the rear (harbour side), hop on one of the free passenger ferries to Amsterdam North and experience the expanse of the IJ. Although it's relatively quiet now, gazing over it you

can try to imagine that in the 17th and 18th centuries this was the busiest harbour in the world – more on the harbour later.

Exiting at the front (city) side, however, you're plunged into the city pretty well immediately. Your first obstacle: tram tracks (please use caution, especially if you're jet-lagged!). To the right you'll spot a spanking new parking garage for 2500…bicycles. Across the tram tracks are branches of the tourist office, VVV (p255), and the local transit bureau, GVB (p245). At these you can collect information, book hotels and purchase transit passes and tickets.

Behind them stretches the Open Havenfront, the harbour where many tour boats dock (Canal Bus, Holland International and Lovers among them).

### ST NICOLAASKERK  Map pp278-9

☎ 624 87 49; Prins Hendrikkade 73; admission free; ☿ vary

Looking from the station, across Prins Hendrikkade (the large street across the harbour) and to your left, you'll see the cupola and twin towers of this neo-baroque edifice, the city's main Catholic church. Designed by AC Bleijs and built in 1887, its impressive interior (wooden vaulting with square pillars of black marble) contains paintings of the Stations of the Cross and a high altar with a representation of the crown of Holy Roman Emperor Maximilian I. As St Nicholas is the patron saint of seafarers, this was an important symbol for the city. This church was the first Catholic Church to be built in the city after restrictions were lifted on Catholic worship (p43).

# DAMRAK

Damrak (Dam Reach; the name refers to both the street and the canal) stretches south towards the Dam, Amsterdam's most historic and important square. Although it's hard to imagine now, Damrak was the city's original harbour, until it became unsuitable for large ships that tied up to palisades along what is now Centraal Station and unloaded onto lighters. Today Damrak is an agonising stretch of gaudy souvenir and sex shops, exchange bureaus, cheap restaurants and claustrophobic, mostly dumpy hotels.

Our advice: see what needs to be seen and move on as quickly as possible.

## BEURS VAN BERLAGE Map pp278-9
☎ 530 41 41; Damrak 243

In the late-19th century the southern half of Damrak was filled in for this new exchange (beurs) building, which was built in 1903 and is considered one of the most important landmarks of Dutch city architecture. It was named after the architect HP Berlage who was still designing it after work began. The large central hall, with its steel and glass roof, was the commodities exchange where coffee, tobacco, sugar, wine and colonial merchandise were traded. Traders eventually deserted the building in favour of the neoclassical Effectenbeurs, or Stock Exchange, built in 1913 by Centraal Station's Pierre Cuypers on the east side of Beursplein.

In the 1970s, the foundations of Berlage's Bourse were sinking and it was slated for demolition, but it was saved by popular outcry. It is now home to the Netherlands Philharmonic Orchestra and occasional museum exhibitions – past shows have included Picasso's paintings, Frank Lloyd Wright's designs and Karel Appel's works that are too large for regular museums. Such is the importance of this building that on '02-02-02', Crown Prince Willem-Alexander married the Argentine Máxima Zorreguïeta here in the regulation civil ceremony, before proceeding to the Nieuwe Kerk (p59) for the church wedding.

Although the functional lines and stark, square clock tower contrast with the more exuberant designs of the age, there are clever details inside and out, visible inside the museum and concert hall. Unfortunately, how-ever, as we went to press these were due to be closed except for special events. If all else fails, the Beurs' Café B van B (p162) is open daily and certainly has worthwhile architectural details of its own (including three 1903 murals by Jan Toorop, representing past, present and future). Enter from the south side of the building.

## SEXMUSEUM AMSTERDAM Map pp278-9
Venustempel; ☎ 622 83 76; Damrak 18; admission €2.50, age 16 & up only; ☒ 10am-11.30pm

Even if it seems rather tame amid the sex shops right down the street, the Sexmuseum gets loads of visitors, and if you're in the right mood it's good for a giggle. Among its treasures: replicas of pornographic Pompeian plates, erotic 14th-century Viennese bronzes, some of the world's earliest nude photographs, a music box that plays 'Edelweiss' and purports to show a couple in flagrante delicto, and an eerie mannequin of Marilyn Monroe re-enacting the sidewalk-grate scene from The Seven Year Itch. The route takes you through a 'bondage room' ('You could be shocked', warns a sign at its entrance), a recreation of a bordello, and mannequins with body hair à la Austin Powers. Welcome to Amsterdam!

## VICTORIA HOTEL Map pp278-9
Cnr Damrak & Prins Hendrikkade

In view of Centraal Station, this grand hotel is nice respite from Damrak's madness. It opened in 1890 to cash in on the station project and has retained much of that old-world flavour to this day. Note the two **17th-century houses** (Prins Hendrikkade 46 & 47) in the façade of the hotel: the owners demanded too much money so the hotel developers simply built around them!

# THE DAM & ROKIN

Damrak ends in Dam square (referred to simply as the Dam) where the original dam was built across the Amstel, giving the city its name. It was the central market square where everything happened. It used to be much smaller than today, reaching its current size only after buildings on all sides were gradually demolished. On busy days, and especially on warm days, the square swarms with visitors – and pigeons!

The original dam was at the eastern end of the current square, with a sluice alongside so ships could pass through. From 1611 they had to lower their masts to pass under the stock exchange, which had been built over the sluice, until it was filled in for good in 1672.

Beyond the Dam, Damrak becomes Rokin (a corruption of *rak-in*, 'inner reach'), most of which was filled in the 19th century. It is considerably more upmarket than Damrak, with office buildings (the modern Options Exchange at No 61), prestigious shops (the wood-panelled tobacconist Hajenius at No 92) and art dealers. However, it may not look it when you read this, due to construction of a new underground (subway) line, for which few locals seem to feel a need.

A column on the pavement at Wijde Kapelsteeg commemorates the Miracle of Amsterdam (p75) that made the city a place of pilgrimage in medieval times. The chapel built on the spot where the miracle of the incombustible Host took place has been demolished, but it occupied this small block between Wijde and Enge Kapelsteeg.

## ALLARD PIERSON MUSEUM
Map pp286-7

☎ 525 25 56; Oude Turfmarkt 127; adult/student/senior/child €4.30/3.20/2.15/1.40; ☿ 10am-5pm Tue-Fri, 1-5pm Sat & Sun

At Grimburgwal, where the water begins again, the bank opposite Rokin is called Oude Turfmarkt, and it is just south of here that you'll find this museum owned by the University of Amsterdam. It has one of the world's richest university collections of archaeological material. You'll find an actual mummy, vases from ancient Greece and Mesopotamia, a very cool wagon from the royal tombs at Salamis (Cyprus) and galleries full of other items providing insight into daily life in ancient times. Each section is explained in a detailed overview via English signage, although most signage on individual items is in Dutch only.

It's not in the same league as the country's largest collection of antiquities in Leiden, let alone the British Museum or the Louvre, but many visitors say that the Allard Pierson's scale and intimacy make it far more accessible and comprehensible.

## MUNTTOREN Map pp286-7
Mint Tower

Rokin terminates at this attractive landmark tower, part of the 15th-century Regulierspoort, a city gate that burned down in 1619. On what was left of the gate, the architect and tower-specialist Hendrick de Keyser built the tower that received its current name in 1672–73,

when the French occupied much of the republic and the national mint was transferred here from Dordrecht for safekeeping.

## NATIONAAL MONUMENT Map pp278-9

This phallic obelisk on the east side of the square was built in 1956 in memory of those who died during WWII. Its many statues symbolise war (the four male figures), peace (woman with child) and resistance (men with dogs); the 12 urns at the rear contain earth from the 11 provinces and the Dutch East Indies. The war dead are still honoured here every year on 4 May.

By the early 1990s the monument had become seriously weakened by rain and frost, and was in danger of falling apart, but it was eventually restored (by a German firm – the irony!).

The monument stands near the site of the old stock exchange (demolished in 1838).

## NIEUWE KERK Map pp278-9

New Church; ☎ 638 69 09; the Dam; admission from €5; ☿ 10am-6pm Fri-Wed, 10am-10pm Thu

Just north of the Royal Palace, this late-Gothic basilica is the coronation church of Dutch royalty, and reckons its origins back to the 14th century, making it the second-oldest church in the city. It is only 'new' in relation to the Oude Kerk (Old Church; p61) – the two competed to be the grandest church in the city. The Nieuwe Kerk was gutted by fire several times, and a

*Nationaal Monument, The Dam*

planned, exceptionally high tower was never completed because funds were diverted to the city hall (now Royal Palace) next door.

Of interest are the magnificently carved oak chancel, the bronze choir screen, massive, gilded organ (1645, designed by Jacob van Campen) and stained-glass windows. The church's oldest stained-glass windows (1650) are directly opposite the entrance, depicting Count William IV presenting the coat of arms to the city founder. The upper portion of the window, with spectators and doves, was not added until 1977. The stained-glass work over the main entrance was created to commemorate the coronation of Queen Wilhelmina, who ascended the throne in 1898 at age 18.

The church also contains the mausoleum of the city's greatest naval hero, Admiral Michiel de Ruijter, who died in 1676 fighting the French at Messina. Several other prominent Amsterdammers are buried here as well, including poets Joost van den Vondel and Pieter Cornelisz Hooft.

The building is used for exhibitions and for organ concerts, but no longer as a church. Opening hours and admission fees may vary, so ring to check.

## ROYAL PALACE Map pp278-9
Koninklijk Paleis; ☎ 620 40 60; the Dam; adult/child or senior/under 6 yrs €4.30/3.60/free, adult ticket with audio tour €6.50; ⏱ 11am-5pm daily mid-Jun-mid-Sep; 12.30-5pm Tue-Thu, Sat & Sun mid-Sep-mid-Jun

The Dam's most imposing building, the palace began life as the grand *stadhuis* (city hall) of republican Amsterdam – in use since 1655, completed 1665. It replaced the old city hall on the same spot, which had burned down. The stunning interior is much more lavish than the stark exterior suggests and is well worth visiting.

The architect, Jacob van Campen, spared no costs for this display of Amsterdam's wealth that rivalled the grandest European buildings of the day. It was described at the time as the eighth wonder of the world, inspired by the Roman Forum (as the many columns of marble attest). The great hall (aka *burgerzaal* or citizens' hall) occupies the heart of the building and was designed to be freely accessible to any citizen. Van Campen envisioned this room as a schematic of the world, with Amsterdam as its centre – look carefully and you'll see motifs representing the four elements: birds (air), fish (water), fruit (land) and fire (er, fire). On the far wall, a clock is constantly set to 11 o'clock, indicating that justice is

possible even at the last hour. This room is still used for large royal functions.

Also worth noting are the balcony room, from where important announcements were made, and the council chamber with its elaborate paintings and murals depicting themes of giving advice, including owls and a painting of Moses by Jacob de Wit.

A century-and-a-half after it was built, the building became the palace of King Louis, Napoleon Bonaparte's brother, who contributed one of the world's richest collections of Empire furniture but had the historic Weigh House in front of the building demolished because it spoiled his view. The building then passed to the members of the House of Orange, who stayed here occasionally. In 1935 the national government bought and restored it for state functions. Officially Queen Beatrix lives here and pays a symbolic rent, though she really lives in The Hague.

The official opening times are only a guideline and depend on government functions, so ring to check. There are free guided tours in English at 2pm Wednesday to Sunday in summer; otherwise, the audio tour is worth the investment. Note that the Royal Palace does not accept the Amsterdam Pass or Museumkaart.

# OUDE ZIJDE (OLD SIDE)
East of the Damrak-Rokin axis is the 'Old Side' of the medieval city. The name is misleading because the 'New Side' to the west is actually older.

Many people are surprised that this gorgeous and historic part of town also contains some of its notorious (and most visited) locales, notably the Red Light District. If you want to head directly toward the red lights, you can skip ahead.

Thanks to the rest of you for reading on. As you wander the district, you'll notice many place names containing *burgwal* (fortified embankment), which attests to the evolution of the city. In the 1380s the Oude Zijde began to expand eastwards towards the Oudezijds Voorburgwal (Old Side Front Fortified Embankment) and soon farther towards the Oudezijds Achterburgwal (Old Side Rear Fortified Embankment).

To the south, the original city stopped at Grimburgwal, where the filled-in part of Rokin ends today. In the 1420s, however, the newly dug Geldersekade and Kloveniersburgwal added more space for the growing population.

## OUDE KERK Map pp278-9

**Old Church;** ☎ 625 82 84; Oudekerksplein 23; adult/
child €4/3; 🕙 11am-5pm Mon-Sat, 1-5pm Sun

A few paces east of Warmoesstraat, through
Enge Kerksteeg, this Gothic church was built
early in the 14th century in honour of the city's
patron saint, St Nicholas – the 'water saint',
protector of sailors, merchants, pawnbrokers
and children. The location of the city's oldest
surviving building (1306) is one of Amsterdam's
great moral contradictions: it's in full view of
the Red Light District, with passers-by getting
chatted up a stone's throw from the church
walls.

The original basilica was replaced in 1340
by an intricately vaulted triple-hall church of
massive proportions that was miraculously un-
damaged by the great fire of 1452. The church's
tower, built in 1565, is arguably the most beautiful in Amsterdam and is well worth climbing
for the magnificent view; special tours (☎ 689
25 65; €40) can be booked for this. The 47-bell
carillon, installed by the carillon master François
Hemony in 1658, is considered one of the finest
in the country. The bell in the top of the tower
dates from 1450 and is the city's oldest.

Also note the stunning Müller organ
(1724), the gilded oak vaults (with remains of
paintings above the southern aisle) and the
stained-glass windows (1555). Check the lively
15th-century carvings on the choir stalls –
some of them are downright rude. As in the
Nieuwe Kerk, many famous and not so famous
Amsterdammers lie buried here under worn
tombstones, including Rembrandt's first wife,
Saskia van Uylenburgh (died 1642). A Dutch
Reformed service is held at 11am Sunday
(doors close at 11am sharp).

Historical notes: the church was once due for
further extensions, but these plans ground to a
halt as funds were diverted to the Nieuwe Kerk.
A century later, Calvinist iconoclasts smashed
and looted many of the Oude Kerk's priceless
paintings, statues and altars. The Calvinist authorities kicked out the hawkers and vagabonds
who had made the church their home, and
changed the official name from St Nicolaaskerk
to Oude Kerk (as it was commonly known anyway). In the mid-17th century the Nieuwe Kerk
took over as the city's main church.

## WARMOESSTRAAT Map pp278-9

Warmoesstraat comprises one of the original
dykes across the Amstel – making it one of
the oldest streets in town. It runs parallel to
Damrak behind the former warehouses that
line the east bank of the river (the southern

extension beyond the Dam is called Nes). The
city's wealthiest merchants lived here, and
anyone else who could afford to.

Today it's a strip of restaurants, cheap hotels, coffeeshops and sex shops, and although
that sounds tawdry (and many of these establishments no doubt are), paradoxically
the street also has a rather well-kept feeling
to it. Condomerie Het Gulden Vlies (p194)
and Geels & Co (p195) are two of the more
interesting shops on the street. For additional
information on these shops and more, see
p192.

# RED LIGHT DISTRICT

This (in)famous area has been sending
sailors broke since the 14th century with
houses of ill repute and countless distilleries. The distilleries have gone, but prostitutes
now display themselves in windows under
red neon lights, touts at sex theatres lure
passers-by with come-ons, and sex-shop
displays leave nothing to the imagination.

All that aside, it is actually a very pretty
part of town – well worth a stroll for the
architecture – and the atmosphere is pretty
laid-back and far less threatening than in
red light districts elsewhere. Crowds of
sightseers both foreign and local mingle
with pimps, drunks, weirdos, drug dealers
and Salvation Army soldiers. Police patrol-
ling on foot chat with prostitutes. Female
sightseers are not assumed to be soliciting
and tend to be left alone if they exercise big-
city street sense.

Colloquially the district is known as the
*wallen* or *walletjes* for the canals that run
down the middle. For a scenic view, face
north on the bridge across Oudezijds Voorburgwal linking Lange Niezel and Korte
Niezel. The formal border is Warmoesstraat
in the west, Zeedijk/Nieuwmarkt/Kloven-
iersburgwal in the east and Damstraat/Oude
Doelenstraat/Oude Hoogstraat in the south.
The best places for strolling window brothels
are along Oudezijds Achterburgwal and in
the alleys around the Oude Kerk, particularly to the south. Advice: don't take photos
of prostitutes or loiterers, or enter into conversation with a drug dealer.

## CASA ROSSO Map pp278-9

☎ 627 89 54; Oudezijds Achterburgwal 106-108; admission €25 or €40 including 4 drinks; 🕙 11am-10pm

You're going to pass this place, with its phallus-
shaped fountain out front, and you're going

## The Red Light District in Facts, Figures & FAQs

- Year prostitution was legalised in the Netherlands: 1810
- Year brothels were legalised: 2000
- Percentage of Dutch public that claims to have 'no problems whatsoever with prostitution': 78%
- Percentage of working prostitutes born in the Netherlands: 5%
- Estimated percentage of prostitutes working illegally in the Netherlands: less than 5%
- Number of windows: approximately 380
- Number of prostitutes working each day in the windows: 1000 to 1200, comprising day, evening and night shifts
- Average rental cost per window (paid by prostitute): €40 to €100 per day, depending on location
- Typical base cost for either 'oral favours' or a 'quickie' in the Red Light District: €30
- Typical base cost for both: €50
- Typical duration of encounter with prostitute: 15 minutes
- Percentage of business from British clients: about 40%
- Most likely time to see prostitutes with Dutch patrons: Monday morning (when many businesses and most shops are closed)
- Do prostitutes pay taxes? Yes
- Are condoms required by law? No, but it's virtually impossible to find a prostitute who'll work without one
- Is there a union? Yes
- Are medical checkups required? No
- Is pimping legal? No
- Is trafficking in prostitutes legal? No
- Penalty for either of the above: maximum six years
- Are accommodations made if a patron can't perform? No
- What happens if a patron gets violent? Prostitutes' quarters are equipped with a button that, when pressed, activates a light outside. The offender had better hope that the police get there before the Hell's Angels do.
- Why red light? Because it's flattering. Especially when used in combination with black light, it makes teeth sparkle. Even as early as the 1300s, women carrying red lanterns met sailors near the port.

to wonder what's inside, so we're going to tell you. Briefly: live sex on stage, or, as we once heard a Casa Rosso barker put it, 'Quality sleaze and filth!'.

Acts can be male, female, both or lesbian (although not gay…sorry boys!). Performers demonstrate everything from positions of the *kama sutra* to pole dances, unbelievable tricks involving candles, and moves we more commonly associate with competitive figure skating. Other acts are comedic, some maybe intentionally so. You may even catch a good old fashioned strip-tease.

Apart from the content of the shows, Casa Rosso could pass for a theatre anywhere, with comfortable cinema-style seating, balcony and bar. Audience members are strictly prohibited from touching the performers.

### EROTIC MUSEUM Map pp278-9

☎ 624 73 03; Oudezijds Achterburgwal 54; admission €5; ⏰ 11am-1am Sun-Thu, 11am-3am Fri & Sat

Ho hum. Your usual assortment of bondage exhibits, erotic photos and cartoons. Although this museum has the advantage of location, it's less entertaining, not as well laid out, more expensive and a little seedy when compared with the Sexmuseum Amsterdam on Damrak (p58).

### HASH & MARIJUANA MUSEUM

Map pp278-9

☎ 623 59 61; Oudezijds Achterburgwal 148; admission €5.70; ⏰ 11am-10pm

Did you know that the first recorded use of marijuana was in 3727 BC in China? We didn't either, but that's just one of the things we learned at this simply designed but informative museum. Exhibits cover pot botany, history, pipes of the world, the relationship between cannabis and religion, and the history of Amsterdam coffeeshops. Queen Victoria was said to have used marijuana for menstrual cramps, and hemp was used to cover wagons in the American Old West.

Dope-smoking is allowed inside, and if you're of a mind to you can watch (and watch and watch…) as the plants grow in a greenhouse in the back. The museum also sells seeds, books and hemp products.

As we went to press, the museum was contemplating a move, down the street to No 130.

### PROSTITUTION INFORMATION CENTRE Map pp278-9

☎ 420 73 28; www.pic-amsterdam.com; Enge Kerksteeg 3; ⏰ noon-7pm Tue, Wed, Fri & Sat

Established by a former prostitute and still staffed by them, for a donation of your choosing, you can view a re-creation of a prostitute's working quarters. The centre caters for study groups from around the world (including police academies) and organises evening Red Light walks – ring for reservations. It also sells pamphlets on prostitution in the Netherlands and a nifty map of the Red Light District, as well as a limited selection of souvenirs.

### MUSEUM AMSTELKRING Map pp278-9
☎ 624 66 04; Oudezijds Voorburgwal 40; adult/student or senior/child €6/4.50/1; ⏰ 10am-5pm Mon-Sat, 1-5pm Sun, extended hours during special exhibits

The highlight of this fascinating museum is Ons' Lieve Heer op Solder (Our Dear Lord in the Attic), one of several 'clandestine' Catholic churches established after the Calvinist coup in 1578. Church property was confiscated and Catholics were permitted to worship only in privately owned real estate so long as it wasn't recognisable as a church and the entrance was hidden. The wealthy hosier Jan Hartman had the house built in 1663, complete with a small church in the attic dedicated to St Nicholas. It remained in use until 1887, when the large St Nicolaaskerk on Prins Hendrikkade diagonally opposite Centraal Station opened its doors.

In 1888 it became a museum and today houses the city's richest collection of Catholic church art, with dozens of liturgical objects, many gilded in silver and gleaming brightly. As you snake through the museum's several floors via tiled staircases, you'll pass the original 'cupboard' bed in the chaplain's room (probably originally used by a servant), the Dutch Classical *sael* (reception hall; note the matching rectangular patterns on the floor, walls and ceiling) and items pertaining to the Miracle of Amsterdam (p75).

When you finally reach the church in the attic, the effect is quite unexpected. Although small, the church is very grand, with marble columns, an elaborate altar, choir, upstairs gallery, even an organ. It is the

---

## Don't even Think about It!

Amsterdam's sex shops offer a virtual horn of plenty (pun intended) for any sexual appetite. In video, DVD and even toy form, you can find anything from plain vanilla to hard-core (S&M, rubber and pain are just the beginning). But one thing is absolutely not tolerated: child pornography. It's illegal even to ask for it.

---

## And in case You Were Wondering...

Several years ago, three men installed themselves behind windows as prostitutes as a sociological experiment. There was intense media interest, but not a single woman dared enter. One of the female prostitutes declared the experiment 'filthy'.

---

only clandestine church preserved as it was originally used, and it is still in use for special ceremonies (weddings, organ concerts and other services).

# ZEEDIJK & NIEUWMARKT

North of the Red Light District is the Zeedijk, the original sea dyke that curved from the mouth of the Amstel to Nieuwmarkt Square and continued from there along what are now St Antoniesbreestraat, Jodenbreestraat and Muiderstraat. The house at Zeedijk 1 dates from the mid-1500s and is one of two timber-fronted houses still left in the city; the other, older one is in the Begijnhof (p75).

In the 1970s, the district's reputation bottomed out when Nieuwmarkt became the centre of Amsterdam's heroin trade. Drug dealers and international mobsters controlled the streets, to the point that a poster signed by the mayor recommended that people visit the miniature model at Madurodam (p235) if they wanted to see this historic part of town. The turning point was the murder of a policeman by a drug addict; the ensuing massive police campaign in the mid-1980s restored legitimate business and much of the old merriment. Although you may still encounter junkies (particularly along Geldersekade to the east), they're much fewer and farther between.

The Zeedijk is also the focus of Amsterdam's 10,000-strong Chinese community, although a New Chinatown east of Centraal Station is on the books for completion by the end of the decade – a combination of residences and entertainment facilities.

### ZEEDIJK

The Zeedijk used to be (and to some extent still is) a street of wine, women and song; the first port of call for sailors after their long voyages. In the 1950s, wine and song predominated and many of the world's great jazz musicians played in pubs such as the **Casablanca** (p181).

On the other side of the street stands the legendary café Het Mandje, a touchstone in the gay rights movement, and an early hangout among Dutch gays and lesbians. It closed in 1983, but if you want to see what it looked like inside, there's a replica at the Amsterdams Historisch Museum (p75).

### GUAN YIN SHRINE Map pp278-9
**Fo Guang Shan He Hwa Temple; ☎ 420 23 57; Zeedijk 106-118; admission free; ☺ noon-5pm Mon-Sat, 10am-5pm Sun**

Near the Nieuwmarkt end of the Zeedijk is Europe's first traditional-style Buddhist temple, completed in 2000. It is dedicated to Guan Yin (aka Kannon), the bodhisattva (Buddhist prophet) alternately depicted in male and female forms, and sometimes known as the goddess of mercy. Guan Yin is commonly shown with many arms, to solve the many problems of supplicants, and this version is no exception. Images on the statue include a prayer bell, a lotus flower and a wheel (said to symbolise the spread of Buddhist teaching), plus Guan Yin's own long ears to facilitate the hearing of prayer.

The building itself is unique. It occupies several lots, and the sections on either end seem to echo the neighbouring row houses. The section in the middle is set back from the

*Guan Yin Shrine*

street and was designed along principles of *feng shui*.

Traditional Chinese-style recitations of the sutras (sayings of the Buddha) are held every Sunday at 10.30am and are open to the public.

### SCHREIERSTOREN Map pp278-9
**Prins Hendrikkade 94-95**

At the mouth of the Geldersekade, the canal east of the Zeedijk, is this small brick tower dating from around 1480 that used to form part of the city fortifications. It's the oldest such tower still standing. Its name comes from an old Dutch word for 'sharp', a reference to this sharp corner that jutted out into the IJ. Tourist literature prefers to call it the 'wailing tower' (from *schreien*, to weep or wail) and claims that sailors' wives stood here and cried their lungs out when ships set off for distant lands, which makes a far more interesting story. The women even have a plaque dedicated to them.

Nowadays there's an attractive **café** ( ☎ 428 82 91) inside the tower.

### NIEUWMARKT SQUARE
In the 17th century, ships used to sail from the IJ down Geldersekade to the Nieuwmarkt (New Market) to take on board new anchors or load and unload produce. Today the square is ringed with cafés, shops and restaurants, and it is the centre of the city's New Year celebrations.

Incidentally, although Nieuwmarkt is very much an open space – arguably the grandest in town after the Dam – nobody adds the word *plein* (square) to the name. It's a little confusing because the whole neighbourhood to the east and southeast is also known as Nieuwmarkt.

### WAAG Map pp278-9
**☎ 422 77 72; Nieuwmarkt 4; admission free; ☺ 10am-1am**

The waag (Weigh House) dates from 1488, when it was known as St Anthoniespoort (St Anthony's Gate) and formed part of the city fortifications. A century later the city had expanded farther east and the gate lost its original function. A section of Kloveniersburgwal was filled in to create the St Anthoniesmarkt (now the Nieuwmarkt). The central courtyard of the gate was covered and it became the city weigh house – the one on the Dam had become too small.

Guilds occupied the upper floor, including the surgeons' guild, which commissioned

## From Old Amsterdam to Nieuw Amsterdam

Among the plaques on the Schreierstoren, one explains that the English captain Henry Hudson set sail from here in 1609 in his ship the *Halve Maen* (Half Moon). The United East India Company (VOC) had enlisted him to find a northern passage to the East Indies, but instead he ended up exploring the North American river that now bears his name. On the return voyage his ship was seized in England and he was ordered never again to sail for a foreign nation.

His reports, however, made it back to base and the Dutch soon established a fort on an island called Manhattan that developed into a settlement called Nieuw Amsterdam; in 1626 an agent of the recently-established Dutch *West* India Company purchased the island from local natives for 60 guilders (often cited as the equivalent of US$24!). In 1664 the West India Company's local governor, the imperious, fanatically Calvinist Pieter Stuyvesant, surrendered the town to the British who promptly renamed it New York. Stuyvesant retired to the Lower Manhattan market garden called Bouwerij, now known as the Bowery.

Fun fact: the distance between the Bowery and New York's Harlem district is about the same as that between Amsterdam and Haarlem. Coincidence? You decide.

Rembrandt to paint *The Anatomy Lesson of Dr Tulp* (displayed in the Mauritshuis in The Hague) and added the octagonal central tower in 1691 to house its new Anatomical Theatre. The masons' guild was based in the tower facing the Zeedijk – note the super-fine brickwork.

Public executions took place at the Waag from the early 19th century, after Louis Napoleon decreed that his palace on the Dam was no longer a suitable spot for such gory displays. In later years it served other purposes – fire station, vault for the city archives, home to the Amsterdam Historical Museum and the Jewish Historical Museum. Today it houses a bar-restaurant illuminated by huge candle-wheels for medieval effect.

The area east and southeast of Nieuwmarkt Square was the centre of Jewish Amsterdam, which was virtually wiped out during the German occupation. Jews were assembled in front of the Waag for deportation.

## SOUTH OF NIEUWMARKT SQUARE

While there are no great monuments or museums in this district, it's a lovely place to stroll and note some historic architecture. Among the best known buildings are:

### DE AGNIETENKAPEL Map pp278-9
**Oudezijds Voorburgwal 231**

Located at the southern end of Oudezijds Voorburgwal is the place that partisans refer to as the Cradle of the University. The complex began life as a convent of St Agnes in 1397, and a beautiful Gothic chapel was added in 1470. When the Calvinists took over it was used as an admiralty warehouse. In 1632 it also became home to the city library (moved from the Nieuwe Kerk) and the Athenaeum Illustre, the Illustrious Athenaeum.

Here students took Latin classes to prepare for higher education elsewhere, especially in Leiden or Utrecht. In 1864 the Athenaeum moved to Singel 421 (part of the present university library) and in 1877 it became the Municipal University of Amsterdam. It seems like a long gestation for the university of such an eminent city, but never fear: by 1895, the UvA had grown to such renown that every few years there was a Nobel Prize awarded among its ranks.

The Agnietenkapel's most recent public incarnation was as a university museum, but it is now closed to the public.

### BINNENGASTHUIS Map pp286-7

A few steps south of the Oudemanhuispoort, at the end of Grimburgwal, another gateway leads to this former inner-city hospital, dating from 1582. In 1981 the university took over and the area is now a mini-campus, with university buildings, living quarters, a large dining hall and an information centre.

### HUIS AAN DE DRIE GRACHTEN
Map pp278-9
**House on the Three Canals; Oudezijds Achterburgwal 249**

Just south of the Agnietenkapel, where the three 'fortified embankments' (*burgwallen*) meet, is this beautiful building (1609). The house was owned by a succession of prominent Amsterdam families and more recently an antiquarian bookshop, but as of writing it had reverted to private property. If no other business opens in its place, you can still easily appreciate the house's steep gables, leaded glass windows and handsome shutters from outside.

### OOSTINDISCH HUIS Map pp278-9
**Cnr Kloveniersburgwal & Oude Hoogstraat; not open to public**

On the west side of Kloveniersburgwal beyond the intersection with Oude Hoogstraat (an extension of Damstraat), the Oostindisch Huis is the former head office of the mighty VOC, the United East India Company. You could easily walk straight past it – there's no sign or plaque to identify it.

The complex of buildings, attributed to Hendrick de Keyser, was built between 1551 and 1643. It was rented to the VOC in 1603 and now belongs to the University of Amsterdam. Enter the stately courtyard through the small gate at Oude Hoogstraat 24 – the only indication of the building's historical significance is the small VOC emblem above the door ahead of you across the courtyard. Along the Kloveniersburgwal frontage, note the gables that defy convention by tilting backwards, making them seem higher.

Districts – Medieval Centre

## OUDEMANHUISPOORT Map pp278-9
### Old Man's House Gate
On Oudezijds Achterburgwal, just east of the Sleutelbrug, is this small, arched gateway leading to a passage of the same name that extends to Kloveniersburgwal. Note the spectacles above the gateway: an almshouse for elderly men and women was built here in 1601 from the proceeds of a public lottery. It was rebuilt in the mid-18th century and in 1879 became the seat of the university. The administration has since moved to other premises, but the buildings here, referred to simply as 'de Poort', can lay claim to being the heart of the university.

A market has operated in the passage since the mid-1700s, specialising in gold, silver, books and knick-knacks, but is now devoted largely to second-hand books. It's well worth a browse (11am to 4pm weekdays). Halfway along, an entrance leads to a lovely 18th-century courtyard dominated by a bust of Minerva. The courtyard is open to the public, but the university buildings surrounding it are closed.

## TRIPPENHUIS Map pp278-9
### Kloveniersburgwal 29
Just south of the Nieuwmarkt, on the east side of Kloveniersburgwal, the Trippenhuis was built in 1660–64 to house the wealthy Trip brothers, Lodewijk and Hendrik, who made their fortune in metals, artillery and ammunition. The greystone mansion with Corinthian pilasters consists of two separate houses with false middle windows, and the chimneys are shaped like mortars to indicate their owners' trade.

## UNIVERSITY DISTRICT
The Oude Zijde south of Damstraat/Oude Doelenstraat/Oude Hoogstraat is distinctly residential, and the Red Light district seems miles away. The southern end of Oudezijds Voorburgwal used to be known as the 'velvet canal' for the wealthy people who lived here.

Both the Oudezijds canals end at Grimburgwal, and the junction is one of the strongholds of the University of Amsterdam (Universiteit van Amsterdam, or UvA). You'll no doubt notice the telltale jumble of parked bicycles. This former municipal university – not to be confused with the orthodox-Calvinist Vrije Universiteit (Free University) in the southern suburbs – has no central campus as such; its buildings number over 110 spread throughout the city, but there's a large concentration of them here.

(Continued on page 75)

## The Winner by a Narrow Margin
Canal-boat commentators and other tourist guides like to point out the narrowest house in Amsterdam. They account for the phenomenon by explaining that property was taxed on frontage – the narrower the house the lower the tax, regardless of the height. There is some truth in this, but it seems as if each guide has a different 'narrowest' house. So which house holds the record?

The house at Oude Hoogstraat 22, east of the Dam, is 2.02m wide and 6m deep. Occupying a mere 12sq metres, it could well be the least space-consuming self-contained house in Europe (though it's a few storeys high). The house at Singel 7 is narrower still, consisting of just a door and a slim, 1st-floor window, but canal-boat commentators fail to point out that it's actually the rear entrance of a house of normal proportions. Farther along and on the other side of Singel at No 144 is a house that measures only 1.8m across the front; it widens to 5m at the rear and experts with nothing better to do will argue whether this counts.

The Kleine Trippenhuis (Small Trippenhouse) at Kloveniersburgwal 26 is 2.44m wide. It's opposite the 22m-wide house of the Trip brothers at No 29, one of the widest private residences in the city. The story goes that their coachman exclaimed, 'If only I could have a house as wide as my masters' door!' and that his wish was granted.

**1** Canal boat tour (p56)
**2** Colourful graffiti, Spuistraat
**3** An Amsterdam café terrace
**4** An Amsterdam tram

1 The Dam and the Royal Palace (p58) 2 Guan Yin Shrine (p64) 3 Begijnhof (p75) 4 Nieuwe Kerk (p59)

1 *The Jordaan, from the Westerkerk (p85)* 2 *Bloemenmarkt, on Singel (p89)* 3 *Waag (p64)*
4 *Stained-glass window, Nieuwe Kerk (p59)*

1 *Noordermarkt (p87)* 2 *Statue of Anne Frank (p80)* 3 *Artis Zoo (p102)* 4 *Greenpeace building, Keizersgracht (p82)*

1 *Prinsengracht (p79)* 2 *Wester-kerk (p83)* 3 *Het Schip (p88)*
4 *Erotic shop, Red Light District (p61)*

1 NEMO science museum (p105)
2 FOAM – Fotografie Museum Amsterdam (p93) 3 Joods Historisch Museum (Jewish Historical Museum; p99) 4 EnergeticA museum (p104)

1 Museumplein (p110) 2 Reguliersgracht (p94) 3 Cyclists in the Vondelpark (p112) 4 CoBrA, museum of modern art (p116)

*1 Blossoming cactus, Hortus Botanicus (p103) 2 Bicycles in the wallen, Amsterdam's Red Light District (p61) 3 A typical gable and furniture hoist, Herengracht 4 Red Light District (p61)*

*(Continued from page 66)*

# NIEUWE ZIJDE (NEW SIDE)

West of the Damrak-Rokin axis is the 'New Side' of the medieval city. It was actually settled slightly earlier than the Oude Zijde – the names date from the construction of the Nieuwe Kerk and the division of the city into two parishes.

The very first houses in Amsterdam probably stood on a dyke no more than 25m wide, on the western bank of the Amstel between the Dam and Oudebrugsteeg. This, the oldest dyke in the city, parallel to the current Damrak, later acquired the name of its northern extension, Nieuwendijk. It used to link up with the road to Haarlem, and its shops and other businesses became adept at fleecing travellers on their way to Amsterdam's market on the Dam. Today this pedestrianised shopping street still suffers from a distinctly downmarket image, though some of the narrow streets leading to the west can be as picturesquely medieval as it gets.

If you'd like to pass through a mini Red Light District without making an ordeal of it, take a quick walk down Oude Nieuwstraat.

South of the Dam is Kalverstraat, the extension of Nieuwendijk and the country's most expensive shopping street rent-wise, at €1500 per square metre per year – shops go broke with depressing regularity. Still, it remains a busy shopping street with a good number of large department stores (and pickpockets – please take care!). It's best to visit on weekdays, unless you don't mind jostling with weekend crowds.

Kalverstraat was one of the original dykes along the Amstel – together with Nieuwendijk, Warmoesstraat and Nes – which makes it one of the oldest streets in the city. The name (Calves Street) presumably refers to the cattle that were led to market on the Dam. (In the 15th century there was a cattle market in the southern section of Kalverstraat beyond Spui, but the name is older.)

## AMSTERDAMS HISTORISCH
## MUSEUM Map pp278-9
☎ 523 18 22; www.ahm.nl; Kalverstraat 92; adult/child/under 6 yrs €6/3/free; ☙ 10am-5pm Mon-Fri, 11am-5pm Sat & Sun

Housed in the former civic orphanage (that existed here till 1960), this museum is quite extensive and pleasant. Begin with the large screen TV depicting an aerial view of the

## Proof that Miracles can Come in Many Forms

The Miracle of Amsterdam has a rather unappetizing start.

In 1345, the final sacrament was administered to a dying man, but he could not keep the Host (communion wafer) down and – and there's no way to put this delicately – vomited it up. Here's the miracle part: when the vomit was thrown on the fire, the Host would not burn. Shortly thereafter, a chapel was built on the site across Kalverstraat from what's now the museum (the Heilege Stede chapel, demolished 1908) and it soon became a pilgrimage area; the final approach is along the street now known as Heilegeweg.

In the Amsterdam Historical Museum is a wooden chest reported to have once contained the Host. In 1578, when Catholic property was parcelled out, the chest ended up in an orphanage, and several children are said to have been cured of illnesses by sitting on it.

evolution of the city from tiny settlement on the mouth of the Amstel, as it was filled in to create the metropolis we now know and love. Excavations, even in the city centre, have yielded well-preserved artefacts: pottery, woollen cloth etc. Exhibited here are models of old homes, religious objects from churches and synagogues (including some relating to the Miracle of Amsterdam, see boxed text), silver and porcelain, exhibits on the trade guilds and a detailed history of Dutch trading. Exhibits on the 20th century include the spread of bicycle use, WWII (naturally) a re-creation of the original Café Het Mandje (p64), well-meaning civic projects like the white cars and white bikes, and an examination of the city's drugs policies.

Even if you give the museum a miss, it's worth walking into the courtyard (note the cupboards in which the orphans stored their possessions).

## BEGIJNHOF Map pp278-9
☎ 623 35 65; admission free; ☙ 8am-11am

Hidden behind the intersection of Spui and Nieuwezijds Voorburgwal, this enclosed former convent dates from the early 14th century. It's a surreal oasis of peace, with tiny houses grouped around a well-kept courtyard. Amsterdam has many such enclosed *hofjes* (literally 'little courtyards') or almshouses (old people's homes run by charities), but this is the only one where the public is still welcome; we hope it endures – in

## Wall Tablets

Before street numbers were introduced in 1795, many of Amsterdam's residences were identified by their wall tablets. These painted or carved stone plaques (dating from the mid-17th century) were practical decorations to identify not only the inhabitant's house but also their origin, religion or profession. Beautiful examples of these stones are still found on many of the buildings along the main canals. Occupations are the most frequently occurring theme: tobacconists, milliners, merchants, skippers, undertakers and even grass-mowers.

As well as being colourful reminders of the city's former citizens, these tablets also provide hints about the city's past. A stone depicting a mail wagon at Singel 74 commemorates the commencement of the postal service between Amsterdam and The Hague in 1660. Farther down the street a tablet portraying the scene of Eve tempting Adam with an apple attests to the time when that part of the street operated as a fruit market (known as the 'apple market').

Many wall tablets dotted throughout the city celebrate the life of famous citizens like the maritime hero Michiel Adriaenszoon de Ruyter and biologist Jan Swammerdam, but the most appealing are memorials to domestic life and common vocations of the age.

2003 local residents got tired of all the visitors, and the hours were curtailed to the present ones.

The Begijnhof is an excellent place to linger before entering the hustle and bustle of the city. Note the house at No 34; it dates from around 1465, making it the oldest preserved wooden house in the country. There's a collection of biblical wall tablets on the blind wall to the left. Some of the other homes around the courtyard have lovely postage stamp–sized gardens.

The Beguines were a Catholic order of unmarried or widowed women from wealthy families, who cared for the elderly and lived a religious life without taking monastic vows; the last true Beguines died in the 1970s. They owned their houses, so these could not be confiscated after the Calvinist coup.

Contained within the hof is the **Begijnhof Kapel** (☎ 622 19 18; Begijnhof 30; admission free; ✦ Eucharist service 9am Mon-Sat, 10am Sun). After the loss of their Gothic church, the Beguines were forced to worship in this 'clandestine' church opposite. Go through the dogleg entrance, and inside this lovely chapel you'll find marble columns, wooden pews, and paintings and stained-glass windows commemorating the Miracle of Amsterdam.

The other church in the Begijnhof is known as the **Presbyterian Church** (Engelse Kerk; ☎ 624 96 65; Begijnhof 48; admission free; ✦ Presbyterian service in English 10.30am Sun), at the southern end of the Begijnhof courtyard. This Gothic church was built around 1392 and was used by the Beguines until it was taken away from them by the Calvinists. It was eventually rented

*Begijnhof (p75)*

out to the local community of English and Scottish Presbyterian refugees – the Pilgrim Fathers worshipped here – and still serves as the city's Presbyterian church. Some of the pulpit panels were designed by a young Piet Mondriaan.

## CIVIC GUARD GALLERY Map pp278-9

☎ 523 18 22; www.ahm.nl; Kalverstraat 92; admission free; 🕑 10am-5pm Mon-Fri, 11am-5pm Sat & Sun

The enormous tableau hanging here represent an entire subgenre of Dutch painting: group portraits of Medieval guard groups. The different divisions – *voetboog* (large crossbow), *kloveniers* (hackbut) etc – protected the city and played a large part in deposing the Spanish government; after the Peace of Munster in 1648, they took on more of a social function. This collection, together with that in the Rijksmuseum (which includes the most famous of these paintings, Rembrandt's *Nightwatch*), is the world's largest, and given the repairs due to the Rijksmuseum over the next few years (see boxed text p111), the Civic Guard Gallery should be the best place in town to view a large number at once. English signage is excellent.

Technically, every man had to serve in these guard units, although not all were able because guardsmen had to pay for uniforms and weapons. Participation in the portraits, however, was voluntary, as each member paid his own way. The size of the paintings was determined by the size of the wall space in the guard houses where the paintings were to be hung.

The gallery used to be a ditch separating the boys' and girls' sections of a previous orphanage. It ends by one entrance to the Begijnhof.

## MAGNA PLAZA Map pp278-9

☎ 626 91 99; Nieuwezijds Voorburgwal 182; 🕑 11am-7pm Mon, 10am-7pm Tue, Wed, Fri & Sat, 10am-9pm Thu, noon-7pm Sun

Back towards the Dam, facing the Royal Palace, this hulk, with its imposing orange-and-white façade, was the former General Post Office. It was built in 1895–99 by the government architect CH Peters, a pupil of Pierre Cuypers. It used to be one of the most-impressive post offices in Europe, but has now been converted into a luxurious shopping centre dominated by clothing boutiques. Pop inside to admire the impressive hall – with three storeys of colonnades and an airy, skylit atrium – and look at some of the interesting shops (see the Shopping chapter, p192, for individual shops).

Adjacent Nieuwezijds Voorburgwal, for its part, was once the country's 'Fleet Street' where many newspapers had their head offices (they're now out in the suburbs).

## POEZENBOOT Map pp278-9

Cat Boat; ☎ 625 87 94; Singel 40; admission free; 🕑 1-3pm

Across the canal, this boat is a must for cat-lovers…and hell for mouse-lovers. It was founded in 1966 by an eccentric woman who became legendary for looking after several hundred stray kitties at a time. The boat has since been taken over by a foundation and holds a mere 30 cats in proper pens, being spayed, neutered, implanted with an identifying computer chip (as per Dutch law) and, hopefully, adopted out. For the meantime, the cats seem endearingly content with life as the boat rocks back and forth on the water, and visitors are welcome to stroke them (donation suggested).

## RONDE LUTHERSE KERK Map pp278-9

Round Lutheran Church; ☎ 623 15 72; cnr Singel 11; admission free; 🕑 9am-1pm Mon-Fri & Sun

This domed church was built in 1668–71 to replace the old Lutheran church on the Spui. It's the only round Protestant church in the country and is pure 17th-century baroque, though the white interior is suitably sober. The church was rebuilt after a disastrous fire in 1822 but falling attendances forced its closure in 1936 (ironically the old church on the Spui is still in use by Lutherans). It now serves as a conference centre for the nearby Renaissance Hotel.

Next door, along the east (odd-numbered) side of Singel, where the former city wall used to run, the house at No 7 (next to the Liberty Hotel) appears to be no wider than its door – except that this is actually the rear entrance of a house of normal proportions.

## TORENSLUIS Map pp278-9

Along the Singel is **Torensluis**, one of the widest bridges in the city. The 'toren' refers to a tower that once stood here and formed part of the city's fortifications; the bridge was later built around it. The tower was demolished in 1829, leaving a 42m-wide esplanade. The view northwards is camera material.

The statue on the bridge represents **Multatuli** (Latin for 'I have suffered greatly'), the pen name of the brilliant 19th-century author Eduard Douwes Dekker. A local captain's son who served in the East Indies colonial administration, Multatuli exposed colonial narrow-mindedness in a novel about a coffee merchant. After being sacked he wrote letters and essays.

## THE SPUI & AROUND
Until 1882, the elongated Spui square (referred to simply as the Spui, pronounced *spow*, approximately) used to be water. In the 14th century it marked the southern end of the city, together with Grimburgwal, its northeastern extension across Rokin. The name means 'sluice' (or rather, the area inside a sluice) and it connected the Amstel with the watercourse running along Nieuwezijds Voorburgwal, the western side of the city, and later with the Singel. A book market is held from 10am to 6pm Friday.

The heart of the square is its western part where Nieuwezijds Voorburgwal and Spuistraat meet. The statuette in the middle, the *Lieverdje* (Little Darling), is an endearing rendition of an Amsterdam street-brat. It was donated by a cigarette company and became the focal point for Provo 'happenings' in the mid-1960s (p51). The area is now a meeting point for the city's intelligentsia, who congregate in the pubs at the western end of the square and in the surrounding bookshops, including the landmark Athenaeum bookshop and newsagency.

### HEILIGEWEG Map pp286-7
Holy Way
This street was the 'Holy Way' travelled by Catholic pilgrims on their annual procession to the chapel of the Miracle of Amsterdam. The route used to extend all the way from the village of Sloten, southwest of the city, along what is now the Overtoom (once a canal for towboats carrying produce) and through the current Leidsestraat, but only this final section has retained the original name. A procession still takes place every year on the Sunday closest to 15 March and attracts Catholics from Holland and abroad.

### KRIJTBERG Map pp286-7
Chalk Mountain; ☎ 623 19 23, Singel 448;
❤ Mass noon & 5pm Mon-Fri, noon & 4pm Sat,
9am & 4.30pm Sun
On the southwestern side of Singel are the soaring turrets of this neo-Gothic church. Officially known as the St Franciscus Xaveriuskerk, it was completed in 1883 to a design by Alfred Tepe and replaced a 'clandestine' Jesuit chapel on the same site. The lavish paintings and statuary, recently restored to their full glory, make this one of the most beautiful churches in the city. Krijtberg's name (chalk mountain) refers to one of the houses that once stood here, which belonged to a chalk merchant.

### MAAGDENHUIS Map pp286-7
Virgins' House; Spui, between Voetboogstraat & Handboogstraat
This classicist building was built in 1787 as a Catholic orphanage for girls and is now the administrative seat of the University of Amsterdam. In 1969 it was occupied by students, a watershed in the development of students' rights in the country. Police cordoned off the building but the occupiers held out for five days, with supplies ferried across a bridge that supportive workers built over the alley. The handsome Lutheran Church across Handboogstraat, on the corner of Singel, was built in 1633. It is still used as a church but also by the university for ceremonies such as doctoral promotions, which benefit from its good acoustics.

### RASPHUIS GATE Map pp286-7
Off Heiligeweg
Halfway along Heiligeweg, on the southeastern side, is a gateway dating from the early 17th century and attributed to Hendrick de Keyser. This once gave access to the Rasphuis, a model penitentiary where beggars and delinquents were put to work to ease their return to society. One of their back-breaking jobs was to rasp brazil wood for the dyeing industry – hence the name, Rasp House. Later it became a normal prison and in 1896 a public swimming pool; now it's a gateway to the Kalvertoren shopping centre (p196).

### UNIVERSITY LIBRARY Map pp286-7
☎ 525 23 01; Singel 421-425; ❤ 8.30am-midnight Mon-Fri, 9.30am-5pm Sat, 11am-5pm Sun
The history of this library is more interesting than its current building, around the corner from the Lutheran Church. Citizens' militias used to meet on the site, the 'hand-bow' militia in No 421 and the 'foot-bow' militia in No 425 (the latter also served as headquarters for the West India Company). The current Handboogstraat and Voetboogstraat are named after the militias. Their firing ranges at the rear reached to Kalverstraat. The building at No 423 was constructed by Hendrick de Keyser in 1606 as the city arsenal and was later used as royal stables.

Today the site is dominated by a concrete hulk, although there's a small gallery that may be worth visiting depending on what's showing.

# WESTERN CANAL BELT, JORDAAN & WESTERN ISLANDS

*Eating p139; Shopping p199; Sleeping p216*

## Orientation

Towards the end of the 16th century, the city burst out of its medieval walls with a flood of Jewish refugees from Portugal and Spain, and Protestant refugees from Antwerp. In the 1580s, after the Calvinists took power and reassessed the city's needs, new land was reclaimed from the IJ and Amstel in the east (see Nieuwmarkt p95). In the west, Singel became a residential canal with the addition of a new moat that was to become Herengracht.

In 1613 the authorities embarked on an ambitious expansion project that more than tripled the city's area. Based on a plan drawn up by the city carpenter, Hendrick Jacobsz Staets, Amsterdam received a belt of parallel semi-circular canals, one after the other like layers of an onion around the medieval city core, beginning and ending at the IJ. These canals were punctuated by 'radial' canals, perpendicular to the semi-circular ones, kind of like spokes on a bicycle. These canals with their many bridges and connecting roads (intended as shopping streets) were all built in one huge effort. Collectively, these new canals are called the Canal Belt (*Grachtelgordel* in Dutch).

Parcels of land were sold along the way to finance the project, and buildings arose gradually. The whole city was enclosed by a new outer moat, the zigzag Buitensingel (outer moat), now known as the Singelgracht. The moat's outer quays became the current Nassaukade, Stadhouderskade and Mauritskade.

Work began at the northwestern end adjoining the new harbour works, and headed south from the radial Brouwersgracht. By 1625 the western canal belt was completed down to the radial Leidsegracht when the money ran out. The project was picked up again later but at a much slower pace, and by the end of the 17th century it petered out just short of its original goal (see the Southern Canal Belt section, p88).

These new canals clearly segregated society into haves and have-nots. Until then, merchants lived more or less in their warehouses, mingling with their labourers and suppliers in the thick of the city's activities. Now the wealthiest among them escaped the sweat and the stench by building residential mansions along the delectable Herengracht (named after the Heeren XVII, the '17 Gentlemen' of the United East India Company, p46). The Keizersgracht (the 'emperor's canal' in honour of Maximilian) was similarly upmarket, though the houses along its later extension beyond Leidsegracht were a bit more pedestrian. Businesses that could be annoying or offensive were banned, and bridges were fixed to exclude large vessels – though this didn't prevent barges from unloading and loading goods at the warehouses that were built even along these canals.

### Transport

Tram lines 13, 14, 17 and 20 travel along Raadhuisstraat/Rozengracht and trams 3 and 10 travel down Marnixstraat, just to the west of the Jordaan, with number 3 going on to the Western Islands.

Bus route 21 travels down Raadhuisstraat/Rozengracht; routes 18 and 22 travel down Nieuwe Westerdokstraat through the Haarlem Quarter.

The Prinsengracht – named for William the Silent, Prince of Orange and forefather of the royal family – was designed as a 'cheaper' canal with smaller residences, warehouses and workshops. It also acted as a barrier against the downmarket Jordaan neighbourhood that lay beyond (p85). That heritage remains today; the Prinsengracht is about the liveliest in the area. Instead of stately offices and banks, there are shops and cafés where you can sit outside in summer. The houses are smaller and narrower than along the other canals, and apartments are still relatively affordable by canal standards; houseboats line the quays. Together with the Jordaan, this is an area where anyone can feel comfortable.

# BROUWERSGRACHT

At the northern end of the canal belt, the Brewers' Canal was named after the breweries that used to operate here. It's one of the most picturesque canals in town and a great place for a stroll, although it wasn't always so: throughout most of its history it was an industrial canal full of warehouses, workshops and factories banned from the residential canal belt. Businesses here included some of the smelliest: breweries, distilleries, tanneries, potash works, and whale-oil and sugar refineries, as well as more fragrant warehouses for spices, coffee and grain.

The buildings were solidly constructed and many were converted to apartments in the 1970s and '80s. Note the almost uninterrupted row of former warehouses from No 172 to 212. Houseboats add to the lazy, residential character.

## BROUWERSGRACHT TO RAADHUISSTRAAT

### ANNE FRANK HUIS Map p277

☎ 556 71 05; www.annefrank.nl; Prinsengracht 276; adult/child/under 10yrs €7.50/3.50/free; ⏰ 9am-9pm Apr-Aug, 9am-7pm Sep-Mar, closed Yom Kippur

### Top Five Western Canal Belt, Jordaan & Western Islands

- Be moved by the story of the **Anne Frank Huis** (below) – get there early or late to avoid the crowds.
- Even non-shoppers may be charmed by the diverse offerings of the boutiques of the **Negen Straatjes** (p84) and the backstreets of the **Jordaan** (p85).
- Find yourself a seat at one of the many brown cafés lining the **Prinsengracht** (p79).
- If the play's your thing, don't miss the excellent, handsome **Theatermuseum** (p82).
- **Het Schip** (p88) is a touchpoint for Amsterdamse School architecture as well as one of Amsterdam's signature buildings.

It's one of Amsterdam's most compelling stories, indeed one of the most compelling of the 20th century: a young Jewish girl forced into hiding with her family and their family friends to escape deportation by the Nazis (see boxed text). The house they used as a hideaway should be a highlight of any visit to Amsterdam; indeed, it gets over 900,000 visitors a year – go early or late in the day to avoid

## Anne Frank

Anne Frank's father, Otto Frank, was a manufacturer of pectin (a gelling agent used in jam) who had the foresight to emigrate with his family from Frankfurt to Amsterdam in 1933. In December 1940 he bought what is now known as the Anne Frank Huis on the Prinsengracht and moved his business here from the Singel. By then the German occupiers had already tightened the noose around the city's Jewish inhabitants, and even though he signed the business over to his non-Jewish partner, Otto was forced in July 1942 to go into hiding with his family – his wife and daughters Anne (aged 13) and Margot (16).

They moved into the specially prepared rear of the building, along with another couple, the Van Daans, and their son Peter, and were joined later by a Mr van Dussel. The entrance hid behind a revolving bookcase, and the windows of the annexe were blacked out to prevent suspicion among people who might see it from surrounding houses (blackouts were common practice to disorient Allied bombers at night).

Here they survived until they were betrayed to the Gestapo in August 1944. The Franks were among the last Jews to be deported and Anne died in the Bergen-Belsen concentration camp in March 1945, only weeks before it was liberated. Otto was the only member of the family to survive, and after the war he published Anne's diary which was found among the litter in the annexe (the furniture had been carted away by the Nazis). Addressed to the fictitious Kitty, the diary – written in Dutch – traces the young teenager's development through puberty and persecution, and displays all the signs of a gifted writer in the making.

In 1957 the then-owner donated the house to the Anne Frank Foundation, which turned it into a museum on the persecution of Jews in WWII and the dangers of present-day racism and anti-Semitism.

The diary, meanwhile, has taken on a life of its own. It's been translated into some 60 languages and was made into a stage play performed in 34 countries, a 1959 Hollywood movie and a 2001 British movie. The diary has been reissued in recent years, complete with passages deleted by Otto about Anne's awakening sexuality and relationship problems with her mother, all of which only rounds out her character and reminds us that she was, among other things, an ordinary girl, unable to swim against the tide of extraordinary times.

*Anne Frank Huis*

the crowds. The house itself is now contained within a modern, square shell.

It took the German army just five days to occupy all of the Netherlands, along with Belgium and much of France. Before long (we learn via Anne's now-famous diary) restrictions were imposed on Jews from riding streetcars to having to turn over bicycles and not being allowed to visit Christian friends; these, of course, were only some of the mildest.

The focus of the museum is the *achterhuis*, the 'rear house' or **secret annexe**. It was here, in this dark and airless space, where the Franks and others observed complete silence during the daytimes, outgrew their clothes, pasted photos of Hollywood stars on the walls and read Dickens, before being mysteriously betrayed and sent to their deaths.

It is, of course, the personalisation of the story that makes it so chilling. If you're like us, by the time you get to the diary itself, sitting alone in its case, you may well have a lump in your throat. And perhaps that's as it should be; you didn't come here to feel the same emotions you can feel at home.

Note that the Anne Frank Huis does not accept the Amsterdam Pass or the Museumkaart. However, if you plan to visit late in the day you can purchase advance tickets (same price as regular tickets) at VVV offices in the city, the Uitburo on Leidseplein and Holland Tourist Information at Schiphol Airport. There's

a separate entrance for **advance ticket holders** (☺ 5pm-8.30pm Apr-Aug, 4pm-6.30pm Sep-Mar). Advance tickets are valid any day.

## GREENLAND WAREHOUSES
Map pp278-9
**Keizersgracht 40-44; closed to the public**

These three warehouses, with their step gables, belonged to the Greenland (or Nordic) Company, which dominated Arctic whaling from the early 17th century when Amsterdam's whalers edged out the Basques. In 1680, Amsterdam's whaling fleet counted 260 ships and employed 14,000 sailors. Whalers from Zaandam proved more competitive after the company's monopoly was lifted in 1642, though Amsterdam continued whaling till the early 1800s.

Whale oil was much sought after for a variety of uses (soap, lamp oil, paint), as was whalebone or baleen (corsets, cutlery). Oil-storage wells in these Keizersgracht warehouses (there were five in a row – the ones at Nos 36 and 38 have been demolished) held 100,000L of the precious stuff, and more barrels sat alongside the whalebone on the top floors. The authorities moved the storage facilities to the Western Islands in 1685 to maintain the upmarket character of the canal belt. Many houses at this end of Keizersgracht used to belong to whaling executives and still bear decorations related to their trade.

81

## GREENPEACE BUILDING Map pp278-9
**Keizersgracht 174-176; closed to the public**
This tall building, which houses the organisation's international headquarters as well as the Dutch branch, is a rare example of Art Nouveau architecture in Amsterdam (The Hague has a much richer collection). It was built in 1905 for a life insurance company – the façade's huge tile tableau shows a guardian angel who seems to be peddling an insurance policy.

## HOMOMONUMENT Map p277
**1987; cnr Keizersgracht & Radhuisstraat**
Behind the Westerkerk a series of three 10m x 10m x 10m triangles are embedded in the ground, straddling the narrow street. Made from pink granite (the pink triangle being the design of the patch the Nazis forced gay men to wear, just as Jews were forced to wear the Star of David), the simple but evocative triangles were designed by Dutch artist Karin Daan to convey past persecution of gays and lesbians while projecting hope for the future.

One of the triangles, the 'water triangle', actually steps down into the Keizersgracht, said to represent a jetty from which gays were sent to the concentration camps, while other interpretations say that stepping up from the canalside creates a rising symbol of hope. Another 'text triangle' is flat on the ground, while the 'podium triangle' rises 60cm from the surface. Walk by the monument without looking for it and you might not know that it's there – an interesting metaphor for homosexuality.

Engraved around the text triangle is a quote from the gay Dutch poet Jacob Israel de Haan (1881–1924), 'Naar vriendschap zulk een mateloos verlangen' ('such an endless longing for friendship').

Just south of the Homomonument is the **Pink Point of Presence** (PPP; noon-6pm Mar-Aug, with limited hours the rest of the year; p203). Part info-point, part souvenir shop, it's a good place to pick up gay- and lesbian-themed publications, news about parties, events and social groups, as well as AIDS info. It's volunteer-staffed, and profits go to the care of the Homomonument and occasionally to other causes (and parties!).

## HOUSE WITH THE HEADS Map pp278-9
**Keizersgracht 123; closed to the public**
Further south on the opposite side of the canal, halfway between Herenstraat and Leliegracht, is one of the finest examples of Dutch-Renaissance architecture. The beautiful step

gable, with its six heads at door level representing the classical muses, is reminiscent of Hendrick de Keyser's Bartolotti House on Herengracht. This is not surprising: the original owner, Nicolaas Sohier, was related to the Bartolottis and commissioned De Keyser to design the house, though the architect died in 1621 and the job was presumably completed by his son Pieter a year later. Folklore has it that the heads represent six burglars, decapitated in quick succession by an axe-wielding maid of Sohier's as they tried to break into the cellar. Appropriately, the building now houses the city's conservation office (Bureau Monumentenzorg), which aims to preserve the city's listed buildings.

## RAADHUISSTRAAT Map pp278-9
The Herengracht is crossed by this street, a 'spoke road' built in 1894–96 to link the Jordaan with the Dam. Note the shopping arcade on the far side, which follows the S-curve of Raadhuisstraat towards Keizersgracht. It was designed by AL van Gendt (the Concertgebouw architect) for an insurance company, with sculptures of vicious animals to stress the dangers of life without insurance. Smoke bombs greeted Princess Beatrix's wedding coach as it passed this arcade in 1966.

## RENÉ DESCARTES HOUSE Map p277
**Westermarkt 6; closed to public**
On the quiet northern side of the square surrounding the Westerkerk is the house where the French philosopher resided in 1634. He was one of many foreign intellectuals who found the freedom to develop and express their ideas in Amsterdam (others included Locke, Comenius, Voltaire and Marx) or who had their works published here. A plaque above the door quotes from a letter he wrote to Balzac: *'Quel autre pays où l'on puisse jouir d'une liberté si entière'* ('In what other country can one satisfy oneself with such complete liberty?'), a sentiment we still support.

Voltaire is said to have had a different view: that local residents were so preoccupied with profit that they'd never notice him even if he spent his entire life here.

## THEATERMUSEUM Map pp278-9
551 33 00; Herengracht 170; adult/student, senior or child €4.50/2.25; 11am-5pm Mon-Fri, 1-5pm Sat & Sun
Theatre buffs will want to spend a good hour here at least, exploring the history of Dutch theatre. Exhibits include dioramas (including

the first theatre built in Amsterdam, 1638); displays of costumes from lush to stark; heady sepia-toned early photographs of 19th-century actors; and video clips of famous modern-day productions. It's also a unique opportunity to learn about one of the most interesting legacies of Dutch theatre: the *rederijkamers* (chambers of rhetoric), medieval literary societies that staged large-scale productions throughout the Netherlands and Flanders. Most signage is in excellent English.

The current exhibit, covering 1000 years of theatre in the Netherlands, is scheduled to run until April 2005. The paper tie-on masks sold in the gift shop are about our favourite souvenir in town.

Even if you're not interested in theatre, the museum is worth visiting for the stunning interior, which was completely restyled in the 1730s, with intricate plasterwork and extensive wall and ceiling paintings by Jacob de Wit and Isaac de Moucheron. A magnificent spiral staircase was added then too. In summer, the lovely garden out the back is the perfect spot to reflect on life. The façade dates back to 1620 (modified 1638) to a design by Philip Vigboons – the building is also known as the **White House**.

The museum spills over into the **Bartolotti House** (Herengracht 170–172), which has one of the most stunning facades in the city – a red-brick, Dutch-Renaissance job that follows the bend of the canal. It was built in 1615 by Hendrick de Keyser and his son Pieter by order of the wealthy brewer Willem van den Heuvel, who later assumed the name of his Bolognese father-in-law so he could inherit his bank and develop it into a trading empire. The house was later split down the middle and both residences were inhabited by prominent Amsterdam families.

### WESTERKERK Map p277

☎ 624 77 66; Westermarkt; church admission free, tower €3 by tour only; ☉ church 11am-3pm Mon-Fri Apr-Sep, tower 10am-5pm Mon-Sat Apr-Sep, church services Sun 10.30am Apr-Sep

The church is the main gathering place for Amsterdam's Dutch Reformed community. It was built as a showcase Protestant church for the rich to a 1620 design by Hendrick de Keyser, who copied his design of the Zuiderkerk but increased the scale. De Keyser died in 1621 and the church was completed by Jacob van Campen in 1630. The square tower dates from 1638 – De Keyser would surely have made it hexagonal or octagonal. The nave, 29m wide and 28m high, is the largest in the Netherlands and is covered

by a wooden barrel vault (the marshy ground precluded the use of heavy stone).

The huge main **organ** dates from 1686, with panels decorated with biblical scenes and instruments by Gerard de Lairesse. The secondary organ is used for Bach cantatas. Rembrandt, who died bankrupt at nearby Rozengracht, was buried in the church on 8 October 1669 but no-one knows exactly where – possibly near his son Titus' grave.

Another highlight of the church is its **belltower**, the highest church tower in the city (85m). It's topped by the imperial crown that Habsburg emperor Maximilian I bestowed to the city's coat of arms in 1489. A tourist logo of Amsterdam today, the tower affords a tremendous view over the city, including the differing layouts of the canal belt and the streets in the Jordaan. The climb during the 60-minute tour is steep (186 steps) and claustrophobic (What do you want? You're in a bell tower!), but there are periodic landings where you can rest while the guide describes the bells and other workings of the massive carillon. Of the 50 bells, the largest is some 7500kg. You can also see the sleeping chamber where the night watchmen slept, between keeping a lookout for fires.

# RAADHUISSTRAAT TO LEIDSEGRACHT

### BIJBELS MUSEUM Map pp286-7

☎ 624 24 36; Herengracht 366-368; adult/child or student/under 6 yrs €5/2.50/free; ☉ 10am-5pm Mon-Sat, 1-5pm Sun

The quartet of sandstone neck-gabled houses at Herengracht 364–370 is known as the Cromhouthuizen, designed in 1662 by Philips Vingboons for Jacob Cromhout. Today, they house the Bible Museum.

The museum originated as the life's work of Leendert Schouten (1828–1905), a minister of the Dutch Reformed Church who built a scale model of the Tabernacle described in Exodus, now on the museum's third floor. So elaborate was the model that it is said to have attracted thousands of visitors even before it was completed in 1851. Schouten also collected Egyptian antiquities and Jewish ceremonial objects, to illustrate the Israelites' 400 years in Egypt. An exhibit on the museum's second floor examines the Temple Mount/Haram al-Sharif in Jerusalem from Christian, Jewish and Muslim perspectives. A collection of Dutch bibles includes the **Delft Bible** printed in 1477.

On the ground floor, you can sniff scents mentioned in the bible and stroll a garden of biblical trees. There are also beautiful 18th-century ceiling paintings by Jacob de Wit in a gallery of 17th-century paintings of biblical scenes.

## HERENGRACHT 380–382
**Closed to the public**

The house at No 380–382 is unique in that it's designed like a French chateau in early French Renaissance style (a fairly faithful copy of the castle at Blois) instead of following Dutch Renaissance lines. It was built in the 1880s for Jacob Nienhuys, who made his fortune as a tobacco planter and wanted to live in the most luxurious canal house that money could buy. It was the first house in Amsterdam with electric lighting and had its own generator room. His neighbours took a dim view of such bright displays and spread the rumour that the authorities had prohibited him placing a solid gold gate in front of the house.

Continuing south along Herengracht, the even-numbered side between Huidenstraat and Leidsegracht shows an interesting mix of architectural styles.

## CHRISTOFFEL BRANTS' HOUSE
Map p277
**Keizersgracht 317; closed to the public**

This is the residence where Tsar Peter the Great of Russia surprised his host, Christoffel Brants, by sailing right up to the house in the passenger barge from Utrecht to pay his respects. The Brants family used to live in Russia and shared Peter's interest in ships. In 1697 the young tsar had already paid an incognito visit to the world centre of shipbuilding to serve as an apprentice shipwright; this time, in 1716–17, his visit was official.

The city dignitaries greeted him with compliments in cultured French; he answered in earthy Dutch expletives, drank beer straight from the jug at the evening banquet and passed out on the floor beside his bed. The next day he moved to the Russian ambassador's house at Herengracht 527 and trashed the place with bouts of drunken revelry over the following months. A similar lot befell Brants' country mansion (called 'Petersburg') along the Vecht River, though Brants received handsome financial recompense and a title.

## FELIX MERITIS Map p277
☎ 623 13 11; www.felix.meritis.nl; Keizersgracht 324;
☼ box office 9am-7pm

This centre for performing arts was built in 1787 by Jacob Otten Husly for an organisation called Felix Meritis (Latin for 'Happy through Merit'), a society of wealthy residents who promoted the ideals of the Enlightenment through the study of science, arts and commerce. It became the city's main cultural centre in the 19th century. The colonnaded façade served as a model for that of the Concertgebouw, and its oval concert hall (where Brahms, Grieg and Saint Saëns performed) was copied as the Concertgebouw's Kleine Zaal (Small Hall) for chamber music.

The building later passed to a printing company and was gutted by fire in 1932. After WWII it became the headquarters of the Dutch Communist Party (and the offices of the party newspaper), and from 1968 to 1989 the Shaffy Theatre Company staged its avant-garde productions here. Today, the reconstituted Felix Meritis Foundation promotes European performing arts and literature; there are often musical performances, and on a sunny morning the café's huge windows make for a comfy warm seat.

## GROOTE KEYSER Map p277
**Keizersgracht 242-252; closed to the public**

This row of houses became famous as a squatters' fortress. Squatters occupied the empty buildings in November 1978 and couldn't be served with eviction notices until the authorities found out their full names. Notices were served a year later, but the squatters stayed put and had a well-organised support network. They fortified the buildings and set up a pirate radio station, the Vrije Keyser (Free Kaiser), which scanned the police frequencies and broadcast instructions to their supporters – the station played a key role in the massive riots that accompanied Queen Beatrix's coronation on 30 April 1980. Eventually the owners and authorities gave up: in October 1980 the council bought the buildings, legalised the squatters and renovated the houses on their behalf.

## NEGEN STRAATJES

The '**nine alleys**' sit like a tic-tac-toe board in an area bounded by Reestraat, Hartenstraat and Gasthuismolensteeg to the north, Prinsengracht to the west, Singel to the east and Runstraat, Huidenstraat and Wijde Heisteeg to the south. Streets like Berenstraat, Wolvenstraat and Oude Spiegelstraat make this perhaps our favourite shopping in town. The *straatjes* (little streets) are full of quirky little shops dealing in antiques, fashions, housewares and one-offs including everything from toothbrushes to antique eyeglass frames. It's all peppered with pubs, cafés and informal dining. Among our favourite shops: Boekie Woekie (which deals in books created by artists; p200), Laura Dols (vintage clothing; p202), Mendo (advertising agency with its own art gallery; p202) and de Kaaskamer (cheese; p201). For cafés, try Hein (p140), de Doffer (p157) or the lovely chocolate and cake shop, Pompadour (p162).

## NETHERLANDS MEDIA ART INSTITUTE Map p277
☎ 623 71 01; www.montevideo.nl; Keizersgracht 264; adult/student €2.50/1.50; ☽ gallery 1-6pm Tue-Sat

From the hilarious to the ridiculous to the deep and the experimental, there's always something different in the gallery's changing exhibits. Don't expect to see works by the hit-makers or TV directors of tomorrow, though. The institute is specifically about video as art; there's even an artist in residence program if you get inspired. The **mediatheek** (admission free; ☽ 1-5pm Mon-Fri) works like a library, complete with librarians to advise you.

## PULITZER HOTEL Map p277
Prinsengracht 315-331

Towards the south of this section of the Prinsengracht is this unique hotel (p217), which began business in 1971 and now occupies 25 canal houses, all connected with internal staircases and passages. In August a free classical concert is held from barges in the canal in

*Netherlands Media Art Institutue*

front of the hotel, as part of the **Grachtenfestival** (p10).

If you continue south along the eastern side of the canal you might notice a number of very narrow **alleyways** between Berenstraat and Leidsegracht, closed off with gates. They were officially intended as side entrances for servants' quarters at the rear, but such quarters were rented out as accommodation and workshops to the city's poor. These hidden slums, in damp cellars and clustered around dark courtyards, violated the municipal codes of the canal belt, but nobody took much notice, probably because they were opposite the southern reaches of the Jordaan – had they been on Herengracht or Keizersgracht it might have been a different story.

# JORDAAN
## Orientation

The Jordaan neighbourhood was planned and built as a working-class district during the canal-belt project in the early 17th century. Here the canal-diggers and bridge-builders, carpenters and stonemasons settled with their families. Here, too, came the tanneries, breweries, sugar refineries, smithies, cooperages and other smelly or noisy industries banned from the upmarket canal belt, along with the residences of the artisans and labourers who worked in them.

The name Jordaan wasn't used until a century later, and its origin is unclear. The most popular theory is that it's a corruption of the French *jardin* (garden). After all, many Huguenots settled here in what used to be the market gardens beyond the city walls – the street pattern follows the original grid of ditches and footpaths, and many streets carry names of flowers. Some historians contend that the name had biblical connotations and referred to the Jordan River. For centuries, the Jordaan remained a thoroughly working-class area and the authorities saw it as the unruly district of the city. It was the first precinct where tarred roads replaced brick paving because the latter could be turned into barricades and police-smashing projectiles during riots. Early in the 20th century, one in seven Amsterdammers lived in the Jordaan, with 1000 people packed to the hectare (100m x 100m) in squalid conditions.

In the late-19th and early 20th centuries many of the Jordaan's ditches and narrow canals were filled in, mainly for sanitary reasons, though their names remain: Palmgracht, Lindengracht, Rozengracht (now a busy thoroughfare) and Elandsgracht. **Bloemgracht** was the most upmarket of the canals (the 'Herengracht of the Jordaan') and, for that reason, was never filled in: here wealthy artisans built smaller versions of patrician canal houses. Note the row of three step gables at No 87–91, now owned by the Hendrick de Keyser Foundation and known as the Three Hendricks, though they were built in 1645, long after the famous sculptor/architect had died.

New housing estates in Amsterdam's northern, western and southern suburbs brought some relief after WWI, and in the 1960s and '70s many Jordaanese moved to the outlying 'garden suburbs'. Their places were taken by students, artists and tertiary-sector professionals who began to transform the Jordaan into a trendy area, though there's still a stronghold of working-class and elderly people. Historically the Jordaan south of Rozengracht was (and to some extent still is) an area of workshops and artists' studios.

Popular conceptions of the Jordaan linger: the 'heart and soul' of the 'real' Amsterdam epitomised in schmaltzy oompah ballads, where life happens on the streets or in corner pubs; where houses are tiny but tidy, with lace curtains and flowers in window boxes, behind which Auntie Greet eyes the street and her front door with the help of a *spionnetje* ('little spy' mirror) attached to the window-sill; and where living, working, shopping, schooling and entertainment are integrated in the one neighbourhood.

Such popular conceptions still hold true, as you will discover when you wander and soak up the atmosphere. Take your time and don't worry if you get lost (which you will); there are plenty of inviting pubs and restaurants, offbeat shops and weird little art galleries to grab your attention.

## HOFJES

Another distinctive historical legacy of the Jordaan is its high concentration of *hofjes*, almshouses consisting of a courtyard surrounded by houses built by wealthy benefactors to house elderly people and widows – a noble act in the days before social security. Some hofjes are real gems, with beautifully restored houses and lovingly maintained gardens. The entrances are usually unobtrusive

and hidden behind doors. Unfortunately, hofjes became such popular tourist attractions that residents complained and they were closed to the public (the one exception being the Begijnhof, p75).

However, if you should find any of the following open, do try to have a peek: the oldest hofje is the **Lindenhofje** (Lindengracht 94–112), dating from 1614; the **Suyckerhofje** (Lindengracht 149–163) is a charming hofje founded in 1670. **Karthuizerhofje** (Karthuizersstraat 89–171) is a hofje for widows, dating from 1650 and on the site of a former Carthusian monastery.

**Claes Claeszhofje** (Eerste Egelantiersdwarsstraat 3), also known as Anslo's Hofje, has three courtyards dating from around 1630. **St Andrieshofje** (Egelantiersgracht 107–141), the second-oldest surviving hofje, was finished in 1617, and founded by the cattle farmer Jeff Gerritzoon. **Venetiae** (Elandsstraat 106–136) was founded in the mid-1600s by a trader with Venice, and features a very pretty garden.

## HOUSEBOAT MUSEUM Map p277

☎ 427 07 50; www.houseboatmuseum.nl; Prinsengracht opposite No 296; adult/child under 152cm €3/2.25; 🕑 11am-5pm Wed-Sun Mar-Oct, 11am-5pm Fri-Sun Nov-Feb, closed 5-30 Jan

Along the canal at Johnny Jordaanplein (which commemorates a popular singer of local ballads), this museum offers a good opportunity to get a sense of life on the water. Housed in a sailing barge built in 1914, the museum's interior epitomises the Dutch term *gezelligheid* (cosiness, conviviality). The collection itself is rather minimal, but you can view the iron hull up close, watch a slideshow of pretty houseboats (and ugly houseboat disasters!), see sleeping, living, cooking and dining quarters with all mod-cons, and try to imagine living here as the water gently rocks beneath. In case you were wondering, houseboat toilets, until this century, could drain directly into the canals, but they now must hook up to the city sewage system.

## NOORDERKERK Map pp278-9

☎ 626 64 36; Noordermarkt 48; admission free; 🕑 11am-1pm Sat, 10am-noon & 7-8.30pm Sun

Near the northern end of the Prinsengracht, this imposing church was completed in 1623, to a design by Hendrick de Keyser, as a Calvinist church for the 'common' people in the Jordaan (the upper classes attended his Westerkerk farther south). It was built in the shape of a broad Greek cross (four arms of equal length) around a central pulpit, giving the whole congregation unimpeded access to the word of God in suitably sober surroundings. This design, unusual at the time, would become common for Protestant churches throughout the country.

A sculpture near the entrance commemorates the bloody Jordaan riots of July 1934, when five people died protesting the government's austerity measures, including a 12% reduction of already pitiful unemployment benefits.

## NOORDERMARKT Map pp278-9
**Noorderstraat; ☺ markets 8am-1pm Mon, 10am-3pm Sat**

A market square since the early 1600s, the plaza in front of the Noorderkerk now hosts a lively flea market on Monday morning where you can find some wonderful bargains. Early on Saturday morning there's a bird market (caged birds, rabbits etc – a holdover from the former livestock market), followed till early/mid–afternoon by a 'farmer's market' (*boerenmarkt*) with organic produce, herbs etc. There's a nice selection of cafés surrounding the square, including Winkel (p143) on the southwest corner, home of some of the city's best apple pie.

## PIANOLA MUSEUM Map pp227
**☎ 627 96 24; Westerstraat 106; adult/child €3.75/ 2.50; ☺ 11.30am-5.30pm Sun**

Although its opening hours are limited, this is quite a special place. You can hear concerts of player pianos from the early 1900s, with rare classical or jazz tunes composed especially for the instrument – some 15,000 rolls. The curator gives demonstrations with great zest.

# WESTERN ISLANDS
## Orientation

The wharves and warehouses of the Western Islands (Westelijke Eilanden), built into the IJ north of the western canal belt, were a focus of the harbour in the first half of the 17th century. The wealthy Bicker brothers, mayors of Amsterdam, even built their very own **Bickerseiland** to cater for their ships.

The area has a character all its own and is well worth a wander. Many warehouses have been converted to residences, and the ones that haven't had much done to them are in demand as studios for sculptors and painters. The **Prinseneiland** and **Realeneiland** (the latter named after the 17th-century

merchant Reynier Reael) are the prettiest of the islands – the narrow bridge linking the two, the Drieharingenbrug (Three Herrings Bridge), is a modern replacement for the pontoon that used to be pulled aside to let ships through.

By all means visit the photogenic **Zandhoek**, the 17th-century sand market on the eastern waterfront of Realeneiland. The Zandhoek escaped demolition this century thanks to Jan Mens' 1940 novel *De Gouden Reael*, named after the bar-restaurant at No 14. Galgenstraat (Gallows Street), which runs across Prinseneiland to Bickerseiland, used to provide a view over the IJ to the gallows at Volewyck, the uninhabited tip of what was to become Amsterdam North, where bodies of criminals executed on the Dam were propped up and left to the mercy of crows and dogs.

## HAARLEM QUARTER

The Haarlem Quarter (Haarlemmerbuurt) between the Western Islands and Brouwersgracht gets few visitors, and as such offers a glimpse of life in central Amsterdam without tourists. **Haarlemmerstraat** and its western extension, **Haarlemmerdijk**, were part of the original sea dyke along the IJ, from the Zeedijk in the east all the way to the western extremities of the IJ north of Haarlem. They have become a lot quieter now that the artery to/from Haarlem runs north of here. Pedestrians have flocked back, mainly local residents lured by a good range of shops, pubs and restaurants.

## HAARLEMMERPOORT Map pp274-5
**Haarlem Gate**

The busy road to Haarlem led through this gate on Haarlemmerplein, where travellers heading into town had to leave their horses and carts. The current structure dates from 1840 and was built as a tax office and a gateway for King William II to pass through on his coronation. It's since been converted to housing. It replaced the most monumental of all the city gates, built by Hendrick de Keyser in 1615 but demolished some 200 years later.

In the 17th century a canal was dug from here to Haarlem to transport passengers on horse-drawn barges. In the 19th century the railways took over, but the original canalside road, Haarlemmerweg, is still a major road (which, for obvious reasons, no longer passes through the gate itself).

### HERENMARKT Map pp278-9

**Haarlemmerstraat**

Halfway along Haarlemmerstraat you'll find this area, which leads to Brouwersgracht at the head of Herengracht. This was planned as a market in the 1613 canal-belt project, but it never took off. Now it's a quiet oasis and a prestigious Amsterdam address. The building at the north end of the square used to be a meat hall before it became the **Westindisch Huis**, head office of the West India Company, from 1623 to 1654. In 1628 Admiral Piet Heyn captured the Spanish silver fleet off Cuba and the booty was stored here in the cellars. Every Dutch person knows the nursery rhyme celebrating Heyn's small name and big deeds, sung by soccer supporters at international matches as a warning not to underestimate this small country.

Walk through the east entrance into the courtyard with its statue of Pieter Stuyvesant, the unpopular governor of New Netherlands (p65). Today the building houses the John Adams Institute, a Dutch–US friendship society.

### HET SCHIP Map pp274-5

☎ 418 28 85; Spaarndammerplantsoen 140; adult/concession €2.50/1.50; ⏱ 2-5pm Wed, Thu & Sun

Several minutes' walk northwest of the Haarlem Quarter (cross under the railway tracks), the housing estate known as het Schip (1920) is one of the signature buildings of Amsterdam School architecture.

This triangular block, loosely resembling a ship, was designed by Michel de Klerk for a housing corporation of railway employees. The pointed tower at the short side of the block has no purpose whatsoever, apart from aesthetically linking the two wings of the complex – and serving as a major symbol of this architectural movement. There are several other Amsterdam School–designed housing blocks in this area.

The former post office at the 'bow' of the 'ship' still has the original interior, all meticulously designed by De Klerk. It now houses the Documentation Centre for Social Housing, with a permanent exhibition of Amsterdam School architecture called **Poste Restante**. It's not a conventional museum, however. The displays mostly take the form of videos at small stands; you listen via headphones (or read the subtitles) to learn about living conditions for the average worker at the turn of the 20th century (squalid doesn't begin to describe it!), and how the Dutch government became responsible for ensuring basic housing standards. Among the other topics covered are Berlage's grand plan for southern Amsterdam, the relationship of the Amsterdam School to socialism, and how the city was laid out via the polder and ditch system. Architecture fans may spend an hour or more here.

Some architectural details: The yellow 'telefooncel', in the section behind the former postal wickets, is where workers would dial the telephone numbers for customers; the 'sprekcel' with its ingenious double doors is where the customer would sit and speak once the call was connected. Also note the geometrical designs of the leadlight windows and cast-iron counters, and the weird shapes of the tiled walls.

Outside on the pavement is a small collection of typical Amsterdam School street fixtures (letterbox, fire alarm etc). On the other side of the post office entrance, be sure to walk into the attractive courtyard through the arch. The fairy-tale garden house with its sculpted roof was intended as a meeting room where residents could discuss housing issues and other matters of common interest.

# SOUTHERN CANAL BELT

*Eating p144; Shopping p203; Sleeping p217*

## Orientation

The canal project (see the Western Canal Belt section, p79) stopped at the radial Leidsegracht in 1625 because of lack of funds, but it was picked up again at a later date. Even then, work on the southern section progressed much more slowly; it had taken a mere 12 years to construct the canals down from Brouwersgracht, along with their various interconnecting roads and the adjoining Jordaan area, but it took another 40 years to complete the southern canal belt towards the Amstel and beyond the opposite bank. Interest then fizzled out

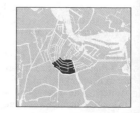

and the only canal that ever made it to the eastern IJ was the (Nieuwe) Herengracht.

The stretch of the Herengracht between Leidsestraat and Vijzelstraat was the site of some of the largest private mansions in the city. Most of them now belong to financial and other institutions. Dutch architectural themes are still evident, but the dominant styles are Louis XIV, XV and XVI – French culture was all the rage among the city's wealthy class.

You can look at the interior of one of these houses by visiting the **Goethe Institut** ( ☎ 623 04 21; Herengracht 470). As large as this house is now, it was much larger when it was built in 1669; it included No 468 next door.

Today, if the Western Canal Belt is upscale and refined, the Southern Canal Belt, while also quite beautiful, has a populist edge. Leidseplein and Rembrandtplein anchor the city's nightlife.

# LEIDSEGRACHT TO VIJZELGRACHT

## ABN-AMRO BANK BUILDING
Map pp286-7

Cnr Herengracht & Vijzelstraat

On the even-numbered side of Herengracht, the corner with Vijzelstraat is dominated by the colossal (some would say monstrous) ABN-AMRO bank building that continues all the way to Keizersgracht. It was completed in 1923 as head office for the Netherlands Trading Society, a Dutch overseas bank (successor to the United East India Company and West India Company) that became the ABN Bank in the mid-1960s and merged with its competitor, the AMRO Bank, in 1991.

## BLOEMENMARKT Map pp286-7
Flower Market; ☿ 9am-5pm; closed Sun in winter

The side of the canal opposite the Munttoren (p59) is occupied by Amsterdam's most famous floating attraction, one of several flower markets since the 17th century (see the boxed text 'Tulipmania', p90). The market here dates from the 1860s and specialises in flowers, bulbs, pots, vases, some plants and, now, lots of souvenirs. It's a very pretty sight and the place is packed with tourists and pickpockets. Prices are steep by Amsterdam standards but the quality is good. Just make sure that your home country allows you to import bulbs (bulbs destined for the USA, for example, are marked with a special label).

## KATTENKABINET Map pp286-7
Cats' Cabinet; ☎ 626 53 78; Herengracht 497; adult/child €4.50/2.25; ☿ 10am-2pm Mon-Fri, 1-5pm Sat & Sun

One Golden Bend house that's open to the public is this museum, devoted to the feline presence in art. It was founded by a wealthy financier in memory of his red tomcat, John Piermont Morgan III. The collection includes cats in art largely from Dutch and French artists (Theopile-Alexandre Steinlen, 1859–1923, figures prominently) as well as a small Rembrandt (a Madonna and Child with cat and snake) and Picasso's *le Chat*. There's also a nice selection of 19th-century magazine covers and circus posters. The museum's also worth visiting for the interior and views of the garden.

A note for the allergic: several real cats also live here.

## KEIZERSGRACHTKERK Map pp286-7
Keizersgracht 566

Beyond Leidsestraat is the solid yet elegant Keizersgrachtkerk. It dates from 1888 and was built to house the orthodox-Calvinist Gereformeerd community who left the Dutch Reformed Church two years before.

---

## Top Five Southern Canal Belt

- Get an aerial view from the café of **Metz & Co Department Store** (p91).
- See a stately home up close at **Museum van Loon** (p94).
- Join the throngs of visitors in the circus-like, busy **Leidseplein** (p90) or chill out at the comfy, quiet **Amstelveld** (p93).
- See cutting-edge photography at **FOAM** (p93).
- Cap your day with a beer or dinner at Café Schiller on **Rembrandtplein** (p95).

# Tulipmania

When it comes to investment frenzy, the Dutch tulip craze of 1636–37 ranks alongside the South Sea Bubble of 1720, the Great Crash of 1929, Enron, Worldcom and the Netherlands' own home-grown Ahold scandal.

Tulips originated as wild flowers in Central Asia and were first cultivated by the Turks, who filled their courts with these beautiful spring blossoms ('tulip' derives from the Turkish for turban). In the mid-1500s the Habsburg ambassador to Istanbul brought some bulbs back to Vienna where the imperial botanist, Carolus Clusius, learned how to propagate them. In 1590 Clusius became director of the Hortus Botanicus in Leiden – Europe's oldest botanical garden – and had great success growing and cross-breeding tulips in Holland's cool, damp climate and fertile delta soil.

The exotic flowers with their frilly petals and 'flamed' streaks of colour attracted the attention of wealthy merchants, who put them in their living rooms and hallways to impress visitors. As wealth and savings spread downwards through society, so too did the taste for exotic products. Tulips were no exception, and growers arose to service the demand.

Ironically, the frilly petals and colour streaks were symptoms of a virus transmitted by a louse that thrived on peaches and potatoes – healthy tulips are solid, smooth and monotone. Turks already knew that the most beautiful tulips grew under fruit trees, but the virus itself wasn't discovered until the 20th century.

The most beautiful tulips in 17th-century Holland were also the weakest due to heavy cross-breeding, which made them even more susceptible to the virus. They were notoriously difficult to cultivate and their blossoms unpredictable. A speculative frenzy ensued, and people paid top florin for the finest bulbs which would change hands many times before they sprouted. Vast profits were made and speculators fell over themselves to outbid each other. The fact that such bidding often took place in taverns and was fuelled by alcohol no doubt added to the enthusiasm.

At the height of the Tulipmania in November 1636, a single bulb of the legendary *Semper augustus* fetched the equivalent of 10 years' wages for the average worker; a couple of *Viceroy* bulbs cost the equivalent of an Amsterdam canal house. One unfortunate foreign sailor made himself rather unpopular with his employer by slicing up what he thought was an onion in order to garnish his herring. An English amateur botanist, intrigued by an unknown bulb lying in his host's conservatory, proceeded to bisect it, and was put in jail until he could raise 4000 guilders.

This bonanza couldn't last, and when several bulb traders in Haarlem failed to fetch their expected prices in February 1637, the bottom fell out of the market. Within weeks many of the country's wealthiest merchants went bankrupt and many more people of humbler origin lost everything they thought they had acquired. Speculators who were stuck with unsold bulbs, or with bulbs that had been reserved but not yet paid for (the concept of options was invented during the Tulipmania), appealed for government action but the authorities refused to become involved in what they considered to be gambling.

The speculation disappeared, but love of the surprising tulip endured and it remained an expensive flower. Cool-headed growers perfected their craft. To this day, the Dutch continue to be the world leaders in tulip cultivation and supply most of the bulbs planted in Europe and North America. They also excel in other bulbs such as daffodils, hyacinths and crocuses.

So what happened to the flamed, frilly tulips of the past? They're still produced but have gone out of fashion, and are now known as Rembrandt tulips because of their depiction in so many 17th-century paintings.

## LEIDSEPLEIN Map pp286-7

One of the liveliest squares in the city and the undisputed centre of nightlife, Leidseplein has always been busy. In the 17th century it was the gateway to Leiden and other points south-west, and travellers had to leave their carts and horses here when heading into town.

There's something here for every taste: The sidewalk cafés at the northern end of the square are perfect for watching interesting street artists and eccentric passers-by. There are countless pubs and clubs in the area that continue till daylight, and a smorgasbord of restaurants in the surrounding streets. Cinemas and other entertainment venues radiate out from its centre, and Kerkstraat, a few streets away, has a cluster of gay establishments.

## MAX EUWEPLEIN Map pp286-7

Steps from Leidseplein, the austere building along the western side used to be a prison. Now there's a Hard Rock Café, the Comedy Café (p184) and an Irish pub. This is also where you'll find Holland Casino Amsterdam (p166), built in the shape of a roulette table.

## MAX EUWE CENTRUM Map pp286-7

☎ 625 70 17; Max Euweplein 30A1; admission free;
🕑 10.30am-4pm Tue-Fri & 1st Sat of month

Max Euwe (1901–81) was the Netherlands' only world chess champion, in the 1930s, and here you'll find a permanent exhibition devoted to the history of chess. You can play against live or digital opponents. An oversized chess board on the pavement of the square is often busy with players and onlookers.

# Bending the Golden Rules

Amsterdam has always had a shortage of land suitable for building. When the authorities embarked on their expensive canal-belt project, they drew up detailed regulations to ensure that this scarce commodity would return maximum revenue.

On the outer bank of Herengracht, plots were limited to a width of 30 feet and a depth of 190 feet (these were pre-metric days). There were no limits to the height of buildings at the front of each plot, but the rear 80 feet could not be built higher than 10 feet to ensure the unprecedented luxury of large gardens (even today, the gardens behind many Herengracht houses are magnificent). Buyers also had to pay for the brick quayside in front of their plots, although the city paid for the street. Subdivisions were prohibited in order to keep these properties desirable and maintain their value.

So much for the theory. In practice, the very wealthiest Amsterdammers got dispensation, as can be seen in the immense palaces along the 'Golden Bend' of Herengracht between Leidsestraat and Vijzelstraat. Elsewhere, regulations were interpreted creatively – for instance, by buying two adjacent plots and building one house with two fronts; or conversely by building one house with two entrances, subdividing the edifice into upstairs and downstairs areas and selling the two separately.

## METZ DEPARTMENT STORE

Map pp286-7
Cnr Keizersgracht & Leidsestraat
This building opened in 1891 to house the New York Life Insurance Company (hence the exterior and interior eagles), but soon passed to Metz, a purveyor of luxury furnishings. The functionalist designer and architect Gerrit Rietveld added the gallery on the top floor where you can have lunch with a view.

## MILK FACTORY Map pp286-7

Prinsengracht 739-741; closed to the public
Unfortunately, the ebullient neo-Renaissance façade is all that remains of the former milk factory, built in 1876 to a design by Eduard Cuypers. Until then, milk was brought into town from the surrounding countryside in wooden barrels and sold on the streets from open buckets.

## MUSEUM WILLET-HOLTHUYSEN

Map pp286-7
☎ 523 18 22; Herengracht 605; adult/child/under 6 yrs €4/2/free; ☺ 10am-5pm Mon-Fri, 11am-5pm Sat & Sun
This impressive house museum, part of the Amsterdams Historisch Museum, dates from 1685 and is named after the widow who bequeathed the property to the city in the late-19th century. The sumptuous interior has been remodelled over the years, including extensive renovations several years ago. Some furnishings and artefacts come from other bequests, which accounts for the mix of 18th- and 19th-century styles.

Highlights include paintings by Jacob de Wit, the *place de milieu* (centrepiece) that was part of the family's 275-piece set of Meissen table service, and the intimate French-style garden with sundial – you can also peek at the garden through the iron fence at the Amstelstraat end. The top floor galleries often hold special exhibitions. Be sure to pick up the notebook of explanations at the front desk; it's got lots of details that make the house come alive (eg how meat was roasted and how windows were cleaned).

## NIEUWE SPIEGELSTRAAT Map pp286-7

Even if you don't have the inclination – or the money – to buy luxury antiques and collectables, this ritzy stretch is worth a look. Many of the shops and galleries feel like museums in their own right. The extension of this street, the pretty Spiegelgracht with more antique shops and especially art galleries, leads to the Rijksmuseum.

One place that's anything but antique is **De Appel** (☎ 625 56 51; www.deappel.nl; Nieuwe Spiegelstraat 10; admission €2.50; ☺ 11am-6pm Tue-Sun), a rather large arts and media space. You'll find ever-changing exhibits of contemporary art: installation pieces, painting, sculpture, media art. Phone or check the website to find out what's on.

## PALEIS VAN JUSTITIE Map pp286-7

Prinsengracht 436
Near the corner with Leidsegracht is the Paleis van Justitie (Court of Appeal), a huge, neoclassical edifice modified in 1829 by the city architect Jan de Greef. It began life in 1666 as the city orphanage and was designed for 800 orphans, but by the early 19th century more than half the city's 4300 orphans were crammed in here.

## The Great Art Fraud

Herengracht 470, which currently houses the Goethe Institut, used to include adjacent No 468. The house was later split, and during WWII a German art dealer 'acquired' No 468.

The Amsterdam painter Han van Meegeren sold him a painting by the 17th-century Delft master Jan Vermeer that the German passed on to Nazi ringleader Hermann Göring in return for two million guilders' worth of paintings plundered elsewhere. After the war, Van Meegeren was accused of collaboration, but he declared that he had painted the Vermeer himself and in fact had painted the other 'Vermeers' that had appeared out of nowhere in recent years. To prove his case he painted another 'Vermeer' under supervision.

His work completely fooled the art historians of the day, including the prestigious Boijmans-van Beuningen Museum in Rotterdam, which bought one of the paintings in 1937 (*Christ at Emmaus*) and gave it top billing. It was the greatest art fraud in Dutch history, all the more remarkable for the fact that Vermeer produced just 35 known paintings in his lifetime. Out of respect for Van Meegeren's talent, and the fact that he had swindled Göring, the judge sentenced him to a lenient one year in prison. Van Meegeren died before serving his sentence. See www.mystudios.com/gallery/han for more on this gifted forger.

### FORMER PC HOOFT STORE Map pp286-7
Keizersgracht 508

Across the Keizersgracht from Metz Department Store, this noteworthy building was built for a cigar manufacturer in 1881 by AC Bleijs (the architect of the St Nicolaaskerk near Centraal Station). The name refers to poet, playwright, historian and national icon Pieter Cornelisz Hooft, whose 300th birthday was commemorated in this Dutch-Renaissance throwback with a Germanic tower. Hooft also has Amsterdam's most renowned shopping street named after him (p110). The playful façade reliefs depict the various stages of tobacco preparation. It now houses a 'smart drug' shop.

### STADSSCHOUWBURG Map pp286-7
City Theatre; ☎ 624 23 11; Leidseplein 26;
☻ advance ticket sales 10am-6pm Mon-Sat

This theatre, with its balcony arcade, dates from 1894. People criticised the building – as they criticised every city theatre before or since – and the funds for the exterior decorations never materialised. The architect, Jan Springer, couldn't handle this and retired.

The theatre is used for large-scale plays, operettas and festivals. South across Marnixstraat, the **American Hotel** is an Art Nouveau landmark from 1902 foreshadowing the Amsterdam School's use of brick. You might grab a coffee in its stylish **Café Americain** (p144).

## VIJZELGRACHT TO AMSTEL

### AMSTELHOF Map p285
Amstel 51; www.hermitage.nl; adult/child under 16yrs
€6/free; ☻ 10am-5pm

The Rijksmuseum and Stedelijk may well have (essentially) closed for years of repairs by the time you read this, but Russia has come to the rescue. At the time of writing, the State Hermitage Museum of St Petersburg was set to open a branch inside a one-time almshouse known as the Amstelhof, the Dutch have taken to calling it '*de Kleine* (little) *Hermitage*'. The *big* Hermitage has the capacity to display only about 5% of its total collection, so it seems like a match made in art heaven.

For now, the Hermitage occupies the Neerlandia building, a small section (about 500 sq metres) of the Amstelhof. When completed (estimated the end of 2007), the Hermitage Amsterdam will encompass the whole Amstelhof, with over 4000 sq metres of exhibition space.

Exhibits in the Neerlandia building will change appoximately twice per year. As we went to press, scheduled exhibitions were Greek Gold (until 29 August 2004), Nicholas and Alexandra (18 September 2004 to 13 February 2005) and Venetian painting (5 March to 4 September 2005).

The Amstelhof itself is noteworthy in its own right. Its origin as an almshouse in 1683 illustrates how the canal project ran out of steam by the time it reached the Amstel. Much of the land was given over to charities or turned into recreational space; the wealthy had already bought their plots and built their mansions, and the Dutch Republic went into consolidation mode against the British and French, which meant there was little new wealth (only increased wealth for those who already had money).

### AMSTELKERK Map pp286-7
☎ 520 00 70; Amstelveld 10; admission free;
☻ 9am-12.45pm & 1.30-5pm

Near the intersection of Prinsengracht and Reguliersgracht is the Amstelveld, a large open square, with this church near its northwestern corner.

The unique, unpainted pinewood Amstelkerk was erected in 1668 as a *'noodkerk'* (makeshift church) under the direction of the city architect, Daniël Stalpaert. This idea was that the congregation would have somewhere to meet while a permanent church arose next to it. City planners had envisaged four new Protestant churches in the southern canal belt, but the only one actually built was the Oosterkerk (p101). It wasn't until the 1840s that plans for the stone church on the Amstelveld were abandoned, and the Amstelkerk's square interior was updated with neo-Gothic alterations, including a pipe-organ.

The Amstelkerk fell into serious disrepair throughout the 20th century, and it even looked as if it would have to be demolished, until it was purchased by the Stadsherstel, a local city restoration group. Reopened in 1990, the building now houses Stadsherstel's offices – glassed-in spaces that complement the Gothic arches surprisingly well – and is a popular venue for concerts, weddings and the like.

## AMSTELSLUIZEN Map p285
### Prinsengracht & Amstel River
If you continue East to the Amstel, you'll see to your right these sluices that date from 1674 and allowed the canals to be flushed with fresh water from the Amstel rather than salt water from the IJ, which made the city far more livable. They were still operated by hand until recently.

## AMSTELVELD Map pp286-7
### Prinsengracht east of Reguliersgracht
Given that authorities never completely dropped their plans for a permanent church, this square was kept free of buildings, and today it remains open and pleasant. In 1876 the Monday market moved here from Rembrandtplein. This lively 'free market' had vendors from out of town peddling a wide range of goods (it still operates in the summer months, focusing on plants and flowers). A small statue by the Amstelkerk commemorates Professor Kokadorus, aka Meijer Linnewiel (1867–1934), the most colourful market vendor Amsterdam has known. People would buy anything from spoons to suspenders ('to hang up your mother-in-law') just to watch his performances interlaced with satirical comments about the politics of the day. The annihilation of the Jewish community in

*Amstelveld*

WWII put an end to the city's rich tradition of creative vending (though if you understand Dutch you can still pick up some great lines in the markets of the Jordaan).

On Mondays there's a **garden market** (🕑 8.30am-2pm Mar-Dec) here with cheap flowers and potted plants. In summer the Amstelveld is a pleasant space where children play soccer, dogs run around, and patrons laze in the sun at Moko restaurant (p145) against the south side of the Amstelkerk.

## DE DUIF Map pp286-7
### The Dove; Prinsengracht 756
This Catholic church, across the canal from the Amstelveld, was first built in 1796, shortly after the French-installed government proclaimed freedom of religion. It was the first Catholic church with a public entrance for over two centuries, and it was rebuilt to its current design in the mid-1800s. In the 1970s the church authorities wanted to sell the building, but the priest and other staff continued to hold services in defiance and saved the church.

## FOAM (FOTOGRAFIE MUSEUM AMSTERDAM) Map pp286-7
🕿 551 65 00; www.foam.nl; Keizersgracht 609; adult/child under 12 yrs €5/free; 🕑 10am-5pm Sat-Wed, 10am-9pm Thu & Fri
Simple and functionalist but large galleries, some with skylights or grand windows for

natural light, are the setting for this impressive new museum of photography. There are two storeys of exhibition space, and a library was in the works at the time of writing. It creates a great setting for admiring changing exhibits from photographers of world renown.

## GEELVINCK HINLOPEN HUIS
Map pp286-7

☎ 639 07 47; Herengracht 518; ☺ by appointment

Beyond Vijzelstraat, east of the mayor's residence at No 502, is a 17th-century house with stylish rooms, a formal garden and art in the coach house. Though not as impressive as Museum Van Loon (below) or Museum Willet-Holthuysen (p91), it's more serene, and worth a look if you can organise a private tour (up to 15 people).

## MAGERE BRUG Map p285
'Skinny Bridge'; Kerkstraat at the Amstel

The most photographed drawbridge in the city links Kerkstraat across the Amstel to Nieuwe Kerkstraat and dates from the 1670s. This one-time pedestrian bridge was rebuilt and widened several times and torn down in 1929 to make way for a modern bridge, only to be rebuilt again in timber. It's still operated by hand and makes a very pretty sight during the day as well as at night when it's lit up. Stand in the middle and feel it seesaw under the passing traffic.

## MUSEUM VAN LOON Map pp286-7

☎ 624 52 55; www.museumvanloon.nl; Keizersgracht 672; adult/child or student/child under 12 yrs €4.50/3/free; ☺ 11am-5pm Fri-Mon

## Worth Noting at the Museum Van Loon

- The balustrade on the staircase, installed by an 18th-century owner named van Hagen – if you look carefully, you can read 'Hagen' in the seemingly random curlicues going up the stairs.
- The trompe-l'oeil door next to the entrance of the bedroom. It was put there in order to give the room a sense of symmetry – there's even a light switch next to the fake door.
- The kitchen equipped with original tiles and some old menus.
- The rococo garden, with roses and a courtyard worthy of picnics (the old stables out back present quite a regal façade).
- Unusually helpful and accessible staff.

Our favourite house museum in town, this house was built in 1672 – along with the house next door, No 674 – for a wealthy arms dealer. The portraitist Ferdinand Bol, a faithful student of Rembrandt, rented the place for a while. In the late 1800s it was acquired by the Van Loons, one of the most prominent patrician families (thanks to the herring trade and the United East India Company of which the original Mr van Loon was a founder). Here they lived in a style befitting their status, and now the museum is a family trust.

Inside hang some important paintings, including the *Wedding Portrait* by Jan Miense Molenaer (1637; note the fine details, the cast of dozens and the fallen chair symbolising a brother who'd passed away before the event) and a collection of some 150 portraits of the van Loon family. But the main point of the museum is to show it as a house. Quiet and unbusy, it allows you to appreciate the fine architectural details and imagine canalside life when money was no object.

Historical note: in the 19th century, the van Loon family was an official representative of Queen Wilhelmina. The present Mrs van Loon is an assistant to Queen Beatrix.

## REGULIERSGRACHT Map pp286-7

Opposite Thorbeckeplein on Herengracht is the beautiful 'canal of the seven bridges', cut in 1664. You can just about count them all when you stand on the Herengracht bridge. Canal tour boats halt here for photos because it's easier to count them from below, especially at night when the bridges are lit up and their graceful curves are reflected in the water.

Luckily, this lovely canal was spared from being filled at the turn of the 20th century to accommodate a tram line. Sights include the house at No 34 with its massive eagle gable commemorating the original owner, Arent van den Bergh (*arend* is one of the Dutch words for eagle) and its unusual twin entrance against the side walls with V-shaped stairway for the upstairs and downstairs dwellings. Grab the camera for the superb scene back towards Herengracht from the east–west bridge at Keizersgracht and the lean of the two houses on the corner (not to mention the 15 bridges visible from here).

Also of interest is the Dutch/German woodwork fantasy at No 57–59, reminiscent of the city's medieval wooden houses. This place was built for a carpentry firm in 1879 and was designed by the same architect, Isaac Gosschalk, who designed the building at No 63. Canal-boat operators fantasize that a midwife lived in the corner house at No 92, decorated with a statuette of a stork.

### REMBRANDTPLEIN Map pp286-7

A very short walk west (and indeed south) of the Amstel, this square is another hub of café culture, nightlife and Amsterdam's gay scene. Originally called Reguliersplein and then Botermarkt (butter market), it now features a proud statue of the painter, gazing pensively towards the Jewish quarter where he lived until circumstances forced him to the Jordaan.

You won't have any trouble finding a café or restaurant on Rembrandtplein or on neighbouring Thorbeckeplein (off Rembrandtplein's southwest corner), but our favourite is **Café Schiller** (p162), an Art-Deco marvel that's popular with the pre-theatre crowd (don't confuse it with Brasserie Schiller, though that's also decent). Gay visitors will want to head north along Halvemaansteeg and to the Amstel for a cluster of bars and cafés; the friendly lesbian café **Vivelavie** (p179) is just east of Rembrandtplein.

The street running west from Rembrandtplein, completing the circle to the Munt, is Reguliersbreestraat. Before the construction of the canal belt, the nuns of the Regulier, or 'Regular', order had a monastery outside the city walls roughly where Utrechtsestraat now crosses Keizersgracht, which explains the frequent use of the name in this area. Reguliersbreestraat is pretty busy, but about a third of the way along on the left you can pause to look at the **Tuschinskitheater** (p183), opened in 1921 and still the most glorious cinema in the country. The building's blend of Art Deco and Amsterdam School architecture, with its recently refurbished interior decorations, is a visual feast. Ring to inquire about 90-minute guided tours at 10am Sunday and Monday in July and August (€7).

*Staircase at Rembrandtplein*

Off the southeast corner of Rembrandtplein is Utrechtsestraat, home to some of the city's favourite restaurants.

### THORBECKEPLEIN Map pp286-7

Southwest of Rembrandtplein, this square is named for Jan Rudolf Thorbecke, the Liberal politician who created the Dutch parliamentary system in 1848. His statue faces outwards from the sqaure, although he might have enjoyed its leafy, car-free atmosphere. There are a number of cafés and clubs on both sides of the market, and the **art market** (☼ 10.30am-6pm Sun Mar-Oct) here offers mostly modern pictorial work. Note that Thorbeckeplein used to be water, part of Reguliersgracht.

# NIEUWMARKT NEIGHBOURHOOD
*Eating p135; Shopping p192; Sleeping p213*

## Orientation

Somewhat confusingly, there's both a Nieuwmarkt Square and a Nieuwmarkt neighbourhood. For information on Nieuwmarkt (the square), see the earlier Oude Zijde section (p64). The Nieuwmarkt neighbourhood lies east of the square, enclosed by the Geldersekade and Kloveniersburgwal in the west, the Amstel in the south, the Valkenburgerstraat (the feeder road of the current IJ-Tunnel) in the east and the IJ in the north.

## Top Five Nieuwmarkt Neighbourhood

- Catch a free lunchtime concert at the **Stopera** (p98).
- Appreciate the understated majesty of the **Portuguese-Israelite Synagogue** (p100).
- At **Museum Het Rembrandthuis** (opposite), see where the painter lived and view his works and other works he inspired.
- Browse the flea market on **Waterlooplein** (opposite).
- Take the kids to the **Marionetten Theater** (p184) for high culture told with puppets, or **Tun Fun** (p101), a new underground play park.

Inside the sea dyke, the 16th-century authorities reclaimed land from the Amstel: the island of Vlooienburg (the current Waterlooplein), with canals and transverse streets that would later become the heart of the Jewish quarter. This was not enough, however, to satisfy the needs of the rapidly growing city and two decades later the authorities gave the go-ahead for the ambitious canal-belt project (see the earlier Western Canal Belt, p79, and Southern Canal Belt, p88, sections for more information).

Until WWII this district was the centre of Amsterdam's thriving Jewish community, which enjoyed more freedom here than elsewhere in Europe and made the city a centre for diamonds, tobacco, printing and clothing. They also gave Amsterdam an exceptional variety of lively markets. The current markets (eg the flea market on Waterlooplein) are mere sad reminders.

If you find the contemporary looking main artery, St Antoniesbreestraat and its continuation, Jodenbreestraat, to be as charmless as the rest of Amsterdam is charming, thank the metro (subway) line. In 1975, after plans for the line were revealed, the neighbourhood became the birthplace of the organised squatter movement (p50). The metro line snaked through much of the neighbourhood and eventually required the demolition of many squatter-occupied houses. New, subsidised housing estates arose after completion of the line and today the west and south of the neighbourhood are dominated by modern inner-city architecture, some of it interesting and some less than successful. The same might be said for the new city hall on Waterlooplein and its surrounds.

## Transport

Tram line 6 travels through Mr Visserplein, near Waterlooplein.
Metro stations are Nieuwemarkt and Waterlooplein.

# LASTAGE

The Nieuwmarkt neighbourhood grew haphazardly. Immediately east of Nieuwmarkt Square, the Lastage district became a jumble of wharves, docks, rope yards and warehouses beyond the medieval city wall and the protective sea dyke that ran along the current Zeedijk, St Antoniesbreestraat, Jodenbreestraat and Muiderstraat.

## GASSAN DIAMOND FACTORY
Map pp282-3

☎ 622 53 33; Nieuwe Uilenburgerstraat 173-175; admission free; ☺ 9am-5pm

In the 1580s, the sudden influx of Sephardic Jews from Spain and Portugal prompted the newly Calvinist authorities to reclaim land from the IJ in the form of several rectangular islands east of Oude Schans, one of which, **Uilenburg**, is still recognisable as an island today. Shipyards that operated here soon moved out to the new Eastern Islands, making way for another wave of Jewish refugees, this time Ashkenazim.

On Uilenburg, the vast Gassan diamond factory was the first to use steam power in the 1880s. The factory was recommissioned in 1989 after thorough renovations (p199).

## HOLLAND EXPERIENCE Map p285

☎ 422 22 33; Waterlooplein 17; adult/child or senior €8/6.85, combination ticket with Rembrandthuis adult/child €12.50/7; ☺ 10am-6pm

Oh dear. Next to the Rembrandthuis, this multimedia hype-fest tries to cram all of this little land's big attractions into an overpriced mishmash of sights and sounds. The audience dons 3-D glasses and sits on a rotating platform that lurches along with a plotless half-hour film from tulips to windmills to threatened dykes. There's no narration or explanation, but a theme from *Swan Lake* gets played ad nauseam and an old-style car (a motif we don't understand) is your spirit guide through the journey. In one instance, a fish wags its tongue at the audience. In another, an on-screen dyke crumbles, room temperature plummets, and a Sony-augmented thunderstorm rages. As filmmaking it leaves a lot to be desired (hint: roll camera from *inside* the roller coaster, not *next* to it!), but we will say this: the six-year-olds in the audience howled with laughter over the sight gags (although even they fell silent after a while).

Our advice: get high first.

## MONTELBAANSTOREN Map pp282-3
**Oude Schaans & Oude Waal; closed to the public**
In the 1510s, after an attack by troops from Gelderland in the east, the Lastage was fortified by means of the wide **Oude Schans** canal and guarded by a gun tower, the Montelbaanstoren, built in 1516. Its octagonal steeple was added in 1606, to a design by Hendrick de Keyser. In addition to being a signature building for the city, it was also a favourite subject of Rembrandt's. Today the tower is used by the city water works.

## MUSEUM HET REMBRANDTHUIS
Map pp278-9
☎ 520 04 00; www.rembrandthuis.nl; Jodenbreestraat 4-6; adult/student/child 6-15/under 6 yrs €7/6/1.50/free, combination ticket with Holland Experience adult/child €12.50/7; 🕑 10am-5pm Mon-Sat, 1-5pm Sun
Rembrandt lived (downstairs) and worked (upstairs) in this beautiful house dating from 1606. He bought the house in 1639 for a fortune thanks to his wealthy wife, Saskia van Uylenburgh, but chronic debt got the better of him and he had to bail out and move to the Jordaan in 1658 (p26). The years spent in this house were the high point of his career, when he was regarded as a star and ran the largest painting studio in Holland, before he ruined it all by making enemies and squandering his earnings.

Although it can be crowded, the museum is well worth visiting for the almost complete collection of Rembrandt's etchings (250 of the 280 he is known to have made), although they are not all on display at once. Shows change a few times per year, often incorporating contemporary paintings that somehow comment on Rembrandt's works – between 20 and 100 etchings are on display at any one time, depending on the exhibit. The collection also includes several drawings and paintings by his pupils and his teacher, Pieter Lastman, and an etching by Albrecht Dürer.

The house itself (always on display) has been completely restored. Thanks to the list of Rembrandt's possessions drawn up by the debt collector, as well as several drawings and paintings by the master himself, the interior now looks as it did when he lived there. Recommended duration of a visit is 45 minutes to one hour.

## PINTOHUIS (OPENBARE BIBLIOTHEEK) Map pp278-9
☎ 624 31 84; St Antoniesbreestraat 69; admission free; 🕑 2pm-8pm Mon & Wed, 2-5pm Fri, 11am-2pm Sat
The street that runs from Nieuwmarkt Square in the direction of Waterlooplein is St Antoniesbreestraat, once a busy street that lost its old buildings during the construction of the metro line – the new houses incorporate rubber blocks in the foundations to absorb vibrations caused by the metro. One exception is the Pintohuis, which used to belong to a wealthy Sephardic Jew, Isaac de Pinto, who had it remodelled with Italianate pilasters in the 1680s. In the 1970s a planned freeway to Centraal Station would have required the demolition of this building, but the controversy stopped the freeway. It's now a library *(bibliotheek)* annexe – pop inside to admire the beautiful ceilings.

## SCHEEPVAARTHUIS Map pp282-3
**Cnr Binnenkant & Prins Hendrikkade;**
**closed to the public**
Heading toward Oosterdok, across Waalseilandsgracht, is the Scheepvaarthuis (Shipping House), completed in 1916 to a design by Johan van der Mey. This remarkable building, which utilises the street layout to resemble a ship's bow, was the first building in the Amsterdam School style and is still one of the finest examples of this architectural movement. Note the many façade sculptures. It used to house a consortium of shipping companies, but is now home to the GVB, the municipal transport company that runs the trams and buses.

# WATERLOOPLEIN & AROUND
South of Jodenbreestraat is Waterlooplein, once known as Vlooienburg and the heart of the Jewish quarter.

The original Waterlooplein covered the eastern portion of Vlooienburg and was created in 1882 by filling a couple of canals. This was the site of the major Jewish flea market, where anything was available. There's still a **flea market** (🕑 9am-5pm Mon-Fri, 8.30am-5.30pm Sat) here, selling a wide range of goods. It's popular, not least among tourists. Prices are a bit higher than at other markets, but it's worth a wander. Beware of pickpockets. Among the more interesting shopping opportunities: along the northern side of the square is Big Red Machine, a shop run by the local Hell's Angels (p193).

### MOZES EN AÄRONKERK Map p285
☎ 624 75 97; Waterlooplein 205

This neoclassical Catholic church, built in 1841 on the northeastern corner of Waterlooplein, shows that this wasn't an exclusively Jewish area. It is still used as a church (with an impressive organ) and also as a centre for social and cultural organisations, which often hold exhibitions. It replaced the 'clandestine' Catholic church that occupied two houses named Mozes and Aäron at what is now the rear of the church along Jodenbreestraat (note the wall tablet of Moses above the street corner).

One of the buildings demolished to make way for the new church was home to the Jewish philosopher Baruch de Spinoza (1632–77), who was born in Amsterdam but spent much of his life making lenses in The Hague after the rabbis proclaimed him a heretic. He is best known for his work *Ethics*, which proposes that the concept of God possesses an infinite number of attributes.

### STOPERA Map pp286-7
☎ 551 81 17; Waterlooplein 22

This jewel in the canal belt dominates the plein. Built in 1986, the 'St' part stands for 'stad' (city) while the 'opera' part is obvious. The part

facing the Amstel is the **Muziektheater** (☎ 551 80 54; Waterlooplein 22; 🕐 advance tickets 10am-6pm Mon-Sat, 11.30am-6pm Sun), while the 'stad' part refers to the *stadhuis* (city hall), facing Waterlooplein.

The building, by the Austrian architect Wilhelm Holzbauer and his Dutch colleague Cees Dam, was the winner of a competition back in 1968. However, opinions are not altogether positive – one critic said that the building had 'all the charm of an Ikea chair', and others sniff at the theatre's acoustics and rehearsal spaces. Our view: yea on the music theatre, nay on city hall.

Music and dance performances take place in the theatre; there are usually free lunch-time concerts on Tuesdays. In any case, have a look at the little display in the arcade between city hall and the theatre that shows the country's water levels (p38).

# SOUTHERN NIEUWMARKT
## JODENBREESTRAAT

St Antoniesbreestraat opens on to the wide Jodenbreestraat, a remnant of the freeway-to-be. Note the leaning lock-keeper's house on the left, Café de Sluyswacht (p156), where you can have a quiet beer out in the sun in summer.

### PENTAGON Map pp278-9
West off St Antoniebreestraat

The former cemetery east of the church adjoins Theo Bosch's 1983 community housing project, the Pentagon. With a very contemporary glass wall that doubles as a waterfall

*Stopera; city hall and opera theatre under the one roof*

(when the water's on) along the courtyard wall, you'll either love it or hate it but you can't ignore it. Visiting architects often have a look.

## VERVERSSTRAAT Map pp286-7
### Painters' Street
South of here, across the beautiful **Raamgracht** that city planners wanted to fill in in the 1950s, is the narrow Verversstraat with a mix of old and new architecture typical of this area. The name refers to the polluting paint factories that were limited to this street (originally a canal) beyond the city walls.

The covered walkway over the street used to link sections of the **Leeuwenberg sewing-machine factory** (Map pp286-7), slated for demolition but saved by squatters who now live here legally (it's an impressive contemporary building viewed from the Zwanenburgwal end). Beneath the covered walkway, note the cat ladder at No 4. At the Staalstraat end of Verversstraat, turn right to the steel drawbridge over the pretty **Groenburgwal**, which affords a good photo opportunity back towards the Zuiderkerk. You can clearly see the slight tilt in its tower.

## ZUIDERKERK Map pp278-9
☎ 552 79 87; Zuiderkerkhof 72; admission free; ☽ 11am-4pm Mon, 9am-4pm Tue, Wed & Fri, 9am-8pm Thu
Off St Antoniestraat, near the Pintohuis, a passageway through a modern housing estate leads to the Zuiderkerk, the 'Southern Church' built by Hendrick de Keyser in 1603–11. His tower, 1m off plumb, dates from 1614. This was the first custom-built Protestant church in Amsterdam – still Catholic design but no choir – and served as a blueprint for the Westerkerk. The final church service was held here in 1929 and at the end of WWII it served as a morgue.

The Zuiderkerk now houses a city government office, the **Municipal Centre for Physical Planning and Public Housing** with occasional, changing exhibits on urban planning and the nature of the city. If you're expecting to be dazzled by magnificent 17th-century church architecture, think again: it's been pretty much modernised and hollowed out. However, you can take a tour up the **tower** (€3; ☽ 2pm, 3pm, 4pm Wed-Sat Jun-Sep) for a great view over the city.

# MR VISSERPLEIN & AROUND
The busy roundabout east of the Mozes en Aäronkerk is Mr Visserplein ('Mr' stands for *meester*, or 'master', the Dutch lawyer's

title). LE Visser was a Jewish president of the Supreme Court who was dismissed by the Nazis. He refused to wear the Star of David and berated the Jewish Council for helping the occupiers carry out their anti-Jewish policies. He died before the Germans could wreak revenge on him.

## JD MEIJERPLEIN Map p285
South of the Portuguese synagogue is the triangular Jonas Daniël Meijerplein, named after the country's first Jewish lawyer (actual name Joune Rintel), who did much to ensure the full emancipation of the Jews in the Napoleonic period.

On the square, Mari Andriessen's **Dockworker statue** (1952) commemorates the general strike that began among dockworkers on 25 February 1941 to protest the treatment of Jews. The first deportation round-up had occurred here a few days earlier. The anniversary of the strike is still an occasion for wreath-laying but has become a low-key affair with the demise of the Communist Party.

## JOODS HISTORISCH MUSEUM Map p285
Jewish Historical Museum; ☎ 626 99 45; www.jhm.nl/ JD Meijerplein 2-4; adult/senior or student/child 13-17/ child 6-12 yrs €6.50/4/3/2; ☽ 11am-5pm, closed Yom Kippur
This interesting and impressive museum (1987) is a beautifully restored complex of four Ashkenazic synagogues linked by glass-covered walkways. These are the Grote Sjoel (Great Synagogue, 1671), the first public synagogue in Western Europe; the Obbene Sjoel (Upstairs Synagogue, 1686); the Dritt Sjoel (Third Synagogue, 1700 with a 19th-century façade); and the Neie Sjoel (New Synagogue, 1752), the largest in the complex, but still dwarfed by the Portuguese Synagogue across the square.

The museum also contains a kosher coffee shop, with handy explanations of the intricate dietary rules.

Parts of the museum are due for a reconstruction through mid-2004, but the rest of the museum was to remain open during that time. The renovations – the first since the museum opened – are designed to make the museum less cerebral and more personal.

The area southeast of here, the 'new' canals (Nieuwe Herengracht, Nieuwe Keizersgracht and Nieuwe Prinsengracht), intersected by the busy Weesperstraat traffic artery, was where the canal-belt project petered out around 1700. The canals on this far side of the Amstel were

# Jewish Amsterdam

It's hard to overstate the role that Jews played in the evolution of civic and commercial life of Amsterdam.

Although some histories trace the presence of Jews in Holland back to Roman times, the first documented Jewish presence goes back to the 12th century. Their numbers remained small through medieval times, but expulsion from Spain and Portugal in the 1580s brought a flood of Sephardic (Jews of Spanish, middle-eastern or north African heritage) refugees. More arrived when the Spaniards retook Antwerp in 1585. These new arrivals eventually settled on the new islands of the current Nieuwmarkt neighbourhood (where land was still affordable).

As in much of Europe, Jews in Amsterdam were barred from many professions. Monopolistic guilds kept most trades firmly closed. But some of the Sephardim were diamond-cutters, for which there was no guild. Other Sephardic Jews introduced printing and tobacco processing, or worked in similarly unrestricted trades such as retail on the streets, finance, medicine and the garment industry. The majority, however, eked out a meagre living as labourers and small-time traders on the margins of society, and lived in houses they could afford in the Nieuwmarkt area, which developed into the Jewish quarter. Yet Amsterdam's Jews enjoyed freedoms unheard of elsewhere in Europe. They were not confined to a ghetto and, with some restrictions, could buy property. Although the Protestant establishment sought to impose restrictions, civil authorities were reluctant to restrict such productive members of society.

The 17th century saw another influx of Jewish refugees, this time Ashkenazim (Jews from Europe outside of Iberia) fleeing pogroms in Central and Eastern Europe. Thus the two wings of the diaspora were reunited in Amsterdam, but they didn't always get on well. Sephardim resented the increased competition posed by Ashkenazic newcomers, who soon outnumbered them and were generally much poorer, and the two groups established separate synagogues. Any antagonism notwithstanding, Amsterdam became the largest Jewish centre in Europe, some 10,000 strong by Napoleonic times.

The guilds and all remaining restrictions on Jews were abolished during the French occupation, and Amsterdam's Jewish community thrived in the 19th century. There was still considerable poverty, and the Jewish quarter included some of the worst slums in the city, but the economic, social and political emancipation of the Jews helped their burgeoning middle class, who moved out into the Plantage area and later into the suburbs south of the city.

All that came to an end, however, with WWII. The Nazis brought about the nearly complete annihilation of Amsterdam's Jewish community. Before the war, about 140,000 Jews lived in the Netherlands. Of these, about 90,000 lived in Amsterdam, or 13% of the city's population. (Before the 1930s this proportion was about 10%, but it increased with Jews fleeing the Nazi regime in Germany.) Only some 5500 of these Amsterdam Jews survived the war, barely one in 16.

The Holocaust left the Jewish quarter empty, a sinister reminder of its once bustling life. Many of the houses – looted by Germans and local collaborators and deprived of their wooden fixtures for fuel in the final, desperate months of the war – stood derelict until they were demolished in the 1970s.

Today there are some 43,000 Jews in the Netherlands; of those around 20,000 live in Amsterdam. Among Dutch Jews, about 85% self-identify as Jewish, although only about 25% are members of synagogues while some 57% are non-practising. The rate of intermarriage among Dutch Jews is about 75%. New Jewish arrivals these days tend to be from Israel and, to a lesser extent, from Russia.

Ironically, Amsterdam's legendary tolerance may also portend difficulty ahead for its Jewish community. Recent decades have seen the arrival of Muslims from the Middle East and North Africa, and while there has not been the same level of friction here as elsewhere in Europe, there's anecdotal evidence of tension.

One lasting legacy of Jewish presence: Amsterdam slang incorporates many terms of Hebrew or Yiddish origin, such as the alternative name for Amsterdam, Mokum (from *makom aleph*, the best city of all); the cheery goodbye, *de mazzel* (good luck); *gabber* (friend, 'mate') from the Yiddish *chaver*, companion; and the put-down, *kapsones maken* (to make unnecessary fuss, from *kapshones*, self-importance).

less in demand among the city's wealthy residents and went to charities or were settled by well-off Jews from the nearby Jewish quarter.

## PORTUGUESE-ISRAELITE SYNAGOGUE Map p285

☎ 624 53 51; www.esnoga.com; Mr Visserplein 3; adult/child 10-15 yrs €5/4; ⏰ 10am-4pm Sun-Fri Apr-Oct, 10am-4pm Sun-Thu &10am-3pm Fri Sep-Mar

This edifice, built between 1671 and 1675 by the Sephardic community, was the largest synagogue in Europe when it was built and is still impressive. The architect, Elias Bouman, was inspired by the Temple of Solomon, but the building's classicist lines are typical of Amsterdam. It was restored after the war and is in use today. Check website for schedule of services.

The soaring interior features massive pillars that stand in contrast with some two dozen

## Tuns of Fun

In addition to being a unique venue for kids, Tun Fun is also a great example of Amsterdam's distinctive local initiative process in action.

'You want your children to play freely and safely in the street,' says Tun Fun founder Adriaan van Hoogstraten, 'but the busy traffic and the lack of space make that impossible in a city like Amsterdam.'

Meanwhile, the tunnel under Mr. Visserplein was languishing, empty, filthy and graffiti-strewn after 11 years of non-use. Van Hoogstraten and another local dad, Edward van der Marel, teamed up to enter the city's competition for the future of the tunnel, and their proposal beat 14 others. It took a year and lots of elbow grease, but Tun Fun opened in 2003. They even brought in their own graffiti artists to decorate the tunnel with new, kid-friendly graffiti.

To hear van Hoogstraten tell it, thanks to processes like these, 'All Amsterdam inhabitants feel as if they own they own part of Amsterdam.'

---

brass candelabra suspended from the ceiling (lit for night-time services). You can catch a short video presentation on some of the synagogue's implements and festivals. Inside you'll find short explanations of the various symbols.

The large library belonging to the Ets Haim seminary, on the synagogue grounds, is one of the oldest and most important Jewish libraries in Europe and contains many priceless works.

**TUN FUN** Map p285

☎ 689 43 00; Mr. Visserplein 7; children aged 1-12yrs/ adults & children under 1 €7/free; ⏰ 10am-7pm

Very odd, very cool and very Amsterdam, this new (2003) indoor playground occupies a former traffic underpass that sat unused and was an eyesore for 11 years. Kids can build, climb, roll, draw, play in a soccer pitch, even watch movies. Note that kids can visit Tun Fun only if accompanied by an adult. It gets rather busy when the weather's bad.

# THE PLANTAGE, EASTERN ISLANDS & OOSTERPARK
*Eating p148; Sleeping p220*

The islands of Kattenburg, Wittenburg and Oostenburg, in the east of the harbour, were constructed in the 1650s as a result of the rapid expansion of seaborne trade in the first half of the 17th century.

The United East India Company (VOC) set up shop on the eastern island of **Oostenburg**, where it established warehouses, rope yards, workshops and docks for the maintenance of its fleet. Private shipyards and dockworkers' homes dominated the central island of **Wittenburg** – city architect Daniël Stalpaert's **Oosterkerk** (1671) on Wittenburgergracht was the last, and the

least monumental, of the four 'compass churches' (the others were the Noorderkerk, Westerkerk and Zuiderkerk). Admiralty offices and buildings arose on the western island of **Kattenburg**, and warships were fitted out in the adjoining naval dockyards that are still in use today.

## Transport

Tram lines 6, 9 and 14 travel though The Plantage; lines 3, 7 and 10 service Oosterpark.

Metro station Weesperplein is on the western edge of Oosterpark, with Wibautstraat further to the south.

Bus lines 22, 32, 39, 43 and 59 spread throughout the Eastern Islands.

The 19th-century discovery of diamonds in South Africa led to a revival of Amsterdam's diamond industry and the Jewish elite began to move into the Plantage (Plantation), where they built imposing town villas.

Until then the Plantage had been a district of parks and gardens. In the 18th century, wealthy residents rented parcels of land here to use as gardens, and the area developed into a weekend getaway with tea houses, variety theatres and other establishments where the upper class relaxed in green surroundings.

Oosterdokseiland will become the temporary home of the Stedelijk Museum from April 2004. The museum will stay in the old TGP (postal) building, to the east of Centraal Station, until 2007 while the original Museum building undergoes renovations.

# THE PLANTAGE

## ARTIS ZOO Map p285

☎ 523 34 00; www.artis.nl; Plantage Kerklaan 38-40; adult/senior/child 4-11/under 4 yrs €14/12.50/10.50/ free; ⏱ 9am-5pm, 9am-6pm in summer

The zoo was founded by an association called Natura Artis Magistra (Latin for 'Nature is the Master of Art') back in 1838, which makes it the oldest zoo on the European continent, as well as the city's oldest park. Famous biologists studied and worked here among the rich collection of animals and plants. Even if some of the cramped enclosures hardly seem to have progressed since the 19th century, the zoo's layout – with ponds, statues and winding pathways through lush surroundings (remnants of some of the former Plantage gardens) – is very pleasant. Concerts and art exhibitions are also held here, in line with the original aim of the association: to link nature and art.

You'll find the usual assortment of apes, gazelles (unlike the city's Gazelle brand bikes, these have legs, not wheels), giraffes and elephants, tropical and polar birds, and an insectarium with creatures icky and alluring (if bugs creep

## Top Five the Plantage & Around

- Be moved over the quiet memorial at the once bustling **Hollandsche Schouwburg** (below)
- Lions and tigers and bears (oh my!) at **Artis Zoo** (left)
- Contemplate the meaning of courage at the **Verzetsmuseum** (opposite)
- Cross the **Entrepotdok** (p104) to **EnergetcA** (p104) for up-close demonstrations of big machinery from the past
- Knock back a couple local brews at **Brouwerij 't IJ** (p104), at the foot of the district's lone windmill.

you out, stick to the butterfly house). Another highlight is the **aquarium**, the oldest in the country (1882, renovated 1997), with some 2000 fish and imposing classical architecture. The zoo's exhibits include an Amazonian flooded forest, a tropical coral reef and an Amsterdam canal. There's also a **planetarium** (Dutch commentary with a summary in English), and zoological and geological **museums**. The entrance fee includes the hourly shows at the planetarium.

Although the zoo covers a vast swath of the Plantage, the only entrance is on Plantage Kerklaan, diagonally across from the Verzetsmuseum.

### HOLLANDSCHE SCHOUWBURG
Map p285

Holland Theatre; ☎ 626 99 45; Plantage Middenlaan 24; admission free; ⏱ 11am-4pm

It's ironic that a place of such joy became a place of such tragedy. Originally the house of the director of Artis zoo, this building became the Artis Schouwburg (Artis Theatre) in 1892 and was soon one of the centres of Dutch theatrical life. In WWII, however, the Germans turned it into a theatre by and for Jews, and from 1942 they made it a detention centre for Jews awaiting deportation. Some 60,000 to 80,000 Jews passed through here on their way to Westerbork transit camp in the east of the country and from there to the death camps.

Artis Zoo

After the war, people felt it unseemly to reopen the site as a theatre, and in 1961 it was demolished except for the façade and the area immediately behind it. Today there's a hollow shell of a lobby and, where the auditorium once provided laughter, a 10m-high memorial pylon dominates a courtyard; the effect is wrenching in its simplicity. Along the wall to the left of the lobby, glass panels are engraved with the names of all the Jewish families deported from the Netherlands. You may see stones at the foot of the panels, following the Jewish custom of placing a stone at a gravesite. On the floor in front of the wall, an inscription in Dutch and Hebrew translates: 'Watch me like you watch the iris of your eye, and hide me under your wings from the evil people lurking around me.'

Upstairs is a small exhibit hall with photos and artefacts of Jewish life before and during the war (signage here in Dutch only). The Hollandsche Schouwburg is part of the Jewish Historical Museum.

## HORTUS BOTANICUS Map p285

☎ 625 90 21; www.hortus-botanicus.nl; Plantage Middenlaan 2A; adult/child €6/3; ☼ 9am-5pm Mon-Fri, 11am-5pm Sat & Sun

This **botanical garden** was established in 1638 as a herb garden for the city's doctors and moved to this southwest corner of the Plantage in 1682. It became a repository for tropical seeds and plants (ornamental or otherwise) brought to Amsterdam by the West and East India Companies' ships. Commercially exploitable plants such as coffee, pineapple, cinnamon and oil palm were distributed from here throughout the world. The herb garden itself, the Hortus Medicus, won world renown for its research into cures for tropical diseases.

The garden is a must-see for anyone with an interest in botany, though it's more a place for study than for pleasant relaxation – if you're after the latter, go to the Vondelpark (p112) or the botanical garden in Leiden (p230). Still, there's a lot to see: the wonderful mixture of colonial and modern structures includes the restored, octagonal seed house; a hyper-modern, three-climate glasshouse (1993) with subtropical, tropical (see if your glasses don't fog) and desert plants; a monumental palm house with a 300-plus-year-old cycad, claimed to be the world's oldest plant in a pot (it blossomed in 1999, a rare event); a butterfly house that's a hit with kids and stoned adults; a newly refurbished café with a very pleasant terrace; and of course the Hortus Medicus, the medicinal herb garden that attracts students from around the

globe. Catwalks in the greenhouses allow you to see the plants from below and up close.

There are guided tours (additional €1) at 2pm Sunday.

## NATIONAAL VAKBONDSMUSEUM
Map p285

National Trade Union Museum; ☎ 624 11 66; Henri Polaklaan 9; adult/concession or union member €2.30/1.15; ☼ 11am-5pm Tue-Fri, 1-5pm Sun, closed public holidays

Several buildings in the area serve as reminders of its Jewish past. This particular building used to house the powerful General Netherlands Diamond Workers' Union (ANDB), one of the pioneers of the Dutch labour movement under the chairmanship of Henri Polak. The displays are of limited interest to all except those with a passion for labour issues (plus, all signage is in Dutch), but the building itself is worth a look.

The architect HP Berlage designed it as the union's headquarters in 1900, and it soon became known as the 'Burcht van Berlage', Berlage's Fortress – a play on Beurs van Berlage, the bourse along Damrak (p58). Berlage considered it his most successful work and it's easy to see why, from the diamond-shaped pinnacle and the magnificent hall with its brick arches, to the murals, ceramics and leadlight windows by famous artists of the day. The soaring, tiled, atrium-style staircase is graced with a three-storey tall chandelier – this Deco marvel was added in 1921 at the phenomenal cost (for the time) of 30,000 guilders.

## VERZETSMUSEUM Map p285

Resistance Museum; ☎ 620 25 35; Plantage Kerklaan 61; adult/child/under 7yrs €5/2.50/free; ☼ 10am-5pm Tue-Fri, noon-5pm Sat-Mon

It took less than one week in May 1940 for the Netherlands to be overrun by the German army, and from that moment the Dutch faced a choice: join or resist?

The choice came on all fronts: political, judicial, medical, scholarly, economic. Germany tried to cosy up to the Dutch at first (eg declaring them part of the 'Germanic brotherhood'). Soon though, came the restrictions – among them: changing the names of streets named for Jews, requiring doctors to join the Nazi Medical Chamber, banning of political movements, confiscation of 80% of radios and, naturally, unspeakable deportations and murders – all of which fomented mass resistance, even if much of it was below the surface.

This museum provides an excellent insight into the difficulties faced by those who fought the occupation from within – as well as the tiny minority who chose to go along with the Nazis. Labels in Dutch and English help with the exhibits, many of them interactive, that explain such issues as active and passive resistance, how the illegal press operated, how 300,000 people were kept in hiding and how such activities were funded (a less glamorous but vital detail). The museum shows in no uncertain terms how much courage it takes to actively resist an adversary so ruthless that you can't trust neighbours, friends or even family. Just as importantly, it gives pause to think how each of us would handle such a situation.

## AROUND THE PLANTAGE

At the eastern end of Plantage Middenlaan, past the Artis aquarium and across the canal, is Alexanderplein with the **Muiderpoort** (Map pp274-5), a grim, Doric city gate dating from 1771. Just northeast of here, along Sarphatistraat, is the 250m façade of the **Oranje-Nassau Kazerne**, barracks built to house the French garrison but only finished in 1814, a year after the French left. They've now been converted to homes, offices and studios. The former drill yard along the Singelgracht accommodates a remarkable row of six modern apartment blocks, each designed by an architect from a different country (from the Muiderpoort end: Japan, Greece, France, USA, Denmark, UK). This was the city's first large-scale experiment in residential architecture in recent times, foreshadowing what's now happening in the Eastern Harbour region (p107).

And as you make your way toward the Eastern Islands to the north, along Valkenburgerstraat you'll see the aluminum-coated Mediamatic Supermarket, an architecturally adventurous extension of the Spar market next door. Its modular structure means it can be removed in case the access road to the IJ Tunnel is widened.

## BIERBROUWERIJ 'T IJ  Map pp274-5
☎ 622 83 25; Funenkade 7; admission free; ❦ 3-8pm Wed-Sun
In 1985, the former public baths alongside the windmill were converted into this small brewery, producing six regular and several seasonal beers. Some are quite strong (up to 9% alcohol by volume), and all can be tasted in the comfortably grungy interior or on the terrace at the foot of windmill. As of this writing, it was the only brewery in town, although de Bekeerde Suster (p161) off Nieuwmarkt may well resume brewing by the time you read this. There are tours 4pm Friday.

## DE GOOYER WINDMILL  Map pp274-5
Funenkade
Northeast of the Muiderpoort homes is this 18th-century grain mill, the sole survivor of five windmills that once stood in this part of the city. Originally southwest of here, it was moved to its present location on Funenkade in 1814 when the Oranje-Nassau barracks blocked the wind from flowing to it.

## ENERGETICA  Map pp274-5
☎ 422 12 27; Hoogte Kadijk 400; adult/child under 12 yrs €3/free; ❦ 10am-4pm Mon-Fri
If it has pistons, gears, wires, cables, tubes or shafts; if it clinks, clanks, buzzes, pops or clunks, you'll find it here. EnergeticA (opened 2003) may be the quirkiest museum in Amsterdam, and it's also one of our favourites. It looks like a power station from the outside (which it was), volunteer docents act like retired engineers (which many are, average age: 70), and they'll enthusiastically escort you through centuries of technological history, demonstrating how things work as they go (some of them speak excellent English).

Galleries are named for pioneering scientists (Marconi, Minckelers et al), and some of the ancient equipment in them – from steamship engines to antique toasters, early washing machines, electric lights and TVs – may remind you of science fiction movies. The early refrigerators are, pardon the expression, very cool.

The highlight, though, is the soaring main hall, several storeys in what was the first power plant for the city's trams. It's filled with large-scale technological marvels from the past: gas streetlamps, antique lifts (elevators) from Vienna and Paris, high-voltage generators that send lightning between enormous v-shaped prongs, and you've never imagined how much fun it can be to ride an escalator.

Note that children under 12 years old need to be accompanied by their parent (one adult supervising a group of kids is not going to do it!).

## ENTREPOTDOK  Map p285
When the Plantage was constructed in the 1680s, the original sea dyke was moved north to what are now the Hoogte Kadijk and Laagte Kadijk (the 'high section' and 'low section' of

the 'quay dyke'). The stretch of water between the Plantage and this new sea dyke is the Entrepotdok, established in the 1820s as a storage zone for goods in transit. The 500m-long row of warehouses, once the largest storage depot in Europe, has been converted into desirable apartments and studios. They've won numerous awards for the preservation of their exteriors, while the interiors have been opened up significantly from the former cramped spaces.

## MUSEUMWERF 'T KROMHOUT
Map pp274-5

☎ 627 67 77; Hoogte Kadijk 147; adult/child €4.75/2.75; ☼ 10am-3pm Tue

On the outer side of the dyke is an 18th-century wharf that still repairs boats in its western hall. The eastern hall is a museum devoted to shipbuilding and even more to the indestructible marine engines that were designed and built here. It reopened in 2001 after a three-year refurbishment. Anyone with an interest in marine engineering will love the place; others will probably want to move on. Signage is almost entirely in Dutch only.

# EASTERN ISLANDS

## ARCAM Map pp282-3
Stichting Architectuur Centrum Amsterdam; ☎ 620 48 78; www.arcam.nl; Prins Hendrikkade 600; admission free; ☼ 1-5pm Tue-Sat

One-stop shopping for all your architectural needs, this foundation is a clearing house of information on architectural history and developments around town. In 2003 it moved into this new waterfront gallery and office

## Top Five Eastern Islands & Eastern Docklands

- Visit **ARCAM** (above) architecture foundation, before starting out on your tour of some of Europe's most adventurous buildings.
- Have dim-sum overlooking the city at the floating **Sea Palace restaurant** (p149).
- Contemplate Amsterdam's shipping heritage at the **Nederlands Scheepvaartmuseum** (right).
- The kids (or you!) can play junior scientist at **NEMO** (right) or relax on its rooftop beach.
- Spend hours learning about world cultures at the **Tropenmuseum** (p108) or see a performer from a faraway land in its theatre.

space designed by Wim Ruigrok. Exhibits vary. They publish (and sell) some of the best books available on architecture in the city (eg *25 Buildings You Should Have Seen*, and *Eastern Docklands Map*). They can recommend tours based on your needs – you can also check the website for information.

## NEDERLANDS SCHEEPVAARTMUSEUM Map pp282-3
Netherlands Shipping Museum; ☎ 523 22 22; Kattenburgerplein 1; adult/senior/child 6-17/under 6 yrs €7/6/4/free; ☼ 10am-5pm Jun-Aug, 10am-5pm Tue-Sun Sep-May

The Republic's naval arsenal was housed in an imposing building completed in 1656 to a design by Daniël Stalpaert. The admiralty vacated the building in 1973, and since 1981 it has housed this museum, with one of the most extensive collections of maritime memorabilia in the world.

The museum covers the history of Dutch seafaring from the ancient past to the present. Early shipping routes, maritime trade, naval combat, fishing and whaling are all explained in interesting displays, paintings and some 500 models of boats and ships. Lovers of charts, maps and navigational material will not want to miss it. There are also films throughout the day.

Moored alongside the museum is a full-scale model of the United East India Company's 700-tonne *Amsterdam*, one of the largest ships of the fleet. It set sail on its maiden voyage in the winter of 1748–49 with 336 people on board, but got stuck off the English coast near Hastings; there it became a famous shipwreck that has been much researched in recent years. Actors in 18th-century costume re-create shipboard life, and you can stroll the cabins and cargo holds – the Great Cabin is set for an elegant dinner. Although it would have taken about six months to build the original *Amsterdam*, this one took six *years* (completed 1991).

Not to be missed is the Royal Barge, in its own gallery. This French-style craft (17m long by 2.6m wide, weight 6 tonnes, built 1818) is decorated from stem to stern in gold filigree, and on the bow there's an elaborate gold figure of Neptune driving a team of half-horse-half-fish beings. It's the oldest existing vessel in the Royal Netherlands Navy.

## NEMO Map pp282-3
☎ 531 32 33; www.e-nemo.nl; Oosterdok 2; adult/student/child under 4 yrs €10/6/free; ☼ 10am-5pm Tue-Sun, Mon Jul & Aug

Districts – The Plantage, Eastern Islands & Oosterpark

## More than Raw Fish in Common

Ask any Japanese: the Dutch have a unique historical relationship with the Land of the Rising Sun. It began around 1660 when a civil war in China (then Holland's source for fine porcelain) caused trade to cease, so Dutch traders turned to Japan.

At the end of the war, the traders returned to China but continued to maintain a presence in Japan as well. This was remarkable because Japan was otherwise isolated from the outside world due to its island geography and, more significantly, the dictatorial, isolationist policies of the Tokugawa shogunate (military rulers).

Not that the Dutch had free run of the place – hardly. Their outpost was on the tiny island of Dejima off the coast of Nagasaki, which is almost as far as one can go in Japan. Still, the Netherlands was the only nation to consistently trade with Japan until its isolation ended in the 1850s. Today travellers to Nagasaki can visit Oranda-mura (Holland Village), a re-created Dutch village.

Perched atop the entrance to the IJ Tunnel (hold that thought) is this rounded-wedge of a museum of science and technology; it's really meant for kids, but grown-ups will probably enjoy it too. There are loads of interactive exhibits, drawing with a laser, 'anti-gravity' trick mirrors and a 'lab' where you can answer questions like 'how black is black?' and 'how do you make cheese?' Signage is in English and Dutch.

Italian architect Renzo Piano (a Pritzker Prize winner whose works also include the Centre Pompidou in Paris, Kansai Airport near Osaka and Potsdamer Platz in Berlin) conceived of this design as the inverse of the tunnel below it (there's the thought you held in the previous paragraph). Less-kind critics had taken to calling this ship-shaped building the *Titanic*, for

its colossal cost, but by all accounts it's doing pretty well, thank you.

In summer, the terraced rooftop plaza hosts **Nemo Beach** (admission €2.50, free with NEMO admission; ☺ vary). The 'beach' itself is actually a rather elaborate sandbox occupying just a small section of the roof, but further up DJs spin, and there's a bar, a convivial atmosphere and nice views. It can get busy.

### STEDELIJK MUSEUM Map pp282-3
☎ 573 27 37; www.stedelijk.nl; Oosterdoksdijk 5; adult/child 7-16 or senior/child under 7 yrs €7/3.50/ free; ☺ 11am-5pm

This building is only the temporary home of the displayed collection; the original Museum building is undergoing renovation until 2007, and is closed to the public.

*A replica of the Amsterdam, and the NEMO museum in the background (p105)*

Districts – The Plantage, Eastern Islands & Oosterpark

The Stedelijk Museum (Municipal Museum) focuses on modern art – paintings, sculptures, installations, videos, photography etc – from 1850 to the present. It's one of the world's leading museums of modern art, with an eclectic collection amassed by its postwar curator, Willem Sandberg.

This includes works by Monet, Van Gogh, Cézanne, Matisse, Picasso, Kirchner and Chagall, as well as other modern 'classics', including a unique collection of some 50 works by the Russian artist Malevich. There are abstract works by Mondrian, Van Doesburg and Kandinsky, and a large, post-WWII selection of creations by Appel (including the former cafeteria decorated by him), De Kooning, Newman, Ryman, Judd, Warhol, Dibbets, Baselitz, Dubuffet, Lichtenstein, Polke, Klee and Rietveld's furniture.

Sculptures include works by Rodin, Renoir, Moore, Laurens and Visser. More recent acquisitions include works by Damien Hirst and Julian Schnabel. The pleasant café-restaurant, with a great mural by Appel, draws the glitterati of the (inter)national arts scene.

## EASTERN DOCKLANDS DISTRICT

North and east of the Eastern Islands, this one-time shipping yard and warehouse district sat derelict for decades, despite some excellent warehouse-style buildings. Recently, though, it's been the focus of a huge amount of attention from architects and architecture critics for the elaborate updates and extremely adventurous new construction. If you're looking for one place to see the cutting edge of Dutch – indeed European – architecture, this is the place to come.

There has been a lot of discussion among urban planners, financiers and council politicians over how to reconcile grandiose projects with affordable housing and the traditional Amsterdam lifestyle. By and large, affordable housing lost out with a relatively low proportion of 30% social housing spread throughout the area. Many of the delectable apartments here are now worth €400,000 and more. When complete, there will be more than 8000 dwellings and 17,000 inhabitants.

### IJBURG Map pp274-5

The 1.5km Piet Heintunnel under the water between Sporenburg and Borneo (the longest tunnel in the country) links the Eastern Harbour District to **IJburg**, a huge new housing project under construction on a string of artificial islands in the IJmeer. Two of these islands

are linked by the stunning Enneus Heerma Brug, a futuristic steel construction designed by Nicholas Grimshaw & Partners. Locals call it the Dolly Parton Bridge, for reasons which will be apparent on sight

On completion, IJburg will be home to 45,000 people in 18,000 dwellings served by 11 primary schools, its own cemetery and even a beach. A majority of Amsterdammers voted against the project in a referendum, but not enough people voted so the plan went ahead – though city planners had to work twice as hard to improve their blueprints. Inhabitants of Durgerdam, a picturesque old village across the water, were furious about losing their view.

### JAN SCHAEFER BRIDGE Map pp282-3

Named after a gung-ho municipal housing councillor in the 1980s who was responsible for an unprecedented number of social-housing projects (favoured motto: 'You can't live in claptrap'), this bridge links this area to Java Eiland farther north. The southern end of the bridge passes through an old warehouse, which had to be reinforced at great expense to withstand the vibrations.

The bridge itself has two removable sections that can be floated out of the way for special events, such as the Sail Amsterdam gathering of tall ships held every five years (next due in 2005). West of this warehouse is another warehouse that's home to a centre for interior design where you can ogle (but not buy) the creative products of the country's top manufacturers.

### JAVA EILAND

Java Eiland consists of new housing estates separated by canals and enclosing sheltered parks. Its western tip is awaiting an as-yet-unknown project befitting its prominent location – municipal planners are looking for a landmark on a par with the Sydney Opera House – and is used meanwhile for temporary events such as the Drum Rhythm Festival (p9).

The eastern third of this island is known as the **KNSM Eiland** (Map p284), named after the Royal Netherlands Steamship Company, which based its ships here in the late colonial period. This, too, has been transformed by apartment blocks that charm visiting architects, with expensive, private housing on the northern side and social housing on the southern side. Some interesting cafés have opened up here too.

### OOSTELIJKE HANDELSKADE

North of Rietlanden park area is the Oostelijke Handelskade (Eastern Trade Quay), where the new passenger terminal caters for enormous cruise ships that dwarf the terminal itself. West of the terminal, the Muziekgebouw Amsterdam (Music Building Amsterdam), due for completion in 2005, will house the Bimhuis (jazz) and IJsbreker (avant-garde) music centres.

## SPORENBURG & BORNEO EILAND
Map p284

South of here, the low-rise housing estates on the former Sporenburg peninsula and Borneo Eiland have the highest density in the world for dwellings that aren't stacked on top of one another, with 100 houses per hectare (100m x 100m). None of the expensive apartments here are freestanding, but they're designed in such a way to ensure privacy. The planning motto could be described as 'green is blue', meaning that instead of gardens there are roof terraces and lots of water and sky – in fact, trees and shrubs planted by residents are often removed because they 'spoil the harbour look' or 'obstruct pedestrians'.

Sporenburg and Borneo have also been described as 'a sea of houses with meteorites', the 'meteorites' being a number of huge apartment blocks, each of them architectural experiments with varying degrees of success. One of the most remarkable is Frits van Dongen's **The Whale** on Sporenburg, a zinc-coated, 12-storey construction that rears its head and tail. It encloses a landscaped garden that's off-limits to visitors and residents alike. A central cable-TV system with four satellite dishes ensures that residents can plug into 180 channels.

A tall pedestrian bridge at the eastern end of Sporenburg links this peninsula to Borneo Eiland. The bridge doesn't have a popular name yet, but the Dinosaur would be apt as it looks like a huge sauropod kissing the other side. It's a work of art (built partly with arts funding) and walking across is quite an experience. Not only is it rather high and exposed (vertigo sufferers take note), and will sway precariously if rocked from side to side, but the steps are of unequal length and you can't see them properly on the way down. Great fun. The bridge is closed in bad weather.

At the far end of Borneo, **Scheepstimmermanstraat** (Ships Carpenter Street) consists of so-called 'free lots', where purchasers were allowed to design and build whatever they liked (within reason). This has resulted in some amazing solutions to problems such as car parking, maximising sun and ensuring an uninterrupted view of water and sky. It's all rather bizarre, and if you're with a friend the two of you will probably disagree strongly on the houses you do and don't like.

# OOSTERPARK

This southeastern district, named after the lush English-style park lying at its centre, was built in the 1880s. At the time, the city's diamond workers suddenly found they had money to spare thanks to the discovery of diamonds in South Africa. About a third of Jewish families worked in the diamond industry in one way or another, and many of these could finally afford to leave the Jewish quarter for this new district beyond the Plantage (the delectable parklands where only the wealthiest could afford to live). Signs of this district's lower-middle-class heritage have long since disappeared and now it's similar to the other 19th-century slums that arose around the canal belt. Much of the real estate in this area is owned by the University of Amsterdam.

## TROPENMUSEUM Map pp274-5
☎ 568 82 15; www.kit.nl; Linnaeusstraat 2; adult/senior or student/child/under 6 yrs €7.50/5/3.75/free; ⏰ 10am-5pm

This impressive complex was completed in 1926 to house the Royal Institute of the Tropics, still one of the world's leading research institutes for tropical hygiene and agriculture. Part of the building became a museum for the institute's collection of colonial artefacts, but this was overhauled in the 1970s to create the culturally aware and imaginatively presented displays you see today.

---

## Our Favourite Place Names in Amsterdam

- **Oude Nieuwstraat** (Old New Street)
- **Nieuwe Nieuwstraat** (New New Street)
- **Java, Sumatra, Borneo etc** (islands in the Eastern Docklands)
- **Dolly Parton Brug** (Dolly Parton Bridge – not the actual name, but everyone calls it that for its anatomical structure)
- **Herengracht** (Gentlemen's Canal – our absolute favourite because it contains every possible way to pronounce a gutteral sound in Dutch: 'Hhherrrrengggrrrrrrrraccccht')

A huge central hall with galleries over three floors offers reconstructions of daily life in several tropical countries (eg African market, Mexican-style cantina, musical instruments which you can hear via recordings). Separate exhibitions focus on theatre, religion, crafts, world trade, textiles and ecology, and there are special exhibitions throughout the year, while others focus on regions (eg Latin America, Southeast Asia, Suriname. For Dutch-speaking children, the children's section, TM Junior, has special guided exhibits (ring for details and prices). There's also an extensive **library** ( ☎ 568 82 54; ☾ 10am-4.45pm Tue-Fri, noon-4.45pm Sun).

There's a shop selling books and gifts and unique CDs, the pleasant **Soeterijn Café** (p150) and the **Ekeko restaurant** ( ☎ 568 86 44) serve cuisine and snacks that reflect current exhibits and performances (despite its name, Ekeko is actually the less formal of the two).

The **Tropeninstituut Theater** (Map pp274-5; ☎ 568 82 15; ☾ box office noon-4pm Mon-Sat) has a separate entrance and screens films but also hosts music, dance, plays and other performances by visiting artists.

Among its other charms, the museum itself is a good place to spend a lazy Monday when most of the other museums around town are closed.

# OLD SOUTH (OUD ZUID)
*Eating p150; Sleeping p222*

## Orientation
The canal belt was a far-sighted project that sufficed for two-and-a-half centuries. There was no real pressure to expand beyond the canals until the 1860s, when the industrial revolution began to attract workers back to the city. In 1830 there were 200,000 inhabitants – 20,000 fewer than in the 18th century, due to Napoleon's disastrous Continental System. In 1860 this had picked up to 245,000, in 1880 to 320,000, and in 1900 to over 500,000.

This time the city's expansion was uncoordinated. There were several grand plans but none of them got past the proposal stage; instead, private initiative and speculation reigned supreme. De Pijp, between the Amstel and Hobbemakade, was the first area to be added, in the 1860s, full of dreary and shoddily built tenement blocks for the city's labourers. Farther west came the Vondelpark in the 1860s and 1870s, surrounded by upmarket housing. The last two decades of the 19th century were a free-for-all as investors grabbed other land beyond the canal belt and built new cheap housing, often with very few restrictions.

In a rerun of the canal-belt scenario, the park and cultural centres were financed by the sale of various plots of land to the highest bidders, who proceeded to build private mansions close to these attractive landmarks. It wasn't until the early decades of the 20th century, however, that the wealthy class deserted these custom-built mansions along Herengracht and Keizersgracht altogether.

In the 1920s, plots farther south that remained empty were filled with Amsterdam School–designed apartments commissioned by subsidised-housing corporations.

---

### Top Five Old South

- **Museum Quarter** (p110) is well worth a visit, even if some of the museums are closed (the Van Gogh Museum, p111, is not closed!).

- In **De Pijp** (p113), one of the city's most diverse, cosmopolitan and interesting neighbourhoods, stroll the **Albert Cuypmarkt** (p113), go for Surinamese food or sip cocktails in a trendy café.

- Laze away the day in the **Vondelpark** (p112), or join hundreds (if not thousands) of skaters here for a Friday night tour of the city (p188).

- Suit up for a grand performance at the **Concertgebouw** (p110).

- Get glam and cruise Amsterdam's classiest shopping strip, **PC Hooftstraat** (p110).

---

109

Prominent architects of these projects were JF Staal and JC van Epen.

Much of the housing here has been renovated or replaced with more-modern social-housing estates – which are decidedly more pleasant. De Pijp has largely gentrified, and it remains an important gathering place for immigrant communities, as well as having the city's largest per capita lesbian and gay population.

# MUSEUM QUARTER

This wedge-shaped district is roughly bordered by the Vondelpark in the west and Hobbemakade in the east. Some call it the Museum Quarter, Concertgebouw area or Vondelpark area, depending on which of these landmarks is closest. Fortunately it escaped the late-19th–century free-for-all. Wealthy investors wanted an upmarket area for themselves and saw to it that tenement blocks or businesses were prohibited here – a suitable spot for a grand national museum (the Rijksmuseum) and an equally grand new concert hall (the Concertgebouw).

## CONCERTGEBOUW Map pp286-7

☎ 671 83 45; www.concertgebouw.nl; Concertgebouw-plein 2-6; ticket prices vary; ⏱ box office 10am-7pm

The Concert Building, at the end of Museumplein, attracts some 800,000 visitors a year to 650 shows, making it the busiest concert hall in the world. It was completed in 1888 to a neo-Renaissance design by AL van Gendt. In spite of his limited musical knowledge, he managed to give the Grote Zaal (Great Hall) near-perfect acoustics that are the envy of concert hall designers worldwide.

The best conductors and soloists consider it an honour to perform here. Under the 50-year guidance of composer and conductor Willem Mengelberg (1871–1951), the Concertgebouw Orchestra (with the epithet 'Royal' since 1988) developed into one of the world's finest orchestras.

In the 1980s the Concertgebouw threatened to collapse because its 2000 wooden piles were rotting. Thanks to new technology, the piles made way for a concrete foundation, and the building was thoroughly restored to mark its 100th anniversary. The architect Pi de Bruin added a glass foyer along the southern side that most people hate, though everyone agrees it's effective.

The Grote Zaal seats 2000 people and is used for concerts. Recitals take place in the 19m x 15m Kleine Zaal (Small Hall), a replica of the hall in the Felix Meritis building.

You can purchase tickets on the telephone between 10am and 5pm, or at the box office till 7pm (after 7pm you can only get tickets for that evening's performance). The VVV and Amsterdam Uitburo (p255) also sell tickets. There are free lunch-time concerts at 12.30pm Wednesdays between September and June.

## PC HOOFTSTRAAT

If you head across Paulus Potterstraat from the Van Gogh Museum and cross Jan Luijkenstraat, you'll soon arrive at Pieter Cornelisz Hooftstraat. For years these few blocks have been the shopping street for the cream of society and the nouveau riche, even if recently there have been a few mob incidents to tarnish its lustre. You'll find some of the world's leading brands here, both in shops of their own name and in others, as well as a few surprisingly friendly cafés for a break. Heading left (westward) on the PC Hooftstraat will deposit you in the lovely Vondelpark.

## RIJKSMUSEUM Map pp286-7

☎ 674 70 00; www.rijksmuseum.nl; Stadhouderskade 42; adult/child under 18yrs €9/free; ⏱ 10am-5pm

Given the museum's scheduled closure (see boxed text), we are presenting here mostly historical and architectural background. Keep in mind, also, that although certain works may not be on display here in Amsterdam, if you're so motivated you may well be easily able to travel to another city to view your area of interest.

The Museum Quarter's gateway – literally, with its pedestrian and bicycle underpass – is the 1885 Pierre Cuypers–designed Rijksmuseum. It bears a striking resemblance to Centraal Station, which was indeed designed by the same architect and completed four years later, with a mixture of neo-Gothic and Dutch Renaissance. The neo-Gothic aspects (towers, stained-glass windows) elicited criticism from Protestants including the king, who dubbed the building 'the archbishop's palace' (Cuypers was Catholic, and proudly so in his approach to architecture).

The Rijksmuseum was conceived as a repository for several national collections, including the royal art collection that was first housed in the palace on the Dam and then in the Trippenhuis on Kloveniersburgwal. It's the country's premier art museum and one that no self-respecting visitor to Amsterdam can afford to miss – in fact, 1.2 million visitors flock here each year.

The collection houses some 5000 paintings, the most important of which are by Dutch and/or Flemish masters from the 15th to 19th centuries, with emphasis on the 17th-century Golden Age. Pride of place is taken by Rembrandt's huge *Nightwatch* (1650), showing the militia led by Frans Banningh Cocq, a future mayor of the city – the painting only acquired this name in later years because it had become dark with grime (it's nice and clean now). Other 17th-century Dutch masters on this floor include Jan Vermeer (*The Kitchen Maid*, also known as *The Milkmaid*, and *Woman in Blue Reading a Letter*), Frans Hals (*The Merry Drinker*) and Jan Steen (*The Merry Family*).

The museum's other collections are Sculpture & Applied Art (delftware, beautiful dolls' houses, porcelain, furniture), Dutch History (though the Amsterdams Historisch Museum and Nederlands Scheepvaartmuseum do this better) and Asiatic Art (including the famous 12th-century *Dancing Shiva*). The print collection includes some 800,000 prints and drawings.

The **garden** at the back of the museum has flowerbeds, fountains and an eclectic collection of statues, pillars and fragments of demolished buildings and monuments from all over the country.

Street musicians perform in the pedestrian and bicycle underpass beneath the museum, their sounds echoing off the cavernous walls. This passage leads to the large **Museumplein**, which hosted the World Exhibition in 1883 and hasn't had a clear purpose since. It has recently been transformed into a huge park, with an underground Albert Heijn supermarket opposite the Concertgebouw, and in fine weather it's not uncommon to see folks playing hackysack of throwing Frisbees, as well as engaging in calmer pursuits like picnicking.

## STEDELIJK MUSEUM Map pp282-3

☎ 57327 37; www.stedelijk.nl; Oosterdoksdijk 5; adult/child 7-16 or senior/child under 7 yrs €7/3.50/ free; ⏰ 11am-5pm

From April 2004 until 2007, the modernist statements of the Stedelijk Museum will appear in an unlikely location: on the 2nd, 3rd and 11th floors of a former post-office high-rise on Oosterdok Island, just east of Centraal Station. For the full review of this excellent collection, please see the Eastern Islands (p106).

The original building on the Paulus Potterstraat will be undergoing renovations during this time, and will not be open to the public.

## VAN GOGH MUSEUM Map pp286-7

☎ 570 52 00; www.vangoghmuseum.nl; Paulus Potterstraat 7; adult/child/under 12 yrs €9/2.50/free, audiotour €4; ⏰ 10am-6pm

The next museum down is the Van Gogh Museum, designed by Gerrit Rietveld (the 1999 expansion onto Museumplein, a separate exhibition wing designed by Kishio Kurosawa, is commonly known as 'the Mussel'). It opened in 1973 to house the collection of Vincent's younger brother Theo, which consists of about 200 paintings and 500 drawings by Vincent and his friends or contemporaries, such as Gauguin, Toulouse-Lautrec, Monet and Bernard.

Vincent van Gogh (pronounced 'fahn khokh', rhyming with Scottish 'loch') was born in 1853 and had a short but very productive life. Through his paintings, the museum chronicles

# Under Construction: Rijksmuseum & Stedelijk Museum

To the chagrin of many art lovers, large parts of two of Amsterdam's most prized museums will be out of site, if not out of sight, for much of this decade.

Most galleries of the **Rijksmuseum** will be closed for a sweeping renovation until 2008. A changing selection of the top 200 attractions are on display in the rear Philips wing overlooking Museumplein – which, they trust, will be enough to satisfy devotees of the Dutch masters. These include Rembrandt's *Nightwatch*, several Vermeers and a selection of Delftware. There will also be travelling exhibits from the Rijksmuseum around the Netherlands (including at Schiphol Airport) and in other countries. You can check the website, www.rijksmuseum.nl, for further details.

The **Stedelijk Museum** building will be shut until 2007 for renovations, although some of its exhibitions will be moving to the old TGP building, an ex-postal high-rise just to the east of Centraal Station on Oosterdokseiland (p106). Mercifully, it's business as usual at the Van Gogh Museum.

his life's journey from Holland (where his work was characterised by a dark colour palette) to Paris (where, under the influence of the Impressionists he discovered colour) to Arles (where it is said his career reached its apotheosis). Astoundingly, his painting career lasted less than 10 years, from 1881 to 1890 when, in a fatal depression, he shot himself (he had already cut off his ear after an argument with Gauguin). Famous works on display include *The Potato Eaters* (1885), a prime example of his sombre Dutch period, and *The Yellow House in Arles* (1888), *The Bedroom* (1888) and several self-portraits, sunflowers and other blossoms that show his vivid use of colour in the intense Mediterranean light. One of his last paintings, *Wheatfield with Crows* (1890), is an ominous work foreshadowing his suicide.

The permanent collection also includes many of the artist's personal effects. He received a milk jug from Theo and used it in several of his works. There are also knots of wool which he used to study contrasts in colours.

His paintings are on the 1st floor; the other floors display his drawings and Japanese prints, as well as works by friends, contemporaries and others he influenced, some of which are shown in rotation. The **library** (☎ 570 59 06; ☺ 10am-12.30pm & 1.30-5pm Mon-Fri) has a wealth of reference material for serious study.

And although we haven't seen any figures, it seems to us that roughly one-third of visitors to Amsterdam end up taking home a triangular box with a poster from the museum inside.

# VONDELPARK & SURROUNDINGS

This pleasant, English-style park, with ponds, lawns, thickets and winding footpaths, is about 1.5km long and 300m wide. Laid out on marshland beyond the canal belt in the 1860s and '70s as a park for the bourgeoisie (when the existing city park, the Plantage, became residential), it was soon surrounded by upmarket housing. It's named after the poet and playwright Joost van den Vondel (1587–1679), the Shakespeare of the Netherlands.

In the late 1960s and early 1970s the authorities turned the park into an open-air dormitory to alleviate the lack of accommodation for hordes of hippies who descended on Amsterdam. The sleeping bags have long since gone and it's now illegal to sleep in the park, but there's still some evidence of Ital-

*Cycling through the Vondelpark*

ian, French and Eastern European tourists stuck in the '70s.

The park is now used by one and all – joggers, in-line skaters, children chasing ducks or flying kites, couples in love, families with prams, acrobats practising or performing, teenagers playing soccer – and can be crowded on weekends but never annoyingly so. There are always people performing music throughout the park, and on a sunny summer day it may seem that everyone is sunbathing.

## DE VONDELTUIN Map pp274-5
☎ 664 50 91; www.vondeltuin.nl; Vondelpark 7
A stand near the Amstelveenseweg entrance at the southwestern end of the park rents in-line skates and gloves. Skate rental for one, two or three or more hours costs €5, €10 or €15. Hours vary, but it is open daily from March to October.

## FILMMUSEUM Map pp286-7
☎ 589 14 00; www.filmmuseum.nl; Vondelpark 3; check website or local listings for details
Close to Constantijn Huygensstraat is the former Vondelpark Pavilion (1881), now home to the Filmmuseum. It's not a museum with displays and such, but it has a large collection of memorabilia and a priceless archive of films that are screened in two theatres, often with live music and other accompaniments. One theatre

contains the Art Deco interior of Cinema Paris-ien, an early Amsterdam cinema. Note that, as of this writing, some screenings were held at the **Filmmuseum Cinerama** (aka Calypso; p183) near Leidseplein; this was on an experimental basis but may be made permanent.

The museum's charming **Café Vertigo** (p161), with its theatrical balcony and great ground-level terrace, is a popular meeting place and an ideal spot to spend a couple of hours watching the goings-on in the park; on sum-mer evenings there are films on the outdoor terrace and jazz on Sunday during winter.

Adjoining the museum is an impressive **information centre** (☎ 589 14 35; Vondelstraat 69-71; admission free; ☺ 10am-5pm Tue-Fri, 11am-5pm Sat) with loads of books and videotapes which can be viewed in viewing booths.

## HOLLANDSE MANEGE Map pp286-7
☎ 618 09 42; Vondelstraat 140; ☺ vary
Just west of the Filmmuseum is the neoclassical Hollandse Manege, built in 1882 and designed by AL van Gendt, an indoor riding school in-spired by the famous Spanish Riding School in Vienna. The building was fully restored in the 1980s, and it's worth walking through the pas-sage to the door at the rear and up the stairs to the café, where you can sip a cheap beer or coffee while enjoying the beautiful interior and watching the instructor put the horses through their paces. Opening times can vary – ring to avoid disappointment.

Nearby is the **Vondelkerk** (1880), built to a design by Pierre Cuypers, which now accom-modates offices.

## OPEN-AIR THEATRE Map pp286-7
☎ 673 14 99; www.openluchttheater.nl
From June to August, the park hosts free concerts in its intimate theatre. Performances range from classical to hip-hop.

## ROUND BLUE TEAHOUSE Map pp286-7
't Blauwe Theehuis; ☎ 662 02 54; Vondelpark 5; lunch €3.50-4, dinner mains €14.50-18.50
The functionalist teahouse from 1936 is a won-derful little multilevel building that serves cof-fee, cake and alcohol; its terrace and balcony are great places for a beer on a sunny day, even in winter when the heaters are on.

## TRAM MUSEUM AMSTERDAM
Map pp274-5
☎ 673 75 38; Amstelveenseweg 264; return ticket adult/child €3/1.50; ☺ 11am-5pm Sun mid-Apr–Oct, 1.45pm & 3.15pm Wed July & Aug

Beyond the southwestern extremities of the park, just north of the Olympic Stadium, is the former Haarlemmermeer Station, which houses the Tram Museum Amsterdam. Historic trams sourced from all over Europe run between here and Amstelveen – a great outing for kids and adults. A return trip takes more than an hour and skirts the large Amsterdamse Bos recreational area (contact the museum for a schedule).

# DE PIJP
This district is enclosed by the Amstel in the east, Stadhouderskade in the north, Hobbemakade in the west and the Amstel-kanaal in the south – it's actually a large island connected to the rest of the city by 16 bridges. The district's name, 'the Pipe' (originally the 'YY neighbourhood'), pre-sumably reflects its straight, narrow streets that are said to resemble the stems of old clay pipes, but nobody really knows. There are a surprising number of attractions for an area that began as the city's first 19th-century slum.

Its shoddy tenement blocks, some of which collapsed even as they were being built in the 1860s, provided cheap housing not just for newly arrived workers drawn by the city's industrial revolution, but also for students, artists, writers and other poverty-stricken individuals. In the 1960s and '70s, as many of the working-class inhabitants left for greener pastures, the government began refurbishing the tenement blocks for im-migrants from Morocco, Turkey, the Neth-erlands Antilles and Suriname. Now these immigrants are also moving out and the Pijp is attracting a wealthier breed of locals who are doing up apartments and lending the neighbourhood a more gentrified air.

In the past as now, the Pijp has often been called the 'Quartier Latin' of Amsterdam thanks to its lively mix of people – labourers, intellectuals, new immigrants, prostitutes (in the city's other and very depressing Red Light District along Ruysdaelkade opposite Hobbemakade), and now gays and lesbians and an increasing number of higher-income professionals.

## ALBERT CUYPMARKT Map pp286-7
Albert Cuypstraat; ☺ 9am-5pm Mon-Sat
This is Amsterdam's largest and busiest market. The emphasis is on food of every description and nationality, but clothes and other general

goods are on sale too, often cheaper than anywhere else. If you want to experience the 'real' Amsterdam at its multicultural best, this market is not to be missed. As always at busy markets, beware of pickpockets.

The surrounding streets hide cosy neighbourhood cafés, small (and usually very cheap) restaurants that offer a wide range of cuisines (check west of the market on Albert Cuypstraat), and an increasing number of stylish shops and bars (especially on Eerste van der Helststraat).

### COOPERATIEHOF Map pp274-5
South of Ceintuurbaan, the Pijp contains some of the most interesting examples of early 20th-century housing estates built in the Amsterdam School style. The imposing Cooperatiehof, surrounded by Burgemeester Tellegenstraat, was designed for the socialist housing corporation De Dageraad (The Dawn) by one of the main Amsterdam School architects, Piet Kramer. Another leading architect, Michel de Klerk, designed the nearby idiosyncratic housing estates at **Henriëtte Ronnerplein** (Map pp274-5) and **Thérèse Schwartzeplein** (Map pp274-5).

As with other architecture of this school, the eccentric details are worth noting: vertically laid bricks, letterboxes as works of art, asymmetric windows, oddly shaped doorways, funny chimneys, creative solutions for corners and so forth. Don't forget to look up: sometimes the most interesting details are above the ground floor.

### GEMEENTEARCHIEF Map pp274-5
Municipal Archives; ☎ 572 02 02; Amsteldijk 67; admission free; ⏱ 10am-5pm Mon-Sat Sep-Jun, 10am-5pm Mon-Fri July & Aug
In the former town hall of Nieuwe Amstel, a town annexed by Amsterdam during the late 19th–century expansion, are the Amsterdam city archives. Anyone interested in their family history or the history of the city can peruse the archives free of charge, and occasionally there are very interesting exhibitions. There's a large library with books about Amsterdam in different languages on everything from housing to legal briefs and sports clubs.

### HEINEKEN EXPERIENCE Map pp286-7
☎ 523 96 66; www.heinekenexperience.com; Stadhouderskade 78; admission €7.50; ⏱ 10am-6pm Tue-Sun
On the site of the one-time (though not the original) Heineken brewery, you can take a self-guided tour through many forms of Heineken

## The World's Ultimate Pickup Line
Apart from his duties as international beer magnate, Freddy Heineken (1924–2002) had a reputation as a ladies' man. As the story goes, an attractive young lady approached the bar and uttered the familiar phrase: 'I'd like a Heineken, please'. Freddy (stationed nearby) replied: 'I'm right here.'

worship. You'll learn the history of the Heineken family, find out how the typeface on the logo evolved, and follow the brewing process from water to malting to the addition of hops etc, all the way through to bottling. Along the way, you get to watch Heineken commercials from around the world, watch a multimedia video of the life of a Heineken bottle and drive a virtual Heineken horse.

Feel a little Heineken-overwhelmed? You can quell it at 'tasting' sessions included in the tour, at which three glasses per person may be consumed. Homer Simpson would feel right at home.

If you're coming in summer or winter, expect lots of company on your tour. Visitors under 18 are only admitted under parental guidance.

The actual brewery closed in 1988 due to inner-city congestion, and since then the building has been used only for the tours and administration; the company's directorate is in the low-key premises across the canal. Heineken beer is now brewed at a larger plant in 's-Hertogenbosch (Den Bosch) in the south of the country that opened in 1950, and since 1975 also at the largest brewery in Europe at Zoeterwoude near Leiden.

### SARPHATIPARK Map pp286-7
South of Albert Cuypstraat is this English-style park named after the energetic 19th-century Jewish doctor and chemist Samuel Sarphati (1813–66). His diverse projects (a waste-disposal service, a slaughterhouse, a factory for cheap bread, trades and business schools, the Amstel Hotel, a mortgage bank) exasperated the dour city council, though many of these ventures survive to this day. The park contains a central fountain, nice lawns for picnicking or sprawling, and enough trees for privacy or shade.

The street running along the south side of the park is Ceintuurbaan, a traffic artery that holds little of interest to the casual observer except for the **Kabouterhuis** (Gnome House; Ceintuurbaan 251–255) near the Amstel. Its whimsical woodwork façade incorporates a couple of gnomes playing ball, a reference to the surname of the original owner, Van Ballegooijen ('of ball-throwing').

# GREATER AMSTERDAM

The city's population stabilised at around 700,000 by 1920, and is about 750,000 today. The authorities at the time didn't foresee this of course and cautiously expected 950,000 by the year 2000. Despite a slight pause during the Depression and WWII, the city kept gobbling up one outlying town after another as increased mobility fuelled urban sprawl.

## NIEUW ZUID (NEW SOUTH)

Map pp274-5

The Housing Act of 1901 set minimum standards for new houses and allowed for the compulsory purchase and demolition of old houses that didn't meet these standards. The act also forced municipal authorities to come up with proper blueprints for city expansion. One such plan was the Plan Zuid of 1917 for the south of the city, drawn up by the progressive architect Berlage and instigated by the Labour Party alderman FM Wibaut. The result was New South, between the Amstel and what was to become the Olympic Stadium.

Urban planners, architects and municipal authorities had not worked together so closely since the canal-belt project, successfully integrating solid housing and wide boulevards that enclosed quiet neighbourhoods with cosy squares. There was even a canal linking the Amstel in the east with the Schinkel in the west: the Amstelkanaal that split in two about halfway along and rejoined again behind the Olympic Stadium. Subsidised-housing corporations provided funding for innovative designs by architects of the Amsterdam School. Many of these architects worked for the city housing department, and the council preferred their designs to the functionalist designs of Berlage himself.

Funding cutbacks in the 1930s meant that these architects couldn't be as creative as they had been in their earlier designs, but even today the area is as elegant as it was then. Streets such as Churchillaan, Apollolaan and Stadionweg are 'good' addresses. The area's main shopping street, Beethovenstraat, is lined with expensive shops and other establishments for elderly women in fur coats.

Among the first residents were Jewish refugees from Germany and Austria, many of them writers and artists, who settled around Beethovenstraat. The Frank family first lived at Merwedeplein farther to the east, where Churchillaan and Rooseveltlaan merge around the **'Skyscraper'** (1930), a 12-storey building with spacious luxury apartments designed by JF Staal.

### RAI EXHIBITION AND CONFERENCE CENTRE Map pp274-5

☎ 549 12 12; www.rai.nl; Europaplein 22

Southwest of Nieuw Zuid is the **RAI** exhibition and conference centre, the largest such complex in the country. It opened in the early 1960s and new halls are still being added. There's always some sort of exhibition or trade fair going on. Attendance varies with economic times, but it gets in the neighbourhood of two million visitors per year.

## AMSTELVEEN

This suburb south of Amsterdam has a long history. In the 12th century it was a moor drained by the Amstel (*veen* means peat). Local farmers built canals to drain the land for agriculture, thus turning the Amstel into a clearly defined river. As the soil along the Amstel compacted, the farming community moved farther west, which is why the west bank of the Amstel at this latitude is relatively uninhabited today. There's not much to draw you to Amstelveen, but a couple of attractions are right up there.

### AMSTERDAMSE BOS Map pp274-5

Amsterdam Woods; visitors centre ☎ 643 14 14; Nieuwe Kalfjeslaan 4; admission free; ☼ visitors centre 8.30am-5pm, Ⓟ 24 hrs

This large recreational area was built as a work-creation project in the 1930s. Amsterdammers flock here on weekends, but it's so huge (940 hectares) that it never gets too crowded. Its only drawback is that it's close to Schiphol Airport and a lot of low-flying aircraft.

There are lakes, wooded areas and meadows, an animal enclosure with bison, a goat farm, paths for walking, cycling and horse riding, a rowing course (the Bosbaan, with several water craft for hire), an **open-air theatre** (p185; ☎ 626 36 47, 640 92 53) with plays in summer, a sports park, a pancake house, a **forestry museum** (☎ 676 21 52; admission free; ☒ 10am-5pm) with displays about the construction, flora and fauna of the area, and much more. To get here, take bus No 170, 171 or 172 from Centraal Station, or the historic tram from the Haarlemmermeer Station (p113). Bikes can be rented at the main entrance at Van Nijenrodeweg.

## COBRA MUSEUM
☎ 547 50 50; www.cobra-museum.nl; Sandbergplein 1; adult/senior/child €6/4/2.50; ☒ 11am-5pm Tue-Sun
The CoBrA artistic movement was formed in the postwar years by artists from Denmark, Belgium and the Netherlands – the name consists of the first letters of their capital cities. Members included Asger Jorn (Denmark), Corneille (Netherlands), Constant (Netherlands) and the great Karel Appel (Netherlands). The group lasted for just three years (1948–51), so changing exhibits feature the work of artists from outside the movement as well as inside.

CoBrA museum

Some critics hailed the CoBrA artists' work as bold, others thought it was derivative.

Especially now with the temporary relocation of the Stedelijk Museum, this contemporary, two-storey building is your best bet to catch the work of this fascinating group, with paintings, ceramics, statuary, creative typography etc. It's really quite an impressive place, even if it doesn't have the history, cachet or location of its bigger siblings.

Take bus No 170, 171 or 172 from Centraal Station or Tram No 5 to the end of the line – from the tram line, walk through or around Vroom & Dreesman department store, through the Binnenhof and Rembrandt Hof shopping centres. Buses stop in front of the museum.

# AMSTERDAM NOORD (NORTH)
Map pp274-5
In the dim, dark past, the area across the IJ now known as Amsterdam North was marshland with shifting contours. Roman sentries may have stared at it and glimpsed the barbarians beyond their empire. Several centuries ago its tip was known as Volewyck, a place where executed criminals were left to be devoured by crows and dogs. Few people actually lived here.

As ships became larger and the sandbanks in the IJ posed more of a problem, engineers built an 80km canal, the Noordhollands Kanaal (North Holland Canal), from Volewyck right up to Den Helder in the northern tip of Holland. It opened in 1824, but by 1876 it was replaced by the more efficient Noordzeekanaal (North Sea Canal) west to IJmuiden. Even so, Amsterdam North wasn't properly colonised until the turn of the 20th century, and the opening of the IJ-Tunnel in 1968 finally established a fixed connection.

The area is predominantly working-class, offering glimpses of authentic Dutch life away from the tourists in the old town, though its character is set to change with large-scale renovation and restructuring over the next decade. If you have time, it's worth spending half a day exploring the older parts of the area on foot or by bicycle.

Take the free pedestrian ferry marked 'Buiksloterweg' (between Pier 8 and Pier 9) from behind Centraal Station across the IJ toward the Shell Oil installations at Buiksloterweg (you can't miss Shell's skyscraper to the left), and you'll disembark next to the Noordhollands Kanaal. The pleasant café and occasional nightspot **Het Ponthuys** (p169) is right across from the dock.

Climb up onto the first lock, the Willemsluis near the ferry wharf, for the view. Return to the main street and walk north 10 minutes toward Van der Pekstraat. If you take the right fork in the road, you might feel as if you've left Amsterdam for a country lane with houseboats lining the canal and plenty of greenery. You might also stop at the cosy café **Ot en Sien**, a great place for local colour. Continuing north on Van der Pekstraat you'll eventually see the massive NH City Hotel North, formerly Amsterdam North's general hospital.

A passageway to the right of the hotel leads into **Mosveld** where a large public **market** (⌚ 9am-5pm Wed, Fri & Sat) takes place. Market days are the best time to do this walk: you can mingle with local residents and will seldom see any tourists. There's a large **Egyptian Coptic Church** on Mosplein.

To return to central Amsterdam, catch bus No 34, 35, 92, 94, 171 or 172 back to Centraal Station.

If you have a bit more time, take any street east to the Noordhollands Kanaal, which you follow north through **Florapark**. You'll pass a public swimming pool and reach a small bridge which crosses another lock on the canal. The old road on both sides of this bridge is lined with picturesque little Dutch cottages. Don't cross the canal but continue north along its west bank and you'll come to a large windmill, the **Krijtmolen**, originally used to grind chalk, with a children's animal park alongside (free). Just north of here is Amsterdam Noord's massive public hospital, from where you can catch a bus back to town.

This diverting walk could easily fill a morning or afternoon; by bicycle it would take a couple of leisurely hours.

# 'GARDEN CITIES' Map pp274-5

The outer suburbs west of Amsterdam – **Geuzenveld**, **Bos en Lommer**, **Slotermeer**, **Osdorp** and **Slotervaart** – were planned in the 1930s as part of the city's grand General Extension Plan. They were fully established after WWII to meet the continued demand for housing, made ever more acute by the demographic shift away from extended families. These spacious new estates, known as 'garden cities' *(tuinsteden)* – with carefully planned traffic systems, lakes, sporting fields, greenery and abundant natural light – represented the latest thinking in suburban living, but seem rather dreary and windswept today.

Similar concepts dominated the massive Bijlmermeer housing project southeast of the city, now simply called the **Bijlmer**. The huge apartment blocks, laid out in a honeycomb pattern around artificial parks, were considered most progressive when the foundations were laid in the mid-1960s. By the time they were finished in the 1970s, however, most people with a choice in the matter avoided such an environment and the area was doomed to become an instant slum, inhabited by Creole immigrants from the Netherlands Antilles, Black immigrants from newly independent Suriname, and anyone else who couldn't afford to live elsewhere.

In 1992 the Bijlmer made world headlines when an El Al freighter jumbo crashed into one of the apartment complexes after take-off from Schiphol, just as residents were settling in to their evening meals. Officially 45 people died in the inferno but the figure was probably higher, despite the subsequent amnesty on illegal immigrants.

The western 'garden cities' as well as the Bijlmer are due for massive renovation and restructuring over the next 15 years, with the pervasive apartment blocks making way for a blend of medium-density housing estates on a more human scale, as well as large commercial venues. In the case of the Bijlmer, building works have already begun. One signature project is the **Amsterdam ArenA** (p186), the large-scale venue where Amsterdam's Ajax football (soccer) club plays, which is also a concert venue (tours are available). The **Heineken Music Hall** (p180) is another new (2001) concert venue nearby.

# Walking & Cycling Tours

# Walking & Cycling Tours

Amsterdam is a joy to discover on foot. Most of the sights are within easy walking distance in the compact city centre. You can also get lost as in Venice, but never as comprehensively.

Cycling is also an ideal way to get around town, but the city is surrounded by some very pretty countryside, often serene, flat and unbelievably green. Church steeples and the occasional windmill dot the horizon. Take a half- or full-day excursion, and you'll begin to understand how Dutch artists were inspired to paint such dramatic skies.

## WALKING TOURS

There are a number of speciality tours (p55), and the VVV publishes handsomely prepared, comprehensive walking/cycling guides to Rembrandt's Amsterdam (€2.50, with two routes) and the city (€2.95). A Jordaan guide was in the works as we went to press.

### THE VEDDY CIVILISED WESTERN CANALS

Far from its farmland beginnings, today the **Dam 1** (p58) is dominated by the **Royal Palace 2** (p60), worth a visit for its grand interior and art collection. To the right, the impressive **Nieuwe Kerk 3** (p59) often stages excellent exhibitions, while **Madame Tussaud Scenerama 4** (good for kids) is to the left.

Head west, and across Nieuwezijds Voorburgwal you'll see the massive shopping complex **Magna Plaza 5** (p77) – check out its atrium lobby and, if you like, dozens of shops. Continue west and then north towards **Torensluis 6** (p77), the bridge over our first canal, the Singel. If you're craving coffee

> **Walk Facts**
> **Start/End** The Dam
> **Distance** 3.9km
> **Time** 3 hours (with time for browsing and relaxing – add more for visiting museums)

and apple pie, **Villa Zeezicht 7** (p138) has about the best in town. The bridge features a statue of the Dutch literary giant **Multatuli 8** (p77); there's a **museum 9** (☎ 638 19 38; Korsjespoortsteeg 20; admission free; ⏰ 10am-5pm Sat & Sun) dedicated to him a few blocks north.

The Singel soon intersects with the pretty **Brouwersgracht 10** (p80). Cross over Brouwersgracht and head west to the head of the Herengracht, one of our favourite views in town, with boats passing in three directions. Behind you, to the north is Herenmarkt, with the 17th-century **Westindisch Huis 11** (p88). On the northern side of this building is Haarlemmerstraat, home to interesting one-off boutiques. You'll also find fancy snacking opportunities galore here, particularly the adventurous chocolates at **Unlimited Delicious 12** (p203).

> **Caution!**
> Statistics show that the Netherlands is Europe's safest country for pedestrians – you're more than twice as likely to be run over by a car in Britain. But beware of bicycles: reddish-coloured pavement is reserved for cyclists, who can get quite angry when pedestrians get in the way, as foreign visitors often do inadvertently. Also, there's a lot of irregular brick or cobblestone paving, so avoid high heels.
> Finally, two important words: dog poo.

Continue west back along Brouwersgracht, then turn south onto the eastern side of Prinsengracht to the imposing **Noorderkerk 13** (p86): on the right day, you can visit a busy **market 14** (p87). Dogleg left into Keizersgracht, with the curious **House with the Heads 15** (p82). At peaceful Leliegracht, by the **Greenpeace Building 16** (p82), return to Prinsengracht to pass the **Anne Frank Huis 17** (p80) and the soaring tower of the **Westerkerk 18** (p83). Behind it is Karin Dann's quietly moving **Homomonument 19** (p82) and to its north the house where **René**

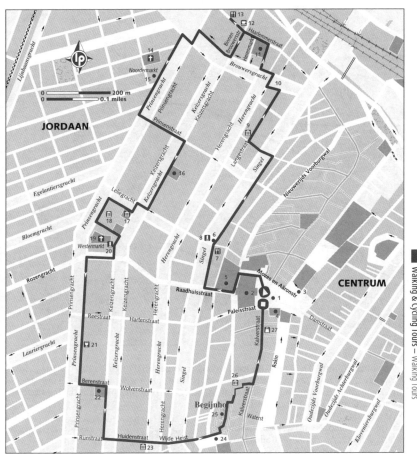

Descartes 20 (p82) stayed during his sojourn in Amsterdam. Further south on Prinsengracht is Van Puffelen 21 (p158), an atmospheric brown café.

Back on Keizersgracht, you can't miss the quirky Felix Meritis building 22 (p161), a one-time enlightenment society turned alternative theatre. Cross the canals again and head east to the Bijbels Museum 23 (p83), with its impressive models of biblical sites, en route to the Spui 24 (p78), for a coffee, be er or weekend book and art markets. The Begijnhof 25 (p75) is just off the square, but check the opening hours first — at time of writing, it was open only in the mornings. The Amsterdams Historisch Museum 26 (p75) is just up the alley. The busy shopping street Kalverstraat 27 (p75) leads you back to the Dam.

## ART & NATURE WALK

Although the Rijksmuseum 1 (p110) will be mostly closed for construction by the time you read this, its grand exterior makes a great starting point. Walk through the beautiful brick underpass to Museumplein, a monumental grassy expanse for lolling, walking and open-air concerts. To your right, on the corner of Hobbemakade, is Coster Diamonds 2 (p199), where you can take a free tour – diamonds are a kind of art, aren't they? Or you can continue along Museumplein to the Van Gogh Museum 3 (p111), with its modern,

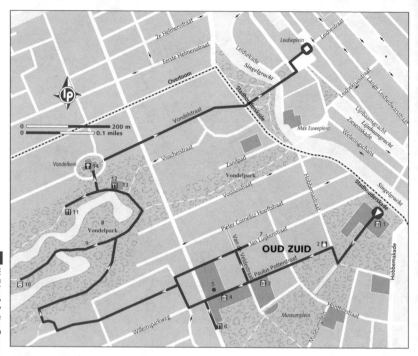

mussel-like- annexe. The **Stedelijk Museum 4** (p111) is next door, though it's also due to be closed for repairs. The neoclassical **Concertgebouw 5** (p110) is in plain view across Van Baerlestraat – check schedules for a free lunch-time concert, otherwise pick up a picnic at the big **Albert Heijn supermarket 6** (p131) on Museumplein.

Weave northwest through a quiet residential quarter (shoppers may detour to **Pieter Cornelisz Hoofstraat 7**, Amsterdam's Rodeo Drive) to the sprawling **Vondelpark 8**; highlights include a **rose garden 9** and an **open-air theatre 10** (p113). Refreshment options abound: enjoy coffee and cake in the **Round Blue Teahouse 11** (p113) or the parkside **Vertigo 12** (p113) at the **Filmmuseum 13** (p112). Step out of the park to admire the **Vondelkerk 14** (p113), a pretty 19th-century church turned office complex, before heading either back into the park or along Vondelstraat towards the buzz of Leidseplein. It's a simple walk, or you can head one block north of Vondelstraat to Overtoom, to catch tram No 1 back towards the central canal belt.

| Walk Facts | |
| --- | --- |
| **Start** Rijksmuseum | |
| **End** Leidseplein | |
| **Distance** 4km | |
| **Time** 4 hours | |

## RED LIGHT RAMBLE

Begin at the **Nationaal Monument 1** (p59) and head north along Damrak past the elegant **Beurs Van Berlage 2** (p58), designed by one of Amsterdam's signature architects, HP Berlage (p39). Heading southeast along Oude Brugsteeg, you'll hit **Warmoesstraat 3** (p61) – here you can get a sample of the city's wild side. If this looks like it will be too much for you, turn back now! The venerable **Oude Kerk 4** (p61) is your gateway to the Red Light District proper. North from here, on this side of Oudezijds Voorburgwal, is the **Museum Amstelkring 5** (p63), with its clandestine Catholic church on the top floor. A jump over to the Oudezijds Achterburgwal and then south takes

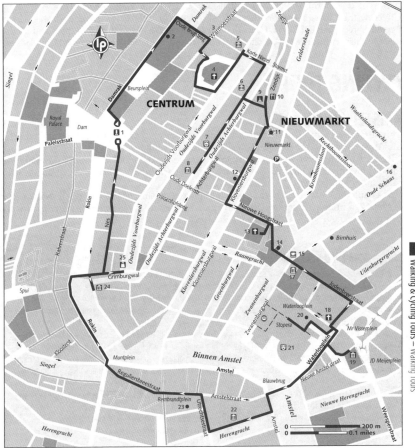

you past the low-key **Erotic Museum 6** (p62), the famous **Casa Rosso 7** (p61) erotic theatre, and the **Hash and Marijuana Museum 8** (p62).

Back up near the Erotic Museum, cross the canal and head east toward the **Guan Yin Buddhist Temple 9** (p64), and a good place to break for Chinese lunch or dinner, **Nam Kee 10** or its compatriots (p135). In Nieuwmarkt Square, you'll find the historic and multitowered **Waag 11** (Weigh House; p64). Heading south from Nieuwmarkt, note the impossibly narrow **Kleine Trippenhuis 12** (p66). Nieuwe Hoogstraat leads you to the elegant **Zuiderkerk 13** (p99), with the 17th-century **Pintohuis 14** (now a library; p97) nearly opposite.

Across the Oude Schans, **De Sluyswacht 15** (p156) makes an ideal beer break, with a classic view of the **Montelbaanstoren 16** (p97).

**Walk Facts**

**Start/End** The Dam
**Distance** 4.5km
**Time** 3 hours

The **Museum Het Rembrandthuis 17** (p97) is across the street. A sweep down Jodenbreestraat takes you past the **Mozes en Aäronkerk 18** (p98); 100m southeast is the **Joods (Jewish) Historical Museum 19** (p99). The **Waterlooplein market 20** (p97) faces the **Stopera 21**(p98), the opera house and city hall; check out the market before crossing the Blauwbrug.

Stop at the charming **Museum Willet-Holthuysen 22** (p91) on Herengracht. Turn right onto Utrechtsestraat toward **Rembrandtplein 23** (p95; plenty of cafés here). Head northwest along Reguliersbreestraat and Rokin. Cross the Amstel to the **Allard Pierson Museum 24** (p59) and its antiquities, inspect the **jewellery shops 25** (p193) of Grimburgwal, then return to the Dam via Nes.

# CYCLING TOURS

## AMSTEL ROUTE

This attractive, convenient route begins in the southern suburb of Amstelveen and takes in the Amstel River and some unexpectedly bucolic surrounds.

Leave from the **Amstelpark 1**, a pretty municipal park, about 300m south of the A10 motorway. Cycling isn't allowed in the park, which has a rose garden, an open-air theatre, cafés and other facilities.

A couple of kilometres south, along the quiet east bank of the Amstel, is **Ouderkerk aan de Amstel 2**, a pretty, affluent village (actually a few centuries older than Amsterdam) with plenty of riverside cafés and handsome houses.

### *Fiets*, don't fail me now!

In Dutch, a bicycle is called a *rijwiel*, or to its friends, a *fiets*. Cyclists are called *fietsers*, a term we adore.

Cycling is our favourite way to get around the city. Although the distances in town are not extreme, saving 20 minutes between venues can buy you time to explore one or two more sights each day. Plus, you'll feel like a native: sling your shopping bag from the Albert Heijn over the handlebars, hold on to the grip with one hand and your sandwich or mobile phone with the other, and you'll fit right in.

Don't bother bringing your bike from home. Your 21-speed racer with handbrakes and toe clips will get you attention all right: (1) for its dashing looks and (2) for the pity you'll receive when it's stolen. Amsterdam's bike of choice seems to be the Gazelle, a gearless, Dutch-made dearie with pedal brakes and – most importantly – a bell. The more trashed the better. And what is this thing you call a 'helmet'? There are plenty of rental shops to set you up (p243); some lodgings also rent bikes.

It all sounds like fun, and indeed it can be, but there are some important rules of the road. So, if we may beg a few moments of your kind attention. . .

- There are 400km of bike paths in Amsterdam. Use them. You can identify them by signage and because they are a different colour (reddish) from the road or the footpaths. Bike paths have their own dedicated traffic signals. Use those too.
- Watch for cars. Cyclists have the right of way, except when vehicles are entering from the right. However, that doesn't mean motorists are as careful as they should be.
- Watch for pedestrians too. Tourists (the poor things) tend to wander in and out of bike paths with no idea of the danger they're putting themselves in.
- The international 'no' sign with a picture of a bike on it (or a blue sign with pedestrians) means you need to walk your bike. If it reads *'fietsers afstappen'* (cyclists dismount), they're putting it in no uncertain terms. If there's a 'no-entry' sign and below it a sign with a picture of a bike and the word *uitgezonderd* (except), you may ride through.
- When approaching tram tracks, be careful. If your wheels get caught, you'll probably fall and it will hurt! Position your wheels as perpendicular to the tracks as possible.
- By law, after dusk you need to use the lights on your bike (front and rear) and have reflectors on both wheels.
- It's polite to give a quick ring of your bell as a warning. If someone's about to hit you, a good sharp *'Heij'* ('hey!') is in order.
- Chain your bike securely. Most bikes come with two locks, one for the front wheel (attach it to the frame) and the other for the back. One lock should also attach to something stationary.

You'll see plenty of locals disobeying these rules, but that does not make it smart. Theoretically you could jump off a bridge and survive that too.

Finally, weather: wind and rain are all-too-familiar features in Holland. A lightweight nylon jacket and cycling trousers or shorts will provide protection, but be sure to use a variety that breathes. On other than warm days, a woollen cap or balaclava is a good idea to keep your ears from freezing.

At Ouderkerk, cross the bridge over the Bullewijk River and turn left (east) opposite the ancient Jewish cemetery, following the right bank of the Bullewijk. You pass under the A9 motorway, and about 1km further on, at a spot with a pleasant restaurant, the Waver River comes in from the right (south) – follow that. You'll have great views of **De Ronde Hoep 3**, a wild, sparsely populated peat area drained by settlers about 1000 years ago. It attracts many birds, impervious to Amsterdam's skyscrapers looming in the distance. The Waver narrows and becomes the Oude Waver, and when you come to the two hand-operated bridges, you'll clearly see that the land is below sea level.

At the southwesternmost part of the route lies a squat riverside **bunker 4**, one of 38 defensive forts built around Amsterdam at the turn of the 20th century (and outmoded by the 1920s). Here you rejoin the Amstel and turn right (north), following the eastern bank back toward Amstelveen. Just north of here, the village of **Nes aan de Amstel 5**, across the river, has some delightful wooden, café-filled terraces – admire them from a distance, as there's no bridge close by.

Crossing north under the A9, the final leg of the journey provides a view towards the western edges of Amsterdam-Zuidoost. You could continue past Ouderkerk and return the way you came, along the east bank of the Amstel, but an interesting diversion takes you across the bridge at Ouderkerk to the west bank and around the fringes of the green Amstelland area, with oodles of all-too-cute garden allotments. The Amstelpark lies just to the north.

# WATERLAND ROUTE

This trip through the eastern half of Waterland is culture-shock material: 20 minutes from the centre of Amsterdam, but back a couple of centuries, with isolated farming communities and flocks of birds amid ditches, dykes and lakes.

Take the free Buiksloterweg ferry from behind Centraal Station across the IJ (p54), and continue 1km along the west bank of the Noordhollands Kanaal. Do a loop onto and over the second bridge, continue along the east bank for a few hundred metres and turn right, under the freeway and along Nieuwendammerdijk past the Vliegenbos camping ground. At the end of Nieuwendammerdijk, do a dogleg and continue along Schellingwouderdijk. Follow this under the two major road bridges, when it becomes Durgerdammerdijk, and you're on your way.

The pretty town of **Durgerdam 1**, spread along the dyke, looks out across the water to IJburg, a major land-reclamation project that will be home to 45,000 people in a few years' time.

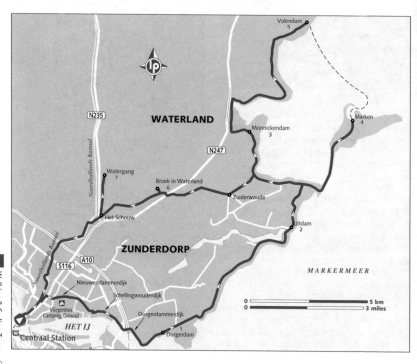

Further north, the dyke road passes several lakes and former sea inlets – low-lying, drained peat lands that were flooded during storms and now form important bird-breeding areas. Colonies include plovers, godwits, bitterns, goldeneyes, snipes, herons and spoonbills. Climb the dyke at one of the viewing points for uninterrupted views to both sides.

The road – now called Uitdammerdijk – passes the town of **Uitdam 2**, after which you turn left (west) towards **Monnickendam 3**, with its many old fishing homes and 15th-century church. Alternatively, you could turn right and proceed along the causeway to the former island of **Marken 4**, a one-time fishing community in an impressive setting, with houses on piles. After visiting Marken, you could take the summer ferry (adult/child €6.25/3.50; 🕒 every 30 to 45 minutes Apr–mid Nov) to **Volendam 5**. This picturesque former fishing port reinvented itself as a tourist town – there are fewer tourists in the pretty streets behind the harbour. From Volendam, backtrack along the sea dyke to Monnickendam, or return over the causeway from Marken and rejoin the tour towards Monnickendam.

After visiting Monnickendam, return the way you came, but about 1.5km south of Monnickendam, turn right (southwest) towards Zuiderwoude. From there, continue to **Broek in Waterland 6**, a pretty town with old, wooden houses. Then cycle along the south bank of the Broekervaart canal towards Het Schouw on the Noordhollands Kanaal. Bird-watchers may want to head up the east bank towards **Watergang 7** and its bird-breeding areas. Otherwise, cross the Noordhollands Kanaal (the bridge is slightly to the north) and follow the west bank back down to Amsterdam Noord; its straight cycling all the way to the ferry to Centraal Station.

**Cycle Facts**

**Start/End** Centraal Station
**Distance** 37km (55km including Marken & Volendam)
**Time** 3½–5 hours (7–10 hours including Marken & Volendam)

# VECHT ROUTE

The Vecht River southeast of Amsterdam was an important waterway to the city of Utrecht before the completion of the Amsterdam Rijnkanaal (Amsterdam-Rhine Canal), but it's peaceful now. The scenery is not as starkly rural as along the Amstel River, though the small towns, woods and 17th- and 18th-century country mansions provide plenty of variety.

Take your bicycle on the train to **Weesp 1**. From Weesp station, follow the west bank south for a few hundred metres and cross the bridge to the opposite bank. Turn left (north) to go to **Muiden 2** if you wish – it's highly recommended, and is only 3.5km along the pleasant east bank of the Vecht. The 13th-century **Muiderslot 3** (Muiden Castle; ☎ 0294-26 13 25; Herengracht 1; adult/child €5.50/4; ⏱ 10am-5pm Mon-Fri, 1-5pm Sat & Sun Apr-Oct, 1-4pm Sat & Sun Nov-Mar) is where the popular count of Holland was murdered in 1296. In the 17th century the multi-talented PC Hooft entertained gatherings of the century's greatest artists and scientists here, including Vondel, Huygens, Grotius, Bredero

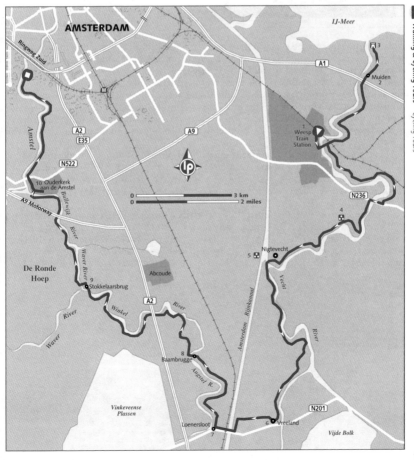

and probably Descartes. The period rooms are open only by guided tour and are quite spectacular even if there are no tours in English.

If you don't want to go to Muiden, head south for 4km as the road winds along the river, with farmland to your left. For the last kilometre or so the road heads inland a bit but returns to a bridge across the river (just bear right when you get to the N236 main road). Cross the bridge to the west bank and continue south along the river.

One kilometre further on you'll pass **Fort Hinderdam 4** , part of a series of forts built before WWI to protect Amsterdam from invasion. The idea was to flood the land to deter approaching troops, but this tactic was already outdated by the start of the 20th century. The forts along this so-called 'inundation line' are now on the Unesco World Heritage List.

Continue along the Vecht and you'll arrive at the town of **Nigtevecht 5**. At the west end of town you cross the sluice to the Amsterdam Rijnkanaal, with another fort across the choppy waters. Stay on the west bank of the Vecht and continue south. This pretty stretch along the Hoekerpolder takes you 6.5km to **Vreeland 6**.

At Vreeland, say goodbye to the Vecht and head west – not along the N201 main road but along a road through farmland a little to the north – until you reach the Amsterdam Rijnkanaal again. Turn left (south) and cross the bridge over the canal. This takes you into the town of **Loenersloot 7**, where you turn right (north) and follow the Angstel River to **Baambrugge 8**. Here you cross the Angstel to the west side and continue northwest in the direction of Abcoude.

Don't go all the way to Abcoude, though: after about 2.5km you should turn left at a T-junction. Proceed under the A2 motorway, past the settlements of Zeldenrust and Holendrecht, and eventually you'll end up at another T-junction at **Stokkelaarsbrug 9**. This is where the Winkel River (which you've been following for the past 3km or so), joins the Waver River.

Here you hook up with the Amstel Route described earlier (p124), except you'll be riding in the opposite direction. Head right along the bank of the Waver and after 1km turn left along the bank of the Bullewijk River, which takes you to pretty **Ouderkerk aan de Amstel 10**. Here you cross the second bridge over the Bullewijk, maybe pause at one of Ouderkerk's many riverside cafés, and head down the east bank of the Amstel River back to Amsterdam.

# Eating

# Eating

Even if Amsterdam is not the food Mecca that other European capitals are, there's a great diversity of choice. Italian, French, Indonesian, Thai and Chinese are commonplace, and sushi, Indian and Turkish are gaining in popularity. Plus there are some cuisines you may never have tried (eg Surinamese) that may pleasantly surprise you. And don't neglect traditional Dutch cooking: while it may not be high cuisine, here you have a unique opportunity to try it.

One of the best things about dining in Amsterdam is the design of its restaurants. From the sumptuously decorated interiors of the city's supper clubs, to places that wear their history like a fine suit, or just convivial canalside seating, you can feast your eyes as well as your stomach.

It's quite common for fine-dining restaurants to change menus seasonally, if not daily. Where we have listed individual dishes, they're either something that is always on the menu or a reference to give you an idea of the creativity of the cuisine. Most restaurants have a few vegetarian choices.

## Opening Hours

Dinner, the main meal of the day, is served between 6pm and 10pm. Most places that refer to themselves as 'restaurants' (as opposed to 'cafés'), open only for dinner, and popular places fill up by 7pm – book ahead, arrive early, or be prepared to wait at the bar. Alternatively you could try arriving late: films and concerts usually start between 8.30pm and 9.30pm, and tables may become available then for a 'second sitting'.

Many kitchens close by 10pm (though the bars and dining rooms may stay open longer); vegetarian restaurants tend to close even earlier. Late-night, there's a smattering of restaurants around Leidesplein and falafel or pizza joints citywide.

For lunch, your best bets are cafés. They're everywhere, and meals tend to be reliable if not life-changing – soups, sandwiches, salads, etc. Many open as early as 10am, and the standard time for serving lunch is 11am to 2.30pm; cafés have the added bonus of staying open late (though usually not their kitchens) and being great places to hang out. Many places listed as serving lunch may also stay open until late afternoon.

Breakfast can be problematic. Unless your hotel serves breakfast, you may need to wait until the cafés open or find a bakery. If you're used to bagels for breakfast, get used to eating them at lunchtime – they're mostly for sandwiches here. On Sundays all bets are off.

Many restaurants are open daily; otherwise the most popular closing days are Sunday and Monday. During the top tourist months of July and (especially) August, some restaurants go on holiday, so phone ahead to avoid disappointment.

## How Much?

Amsterdam used to be known as one of Western Europe's least-expensive capitals. It remains reasonable by comparison to some other places (hello, London and Paris), but prices have gone up significantly – particularly, locals complain, since the introduction of the Euro.

Lunch prices hover between €2.50 for a simple cheese sandwich and €10 for an elaborate salad; most sandwiches are under €5. Main courses at moderate restaurants run between €8 and €20 (lunch or dinner) – to keep costs down, look for the *dagschotel* (dish of the day). For heartier appetites, many restaurants offer the *dagmenu*, a set menu of three or more courses for around €9 to €15 (lunch) and from about €20 (dinner). Except at top-end restaurants, it's rare to see a main course above €27.50 (usually something like lobster) or a four course menu above €50. Main course servings are usually generous.

Breakfast out is the one meal of the day we find almost universally overpriced: at a café, you can expect to pay upwards of €5 for a meagre meal of coffee, something baked and maybe some orange juice. Insider tip: for about twice that, some hotels offer generous buffet breakfasts. At bakeries, muffins and croissants start from about €0.80.

For snacks and light meals, there are plenty of small shops and stands serving *broodjes* (sandwiches), starting around €1.75 – many sandwich shops are 'build-your-own' affairs, and prices rise according to the ingredients you add, some also specialise in fish. Virtually any butcher shop, fishmonger or supermarket with a deli counter will also make sandwiches.

A beer will generally set you back around €2, with non-alcoholic drinks slightly less. House wines by the glass are generally €3 to €5, although the sky's the limit on bottles of wine – bottles that cost €4.50 in the shops can sell for up to €20 in a café.

Beware that many restaurants do *not* accept credit cards; check in advance.

*Winter Garden, Grand Hotel Krasnopolsky (p138)*

## Booking Tables

Except at the busiest, most-uppercrust restaurants, booking a table is rarely a problem, and virtually everyone speaks excellent English. Apart from Fridays and Saturdays, a simple phone call a day or two before your arrival should do the trick. Seating at most cafés is first-come-first-served.

## Tipping

If you're from a 'service-with-a-smile', kind of society, service in Amsterdam may strike you as inattentive, impersonal, off-putting and just plain slow. This is not confined to restaurants.

Our advice: (1) don't take it personally – it's not directed at you; and (2) turn it to your advantage. If it's taking forever for the waitress to bring your main course, savour the delicate bouquet of your beer. If you and your friends have to wait an eternity for the bill, just be *gezellig* – you're enjoying each other's company, so what's the problem?

Service is included in the bill, but unless your server does something truly rude, inept or egregious, a modest tip is in order. A good guideline is to round up to the next round-ish number around 5%; 10% is considered very generous. In practical terms, if your bill comes to €9.55, you can leave €10; if it's €14.75, round up to €15.50. Tax is always figured into the bill before it's presented to you.

If you're paying by credit card or need change, state the amount you want to pay, including tip, as you hand your payment to your server (this will usually elicit a proper 'thank you'!). Credit card users: note that servers generally appreciate being tipped in cash – in some restaurants they do not receive tips until after the credit card payment clears.

## Self Catering

Amsterdam is blessed with a number of excellent takeout shops; many are *traiteurs* (caterers) that operate out of storefronts. The current trend is mostly Mediterranean, but you might well find Middle Eastern or Indonesian. See Pasta di Mamma (p145), Small World Catering (p143), Sterk Staaltje (p138), Uliveto (p147) and van Dam (p147). Department stores like de Bijenkorf (p193) and Vroom & Dreesman (p199) have worthwhile cafeterias.

The supermarket chain Albert Heijn is pretty much everywhere, although it's known for being a tad expensive (look for a white logo that looks something like a bow, on a blue background).

Less-expensive supermarkets include Dirk van den Broek and Aldi, though the latter is somewhat downmarket. And of course there are farmers markets throughout town (p192).

The chain Gall & Gall sells wine and alcohol – it's often found near an Albert Heijn. We have also listed some finer wine shops in the shopping chapter.

Bottles made of heavy plastic are subject to a deposit (€0.25) but do not have to be returned to the store where they were purchased. Glass bottles can be recycled in receptacles all over town, especially in residential districts. Given the otherwise generally progressive nature of the Netherlands on environmental issues, it's surprising that Amsterdam does not recycle other types of plastic or metal containers, especially those for soft drinks.

# Cuisines

## DUTCH

Traditional Dutch cuisine concentrates on filling the stomach rather than titillating the taste buds, based on a rudimentary meat, potato and vegetable theme and served in large portions. That said, contemporary Dutch chefs have made some great strides, and what's now called 'Dutch' may have echoes of the Mediterranean. Even contemporary Dutch kitchens might include some Dutch staples, especially in winter, that are filling and good value.

Some of the more traditional Dutch dishes include *Stamppot* (mashed pot), which is potatoes mashed with vegetables (usually kale or endive) and served with smoked sausage or strips of pork. *Hutspot*, similar to *stamppot* but with carrots, onions and braised meat, is a popular winter dish. *Erwtensoep* is a thick pea soup (a spoon stuck upright in the pot should fall over slowly) with smoked sausage and bacon.

White *asperges* (asparagus), served with ham and butter, is very popular in the spring. *Mosselen* (mussels) are best eaten from September to April; the classic preparation is to cook them with white wine, chopped leeks and onions, and serve with a side of *frites* or *patat* (French fries). Use an empty shell as a pincer to pluck out the bodies, and don't eat mussels that haven't opened properly as they can be poisonous.

Year-round favourites include the ever-present *broodjes*, about which the translation of 'sandwiches' doesn't begin to tell the story. Quality *broodjeswinkels* or *broodjeszaken* (sandwich shops) are small but elaborate delis. Pile your choice of hot or cold ingredients onto a choice of breads and rolls, from roast beef or fish salads to cheeses and *kroketten* (croquettes) and *osseworst* (raw beef sausage, a Dutch delicacy). Wash it down with a beer or a cool glass of *melk (milk)*. *Kroketten* (croquettes) are a Dutch classic and consist of dough-ragout with meat (sometimes fish or shrimp) that's crumbed and deep-fried, they are also served in the form of small balls called *bitterballen* and served with mustard – a popular pub snack. *Pannenkoeken* translates as 'pancakes', although North Americans will be in for a surprise – the Dutch variety are huge and a little pully. In form they look like French crepes, served flat, one to a plate and topped from among hundreds of combinations of ingredients both sweet and savoury. Often they're a meal rather than a snack or dessert.

There's plenty of seafood, even if it doesn't feature as prominently as you'd expect in a seafaring nation. It's often available at stalls at strategic locations around the city. *Haring* (herring) is a national institution, eaten lightly salted or occasionally pickled but never fried or cooked – your Dutch friends may well point out that their nation was centuries ahead of the raw fish trend that became fashionable with sushi. Don't expect elegant slivers over vinegared rice, however; a Dutch herring is decapitated, split, filleted, and served pretty much as is, with diced onion and sometimes sweet pickle chips as a garnish, and that's the way we like it. *Paling* (eel) is another favourite, usually smoked. Don't dismiss either of these until you've tried them!

Other popular fish include *schol* (plaice), *tong* (sole), *kabeljauw* (cod) and freshwater *forel* (trout). *Garnalen* (shrimps, prawns) are also found on many menus, large species are often called by their Italian name of *scampi*. On Mondays, fish tends to be old and the locals avoid it – fish shops and herring stalls are closed then too.

Some typically Dutch desserts are fruit pie (apple, cherry, banana cream or other fruit), *vla* (custard) and pancakes. Many snack bars and pubs serve *appeltaart* (apple pie) and coffee throughout the day – there's a reason Dutch apple pie is so admired. Good places to try it are Villa Zeezicht (p138) and Winkel (p143).

# Traditional Dutch Dishes

## Dutch Pea Soup

This thick soup tastes even better the next day. Serve with hot, crusty bread.

3 cups split green peas
1 pig's trotter
1 pig's ear
1 cup diced bacon
1kg potatoes
2 leeks
2 onions
1 celeriac
4 frankfurters
salt and pepper to taste

- Wash peas, cover with water and soak overnight.
- Boil softened peas in 3L of water for one hour.
- Add pig's trotter, ear and bacon and continue to cook for two hours.
- Add sliced potatoes, diced leeks, diced onions and diced celeriac and simmer for a further one hour.
- Add sliced frankfurters to soup for the last five minutes. Season with salt and pepper.

## Dutch Appeltaart

1 packet shortcrust pastry
1½ tsp gelatine
1kg/2.2lbs apples
1 tbsp lemon juice
2 tbsp sugar
2 tsp cinnamon
150g/5¼ ounces of dried fruit soaked in 3 tbsp rum
¼ cup butter
1 tbsp milk
1 tsp caster sugar
½ cup whipped cream

- Preheat oven to 175ºC/350ºF.
- Use three-quarters of the shortcrust pastry dough to line base and sides of a 24cm/9in greased round cake tin; sprinkle with the gelatine.
- Peel and core apples, slice thinly, sprinkle with lemon juice and mix in sugar and 1 tsp of cinnamon.
- Place alternate layers of apple slices and dried fruit in tin, sprinkling each layer with some cinnamon and sugar. Use apples for the top layer and dot with butter.
- Roll the remaining dough into a rectangle, cut into 1cm-wide strips and lay in a lattice over fruit, sealing at ends; brush with milk, and sprinkle caster sugar mixed with remaining cinnamon on top.
- Bake for 45 minutes or till golden.
- Cool and serve with a generous amount of whipped cream.

Eating

## INDONESIAN

A tasty legacy of Dutch colonial history. Some dishes, such as the famous *rijsttafel* (rice table – white rice with lots of side dishes), are colonial concoctions rather than traditional Indonesian, but that doesn't make them less appealing. If you're not up for a large, expensive *rijsttafel* meal, consider *nasi rames* (literally, boiled rice), a plate of rice covered in several accompaniments that would be served in separate bowls in a *rijsttafel*. The same dish with thick noodles is called *bami rames*.

*Gado-gado* (lightly steamed vegetables and hard-boiled egg, served with peanut sauce and rice) feels good in all respects. *Saté* or *sateh* (satay) is marinated, barbecued beef, chicken or pork on small skewers; the best versions are cooked over a grill and coated lightly (not smothered) in peanut sauce. Other stand-bys are *nasi goreng* (fried rice with onions, pork, shrimp and spices, often topped with a fried egg or shredded omelette) and *bami goreng* (the same thing but with noodles).

Indonesian food is usually served mild for Western palates. If you want it hot (*pedis*, pronounced 'p-*dis*'), say so but be prepared for the ride of a lifetime. If you're unsure, you can play it safe by asking for *sambal* (chilli paste – it may already be on the table) and helping yourself. Usually it's *sambal oelek*, which is red and hot; the dark-brown *sambal badjak* is based on onions and is mild and sweet. If you overdo it, a spoonful of plain rice will quench the flames; drinking distributes the sambal and only makes things worse.

Indonesian food should be eaten with a spoon and fork (chopsticks are Chinese, Japanese or Korean) and the drink of choice is beer or water.

Note: many places serving Indonesian food call themselves Chinese-Indonesian and usually end up serving bland dishes to suit Dutch palates. The food is OK and can be great value, but if you want the real thing, go to a place without *Chinees* in its name.

### SURINAMESE

Food from this former South American colony is similar to Caribbean food – a unique African/Indian hybrid – with Indonesian influences contributed by indentured labourers from Java. Chicken features strongly, along with curries (chicken, lamb or beef), potatoes and rice, and delicious *roti* (unleavened pancakes). It can be hot and spicy, but it's always wholesome and good value. Surinamese restaurants are small and specialise in takeaway food, though there might be a few tables and chairs. Most close early and some are only open for lunch.

### INTERNATIONAL

Many restaurants fall into this category, with menus looking like a roll call for the United Nations. Sometimes you see them all on the same menu, or at least you'll see their influence. Main courses usually come with salads that can be quite imaginative.

## Drinks

Amsterdam tap water is fine but it does have a slight chemical taste, so mineral and soda waters are popular. Dairy drinks include chocolate milk, Fristi (a yogurt drink), *karnemelk* (buttermilk) and of course milk itself, which is good and relatively cheap. A wide selection of fruit juices and soft drinks are available too.

### TEA & COFFEE

For a city with such a rich tradition in the tea and coffee trade, the tea is a bit of a disappointment. It's usually served as a cup of hot water with a tea bag, though many places do offer a wide choice of bags. If you want milk, ask '*met melk, graag*' (with milk, please); many locals add a slice of lemon instead.

The hot drink of choice is coffee – after all, it was the merchants of Amsterdam who introduced coffee to Europe in a big

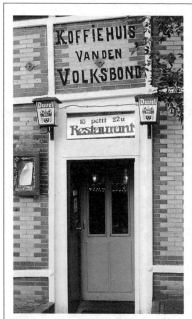

*Koffiehuis van den Volksbond (p149)*

way, in the early 1600s. It should be strong and can be excellent if it's freshly made. If you simply order *koffie* you'll get a sizeable cup of the black stuff with a small airline container of *koffiemelk*, a slightly sour tasting cream similar to unsweetened condensed milk. *Koffie verkeerd* (coffee 'wrong') comes in a bigger cup or mug with plenty of real milk. *Espresso* or *cappuccino* are also available. The Coffee Company chain has locations throughout town, and Starbucks is due to move in soon.

Remember, there's a *big* difference between a *koffiehuis* (coffee house) and a 'coffeeshop'; the latter may have nothing to do with coffee (and a lot to do with cannabis), while lighting up in the former will get you a tongue-lashing at best.

# MEDIEVAL CENTRE

You'd expect the city hub to have the most options, and indeed it does, from supremely elegant Dutch and international options to the hippest restaurant/DJ clubs, and even some downmarket classics. Befitting this part of town, some of the highest-end places are where you'd least expect them, such as the Red Light District. Spuistraat also has a number of offerings.

For Chinese with the freshest ingredients at affordable prices, visit little Chinatown along the Zeedijk near Nieuwmarkt Square. Roasted ducks and meats hang in the windows, and menus are the length of small-town phone books. Don't worry about reservations – if one place is full, the one next door will have space.

### CAFÉ BERN Map pp278-9 — *Swiss*
☎ 622 00 34; Nieuwmarkt 9; mains €5.45-12.25;
Ⓨ dinner
Indulge in a fondue frenzy at this delightfully well-worn brown café. People have been flocking here for nearly 30 years for the gruyère fondue as well as the entrecote. Note: it's generally closed for a large part of the summer, but you're unlikely to want to eat fondue in hot weather anyway. Reservations advised.

### BLAUW AAN DE WAL
Map pp278-9 — *International*
☎ 330 22 57; Oudezijds Achterburgwal 99; mains €23-25.50, 3-course menu €37.50; Ⓨ dinner Mon-Sat
Oasis, rose among thorns, minor miracle: in the middle of the Red Light District a long, often graffiti-covered hallway leads you to a place of unexpected refinement. Originally a 17th-century herb warehouse, the whitewashed, exposed brick, multilevel space still features old steel weights and measures, plus friendly, knowledgeable service and contemporary French- and Italian-inspired cooking. Order the chocolate brownie, with its molten centre. In summer, grab a table in the romantic garden.

### DE ROODE LEEUW Map pp278-9 — *Dutch*
☎ 555 06 66; Damrak 93; mains €17.50-25;
Ⓨ breakfast, lunch & dinner
To escape the cacophony that is Damrak, duck into this dark, formal dining room. Note the striking carvings of horse carriages hanging from the ceiling (carved in 1911 by a Hungarian guest) as you linger over old-fashioned dishes like fish stew and marrowfat peas.

### DORRIUS Map pp278-9 — *Dutch*
☎ 420 22 24; Nieuwezijds Voorburgwal 5;
mains €15.40-26; Ⓨ dinner Mon-Sat
Dressed-up diners head to Dorrius for its fab old-world surroundings (marble floor, leather wallpaper and velvet upholstered chairs) and upscale Dutch dishes like old-fashioned stockfish.

### D'VIJFF VLIEGHEN Map pp278-9 — *Dutch*
☎ 530 40 60; Spuistraat 294-302; mains €21-29;
Ⓨ dinner
So what if every tourist and business visitor eats here? Sometimes the herd gets it right. 'The Five Flies' is a classic dining experience spread out over five 17th-century canal houses. Old-wood dining rooms teem with character, Delft tiles and works by Rembrandt and Breitner.

## Top Five Medieval Centre Dining

- **Blauw aan de Wal** (this page) Sophisticated French dining in a most unexpected place.
- **Lucius** (p137) Fish and seafood prepared simply in an understated setting.
- **Nam Kee** (p137) For anything Chinese and roasted (though don't expect the royal treatment).
- **d' Vijff Vlieghen** (this page) Everyone visits this old line Dutch place, with good reason.
- **Vlaams Friteshuis** (p138) Because everyone should try Flemish-style fries once (or twice, or three times…).

## Top Five Eat Streets

- **Utrechtsestraat** (Southern Canal Belt) Hands down, our favourite dining street, with some of the city's culinary highlights.
- **The Negen Straatjes** (Western Canal Belt) A great place to browse for clothing or lunch, home wares or dinner. There's a new crop of fashionable cafés.
- **Reguliersdwaarstraat** (Southern Canal Belt) Amid some of Amsterdam's prime gay establishments are some of the city's prime dining establishments, including a Michelin-rated Chinese spot. Gay men have taste.
- **Leidseplein and surrounds** (Southern Canal Belt) Included for quantity if not necessarily quality. There's absolutely everything here, prices are reasonable, and it's minutes' walk from entertainment.
- **Albert Cuypstraat** (Old South) West of the famous market you'll find an unparalled assortment of exotic choices including Cambodian, Kurdish and Surinamese.

Some chairs have brass plates commemorating celebrities who've sat in them, but you don't have to be famous to receive silver service and chichi contemporary Dutch food.

### GETTO

Map pp278-9     *International, Gay Following*
☎ 421 51 51; Warmoesstraat 51; mains €9.50-14.50; ☺ dinner Tue-Sun

Getto's fab-trashy, disco-pad interior is a great place to chill while you indulge in a few cocktails, a burger or the cranberry crumble. There are cool tunes, a lounge room in the back, customers from twinks to leather boys, and some of Warmoesstraat's best people-watching.

### GREEN PLANET Map pp278-9   *Vegetarian*
☎ 625 82 80; Spuistraat 122; mains €12.50-16.50; ☺ dinner Mon-Sat

This modern veggie eatery cares – about your health, biodegradable packaging, peace, love and quite decent food. Come for a soup, salad, antipasti or homemade cake. Mains include goulash, dumplings and Indian masala.

### GREKAS Map pp278-9      *Greek*
☎ 620 35 90; Singel 311; mains €9.50-11.50; ☺ dinner Wed-Sun

What started as a catering shop has morphed into one of A'dam's best loved Greek restaurants. You can still get takeaway, or sit down in the informal but pleasant dining room for generous portions of Greek home cooking: moussaka, roasted artichokes, chicken in lemon sauce...

### HAESJE CLAES Map pp278-9   *Dutch*
☎ 624 99 98; Spuistraat 275; mains €13.30-20, menus from €28.50; ☺ lunch & dinner

Haesje Claes' warm surrounds, lots of dark wooden panelling and antique knick-knacks, is just the place to sample comforting pea

soup and endive *stamppot*. The fish starter has a great sampling of Dutch fishes. It gets lots of tourists, but with good reason.

### HEMELSE MODDER

Map pp282-3      *Dutch, Dessert*
☎ 624 32 03; Oude Waal 9; mains €16, set meals €26; ☺ dinner Tue-Sun

This gay-run restaurant has floor-to-ceiling velvet curtains and displays of tropical flowers. The speciality is chocolate mousse ('heavenly mud', hence the restaurant's name). Extraordinary care goes into dishes; the repertoire might include *pot au feu* with chicken or polenta soufflé.

### KANTJIL EN DE TIJGER

Map pp286-7      *Indonesian*
☎ 620 09 94; Spuistraat 291-3; mains €3.40-14.50; ☺ dinner

Although the look of this large place is more contemporary Deco than old Indo, it's crowded nightly, the service is sprightly, and *rijsttafel* means that you needn't eat lightly.

### KING SOLOMON Map p285   *Kosher*
☎ 625 58 60; Waterlooplein 239; mains €13.75-21.50; ☺ lunch & dinner except Jewish Sabbath & holidays

Close your eyes and you could be in Israel, thanks to the Hebrew-speaking staff and patrons, informality, streetside seating and, of course, food. Locals come for the veal schnitzel, as well as small plates including hummus, falafel and gefilte fish imported from the Holy Land. It's also right near many sights of Jewish interest.

### KRUA THAI Map pp286-7      *Thai*
☎ 622 95 33; Staalstraat 22; mains €16.50-24.50, course menus from €22.50

Top-shelf soups, duck or shrimp curries, and noodle dishes are the order of the day at this sophisticated restaurant with bright art. Note:

some locals refer to it by its old name, Tom Yam. A pre-theatre menu is available.

## LA STRADA

Map pp278-9        *International, Gay Following*
☎ 625 02 76; Nieuwezijds Voorburgwal 93-95; mains €10.90-16.80, 2-/3-course menu €13.50/23.50; ☽ lunch Fri-Sun, dinner Wed-Sun

A mixed lesbian, gay and hetero crowd enjoy the mixed Euro-styled food, pleasant ambience and friendly service at this split-level restaurant. Fish dishes are reliably good. Given its central location, it can get quite busy.

## LUCIUS Map pp278-9       *Seafood*
☎ 624 18 31; Spuistraat 247; mains €19.50-25; ☽ dinner

Simple, delicious and simply delicious, Lucius is known for fresh ingredients and not mucking them up with lots of sauce and spice. The interior, all fish tanks and tile, is workmanlike and professional, just like the service.

## NAM KEE Map pp278-9      *Chinese*
☎ 639 28 48; Zeedijk 115; mains €6-16.50; ☽ lunch & dinner

It won't win any design awards, but year in, year out, Nam Kee's the most-popular Chinese spot in town. And why not: there's good roast anything, and service is snappy.

## NEW KING Map pp278-9      *Chinese*
☎ 625 21 80; Zeedijk 115; mains €4-15; ☽ lunch & dinner

If you want Chinese on the Zeedijk but don't want to feel like you're slumming it, New King is about the fanciest on the block. Try the steamed fish with mushrooms or sizzling aubergine.

## ORIENTAL CITY Map pp278-9    *Chinese*
☎ 626 83 52; Oudezijds Voorburgwal 177-9; mains €8.50-23.50; ☽ lunch & dinner

This huge, unpretentious Hong Kong–style restaurant is always lively; join gaggles of local Chinese for daily dim sum (11.30am to 4.30pm) and classic Canto cuisine.

## PINTO Map p285         *Kosher*
☎ 625 09 23; Jodenbreestraat 144; mains €10.50-25, sandwiches €4.50-5; ☽ lunch & dinner except Jewish Sabbath & holidays

If King Solomon is Israel, Pinto is Paris, with an upscale yet comfortable setting of open-backed wooden chairs and pleasant lighting. Food is both French and Israeli, from oven-baked fish to

various chicken dishes and a huge falafel platter. Male Jewish visitors may be invited to put on *tefillin* (phylacteries) and say a quick prayer.

## RAAP & PEPER

Map pp282-3      *International, Gay Following*
☎ 330 17 16; Peperstraat 23-35; 3-course menus €31.75; ☽ dinner Tue-Sat

Equally known for the quality of the Mediterranean cuisine (eg duck, fish, game), its romantic, candlelit setting and staff friendliness; this out of the way place gets rave reviews. It's also one a favourite for lesbian wedding banquets.

## STEREO SUSHI Map pp278-9    *Japanese*
☎ 777 30 10; Jonge Roelensteeg 4; prices vary; ☽ dinner Thu-Sat

It ain't the most authentic sushi bar in the city, but this blink-and-you'll-miss-it place is definitely the most fun. Get sozzled on sake as DJs spin deep house. That way you won't notice how small the serves of sushi and sashimi are.

## SUKASARI Map pp278-9     *Indonesian*
☎ 624 00 92; Damstraat 26-28; mains €5.25-16.25; ☽ lunch Thu-Sat, dinner Mon-Sat

With its requisite Indonesian-style decorations, this unpretentious but neat spot does a mini-*rijsttafel* (€10.75) and an authentic mixed meat satay (€9.75). Service is reliable and efficient. If you want the spice toned down, make sure to ask. Lunch specials start at €7.

## SUPPER CLUB Map pp278-9    *DJ Restaurant*
☎ 638 05 13; Jonge Roelensteeg 21; 5-course menu €60; ☽ dinner

If you're looking for a scene, you'll find one here. Enter the theatrical, all-white room, snuggle up on enormous mattresses and snack on platters of victuals as DJs spin platters of house music. Even if the food and service are so-so and the prices are expensive (though you save on club admission you'd otherwise have spent later!), it's an experience that's hard to forget.

## PANNENKOEKENHUIS UPSTAIRS

Map pp278-9          *Dutch*
☎ 626 56 03; Grimburgwal 2; mains €4.10-9.15; ☽ lunch

Climb some of the steepest stairs in town to reach this small-as-a-stamp restaurant. The lure? Pancakes that are flavoursome, inexpensive (most under €7.50) and filling. We like the one with bacon, cheese and ginger. It's a one-man show, so service operates at its own pace.

### VILLA ZEEZICHT Map pp278-9     *Café*
☎ 626 74 33; Torensteeg 7; mains €3-21;
✆ lunch & dinner

Although you *could* try sandwiches and pastas here, half the patrons are eating the famous apple pie. €3.50 buys a mountain of apples dusted in cinnamon, surrounded by warm pastry and fresh cream. In warm weather, they set up tables on the bridge over the Singel.

### WINTER GARDEN
Map pp278-9     *Breakfast & Lunch*
☎ 554 91 11; Dam 9; breakfast/lunch €21/30

The soaring one-time ballroom of the Grand Hotel Krasnapolsky is one of Amsterdam's most splendid spaces; you can get a buffet breakfast or lunch teeming with meats, fishes, salads and the usuals, both hot and cold. Sunday brunch (€33) is by reservation only.

# CHEAP EATS

### DOLORES Map pp278-9     *Organic*
☎ 620 33 02; opposite Nieuwezijds Voorburgwal 289;
mains €2-6.50; ✆ lunch & afternoon

*Biologische* (organic) is the name of the game at this tiny shop, resembling a kiddie-train station in the traffic island. Try organic burgers, tostis, chicken and *frites* (though not with organic mayo – taste does matter!). Service can take its time, but you can watch the world go by at picnic table seating outdoors.

### DUTCH FOUR Map pp278-9  *Sandwich Shop*
☎ 626 33 88; Zoutsteeg 6; sandwiches €2.05-4.30;
✆ breakfast & lunch

This three-table shop has a 20-plus year history, a kindly owner, immaculately fresh fish

*Vlaams Friteshuis*

and a great, central location – a quiet refuge from the madness of Damrak.

### SOUPKITCHEN Map pp278-9     *Soup*
☎ 528 71 75; Nieuwendijk 50; soups €2.95-5.50;
✆ lunch & dinner

From chicken noodle to clam chowder, this cool, high-tech place not far from Central Station is busy all day. You can also find bagel sandwiches, fruit smoothies, and extra-large 32-ounce (946ml) cups for €8.40.

### STERK STAALTJE
Map pp286-7     *Takeaway/Traiteur*
☎ 624 9065; Staalstraat 12; prices vary; ✆ lunch

Squarely between the Amstel, the Red Light District and Nieuwmarkt is this handsome, *rustique* takeout shop with lasagne, savoury pies, and lovely olives and cheeses. Lunch will set you back about €5.

### VAN DEN BERG'S BROODJESBAR
Map pp278-9     *Sandwich Shop*
☎ 622 83 56; Zoutsteeg 4; sandwiches €1.60-4.45;
✆ 9am-6pm Mon-Fri

Tiny, friendly, clean, family-run and utterly without pretension, you can linger over the newspaper and commune with local office people. Our favourite sandwich is the *gehakt*, thin slices of a giant meatball, served warm and eaten with killer-hot mustard.

### VILLAGE BAGELS
Maps pp278-9 & pp286-7     *Sandwich Shop*
☎ 528 91 52; Stromarkt 2; ☎ 427 22 13; Vijzelstraat
139; bagel sandwiches €2.30-5.10; ✆ breakfast & lunch

The shop that brought bagel-chic to Amsterdam is still going strong. You may feel like a New Yorker as you dive into a bagel with salmon, chive cream cheese and capers, especially if you grab a copy of the *Herald Tribune* (they keep it on hand at the Stromarkt location).

### VLAAMS FRITESHUIS
Map pp286-7     *French Fries*
☎ 624 60 75; Voetboogstraat 33; small/large €1.50/
1.90, sauces €0.40; ✆ 11am-6pm Tue-Sat, noon-6pm
Sun & Mon

At this hole-in-the-wall takeaway off the Spui, join queues of locals for Amsterdam's best-loved *frites* (french fries). The standard is smothered in mayonnaise, though you can ask for ketchup, peanut sauce or various spicy mayos including our favourite, with green peppercorns. It's been an institution since 1887.

# WESTERN CANAL BELT & JORDAAN

It may not have the ethnic dining diversity of the Centre, but this part of town makes up for it with some lovely and surprisingly fashionable options. Negen Straatjes are filled with cafés and small restaurants to match their lovely boutiques, while the restaurants of the Jordaan are typified by the conviviality that has been a hallmark of the area since its beginning.

Alongside the western canals and in the alleys of the Jordaan, it's easy to lose one's way. Let it happen. In this rapidly changing area, you may even discover the next hot spot.

## WESTERN CANAL BELT

**BLAKES** Map p277                              *French*
☎ 530 20 10; Keizersgracht 384; mains €28-38;
😊 breakfast daily, lunch Mon-Fri, dinner Mon-Sat
It's swank central, baby, thanks to the dazzlingly elegant interior with well-spaced power tables, ultra-smooth service, cuisine fusing French, Italian, Japanese and Thai, and an ever-present smattering of international celebs. Diners also get access to one of Amsterdam's most excellent lounge scenes. Reserve.

**DE BOLHOED** Map pp278-9           *Vegetarian*
☎ 626 18 03; Prinsengracht 60-2; mains €12-15.70,
3-course menu €18-20; 😊 lunch & dinner
The 'Charlie Brown's pumpkin patch goes to India' interior is a nice setting to tuck into enormous, organic Mexican and Italian-inspired dishes; in warm weather, there's also a verdant little canalside terrace, surrounded by wild rose bushes. Leave room for the ice-cream sundaes or banana cream pie. Although carnivores will find the cooking a little, well, veggie, vegans and vegetarians swear by it – reserve.

**CHRISTOPHE** Map pp278-9               *French*
☎ 625 08 07; Leliegracht 46; mains €30-50, 4-course menus €51-65; 😊 dinner Wed-Sat
Jean-Christophe Royer's Michelin star, lobster dishes, duck liver terrine and unusual elegance

### Top Five Western Canal Belt & Jordaan Dining

- **De Belhamel** (this page) Especially on a summer night sitting canalside.
- **Christophe** (this page) This Michelin-rated restaurant is a splurge and worth it.
- **Cinema Paradiso** (p142) Italian that's new, hot and loads of fun.
- **Local** (p142) Convivial setting, food on skewers and cocktails for dessert.
- **Nomads** (p141) Between the food and the DJs, a scene par excellence.

keep it busy nightly. However, the excellent, caring service puts it over the top in our book, making this an extraordinary restaurant by world, and not just Amsterdam, standards.

**CILUBANG** Map p286-7               *Indonesian*
☎ 626 97 55; Runstraat 10; mains €7.25-18, rijsttafel €19.90-34.40; 😊 dinner Tue-Sun
Cute, cosy and slightly romantic, celadon-hued Cilubang soothes the stomach and soul with *rijsttafel* and attentive, personal service.

**DE BELHAMEL** Map pp278-9             *French*
☎ 622 10 95; Brouwersgracht 60; mains €18-20, set menu €31; 😊 dinner
In warm weather the canalside tables at the head of the Herengracht are an aphrodisiac, and inside the sumptuous Art Nouveau interior is the perfect backdrop for excellent, French-inspired dishes like silky roast beef.

**DE STRUISVOGEL** Map p277               *French*
☎ 423 38 17; Keizersgracht 312; 3-course dinner €17.50; 😊 dinner
This former kitchen to some of the large canal houses in the neighbourhood offers our favourite deal in town. It's in the cosy basement (hence 'struisvogel' means 'ostrich'), and yes they do serve the bird, along with a nightly-rotating menu – generous portions of more conventional French-inspired choices. It gets crowded, so book ahead.

**DE 2 GRIEKEN** Map pp278-9               *Greek*
☎ 625 53 17; Prinsenstraat 20; mains €12-17; 😊 dinner
Craving a big plate of stewed mountain goat or some juicy lamb chops? This relaxed, family-run bistro caters to your carnivorous desires with great grills and gets '*opa!*'s from locals. In nice weather, grab a seat on the flower-lined terrace out back.

**DIMITRI'S** Map pp278-9            *International*
☎ 627 93 93; Prinsenstraat 3; mains €2.50-11;
😊 breakfast, lunch & dinner
Resembling a mini Parisian brasserie, sophisticated Dimitri's serves an international menu

of gargantuan salads, pastas and burgers. Mornings see fashionable types nibbling on croissants. The Dexter's Lab sandwich contains a parsley omelette with fresh ham and tomato, and they serve fajitas for dinner.

### 5 Map pp278-9 *French*
☎ 428 24 55; Prinsenstraat 10; mains €16.50-19.50, 5-course menu €35; ☼ dinner Wed-Mon

This one-time blacksmith's shop and bookstore has been given an airy update, and a changing menu of modern Mediterranean mains keeps things interesting. Better yet, order the chef's choice and be surprised. It's also known for its wine selection. By the time you read this, it may be open at lunchtime too.

### FOODISM Map pp278-9 *Café*
☎ 427 51 03; Oude Leliestraat 8; mains €3.50-9.50; ☼ lunch & dinner

A hip, colourful little joint run by a fun, relaxed crew of chefs and waiters. All-day breakfasts, sandwiches and salads make up the day menu; night-time sees patrons tucking into platefuls of pasta – try the 'Kung Funghi' (with mushrooms, parsley, walnuts and cream).

### GOODIES Map pp286-7 *Café*
☎ 625 61 22; Huidenstraat 9; mains €4.50-14.50; ☼ lunch & dinner

This once-country place with rustic picnic tables has gone glam with a slick makeover, a bar and occasional DJ nights. It's still popular for creative sandwiches like grilled chicken with salad and pine nuts, or main courses in-

cluding pastas and salmon. The picnic tables are still there, but now with cool embossed paint jobs.

### HEIN Map p277 *Café*
☎ 623 10 48; Berenstraat 20; mains €4-10; ☼ breakfast & lunch

Hein simply loves to cook, and it shows in her simple, stylish, skylit café – you have to walk through the kitchen to reach the dining room. Media types, doing business over brunch, comment that she has a great touch with simple dishes: *croque monsieur* or *madame*, smoked salmon etc.

### KOH-I-NOOR Map p277 *Indian*
☎ 623 31 33; Westermarkt 29; mains €10-17.50; ☼ dinner

Longstanding Koh-I-Noor's interior is all cinnabars and blue-and-white tapestries, and the curries, tandoori and biryani dishes (especially the king prawn biryani) are about as good as you get in town. Tables are rather close together, but hospitable staff helps alleviate any pressure.

### L'INDOCHINE Map pp286-7 *Indonesian*
☎ 627 57 55; Beulingstraat 9; mains €19.50-24.50; ☼ dinner Tue-Sun

A swanky, white-linen Thai-Vietnamese place, known for using only the finest ingredients. This would be enough to get upscale diners into this restaurant, but the nice crockery and nicer service keep them coming back. Course menus are available for around €35.

### LULU Map pp286-7 *International*
☎ 624 50 90; Runstraat 8; 3-/4-course menu €32.50/ 37.50; ☼ dinner

Lulu's decorations – gaudy chandeliers and tacky cupids – are the perfect foil for the kitchen's serious French- and Italian-accented dishes coming from the open kitchen. The beef carpaccio is a perennial favourite, and the rest of the menu is good ol' comfort food.

### LUST Map pp286-7 *Café*
☎ 626 57 91; Runstraat 13; mains €3.50-8.95; ☼ breakfast & lunch

Parquet floors and walls, super-mod ceiling lamps, and beats from thumping dance to Brazilian animate this glam café. It's a fair bet you'll spot models nibbling focaccia sandwiches, *tostis* (grilled sandwiches), generous salads or the grilled chicken club with avocado.

Eating – Western Canal Belt & Jordaan

### NEW DELI Map pp278-9 *Café*
☎ 626 27 55; Haarlemmerstraat 73; mains €4.25-11.50; ⏰ lunch & dinner daily, breakfast Mon-Sat
Slick, hip couples congregate at this modern and minimal café to air-kiss, read design magazines, gossip and share Italian and Asian-inspired dishes, fruit shakes and focaccia tuna melts.

### NIELSEN Map p277 *Café*
☎ 330 60 06; Berenstraat 19; dishes €2.30-8.50; ⏰ breakfast & lunch Tue-Sun
This sunny café, with its bright interior filled with fresh flowers, has a tasty set breakfast – eggs, toast, fruit, juice and coffee (€7.50). During lunch a large variety of salads and sandwiches are served: try the BLT or gigantic chicken club sandwich, and top it off with lemon cake. And – get this – it opens at 8am!

### NOMADS Map p277 *Middle Eastern*
☎ 344 64 01; Rozengracht 133; mezze plates €2.25-8, 3-course set menu €42.50; ⏰ dinner Tue-Sun
It's the Supper Club concept on the road to Morocco. Wine, dine and recline on mattresses amid decadent decorations, and graze on platters of mod Middle Eastern snacks while being entertained by belly dancers and DJs. Fancy-trancey and superbly sexy.

### RAKANG THAI Map p277 *Thai*
☎ 627 50 12; Elandsgracht 29; mains €17.50-20-50, 4-course menus €26.50-31.50; ⏰ dinner
Chairs that fit like straitjackets, bright art on the walls, a *mai pen rai* ('no problem') atmosphere and delicious cooking (go for the crunchy, spicy duck salad) keep it busy here night after night.

### SPANJER & VAN TWIST
Map p277 *International*
☎ 639 01 09; Leliegracht 60; mains €10.25-14.25; ⏰ lunch & dinner
Inside, find Mondrianesque stained-glass panelling, a big bar and an open kitchen; outside are tables along one of Amsterdam's prettiest canals. Add to these a spin-the-compass menu (eg. fish and sweet-potato chips, pastas, Thai cucumber salad) and you've got a very popular spot, even if service can be slow.

### ZUID ZEELAND Map pp286-7 *International*
☎ 624 31 54; Herengracht 413; mains €24-26, 3-/4-course menu €29.50/34; ⏰ lunch Mon-Fri, dinner nightly
Popular with artists, authors, Bohemians and the US Democratic Party, Zuid Zeeland is

known for cuisine that whispers quality and its low-key celebrity clientele. The contemporary room is attractive but not imposing, much like the French-international cuisine.

# JORDAAN

### ALBATROS Map p277 *Seafood*
☎ 627 99 32; Westerstraat 264; mains €16-24; ⏰ dinner Thu-Mon
Albatros' garish decorations (plastic lobsters in fishing nets) fall into the 'so-bad-it's-good' camp. But the seafood dishes – *real* lobsters, prawns, fishpot with white wine and cream sauce – fall into 'so-good-it's-good'. They dispense the house white wine by the centimetre.

### BALTHAZAR'S KEUKEN
Map pp278-9 *French*
☎ 420 21 14; Elandsgracht 108; 3-course set menu €23.50; ⏰ dinner Wed-Fri
Don't go expecting a wide-ranging menu – the byword is basically 'whatever we have on hand', but whatever they have is usually really good French/Mediterranean. Plus, there's a modern-rustic look and attentive service. Limited opening hours mean that a reservation is recommended.

### BORDEWIJK Map pp278-9 *French*
☎ 624 38 99; Noordermarkt 7; mains €24-31; ⏰ dinner Tue-Sun
The interior here is so minimal that there's little to do but appreciate the spectacular French/Italian cooking. Many locals consider it the best in town, and you'd do best to go with one of them, as Bordewijk is known for favouring repeat customers.

### BURGER'S PATIO Map p277 *International*
☎ 623 68 54; Tweede Tuindwarsstraat 12; mains €10.50-18.50, 3-course menu €25; ⏰ dinner
Despite its name, this is no hamburger joint but rather an Italian-inspired restaurant with an air of subdued cool. The post-industrial-tile-meets-Dutch-modern interior has great art on the walls, and the namesake patio (out back) is a fun hideout. Sensibly priced mains usually include lamb or pastas.

### CAFÉ REIBACH Map pp278-9 *Café*
☎ 626 77 08; Brouwersgracht 139; mains €2.70-12.50; ⏰ breakfast & lunch
This window-lined corner place in the Jordaan serves a magnificent breakfast (€12.50), laden

with Dutch cheese, pâté, smoked salmon, eggs, coffee and fresh juice. It's also pleasant for afternoon cake and coffee (try the cheesecake or nut tart), and we love the sassy service that describes itself as 'straight-friendly'.

### CINEMA PARADISO Map p277 *Italian*
☎ 623 73 44; Westerstraat 184-186; mains €6.75-16; ☽ dinner Tue-Sun
*Action!* Cinema Paradiso opened 2002 in a former movie theatre, and glitterati have been appearing in the dining room ever since. Direct yourself into a booth or table near the open kitchen, and enjoy pastas, pizzas, *rosticceria (roasted meats)* and stargazing.

### DE BLAFFENDE VIS Map p277 *Dutch*
☎ 675 17 21; Westerstraat 118; mains under €10; ☽ dinner
Meals (contemporary Dutch, changing daily) are better than they need to be at this rowdy, corner brown café. Students and thirtysomethings happily bop and swish beer while listening to music with a beat (think Macy Gray) – it can get busy on weekend nights.

### DE VLIEGENDE SCHOTEL
Map p277 *Vegetarian*
☎ 625 20 41; Nieuwe Leliestraat 162; mains €7.50-11.50; ☽ dinner
Service can be spotty at 'the flying saucer', but if you're prepared to take your time in the summer-camp-chic dining room, you'll enjoy some of the city's favourite veggie gratins, lasagnes and Indian-inflected meals, as well as some fish dishes. There's also a decent wine list.

### DUENDE Map p278-9 *Spanish*
☎ 420 66 92; Lindengracht 62; tapas €2.05-8.50; ☽ dinner
Flamenco music (Saturday night), big shared tables and reasonably priced tapas guarantee Duende's popularity. It's great for a party with a big group of friends – or strangers. The front room is the more lively (and attractive) of the two. Note: you have to order at the bar.

### JEAN JEAN Map p277 *French*
☎ 627 71 53; Eerste Anjeliersdwarsstraat 14; mains €14-19; ☽ dinner Tue-Sun
One of the hottest places in town, this cosy neighbourhood bistro offers honest and affordable Gallic comfort food: traditional crepes, soups, meat and fish dishes, etc. The

setting is understated yet sophisticated, and service is predictably professional. Be sure to reserve.

### LOCAL Map p277 *International*
☎ 423 40 39; Westerstraat 136; mains €8-16; ☽ dinner
Our favourite new restaurant, this eel's nest of contempo-cool, with long tables stretching its entire length, ensures you'll never eat alone – go with friends and it's an instant party. In keeping with the 'long and thin' theme, main dishes are grilled on skewers: an international selection from yakitori to beef stroganoff, all with potatoes, salad and appropriate sauces. Dessert: cocktails!

### LOF Map p278-9 *Fusion*
☎ 620 29 97; Haarlemmerstraat 62; mains €20, 3-course menu €35; ☽ dinner Wed-Sun
Chef Sander Louwerens combines Southeast Asian and Mediterranean flavours in complex and complementary ways. This is evidenced in dishes like pike served with fennel and miso sauce. Schoolhouse-surplus décor manages to feel cool.

### MOEDER'S POT EETHUISJE
Map p278-9 *Dutch*
☎ 623 76 43; Vinkenstraat 119; mains €3.60-11.35; ☽ dinner Mon-Sat
*Moeder* (mother), probably in his 60s (yes, his…he's big and gruff and probably a sweetheart inside), has been serving up solid, inexpensive meals for about 35 years. His tiny shop is loaded with kitsch and is no gourmet experience, this is home cookin': beefsteaks, schnitzels and chicken with vegetables (some canned) and potatoes like your own *moeder* always wanted you to eat. Six-course set menus (€12.50 to €14.75) are a steal.

### PATHUM THAI Map p278-9 *Thai*
☎ 624 49 36; Willemsstraat 16; mains €10.50-16.75; ☽ dinner
This sweet, little neighbourhood restaurant serves much-loved and authentically cooked Thai standards like tom yum soup, pad thai and a good selection of green and red curries. It ain't flash, but nobody seems to mind.

### STOOP Map p277 *International*
☎ 639 24 80; Eerste Anjeliersdwarsstraat 4; mains €18-21, 3-course menu €29.50; ☽ dinner
Locals may actively discourage you from visiting Stoop. Why? It seems they want to keep this modestly priced bistro all to themselves –

with its robust, tasty mains (think organic roast chicken), creative vegetarian dishes and comfortably contemporary décor.

### SUMMUM Map p278-9 *Fusion*
☎ 770 0407; Binnen Dommersstraat 13; mains €17.50-21.50; 🕑 dinner Mon-Sat
Punchy mostly-Mediterranean creations (with some Asian touches), spunky waiters and sophisticated décor mean bookings are essential on weekends. Try the melt-in-your-mouth ceviche. If there's no large party, the communal table is great for meeting new friends.

### THE PANCAKE BAKERY Map p278-9 *Dutch*
☎ 625 13 33; Prinsengracht 191; mains €6.35-10; 🕑 lunch & dinner
This basement restaurant – in a restored warehouse – features 79 varieties of this Dutch speciality from sweet (chocolate) to savoury (the 'Egyptian', topped with lamb, sweet peppers, garlic sauce). There are also omelettes, soups, desserts and lots of tourists, but you'll find plenty of locals here too.

### TOSCANINI Map p278-9 *Italian*
☎ 623 28 13; Lindengracht 75; mains €11-35; 🕑 dinner Mon-Sat
There's a seasonal menu of very contemporary Italian selections to match the very contemporary redo of this former horse-carriage house. Urbane, hip and lively, but somehow also warm.

## CHEAP EATS
### BROODJE MOKUM
Map p277 *Sandwich Shop*
☎ 623 19 66; Rozengracht 26; sandwiches from €1.80; 🕑 breakfast & lunch Mon-Sat
With several tables and outdoor seating, it's larger than your average *broodjeswinkel* but has a great workaday feeling that may remind you of your favourite burger or chip stand at home. Our strategy for ordering: point at what you want, and the staff will tell you how much it is.

### GARY'S MUFFINS
Maps pp286-7 & p285 *Bakery, Sandwiches*
☎ 420 14 52, Prinsengracht 454; ☎ 421 59 30, Jodenbreestraat 15; dishes €1.50-4.35; 🕑 breakfast & lunch
Fresh bagels and bagel sandwiches, freshbaked chocolate brownies from Gary's grandma's recipe, and sweet and savoury muffins for anyone craving a healthy(ish) mini-munch.

*Winkel on Noordermarkt*

### HET KUYLTJE Map pp278-9 *Sandwich Shop*
☎ 620 10 45; Gasthuismolensteeg 9; sandwiches €1.90-3; 🕑 breakfast & lunch
An antiseptic-atmospheric, tile-lined sandwich shop that takes you back to the early 20th century. Plus, the menu tops out at €3.

### SMALL WORLD CATERING
Map pp278-9 *Takeaway/Traiteur*
☎ 420 27 74; Binnen Oranjestraat 14; sandwiches €5.45-7.50, other mains €4-6; 🕑 lunch & dinner Tue-Sun (closing time 8pm)
This Australian-run company is known for quality. Small cases house gorgeous prepared vegetables and meat dishes, and you can get a variety of quiches and sandwiches including fresh tuna, tapenade and artichoke hearts.

### WINKEL Map pp278-9 *Café*
☎ 623 02 23; Noordermarkt 43; mains €2.50-6; 🕑 breakfast & lunch
This sprawling, indoor-outdoor space is great for people watching, popular for coffees and small meals, and out-of-the-park for its tall, cakey apple pie (€2.50). On market days (Mondays and Saturdays) there's almost always a queue out the door. A move to open for dinner was in the works as we went to press.

## WORTH THE TRIP
### BLENDER Map p277 *International*
☎ 486 98 60; Van der Palmkade 16; mains €19.50-22; 🕑 dinner daily, lunch Sat & Sun
Blender's, cheeky, curvy, 1970s airport-lounge interior (think lots of orange swivel chairs) is just the place to sip cocktails, sample inventive French-Med food and socialise as DJs spin deep house and soul.

## CAFÉ-RESTAURANT AMSTERDAM

Map pp274-5                          *French International*

☎ 682 26 66; Watertorenplein 6; mains €9.05-20.40;
⊙ lunch & dinner

One of the city's hippest eateries is housed in a former water-processing plant. Expect classic French brasserie food (steak bearnaise, mussels, sweetbreads, roasted garlic chicken) served in a vast, industrial-style space. Note the 100ft wooden ceilings (with hanging metal hooks and chains) and the huge floodlights rescued from the former Ajax and Olympic stadiums.

## CANTINE WEST Map p274-5      *International*

☎ 488 77 78; Haarlemmerweg 8-10; 3-course menu
€32; ⊙ dinner Mon-Fr

Amsterdam is changing. What was once Café West Pacific, a leader of the restaurant-that-turns-into-a-nightclub trend, has gotten rid of the DJ, toned down its cavernous, tiled space in the edgy Westergasfabriek, and reclaimed its chef credentials. They serve oysters daily; otherwise it's a market menu. French and Italian preparations are accented with world flavours.

# SOUTHERN CANAL BELT

You may well pass through Leidseplein, but we don't really recommend eating there. While cheap and cheerful, establishments there tend to be not particularly distinctive. A short walk away, however, are some very attractive options (Iguazu, NOA and Pastini, for starters).

Much the same could be said for Rembrandtplein. Instead of eating there, walk a few steps to Utrechtsestraat, Amsterdam's finest restaurant row.

## BOJO Map pp286-7                       *Indonesian*

☎ 622 74 34; Lange Leidsedwarsstraat 51; mains
€7.25-11.50; ⊙ lunch Sat & Sun, dinner daily

After a night on the town, there's nothing like a little Indonesian. Bojo is a late-night institution (open until 2am). Clubbers come for sizzling satays, filling fried rice and steaming bowls of noodle soup. The quality may be uneven but the food is certainly well priced.

## CAFÉ AMERICAN Map pp286-7              *Café*

☎ 556 30 00; Leidsekade 97; buffet breakfast €9.95;
⊙ breakfast, lunch & dinner

This is that reasonably priced hotel breakfast we were telling you about, a diverse (though not overwhelming) buffet with meats, fishes, cheeses, cereals, breads and baked goods. Bonuses: the Art Deco dining room (one of

Amsterdam's loveliest spaces) and interesting people-watching on Leidseplein.

## CAFÉ MORLANG

Map p286-7                        *Café, Gay Following*

☎ 625 26 81; Keizersgracht 451; mains €5.90-10;
⊙ lunch & dinner daily except Mon winter

Around the corner from Metz & Co, grab a fashion magazine, order tomato soup or tarte tatin, or choose from a rotating menu with influences from Italy to India. Enjoy the gorgeous canalside terrace in warm weather, or indoors you can take in the silver wallpaper and gigantic portraits of staff members painted on the back wall. On Friday nights, it's known as a gay hangout.

## CAFÉ WALEM Map pp286-7                  *Café*

☎ 625 35 44, Keizersgracht 449; mains lunch €4.50-
9.50, dinner €9.50-17.50; ⊙ breakfast, lunch & dinner

Industrial-mod décor, friendly service and a changing menu keep this place busy. There's a popular *carpaccio* sandwich, mains including fish and duck, a neat line of soups and salads, and coffee from Illy. If the weather's nice, sit in the garden courtyard or at canal-side tables out front.

## DYNASTY Map pp286-7                       *Thai*

☎ 626 84 00; Reguliersdwarsstraat 30; mains €18.50-
28; ⊙ dinner Wed-Mon

Decorated on a lavish *King and I* budget, Dynasty is resplendent with orchids, colourful murals and hundreds of rice-paper fans. The

> ### Top Five – Southern Canal Belt
>
> - **Iguazu** (p145) Friendly, informal Argentine/Brazilian with steaks – and service – a cut above.
> - **La Rive** (p145) It's hard to get more elegant than the Amstel Hotel's top-flight restaurant.
> - **Pata Negra** (p145) Tapas and only tapas, and boy do they do it well.
> - **Tempo Doeloe** (p147) Some of the city's best Indonesian.
> - **Uliveto** (p147) Our favourite take-out/eat-in shop in town.

menu, a heady mix of Southeast Asian cuisines (eg 'thousand flower duck', 'three meats in harmony') is as embellished as the interior.

## GOLDEN TEMPLE Map pp286-7 *Vegetarian*
☎ 626 85 60; Utrechtsestraat 126; mains €6.85-13.15; ☾ dinner

Friendly, family-run Golden Temple is a real find. Its international menu of Indian thali, Middle Eastern and Mexican platters is consistently good and inexpensive, and the place has a polished feel to it. Leave room for the wicked banana cream pie.

## IGUAZU Map pp286-7 *Argentine/Brazilian*
☎ 420 39 10; Prinsengracht 703; mains €11-32; ☾ lunch & dinner

In a city where impersonal Argentine chains dominate, Iguazu offers quality and personal service. In addition to great Argentine steaks – from special butchers and served with powerful *chimchurri* sauce – you'll find Brazilian specialities like *feijoada*, a homey stew of black beans and meats. Service is friendly, and you can sip *caipirinhas* or South American beers with your meals (by the canal in nice weather).

## LA RIVE Map p285 *French*
☎ 622 60 60, Amstel Inter-Continental Hotel, Professor Tulpplein 1; mains €21.50-50; ☾ breakfast daily, lunch Mon-Fri, dinner Mon-Sat

Two Michelin stars and a formal dining room with graciously spaced tables and views over the Amstel make La Rive the perfect venue for an out-to-impress lunch or dinner. Standbys include turbot and truffle in potato pasta, or a starter of salt cod, potato and oyster croquettes.

## M CAFÉ Map pp286-7 *Café*
☎ 520 78 48; Keizersgracht 455; mains €6-18.50; ☾ lunch & afternoon

Drink in that amazing, panoramic view! Although the food is nothing you can't find elsewhere (and a tad pricey), it's hard to put a value on enjoying soup, salads or sandwiches from the top floor gallery of ritzy Metz & Co department store, high above the Keizersgracht. Mains include veal and tuna, and high tea (€16.50) is served from 2.30pm.

## MOKO Map pp286-7 *International*
☎ 626 11 99; Amstelveld 12; sandwiches & salads €4.50-13, mains €13-18; ☾ lunch & dinner

Set back from the Prinsengracht, with one of the most stunning, scene-filled terraces in Amsterdam, Moko's super-size cushions and long outdoor tables are *the* place to spend summer evenings. Inside it's equally hip with a lounge-y feel including bamboo-slat accents and big fish tanks. Oh yes, they also serve food (Asian-inspired).

## NOA Map pp286-7 *International*
☎ 626 08 02; Leidsegracht 84; mains €12.50-16.50; ☾ dinner Tue-Sun

NOA stands for 'noodles of Amsterdam', and are they ever. This chic, cavernous space (with its open kitchen, silver foil walls, richly grained wood and glass sculptures) offers a share-a-bowl menu of noodles from pad thai to lasagne. Neighbourly seating encourages sharing, slurping and flirting.

## PASTA DI MAMMA
Map pp286-7 *Takeaway/Traiteur*
☎ 664 83 14; PC Hooftstraat 52; sandwiches €3.10-5; antipasti per 100g €2.60-3.30; ☾ lunch & afternoons

Casual, friendly Pasta di Mamma is supremely located for picking up a picnic to take to the Vondelpark. Choose from dozens of antipasti, gorgeous salads and more substantial plates. The countrified-cafeteria space is also pleasant for eating in.

## PASTA E BASTA Map pp286-7 *Italian*
☎ 422 22 26; Nieuwe Spiegelstraat 8; 3-course set menu €35; ☾ dinner

Go with a large group to be serenaded with live opera performed by singing waitstaff. Although there are better-regarded Italian places in town, regulars swear by the antipasto buffet and grilled meats. It's always busy; be sure to reserve well in advance.

## PASTINI Map pp286-7 *Italian*
☎ 622 17 01; Leidsegracht 29; mains €9.75-14.75; ☾ dinner

With a *gezellig*, rustic-meets-renaissance interior and a can't-beat-it location on two canals, Pastini wins praise for its looks, perfectly cooked pastas and reasonable prices. Another speciality is the antipasto starter (€10.25 for five choices), but save room for dessert.

## PATA NEGRA Map pp286-7 *Spanish*
☎ 422 62 50; Utrechtsestraat 142; tapas €3-15.90; ☾ lunch & dinner

They serve tapas and only tapas, and that's the way we love it. The alluringly tiled exterior is matched by a vibrant crowd inside, especially on weekends downing sangria by the jug and all those small plates (the garlic-fried shrimps and grilled sardines are standouts). Margaritas are made with fresh-squeezed lime juice, as they should be. Arrive before 6.30pm or reserve.

### PYGMA-LION Map pp286-7 *African*
☎ 420 70 22; Nieuwe Spiegelstraat 5A; mains €18-22.50; ☽ lunch & dinner Tue-Sun

This modern South African bistro plates up animals you normally have to go to a zoo to see, eg, ostrich, springbok, zebra (the latter might be in a quince-port sauce). Squeamish stomachs will find more domesticated options: vegetarian dishes, 'tipsy' tart and black-currant scones.

### RISTORANTE D'ANTICA
Map pp286-7 *Italian*
☎ 623 38 62; Reguliersdwarsstraat 80-82; mains €11-41.50, course menus from €34.50; ☽ dinner Tue-Sun

Although D'Antica's three dining rooms get their share of celebrities, you'd be hard pressed to find a more welcoming restaurant in town. There's a familiar selection of Italian pasta and meat (eg veal marsala), but *cognoscenti* order spaghetti al parmigiano (not on the menu) assembled tableside – the entire room may pause to watch as waiters whirr steaming green pasta inside a huge wheel of cheese.

### ROSE'S CANTINA Map pp286-7 *Mexican*
☎ 625 97 97; Reguliersdwarsstraat 38; mains €6.90-22.20; ☽ dinner

Even if the Californians and Texans (not to mention Mexicans) among us wouldn't recognise the food as authentic, it's hard not to love the gorgeous garden courtyard and fiesta interior. Fajitas, quesadillas and enchiladas are super-sized, and margaritas taste good on any continent.

### SATURNINO
Map pp286-7 *Italian, Gay Following*
☎ 639 01 02; Reguliersdwarsstraat 5; mains €11.35-22.45; ☽ lunch & dinner

It's all the usual suspects menu-wise at this Italian bistro. Stunning gay couples pack the different levels of this Art Nouveau tiled-and-styled space for pizzas, pasta and playful flirting.

### SEGUGIO Map pp286-7 *Italian*
☎ 330 15 13; Utrechtsestraat 96; mains €15-36; ☽ dinner Mon-Sat

This new restaurant, in a fashionably minimalist storefront with two levels of seating, is the sort of place other chefs go for a good dinner. It's known for risotto and for quality ingredients. Book ahead – it's almost always busy.

### SHIVA Map p286-7 *Indian*
☎ 624 87 13; Reguliersdwarsstraat 72; mains €4.50-12.50; ☽ dinner

There are flashier Indian restaurants, but Shiva, neither gaudy, overdone nor underdone, is admired by those in the know. Honest prices and unusually friendly service go well with Punjabi specialities, including super-spicy *bhuna* curries and onion *bhaji* (fritters) as starters.

### SICHUAN FOOD Map p286-7 *Chinese*
☎ 626 93 27; Reguliersdwarsstraat 35; mains €17.50-22.50, menus from €30.50; ☽ dinner

Despite the unglamorous name, this spot has a Michelin-star and a suitably formal setting that might be filled with upscale tourists one night and gay locals the next. There's a large selection of great fish dishes and a perfectly crisp Peking duck.

### SLUIZER Map pp286-7 *International*
☎ 622 63 76; Utrechtsestraat 43-45; mains €12.50-32.75; ☽ lunch Mon-Fri, dinner nightly

This lively Amsterdam institution – with its super-romantic, enclosed garden terrace – comprises two restaurants: a Parisian-style 'meat' restaurant (No 43) and a fish restaurant (No 45) though both menus are offered in either. Spareribs are the speciality of the former and bouillabaisse in the latter.

### SZMULEWICZ Map p286-7 *International*
☎ 620 28 22; Bakkersstraat 12; mains €9.80-16.80; ☽ dinner

Szmulewicz's décor is at once slick and breezy (trompe l'oeil marble walls, sculpted lighting), a diversity reflected in its menu of reliable, ever-changing international cooking: pastas, tapas, Greek, beef fillets, and vegetarian specialities. In summer, buskers play on the terrace on this quiet block off Rembrandtplein.

### TAKE THAI Map p286-7 _Thai_
☎ 622 05 77; Utrechtsestraat 87; mains €11.25-20, menus €24.50-37.50; 🕑 dinner
This modern, all-white restaurant plates up some of the best Thai food in the city. Choose from a variety of curries spiced according to your palate. The Penang beef curry is a winner, as is the fish fried in lemongrass and Thai basil.

### TEMPO DOELOE Map pp286-7 _Indonesian_
☎ 625 67 18; Utrechtsestraat 75; mains €12.50-21.50, rijsttafel €27-43; 🕑 dinner Mon-Sat
It's known as one of the best Indonesian restaurants in the city, and it charges accordingly. Dishes are spicy, yet you can still taste all the subtle flavours in mains like giant shrimps in coconut-curry sauce. Plus, there's an extraordinary wine list. Downside: a bit supercilious – reservations are essential, and even with one you'll probably have to ring the doorbell to enter.

### THAI CORNER Map pp286-7 _Thai_
☎ 320 66 84; Kerkstraat 66; mains €9.50-19.50; 🕑 dinner
Don't dismiss this cute little place: it does seriously authentic Thai. Locals and restaurant critics swoon over squid with garlic pepper and tofu with Thai basil, and stare agog at the over-the-top, carved wooden bar at the back of the room.

### TUJUH MARET Map pp286-7 _Indonesian_
☎ 427 98 65; Utrechtsestraat 73; mains €13-17, rijsttafel €19-23.50; 🕑 lunch Mon-Sat, dinner nightly
Dare we say it? Tujuh Maret, next door to Tempo Doeloe, is just as good but attitude-free and cheaper. Grab a wicker chair and tuck into spicy Sulawesi-style dishes like dried, fried beef or chicken in red pepper sauce. The _rijst-tafel_ is laid out according to spice intensity.

### ULIVETO Map pp286-7 _Takeaway/Traiteur_
☎ 423 00 99, Weteringschans 118; mains €4.50-10.50; 🕑 lunch & afternoons Mon-Sat
In a capacious, spare atmosphere of under-stated luxury, this shop is lined with huge crocks

of olive oil and splendid displays of Italian specialities. If you prefer to dine in, try the long white marble table when they're not doing cooking demonstrations or classes there.

### VAN DAM Map pp286-7 _Takeaway/Traiteur_
☎ 670 65 70; Cornelius Schuystraat 8; prices vary; 🕑 lunch & afternoons Tue-Sat
Van Dam's caters some of the city's ritziest parties, and the rest of us can shop or lunch here. Ever-changing selections are Italian- and French-inspired, with salads, innovative soups (eg tomato brie) and gorgeous desserts.

### WAGAMAMA Map pp286-7 _Japanese/Noodles_
☎ 528 77 78; Max Euweplein 10; mains €7.55-12.95; 🕑 lunch & dinner
This Japanese-inspired noodle house started in London, and it's monstrously popular here as well. Its long rows of spare, rectangular tables, laid out cafeteria-style, are often filled with hipsters and assorted young'uns fortifying themselves for days or nights on the town. Staples include chicken ramen, Japanese curries and fried noodles or rice. Some of the dishes have been prettied up for Western palates, but that doesn't stop them from being good.

### YOICHI Map pp286-7 _Japanese_
☎ 622 68 29; Weteringschans 128; mains €9-25.50, set menu €29-45.50; 🕑 dinner
Classic Yoichi specialises in fastidiously pre-pared sushi and sashimi. Book the upstairs tatami room and order the 'Shogun Deluxe': this all-round winner features tasty morsels of yakitori, tempura, miso, sukiyaki and sashimi.

### ZUIDLANDE Map pp286-7 _French_
☎ 620 73 93, Utrechtsedwarsstraat 141; mains €22.50-24, 4-course menu €40; 🕑 dinner Tue-Sat
Creative and flavoursome French-Med dishes (the oven-baked onion with Romano, thyme and Parma ham is a long-standing favourite) are served in this romantic, upscale restaurant. It's a memorable splurge.

### ZUSHI Map pp286-7 _Japanese_
☎ 330 68 82, Amstel 20; dishes €2.20-5.50; 🕑 lunch & dinner
You're heading to the Stopera or returning from a bike ride and you need sushi, stat. This conveyor belt sushi shop features post-industrial chic décor (stainless steel, brick and blondwood), reasonably priced plates and lightning service.

## Top Five Broodjeswinkels

- **Broodje van Kootje** (below)
- **Dutch Four** (p138)
- **Het Kuyltje** (p143)
- **Van Dobben** (this page)
- **Van den Berg's Broodjesbar** (p138)

# CHEAP EATS

### BROODJE VAN KOOTJE
Map pp286-7                                *Sandwich Shop*
☎ 623 20 36, Leidseplein 20 & ☎ 623 74 51,
Spui 28; broodjes from €1.75; ☽ lunch & dinner
This is Amsterdam's longest-running sandwich bar, although you'd never know it by its appearance (Micky D's has more charm). Still, it's open from lunch until late, the quality is solid, and you can't beat the central locations.

### MAOZ FALAFEL Map pp286-7          *Israeli*
☎ 420 74 35; Muntplein 1; sandwiches €1.50-3.50;
☽ lunch & dinner
Its flagship falafel sandwich is always crispy, hot and very authentic, with endless toppings from the self-service salad bar. There's a half-dozen branches around town, most open good and late.

### VAN DOBBEN Map pp286-7    *Sandwich Shop*
☎ 624 42 00; Korte Reguliersdwarsstraat 5; dishes €1.75-6; ☽ breakfast, lunch & dinner
This tiny stand has been kicking around since 1945 and also serves Amsterdam's *kroketten* of record (€2) – most other places seem to get theirs supplied from here. It's also much beloved for sandwiches, soups and omelettes, and its location just off Rembrandtplein makes it an compulsory stop on a pub crawl.

### Febo A-Go-Go

Our approach to the fast-food chain **Febo** (say '*fay*-bo') is pretty much the way Amsterdammers approach sex and drugs: you may well encounter it while you're in town, so you might as well educate yourself before you decide whether to partake.

Febo's grease-laden snacks are much-maligned but also secretly loved, not least of which because they're cheap (mostly between €1 and €2). Then there's the presentation: along one wall of these tiny shops, these delicacies practically wink at you from behind little glass doors like ugly kids on the make at a school dance: *kroketten* of veal or beef, the *kipburger* (made from chicken), the Feboburger (beef with grill sauce and lettuce) and a half-dozen others. Insert a euro or two into a slot, open the door, and pull out your snack.

It's down and dirty, all right, but as long as you keep your wits about you, there's nothing wrong with an occasional dalliance; plus, if you duck in and out quickly, who's gonna know?

# THE PLANTAGE, EASTERN ISLANDS & OOSTERPARK

In this district, a lot of our favourite places are by or (in some cases, literally) on the water. Choices range from the historic and homely of the Eastern Islands to the super-stylish of the Eastern Docklands; options in the Plantage are superbly located to sights and often great surprises in and of themselves.

### ABE VENETO Map p285                *Italian*
☎ 639 23 64; Plantage Kerklaan 2; mains €6.50-12.50; ☽ lunch & dinner
Sometimes you just want a corner place with good solid food at honest prices, and Abe Veneto is old-shoe comfy up to the vines hanging from the ceiling. The pizza menu tops out at €9.50 and has 45 choices – the gorgonzola pizza puts this stinky cheese to excellent use. Other options include pastas, salads and meat dishes. In summer, they set up a nice terrace by the canal.

### A TAVOLA Map pp282-3               *Italian*
☎ 625 49 94; Kadijksplein 9; mains €12-21; ☽ dinner
Overlooked by most tourists, this authentic Italian restaurant near the Shipping Museum serves mouth-wateringly tender meats and superb pastas that cry out for a selection from its excellent wine list. Reservations are a must.

**GARE DE L'EST** Map pp274-5 *International*
☎ 463 06 20; Cruquiusweg 9; 4-course set menu €26; 🕑 dinner

Gare de l'Est has both the smallest menu in Amsterdam and also the largest. They say that because four chefs (from traditions including North African, Asian and Mediterranean) take turns nightly in the kitchen, and what their course menus lack in length they make up in variety over the course of a year. Portuguese tiles and glowing Middle Eastern lamps adorn the interior, and courtyard seating exudes good vibes.

## KOFFIEHUIS VAN DEN VOLKSBOND

Map pp282-3 *International*
☎ 622 12 09; Kadijksplein 4; mains €9.50-15; 🕑 dinner

This laid-back place began life as a charitable coffee house for dockers, and it still has a fashionably grungy vibe – wood floors, a giant red rose mural and tall candles on the tables. The menu is huge plates of comfort food with ingredients like mussels and merguez, or try the risotto. The Belgian chocolate terrine has fans all over town.

**LA SALA** Map p285 *Portuguese/Spanish*
☎ 624 48 46; Plantage Kerklaan 41; mains €14.80-16.90; 🕑 dinner Tue-Sun

Amid a city full of Spanish tapas bars, La Sala serves Portuguese dishes as well; *bacalhão* (salt cod) and *espetada de porco* (skewered pork) are favourites. Tapas are generous, varied and colourful. The simple, blue-tiled room is more functional than exotic, but there's busy sidewalk seating in warm weather.

**PANAMA** Map pp282-3 *International*
☎ 311 86 86; Oostelijke Handelskade 4; mains €10-23; 🕑 dinner Wed-Sun

The Eastern Harbour's first grown-up restaurant has an enormous, sleek dining room, Mondrian colour scheme and circular, steel light fixtures. Gucci-garbed couples splurge on oysters and a weekly-changing menu of pastas and grills in European and Asian preparations.

**PLANCIUS** Map p285 *International*
☎ 330 94 69; Plantage Kerklaan 61A; mains €13.50-18; 🕑 lunch & dinner

Next to the Resistance Museum opposite the Artis Zoo, this dramatically stylish space (bright red bar at the back) is where TV execs head to cut deals over big serves of upmarket comfort

food. The menu changes quarterly, and there are friendly, good-looking waiters.

**SEA PALACE** Map pp282-3 *Chinese*
☎ 626 47 77; Oosterdokskade 8; mains €8.20-38.65; 🕑 lunch & dinner

The funny thing about floating Chinese restaurants: they look like tourist traps and may well be, but from Hong Kong to Holland many are admired for good food. The Sea Palace is no exception – its three floors are busy with Chinese and non, who come not just for great views of the city from across the IJ. You may have to order dim sum from a menu instead of a cart, but the shrimp in the *ha kow* dumplings go pop in your mouth just the same.

**TO DINE** Map p285 *Fusion*
☎ 850 24 00; 's Gravesandestraat 51; mains €15-19.50; 🕑 lunch & dinner

The main restaurant of the super-hip Hotel Arena offers a variety of dishes (veal, tenderloin, lamb, fish, etc) with influences from France, Spain, the Middle East and Japan. Dance your dinner off at the hotel's ToNight club next door.

# WORTH THE TRIP

**DE KAS** Map pp274-5 *International*
☎ 462 45 62; Kamerlingh Onneslaan 3, Frankendael Park; 5-course menu €42; 🕑 lunch Mon-Fri, dinner Mon-Sat

Admired by food lovers city-wide, De Kas has an organic attitude to match its chic glass greenhouse setting – try to go during a thunderstorm! They grow much of their own herbs and produce right there (if it's not busy you may be offered a tour), and the result is incredibly pure flavours and innovative combinations. Romantic and tony.

**ODESSA** Map p284 *International*
☎ 419 30 10; Veemkade 259; mains €15-21.50; 🕑 dinner

Odessa rocks. Literally. This groovy boat, with indoor and outdoor eating decks and a 1970s-themed, 'plush-porno' décor, is just the sort of place where Hugh Hefner would hold a debauched pyjama party – as if to emphasise that fact, DJs take over late at night. The menu changes frequently, and although opinions on food and service run the gamut from 'love-it' to 'hate-it', there's no denying it's a scene.

*Eating – The Plantage, Eastern Islands & Oosterpark*

## SOETERIJN CAFÉ-RESTAURANT

Map pp274-5        *International, Eclectic*

☎ 568 83 92; Linnaeusstraat 2; course menus around €25; ☺ lunch Tue-Fri, dinner Tue-Sat

It's fun to dine here before there is a performance in the adjacent Tropeninstituut Theater, as the meals served are inspired by the current performers' country of origin – you can expect anything from Turkish, Vietnamese, Indian or even Tibetan-themed meals.

## VOORBIJ HET EINDE Map pp282-3    *French*

☎ 419 11 33; Sumatrakade 613; mains €22.75, 3-6 course menus €32-58; ☺ dinner Wed-Sat

It means 'beyond the end', and on your trek out here to Java Eiland you may begin to question your judgement. Don't. This new place, with its super-mod architectural interior (frosted glass walls, lots of right angles), wins high praise for high French in high style. Chef's choice is a popular option. Lunch is by appointment only.

# OLD SOUTH

As you'd expect in the part of town that hosts the Concertgebouw and Rijksmuseum, the Old South is home to some very chichi places. It's also adjacent to De Pijp, where anything can happen – funky, frilly, fashionable and fun. Also in De Pijp, particularly along Albert Cuypstraat, you'll find some wonderful and diverse ethnic choices.

## CAFÉ DE PIJP Map pp286-7       *Café*

☎ 618 16 69; Ferdinand Bolstraat 17-19; mains €13.75-15; ☺ lunch & dinner

De Pijp the restaurant is a fitting emblem of De Pijp the neighbourhood: bright, young, cheerful, colourful, reasonably priced and good-looking both outside and in. You might see skinny young things digging into enormous plates of dishes like fish paella and tempura-style shrimp. Open lunch, dinner and happy hour.

## CAFFE PC Map pp286-7       *Café*

☎ 673 47 52; PC Hooftstraat 87; mains €5.90-10.20

On Amsterdam's most-fashionable shopping street, join fashionistas and browsers amid snappy music – designed with forethought but not overthought. Dine on fine salads (Kim Oh Kim is chicken, avocado and mozzarella), omelettes and sandwiches like the Monte Cristo.

## CAMBODJA CITY Map pp286-7   *Cambodian*

☎ 671 49 30; Albert Cuypstraat 58-60; mains €3.50-13.50; special dinner for 2 from €24; ☺ dinner Tue-Sun

The owner's welcome is warm and friendly, and the flavours are from across southeast Asia – *loempias* (spring rolls), Vietnamese noodle soups, Thai curries, etc. Set menus also reflect the different traditions, and there are fab displays of takeaway foods in case you don't feel like eating in.

## COBRA CAFÉ-RESTAURANT

Map pp286-7        *International*

☎ 470 01 11; Hobbemastraat 18; mains €5.50-15; ☺ lunch & dinner

## Top Five – Old South & De Pijp

- **CoBrA Cafe** (this page) We nominate this one for the setting, because sometimes you just want to relax overlooking the Museumplein.
- **Nieuw Albina** (p152) If you've never tried Surinamese, you may be pleasantly surprised.
- **Lalibela** (this page) A tiny Ethiopian spot that's a real adventure.
- **Mamouche** (p151) Super-popular neo-Moroccan in a very cool space.
- **Taarte van m'n Tante** (p152) Which are more kitsch? The tasty cakes or the pink decor?

This arty, glass cube of a restaurant, full of original works by Corneille and Appel, sure is touristy. But when you're all museumed out and need a salad, massive club sandwich or slice of 'Karel Appel pie', you'll hardly notice. The high-tech toilets are almost worth the €0.50 admission.

## LALIBELA Map pp274-5       *Ethiopian*

☎ 683 83 32; Eerste Helmersstraat 249; mains €8-12.50; ☺ dinner

This storefront off Overtoom was the Netherlands' first Ethiopian restaurant and it's still our favourite in town. See the Aksumite hide paintings with Christian motifs on the walls, drink Ethiopian beer from a half-gourd, and touch your meals – stews, vegetable and egg dishes eaten with your hands using *endjera*, a spongy pancake, instead of utensils. The unique, trippy music rounds out the experience.

### LE GARAGE Map pp274-5 French
☎ 679 71 76; Ruysdaelstraat 54; set menus €32.50-
48.50; ☺ lunch Mon-Fri, dinner nightly
Spy Dutch soap stars, media biz-kids and
a couple of international celebrities at this
glamorous joint. The semicircular room – with
bold red banquettes and mirrored walls – is
a great place to indulge in French-inspired
cuisine (standards include the raw tuna pizza
and rotisserie chicken), and the creamiest
crème brulée in town.

### ZABAR'S Map pp286-7 International
☎ 679 88 88, van Baerlestraat 49; mains €8.25-17.25;
☺ lunch Mon-Sat, dinner nightly
In this airy stucco and tile space spread over
two levels, the native Moroccan chef works
magic with Mediterranean ingredients to come
up with a rotating selection of dishes – chicken
tajine is a perennial favourite. The cooking
is flavourful and inspired, and the service is
friendly. Note: it's not affiliated with the New
York gourmet market of the same name.

# DE PIJP

### ALBERT CUYP 67 Map pp286-7 Surinamese
☎ 671 13 96; Albert Cuypstraat 67; mains €3.20-8.40;
☺ lunch & dinner
If you're looking for stylish surrounds, turn
away now. If, however, you're after quality
examples of Surinamese food, take a seat. A
colossal portion of roti kip (chicken curry, flaky
roti bread, potatoes, egg and cabbage) is a
fine replenishment after a couple of hours at
Albert Cuyp market.

### BAHTI HOUSE Map pp286-7 Indian
☎ 470 89 17; Albert Cuypstraat 41; mains €10-18;
☺ dinner
One of the best-kept secrets in De Pijp is this
exceedingly friendly, quick-serving, always-
tasty spot. The butter chicken masala (€12.50)
is consistently smooth and tender but the fiery
tandooris and biryanis won't disappoint either.
Start with a rich mango lassi and a chapatti
amuse-bouche on the shady terrace.

### DISTRICT V Map pp274-5 International
☎ 770 08 84; Van der Helstplein 17; 3-course menu
€28.50; ☺ dinner
You like the dishes? Buy 'em! Tables, lamps, even
the toilets were designed by local artists, and all –
or recreations thereof – can be purchased at
this gallery-cum-fine restaurant. The split-level
room (off a pretty square) has an eclectic feel

to match the cuisine – a daily-rotating stable of
chefs comes from traditions as diverse as France
and Brazil. Reservations suggested.

### EUFRAAT Map pp286-7 Middle Eastern
☎ 672 05 79; Eerste van der Helststraat 72;
mains €8-13.90; ☺ lunch & dinner
This no-frills, friendly eetcafé may not look like
much but it's hailed far and wide for its excellent
Assyrian food. It's a great place for starters like
hummus and baba ganoush (try an assortment
in a mezza combo); Assyrian pancakes stuffed
with chicken and cheese are a good value, as
is a fuel-injected cup of Arabic coffee. It's in
the middle of a lively pedestrian block.

### LOKAAL 4 Map pp274-5 International
☎ 675 26 20; Karel du Jardinstraat 47; mains €15;
☺ dinner
This newly opened, hardwood place with an
open kitchen features house-baked bread,
an antipasto selection (€10 to €15) and a
Mediterranean-influenced menu that changes
daily. Look out the huge windows to see a typical
Pijp neighbourhood backyard. Caffe speciaal
comes with three small serves of cakes.

### MADAME JEANETTE
Map pp286-7 International
☎ 673 33 32; Eerste van der Helststraat 42;
mains €14-22; ☺ lunch & dinner
Once the province of foxy models, now
everyone from bankers to kids can get the
model treatment in this hip, multiroom space.
Be seen in a lounge chair or against the backlit
bar, or see the action up close at the long table
near the kitchen. Even the chefs are good
looking. Menu (pastas, lamb, Mediterranean)
changes seasonally.

### MAMOUCHE Map pp286-7 Moroccan
☎ 673 63 61; Quellijnstraat 104; mains €14.50-21;
☺ dinner Tue-Sun
Since bursting onto the scene in 2002, Mamouche has met serious acclaim for modern
Moroccan 'midst minimalism. Exposed flooring,
mottled walls, a long leather banquette,
slat-beam ceiling and tables at right angles
complement the changing selection of cous-
cous, lamb and fish dishes. Check out the
brass fixtures in the loo – if you can find it.
Reservations are a must.

### MÁS TAPAS Map pp286-7 Spanish
☎ 664 00 66; Saenredamstraat 37; tapas from €3 per
plate; ☺ dinner

While 'tapas' has become Amsterdamese for anything served on a small plate, this cool, whitewashed room serves the real thing and is full of funsters having a garlicky good time.

### NIEUW ALBINA Map ppp286-7 *Surinamese*
☎ 379 02 23; Albert Cuypstraat 47-9; mains €4.50-11.50; ☽ lunch & dinner Wed-Mon
Down the block, Nieuw Albina is more polished and more expensive than Albert Cuyp 67, but the flavours are just as bold. One of the cheapest dishes on the menu, *moksi meti* (roast mixed meats over rice) is also one of the best.

### ZAGROS Map pp286-7 *Kurdish*
☎ 670 04 61; Albert Cuypstraat 50; mains €10.50-15.50; ☽ dinner
Never tried Kurdish food? Neither had we, but we're glad we did. Just as Kurdistan straddles Greece and Persia, so does the cuisine, familiar yet exotic with grills and stews (mostly lamb and chicken), salads of cucumber, tomato or onion, and starters like hummus and *dumast* (thick, dry yoghurt). There's nothing fancy about the atmosphere, so you can concentrate on the food.

# WORTH THE TRIP
## BETTY'S PETIT RESTAURANT
Map pp274-5 *Vegetarian*
☎ 644 58 96; Rijnstraat 75; 3 courses €23.50; ☽ dinner Tue-Sat
Some consider it the number one vegetarian restaurant in the country (the menu's small on any given day, but there's always something new). It's rounded out by tiny tables and commendably warm and friendly service. *Everyone* says to save room for dessert.

# CHEAP EATS
## BAGELS & BEANS
Map pp286-7 *Bakery, Sandwiches*
☎ 672 16 10, Ferdinand Bolstraat 70; ☎ 330 55 08;

Keisersgracht 504; bagel sandwiches €2.30-5.30; ☽ breakfast & lunch Mon-Fri, lunch Sat & Sun
At the Ferdinand Bolstraat location, join the crowds on the square near the Albert Cuyp Market for bagels with all the usual toppings, plus some new-fangled ones (smoked chicken with avocado and pesto). In poor weather the interiors at both locations are light and airy. Top it all off with a slice of dense fig cake; it goes exceedingly well with coffee.

### DE SOEPWINKEL Map pp286-7 *Soup*
☎ 673 22 93; Eerste Sweelinckstraat 19F; soups €3.50-10; ☽ lunch & early dinner Mon-Fri, lunch Sat
Slurping out loud is positively encouraged at sleek De Soepwinkel. A welcome alternative to fast-food joints, this airy, modern eatery does an ever-changing selection of seasonal soups, as well as homemade quiches, cakes and tarts. Note that they close around 7pm or 8pm, so early dinner means just that.

### GELATERIA ITALIANO PEPPINO
Map pp286-7 *Sweets*
☎ 676 49 10; Eerste Sweelinckstraat 16; gelati from €0.75
Ignore those packaged ice cream cones at the Albert Cuypstraat Market and head around the corner for a cone of lemon, mango, Malaga wine or a dozen-plus other flavours. What the heck – take a gamble and let them scoop you some of whatever's spinning in the ice-cream maker.

### TAARTE VAN M'N TANTE
Map pp286-7 *Sweets*
☎ 470 07 87; Ferdinand Bolstraat 10; desserts €2-3.75
One of Amsterdam's best-loved cake shops has opened this über-kitsch parlour at the edge of De Pijp selling apple pies (Dutch, French or 'tipsy'), pecan pie, and tarts with ingredients including truffles, marzipan with strawberry liqueur. Savouries include the mozzarella pesto quiche. Hot-pink walls accent cakes dressed like Barbie dolls – or are they Barbies dressed like cakes?

Eating – Old South

# Entertainment

# Entertainment

Amsterdam: Party capital of Europe, Sin City, Libertine.

There's certainly something to that. Whatever your scene, chances are Amsterdam has a way to fulfil it: from cosy bars to wild party nights, marijuana and the Red Light District, major sporting events, stadium concerts, intimate jazz pubs, Afro-Latino-electro-boho-trendo, gay, straight or undecided. You name it.

However...

Amsterdam is part of the Netherlands, where overall the shift is toward the right. And the Netherlands is part of Europe, from where there's pressure to clamp down on drugs. All this means the beginnings of change. We're not talking fascism (this *is* the Netherlands), but whereas the authorities once had an attitude of *gedoogbeleid* (turning a blind eye) to illegal activities (eg drugs), now that eye is not quite so blind.

The city's nightlife community is currently negotiating one perceived bullet. At the time of writing, the hospitality industry and the Dutch health ministry were in a heated debate over the potential ban on smoking in bars, cafés and restaurants. The health minister was pushing to have it start on 1 January 2006. However, that could all change by the time you read this. It would hardly be the first time.

Although, viewed from the streets, the city's nightlife hardly seems to have flagged, the next few years are bound to be interesting times. For now, the trend seems to be toward smaller clubs with DJs spinning and large raves in at the beach or out in the open. Amsterdammers, it seems, always find ways to party on.

## DRINKING

Given Amsterdam's wild reputation, it may surprise the first-time visitor that, in the mainstream, Amsterdam is very much a café society.

When the Dutch say 'café', they mean a pub, and there are over 1000 of them in the city. But more than just drinking houses, they're places to go and hang out for hours if you like. Amsterdam's cafés are stunning in their variety; some have regular customers or a certain type of clientele that's been coming there for years, if not generations.

Once upon a time, cafés only served a few perfunctory snacks, but many these days have proper menus. Less adventurous chefs get by on soups, sandwiches, salads, *tostis* (ingredients such as cheese and tomato or pesto grilled between two slices of bread) and the like. Those that take their food seriously (or would like their customers to think they do) call themselves *eetcafé* and their food can be very good indeed.

The most historic and famous type is the brown café *(bruin café)*. The name comes from the interior, stained with smoke from a century-plus of use (recent aspirants simply slap on the brown paint). You may well find sand on the wooden floor or Persian rugs on the tables to soak up spilled beer, and some sell snacks or full meals. Most importantly though: they provide an atmosphere conducive to deep, meaningful and often convivial conversation.

Grand Cafés are spacious with comfortable furniture. They're all the rage, and any pub that installs a few solid tables and comfortable chairs will call itself a grand café. A good tradition in many grand cafés is the indoor reading table with the day's papers and news magazines, including one or two in English. Another difference: they all have food menus, some quite elaborate. Some are very grand indeed, and when they open at 10am they're perfect for a lazy brunch with relaxing chamber music tinkling away in the background.

Theatre cafés are normally attached or adjacent to theatres, serving meals before and drinks after performances. Generally they're good places to catch performing artists and other types who do a lot of drinking. Women's cafés cater to a mainly gay clientele, but straight women will feel perfectly comfortable there too (see the later Gay & Lesbian venues, p169, for listings).

There are also a few tasting houses *(proeflokalen)*, generally small affairs where you can try dozens of genevers (Dutch gin) and liqueurs. Some are attached to distilleries (a holdover from the 17th century when many small distilleries operated around town), while others are simply affiliated. Beer cafés specialise in the brew, with many seasonal and potent brands on tap and in the bottle.

Irish and English pubs are currently so popular in Amsterdam that many pubs are undergoing extensive renovations and reopening with Guinness on tap and some Gaelic decorations. Don't worry though, we've only listed authentic ones. There's also been an explosion of ultra design-conscious, 'loungey' designer bars in the past several years. Some are ultra-modern, some retro, others shabby-chic.

Still other cafés straddle a few of these categories and others are so unique – New-Age tearooms for instance – that they defy easy classification.

Many cafés have outside seating on a *terras* (terrace) that may be covered and heated in winter. These are great places to relax and watch passers-by, soak up the sun, read a paper or write postcards. Once you've ordered a drink you'll be left alone, but you might be expected to order the occasional top-up. If all tables are occupied, don't be shy about asking if a seat is taken and sharing a table.

The price for a standard beer varies from around €1.25 in the outer suburbs to €2.50 in the popular Leidseplein and Rembrandtplein areas; a mixed drink (eg scotch and coke) will set you back €3 to €5. If you occupy a table or sit at the bar, it's common to put drinks on a tab and to pay when you leave.

Virtually every café in town opens at 10am and closes at 1am, extended until 3am on Friday and Saturday nights. Where the hours diverge significantly, we've let you know.

## Alcoholic Drinks

Lager beer is the staple, served cool and topped by a two finger–thick head of froth – supposedly to trap the flavour. Requests of 'no head please' will meet with a steely response. *Een bier*, *een pils* or *een vaas* will get you a normal glass; *een kleintje pils* is a small glass and *een fluitje* is a small, thin, Cologne-style glass. Many places also serve half-litre mugs *(een grote pils)* to please tourists, but somehow draught lager doesn't taste the same in a mug and goes flat if you don't drink quickly!

Popular brands include Heineken, Amstel, Grolsch, Oranjeboom, Dommelsch, Bavaria and the cheap Brouwersbier put out by the Albert Heijn supermarket chain. They contain about 5% alcohol by volume, so a few of those seemingly small glasses can pack quite a wallop. Tasty and stronger Belgian beers, such as Duvel and Westmalle Triple, are also very popular and reasonably priced. *Witbier* (eg the Dutch Wieckse Witte, the Belgian Hoegaarden) is a somewhat murky, crisp blonde beer that's drunk in summer with a slice of lemon. The dark, sweet *bokbier* is available in autumn. Don't be surprised if the beer sold in supermarkets is not much cheaper than beer in pubs.

*Glass of Heineken*

Dutch gin (*genever*, pronounced ya-NAY-ver) is made from juniper berries and is drunk chilled from a tiny glass filled to the brim. Most people prefer *jonge* (young) genever, which is smooth and relatively easy to drink; *oude* (old) genever has a strong juniper flavour and can be an acquired taste. A common combination, known as a *kopstoot* (head banger), is a glass of genever with a beer chaser – few people can handle more than two or three of those. Brandy is known as *vieux* or *brandewijn*. There are plenty of indigenous liqueurs, including *advocaat* (a kind of eggnog) and the herb-based *Beerenburg*, a Frisian schnapps.

Wines in all varieties are very popular thanks to European unity, which has given French vintners and their overpriced products a run for their money. The average Amsterdam supermarket stocks wines from every corner of Europe (with excellent value from Spain and Bulgaria) and many countries farther afield, such as Chile, South Africa and Australia. The most expensive bottle in a supermarket rarely costs more than €8 and will be quite drinkable.

# BROWN CAFÉS
## Medieval Centre
### DE DOELEN Map pp286-7
☎ 624 90 23; Kloveniersburgwal 125
On a busy canalside crossroads between the Amstel and Red Light District, this café dates back to 1895 and looks it: carved wooden goat's head, stained leaded glass lamps, sand on the floor. Still, it's far from stuffy, and there's a fun, youthful atmosphere here.

### DE SLUYSWACHT Map pp278-9
☎ 625 76 11; Jodenbreenstraat 1
Listing like a ship in a high wind, this tiny black building was once a lock-keeper's house on the Oude Schans. Today, the canalside terrace is one of the nicest spots we know in town to relax and down a beer (Dommelsch is the house specialty) with gorgeous views of the Montelbaanstoren (p97).

### LOKAAL 'T LOOSJE Map pp278-9
☎ 627 26 35; Nieuwmarkt 32-34
With its beautiful etched-glass windows and tile tableaux on the walls, this is one of the oldest and prettiest cafés in the Nieuwmarkt area. It attracts a vibrant mix of students, locals and tourists.

### OPORTO Map pp278-9
☎ 638 07 02; Zoutsteeg 1
This tiny brown café is worth visiting just for the inlaid woodwork behind the bar (check out the Zodiac signs). Its wrought-iron-and-parchment lighting fixtures are said to have been the same for 60 years. Thursdays and Fridays after work are the busiest times.

Near the Spui are quite a few brown cafés worth seeking out:

### DE SCHUTTER Map pp286-7
☎ 622 46 08; Voetboogstraat 13-15
This large student eetcafé has a brown café look, a relaxed vibe and inexpensive, tasty *dagschotels* (dishes of the day). It's open lunch and dinnertime and is a good place to fortify yourself on the cheap before a night on the town.

### DE ZWART Map pp286-7
☎ 624 65 11; Spuistraat 334
'Not everyone has knowledge of beer, but those who have it drink it here', is the translation of the slogan on a panel above this atmospheric bar with the original tile floor from 1921. Just across the alley from Hoppe (see following), de Zwart gets a different (though amicable) crowd of left-wing journalists and writers, as well as local government people.

### HOPPE Map pp286-7
☎ 420 44 20; Spui 18-20
Go on. Do your bit to ensure Hoppe maintains one of the highest beer turnovers in the city. Since 1670, drinkers have been enticed behind that velvet curtain into the dark interior to down a few glasses – the entrance is to the right of the pub-with-terrace of the same

---

**Top Five Drinking**

- Take in the art of legendary club promoter Herman Brood at **Café Dante** (p158).
- Feel like you're part of history over a beer at **Hoppe** (see right).
- Taste Amsterdam's own at **Bierbrouwerij 't IJ** (p104).
- Listen to Irish music (or make your own) at **Mulligans** (p160).
- Contemplate the gorgeous canal outside **'t Smalle** (p157).

---

name. In summer, Hoppe's crowd of boisterous business boys spills over onto the pavement of The Spui.

## PILSENER CLUB Map pp278-9
☎ 623 17 77; Begijnensteeg 4
Also known as Engelse Reet (ask the bartender for a translation), this small, narrow and ramshackle place doesn't allow you to do anything but drink and talk, which is what a 'real' brown café is all about. It opened in 1893 and has hardly changed since. Beer comes straight from the kegs in the back via the 'shortest pipes in Amsterdam' (most places have vats in a cellar or side room with long hoses to the bar); connoisseurs say they can taste the difference.

# Jordaan & Western Canal Belt
The Jordaan, the area adjoining Prinsengracht and nearby side streets, is packed with wonderful cafés:

## CAFÉ HET MOLENPAD Map pp286-7
☎ 625 96 80; Prinsengracht 653
This place attracts a nice mix of artists, students and tourists – some of whose work adorns the walls of this gallery-café. Lunch is the standard sandwich-and-salad affair, but dinner dishes are more interesting, with a mix of Dutch and Mediterranean flavours.

## CAFÉ 'T MONUMENTJE Map p277
☎ 624 35 41; Westerstraat 120
Diagonally opposite Café Nol, this slightly scruffy café is always full of barflies, backgammon players and locals. It's a good spot for a beer and a snack after shopping at the Westermarkt.

## CAFÉ 'T SMALLE Map p277
☎ 623 96 17; Egelantiersgracht 12
Take your boat and dock right on 't Smalle's pretty terrace – there's hardly a more convivial setting in the daytime or a more romantic one at night. It's equally charming inside – dating back to 1786 as a genever distillery and tasting house, and restored during the 1970s with antique porcelain beer pumps and leadlight windows.

## CAFÉ NOL Map p277
☎ 624 53 80; Westerstraat 109; 🕒 Wed-Mon from 9pm
Hipsters may cringe, but Café Nol epitomises the old-style Jordaan café with a must-see, kitsch interior. It's the sort of place where the original Jordaanese (ie before students, artists

and professionals moved in) still sing oompah ballads with drunken abandon; nowadays, everyone from athletic types to drag queens might join in. Here comes the neighbourhood.

## DE DOFFER Map pp286-7
☎ 622 66 86; Runstraat 12-14
Writers, students and artists congregate at this popular café (with adjoining bar) for affordable food and good conversation. The dining room with its old Heineken posters, large wooden tables and, occasionally, fresh flowers, is particularly ambient at night.

## DE PIEPER Map pp286-7
☎ 626 47 75; Prinsengracht 424
Considered by some to be the king of the brown cafés, De Pieper is small, unassuming and unmistakably old (1665). The interior features stained-glass windows, fresh sand on the floors, antique Delft beer mugs hanging from the bar and a working Belgian beer pump (1875). It's a friendly, sweet place for a late-night Wieckse Witte.

## DE PRINS Map p277
☎ 624 93 82; Prinsengracht 124
Close to the Anne Frank Huis, this pleasant and popular brown café prepares good lunch-time sandwiches, a terrific blue cheese fondue at night, and international dishes like vegetarian wraps.

## DE REIGER Map p277
☎ 624 74 26; Nieuwe Leliestraat 34
Assiduously local but highly atmospheric, this café has a quiet front bar and a noisy, more spacious dining section at the back serving a short menu (eg steaks, duck with peppercorns).

## DE TUIN Map p277
☎ 624 45 59; Tweede Tuindwarsstraat 13
Always a good place to start the evening – join the youngish clientele enjoying the wide selection of Belgian beers, good food and funky soul music.

## DE II PRINSEN Map pp278-9
☎ 624 97 22; Prinsenstraat 27
With its large windows, chandelier, mosaic floor and big terrace, this café looks suitably restrained. You may be surprised then by the pumping disco music inside; all those students munching on tasty sandwiches don't seem to mind.

### DE TWEE ZWAANTJES Map p277
☎ 625 27 29; Prinsengracht 114;
🕑 from 8pm Thu-Fri, from 3pm Sat-Sun
The small, authentic 'Two Swans' is at its hilarious best on weekend nights, when you can join some one hundred people belting out torch and pop standards, accompanied by René on the electric piano. Singing begins at 10pm on Fridays and Saturdays, and 5pm on Sundays.

### HET PAPENEILAND Map pp278-9
☎ 624 19 89; Prinsengracht 2
You won't be the only tourist visiting this café, but that doesn't make it any less worthwhile. It's a 1642 gem with Delft-blue tiles and a central stove. The name, 'Papists' Island', goes back to the Reformation when there was a clandestine Catholic church across the canal, allegedly linked to the other side by a once-secret tunnel that is still visible from the top of the stairs.

### VAN PUFFELEN Map p277
☎ 624 62 70; Prinsengracht 377
This large café-restaurant, popular among cashed-up professionals and intellectual types, has lots of nooks and crannies for nice, cosy drinks and big, communal tables for sharing meals like the antipasto and large salads on offer.

*Outdoor tables at café 't Smalle (p157)*

## Southern Canal Belt
### EYLDERS Map pp286-7
☎ 624 27 04; Korte Leidsedwarsstraat 47
During WWII, Eylders was a meeting place for artists who refused to toe the cultural line imposed by the Nazis, and the spirit lingers on. It's still an artists' café with exhibits, and makes a nice quiet retreat from the Leidseplein.

### OOSTERLING Map pp286-7
☎ 623 41 40; Utrechtsestraat 140
Opened in the 1700s as a tea and coffee outlet for the United East India Company, Oosterling is as authentic as it gets – run by the same family since 1877. These days it's packed with the after-work drinks crowd from the bank across the square and is one of the very few cafés that has a bottle-shop (liquor-store) permit.

### REYNDERS Map pp286-7
☎ 623 44 19; Leidseplein 6
This venerable (1897) establishment has undergone a touristy Irish makeover. It still retains a smidgen of old-world charm though, and the pleasant terrace (heated in winter) makes for good people-watching. Today, it shares a kitchen with the two neighbouring Irish (-style) pubs.

## The Plantage
### DE BAMBOESEUR Map p285
☎ 625 47 21; Plantage Parklaan 10
This one-time corner post office and bookstore has been reincarnated as a cheery brown café. Its decent menu (mains €9 to €13.50, including chicken sate, steaks and house-made spare ribs) makes it the de facto caféteria for the small hotels in the neighbourhood.

## GRAND CAFÉS
## Medieval Centre
### CAFÉ DANTE Map pp286-7
☎ 638 88 39; Spuistraat 320
This big, Art Deco–style space is peaceful during the day, but after 5pm weeknights it transforms into a lively bar full of stockbrokers and suits. Plus, you get your choice of outside views: The busy Spui out front or the lovely Singel in the back. Upstairs is the Herman Brood Galerie.

### CAFÉ DE JAREN Map pp286-7
☎ 625 57 71; Nieuwe Doelenstraat 20
Watch the Amstel float by from the balcony and waterside terraces of this huge, bright

and *very* grand café. Find a foreign publication at the great reading table and settle down for Sunday brunch (try the smoked salmon rolls) or an afternoon snack like banana cream pie.

### CAFÉ-RESTAURANT DANTZIG
Map pp286-7

☎ 620 90 39; Zwanenburgwal 15

In the Stopera building, Dantzig doesn't have the history of some other cafés in town, but that doesn't make it any less appealing. The great Amstel-side terrace is always busy in summer, with excellent views over the water and lots of sunlight. It's just the place to unwind after shopping at Waterlooplein market before catching a show, or to watch the Friday night skate.

### LUXEMBOURG Map pp286-7

☎ 620 62 64; Spui 24

Join gaggles of glam locals and tourists at this permanently busy café. Our advice: grab a paper (from the reading table or the Athenaeum newsagency across the square), procure a sunny seat on the terrace, order the 'Royale' snack platter (bread, cured meats, Dutch cheese and deep-fried croquettes) and watch the world go by. Inside is handsome, with parquet floors, a marble bar and Art-Deco stained-glass skylight.

## Western Canal Belt
### CAFÉ DE VERGULDE GAPER Map pp278-9

☎ 624 89 75; Prinsenstraat 30

Decorated with old chemists' bottles and vintage posters, this former pharmacy (it translates as 'the golden mortar') has amiable staff and a terrace with copious afternoon sun. It gets busy late afternoons with 20- and 30-somethings, as well as media types meeting for after-work drinks and big plates of fried snacks or dinner salads.

### DULAC Map pp278-9

☎ 624 42 65; Haarlemmerstraat 118; ☺ from 4pm

This former bank building is outrageously decked out in a kooky, kind of spooky mixture of styles (think Turkish, Art Nouveau and Amsterdam School with Gothic accents). There are DJs Friday and Saturday nights, plus a pool table. Note: as of our visit, they were contemplating opening for lunch.

## Southern Canal Belt
### CAFÉ AMERICAIN Map pp286-7

☎ 556 32 32; Crowne Plaza American Hotel, Leidsekade 97

This Art Deco monument, opened in 1902, is the oldest grand café in Amsterdam, with huge picture and stained-glass windows overlooking Leidseplein, a marvellous, library-like reading table and a great terrace. It's the sort of place that attracts rafts of celebrities, as the photos lining the walls of the adjacent Euro-contempo Nightwatch bar will attest. Café prices are stiff, but it's worth visiting for a drink, a snack or the excellent breakfast buffet (€10).

### DE KROON Map pp286-7

☎ 625 20 11; Rembrandtplein 17-1

A popular venue for media events and movie premiere parties. High ceilings, velvet armchairs, taxidermic specimens on the walls, and the opportunity to feel like a star yourself on the covered balcony. You can wave at the Little People below on the Rembrandtplein. There's a lift to get up the two storeys, but climb the two flights instead and you'll be rewarded with an Art-Deco tiled staircase.

## Old South
### DE ENGEL Map pp286-7

☎ 675 05 44; www.de-engel.net; Albert Cuypstraat 182

Let the golden angel above the Albert Cuyp Market be your beacon. The understated Dutch façade gives little clue as to the soaring space inside, with deep dangling chandeliers, a loooong bar and balconies ringing the second level. There are Sunday brunch concerts, frequent jazz and classical performances, and occasional DJ nights.

## IRISH & ENGLISH PUBS
## Medieval Centre
### BLARNEY STONE Map pp278-9

☎ 623 38 30; Nieuwendijk 29

This reputable Irish pub is much loved for its country-style interior bursts with Irish, Australians and locals enjoying a pint.

### DURTY NELLY'S Map pp278-9

☎ 638 01 25; Warmoesstraat 117; ▢

Huge, dark and always busy, this Red Light District pub attracts foreign visitors from the cheap hotels in the area with fun, drinks, darts and pool. It serves a first-rate Irish breakfast too.

### LAST WATERHOLE Map pp278-9

☎ 624 48 14; Oudezijds Armsteeg 12

Hankering to hang out with Hell's Angels and homesick Brits? This has three pool tables, jam sessions and rock or blues cover bands. If you're really enjoying your self book a hostel bed (from €14). Note: enter off the small alley.

### MOLLY MALONE'S Map pp278-9
☎ 624 11 50; Oudezijds Kolk 9
Regularly packed with Irish folk, this dark, woody pub holds spontaneous folk music sessions – bring your own guitar.

## Southern Canal Belt
### MULLIGANS Map pp286-7
☎ 622 13 30; www.mulligans.nl; Amstel 100
This is probably the most 'authentic' pub, at least music-wise. There's a congenial atmosphere, Guinness on tap and live Irish music most nights from 9pm (no cover charge). Sunday *sesiàns* let you participate. BYOI (instrument) and T (talent).

### OLD BELL Map pp286-7
☎ 620 41 35; Rembrandtplein 46
A comfortable English pub full of beamed ceilings and ephemera like heraldry, old signs and drinking mugs. Meals include omelettes, smoked fish and grilled meats, and there's a big screen TV for sports. It's popular among businesspeople (especially for the business lunch) and tourists.

## Old South
### O'DONNELL'S Map pp286-7
☎ 676 77 86; Ferdinand Bolstraat 5 at Marie Heinekenplein
This large Irish pub, just south of the Heineken Experience, has a few snugs (great if you can grab one), live football, cricket and rugby on TV, and a terrace full of sociable types.

## TASTING HOUSES
### Medieval Centre
### DE BLAUWE PARADE Map pp278-9
☎ 624 48 60; Nieuwzijds Voorburgwal 176-180;
🕑 tastings nightly
The building, now the hotel Die Poort van Cleve, was the site of the original Heineken brewery, so it seems an appropriate place for tastings (of genevers though, not beers), with Dutch snacks like herring. While there, your eye can feast on the Delft blue-tile mural (1870s), a parade of children bearing gifts to an emperor. Tasting courses run from €14.50.

### DE DRIE FLESCHJES Map pp278-9
☎ 624 84 43; Gravenstraat 18;
🕑 Mon-Sat noon-8pm, Sun 3-7pm
Behind the Nieuwe Kerk, De Drie Fleschjes dates from 1650, and is dominated by 52 old vats that are rented out to businesses who take their clients here. It specialises in liqueurs (although you can also get genevers) – the macaroon liqueur is quite nice. Also, take a peek at the collection of *kalkoentjes*, small bottles with hand-painted portraits of former mayors.

### PROEFLOKAAL WIJNAND FOCKINCK Map p277
☎ 639 26 95; Pijlsteeg 31; 🕑 5-9pm
This small tasting house (dating from 1679) has scores of genevers and liqueurs – some quite expensive and potent! Fockinck is located on an arcade behind Grand Hotel Krasnapolsky, and although there are no seats or stools, it is an intimate place to knock back a taste or two with a friend or two. We particularly enjoy the *boswandeling* (walk in the woods; €2.50), a vivacious combination of young genever, herb bitters and orange liqueur – the effect is like cloves. Plus, the name sounds like what you think it sounds like (and how fun is that?). Note: large groups are not welcome.

## Western Canal Belt
### DE ADMIRAAL Map pp278-9
☎ 625 43 34; Herengracht 319;
🕑 5pm-midnight, Mon-Sat
The grandest and largest of Amsterdam's tasting houses, de Admiraal is also a restaurant and party venue. Although some grumble that they pour only their own house brands (16 genevers and 60 liqueurs made by van Wees, an Amsterdam distiller), it's hard to quibble over the lovely setting and pleasant staff.

## BEER CAFÉS
### Medieval Centre
### IN DE WILDEMAN Map pp278-9
☎ 638 23 48; Kolksteeg 3
This former distillery tasting house has been transformed into an atmospheric yet quiet beer café with over 200 bottled beers, 18 varieties on tap and a longstanding smokefree area. Locals rave about the choice of Trappist ales, the huge selection from Belgium and the Netherlands, and the potent French 'Belzebuth' (13% alcohol!).

# Western Canal Belt

## GOLLEM Map pp278-9

☎ 626 66 45; Raamsteeg 4

Gollem, the pioneer of Amsterdam's beer cafés, is a minuscule space covered in beer paraphernalia (old coasters, bottles and posters). The 200 beers on tap or in the bottle attract lots of drinkers.

## 'T ARENDSNEST Map pp278-9

☎ 421 20 57; Herengracht 90

This gorgeous, re-styled brown café, with its glowing, copper genever boilers behind the bar, specialises in Dutch beer. Be sure to try the herby, powerful 'Jopen Koyt', brewed from a 1407 recipe.

# The Plantage

## BROUWERIJ 'T IJ Map pp274-5

☎ 622 83 25; Funenkade 7; 🕑 3-8pm Wed-Sun

The tasting room of Amsterdam's leading micro-brewery (p104) has a cosy, down-and-dirty beer hall feel (walls lined with bottles from around the world, dried hops) and the house brews on tap. In nice weather you can enjoy your beer on the terrace at the foot of the windmill. Where better to sample a *zatte* (drunk) or a sweet, orange-coloured *struis* (ostrich)?

---

### Worth Noting

- **De Bekeerde Suster** (Map pp278-9; ☎ 423 01 12; Kloveniersburgwal 6-8) It's got the brew tanks, it's got the beautiful hardwood interior, it's even got the history: a 16th-century brewery/ cloister run by nuns. They reopened under new management (with new beers) as we went to press. Try one and tell us how you liked it.

---

# THEATRE CAFÉS

## Medieval Centre

### DE BRAKKE GROND Map pp278-9

☎ 626 00 44; Nes 43

Part of the Flemish Cultural Centre, this café overlooking a quiet square does an honest trade in Flemish beer (try a magnum bottle from a Belgian abbey) and home-style food (largely fish and veal dishes).

# Western Canal Belt

## FELIX MERITIS CAFÉ Map p277

☎ 626 23 21; Keizersgracht 324

Join performing artists from around Europe and the city's cultural cognoscenti imbibing in this high-ceilinged, quietly refined room (think theatrical lighting). Huge windows overlooking the canal make it a sunny place for breakfast (from 9am).

# Southern Canal Belt

## DE BALIE Map pp286-7

☎ 623 36 73; Kleine-Gartmanplantsoen 10

In the Balie performance space, lovely Deco-meets-industrial design attracts a diverse crowd of artists, politicians, journalists, actors, filmmakers and anyone else looking for a decent lunch.

## DE SMOESHAAN Map pp286-7

☎ 625 03 68; Leidsekade 90

Theater Bellevue's café gets pretty lively before and after the shows, with theatre visitors and performers. During daytimes it's a nice place to relax by the Singelgracht. The pub food is better than it needs to be (try the *gehakt* at lunchtime) and there's a good full-on restaurant upstairs too (restaurant closed July to mid-August).

# Old South

## VERTIGO Map pp286-7

☎ 612 30 21; Vondelpark 3

Bonus: this is both a theatre café (at the main hall of the Filmmuseum, p112) and, in nice weather, a great place to linger for hours watching the goings-on in the Vondelpark. Try the *Uitsmijter* Vertigo (with bacon, mushrooms, peppers, carrots and melted cheese); other main dishes: €14 to €20.50.

# Oosterpark

## KRITERION Map p285

☎ 623 17 08; www.kriterion.nl; Roeterstraat 170

Come to the UvA's Kriterion movie theatre for film premieres and film-themed parties. It's in a former diamond factory – and a very cool Amsterdam School space. It's student run, so drinks are cheap, and there's a limited food menu. Check website for films, events and hours.

Entertainment – Drinking

# OTHER CAFÉS
## Medieval Centre
### B VAN B CAFÉ Map pp278-9
☎ 638 39 14; Beursplein 1; ⏰ 9am-5pm Mon-Wed, 10am-6pm Thu-Sat, 11am-6pm Sun

The café in the Beurs van Berlage (p185), one the city's most spectacular buildings, boasts fabulous original brick and tilework, and murals by Jan Toorop (1903) representing past, present and future. Food includes the Beurs burger (minced veal) and the usual assortment of sandwiches and salads. Unless the main building is reopened to the public, this is your only sure way to get inside.

### CAFÉ CUBA Map pp278-9
☎ 627 26 35; Nieuwmarkt 3

If a brown café were beamed to the tropical Atlantic, it would probably have Café Cuba's air of faded elegance. Slouch into a table with names etched into it, and quaff blender drinks like mai-tais and planter's punch. It may remind you of Hemingway or the Buena Vista Social Club, although we wonder whether Café Cuba's attractive 20- and 30-something crowd have even heard of them.

### CAFÉ-RESTAURANT KAPITEIN ZEPPO'S Map pp278-9
☎ 624 20 57; Gebed Zonder End 5

This site, off Grimburgwal, has assumed many guises over the centuries: a cloister during the 15th, a horse-carriage storehouse in the 17th and a cigar factory in the 19th. These days it's festive, attractive and almost romantic, with a beautiful garden and Belgian beers. There's live music Sunday from 4pm (cover groups and big bands).

### WAAG Map pp278-9
☎ 422 77 72; Nieuwmarkt 4

This former 15th-century weigh house (and later, gallows!, p95) is now an impressive café-restaurant combining old-world accents (massive, circular wrought-iron candelabras) with new-world drinks and food, though it's rather expensive (€4 for a Corona?!?). It serves pretty good sandwiches (try the Club) and salads too, plus more elaborate mains.

## Western Canal Belt
### CAFÉ THIJSSEN Map pp278-9
☎ 623 89 94; Brouwersgracht 107

The glowing umber, Art Deco inspired interior with stained-glass windows and big tables is a crowd-puller. It's busy on weekends with groups of convivial neo-Jordaanese yuppies meeting up for a late brunch and staying on until dinner.

### POMPADOUR Map pp286-7
☎ 623 95 54; Huidenstraat 12

Join society ladies sipping top-notch tea and nibbling away at house-made Belgian-style chocolates and pastries at this chichi little tearoom. If you just want the chocolates, they're €4.30 per 100g.

## Southern Canal Belt
### AMSTEL BAR & BRASSERIE Map p285
☎ 622 60 60; Amstel Hotel, Professor Tulpplein 1

Appropriately clubby and intimate, this riverside bar is a very dignified place to enjoy a quiet drink or rub elbows with famous financiers.

### AMSTEL HAVEN Map p285
☎ 665 26 72; Mauritskade 1

Bike up or boat up to where the Amstel meets the Singelgracht, snag a canalside table under an umbrella, and have yourself a swell view of the water and skyscrapers. Daytimes, munch on *uitsmijters*, sandwiches and mains (€7 to €18), and on weekend nights, the dining room becomes a dance floor with DJs or live music.

### CAFÉ SCHILLER Map pp286-7
☎ 624 98 46; Rembrandtplein 26; ⏰ from 4pm

Most cafés would pay a fortune to have Schiller's fabulous Deco interior, but this is original. Walls are lined with portraits of Dutch actors

---

## Worth Noting

- **Café De IJsbreker** (Map 285; ☎ 468 18 08; Weesperzijde 23) This café is named for the centre for contemporary music, which currently shares its building. At the time of writing it was due to move to the Eastern Docklands in 2005. There is a great riverside terrace that's glorious in summer for a long lunch. In cooler weather: cheese fondue.
- **Himalaya** (Map pp 278-9; ☎ 626 08 99; Warmoesstraat 56; ⏰ Mon-Sat) Just the place to put some yin back into your yang. Sip a cup of 'vitality' tea, snack on a vegie burger and contemplate the Buddha statues at this calm, tearoom in the New-Age shop overlooking Damrak. See Shopping (p000).

and cabaret artists from the 1920s and '30s. Bar stools and booths are often occupied by tippling journalists and artists, and folks tucking into pre- and post-theatre menus.

### DE KOE Map pp286-7
☎ 625 44 82; Marnixstraat 381; ☻ from 4pm
'The Cow' is loved by a 25-plus crowd of locals for its *gezellig* atmosphere, fun pop quizzes, darts tournaments, good (cheap) restaurant and free performances by local rock bands.

# DESIGNER BARS
## Medieval Centre

### BAR BEP Map pp278-9
☎ 626 56 49; Nieuwezijds Voorburgwal 260
With its olive-green vinyl couches and ruby-red walls, Bep resembles a kitsch, 1950s Eastern European cabaret lounge. It gets groovy with filmmakers, photographers and artists.

### DIEP Map pp278-9
☎ 420 20 20; Nieuwezijds Voorburgwal 256
Located just next door to Bar Bep, Diep does first-rate quirky decorations. You might find chandeliers made of bubble wrap, a six-foot fibreglass hammerhead shark, illuminated electronic signs above the bar and a similarly creative crowd.

### LIME Map pp278-9
☎ 639 30 20; Zeedijk 104
Small but perfectly formed Lime, with its ever-changing, kitsch-cool interior and upbeat grooves, is the perfect pre-club pit stop.

### NL LOUNGE Map pp278-9
☎ 622 75 10; Nieuwezijds Voorburgwal 169
NL's 13m-long, solid-glass bar, underlit for dramatic effect, is rather special. So, too, is the wallpaper (Tang Dynasty, anyone?) and the gangs of glamourpusses grooving to deep house and deep soul on the weekends.

## Western Canal Belt

### BLAKE'S Map p277
☎ 530 20 10; Keizersgracht 384
Like the hotel and restaurant surrounding it, Blake's lobby bar is super-posh – sleek black and white (with Indonesian influences) and a great place to stand and pose…if you can get in. Restaurant patrons get seating priority, but if you make it you might swear that the beautiful people surrounding you stepped off the pages of the fashion mags on the coffee tables.

### FINCH Map pp278-9
☎ 626 24 61; Noordermarkt 5
This funkalicious bar, with its retro décor (deliberately mismatched yet somehow harmonious) is just the spot to hang out and knock back a few beers after a visit to the market. It's known for an arty-design-y clientele, and lipstick lesbians.

### PROUST Map pp278-9
☎ 623 91 45; Noordermarkt 4
Next door to Finch, this bar is sleek and hip with mod colours, and the crowd changes as the hour does – families in the daytime, students (and older) at night. It's also known for its hot chocolate.

### WOLVENSTRAAT 23 Map pp278-9
☎ 320 08 43; Wolvenstraat 23
Part 1970s love-pad, part slick lounge, this fun day-into-night bar plays host to students, biz-kids and hipsters. The restaurant serves very uppity, contemporary Chinese – lots of fun.

### ZULU Map pp278-9
Westerstraat 30
There's not a right angle in this new café, decorated like Art Nouveau at full flower. Cocktails are the specialty of the bar, the kitchen (open from 11am) serves vegetarian, fish and meat mains, and the coffees are organic. At night, DJs play a variety of music for a 20-to-40 crowd.

Entertainment – Drinking

## Places to Play

You'll have ample opportunity for mind games at Amsterdam's bars and clubs, but if you're after more traditional games, try one of the following. Some are pretty down & dirty, and that's the way we like 'em.

- **Snookerclub Final Touch** (Map pp286-7; ☎ 620 92 52; Prinsengracht 735; ☜ from 2pm; pool tables before/ after 7pm €5/7, snooker tables €7/7.50) This two-storey spot with six snooker tables and five pool tables feels student-y but gets a mixed crowd. Other games include backgammon, darts and chess.
- **Schaakhuis Gambit** (Map p277; ☎ 622 18 01; Bloemgracht 20; ☜ from 1pm) Chess players won't want to miss Gambit's 10 intimate, well-worn tables. Daytimes the crowd skews older, while the sharks come out at night. Refreshments include coffee, beer and tostis.
- **Snookerclub De Keizer's** (Map p277; ☎ 623 15 86; Keizersgracht 256; ☜ from 1pm) De Keizer's five storeys feel like something out of The Shining, a once-grand 18th Century canal house whose huge rooms now contain just one or two tables each. You can get drinks and bar snacks, and it's always pretty quiet. It's bittersweet to see such faded glory; on the other hand, it's soooo cool that it exists.
- **Poolcafé De Keu** (Map pp286-7; ☎ 689 14 49; Eerste Helmerstraat 5; ☜ from 4pm; tables €5 per hour; reservations suggested Thu-Sat) In this one-time carriage house off the Overtoom, you'll rub elbows with students, 20-somethings and travellers at over 12 pool tables and a billiard table. Bonus: cheap beer.

  **Max Euweplein** (p90) Enthusiastic chess players can play and schmooze around the oversized outdoor chessboard.

## Southern Canal Belt

### DE HUYSCHKAEMER Map pp286-7
☎ 627 05 75; Utrechtsestraat 137

A one-time restaurant, de Huyschkaemer has made the transition to a full-time designer bar, with a mixed crowd – gay and straight, expat and local, old and young. The setting is minimalist, with spare walls and booths, and if you get hungry, they can bring in excellent tapas from Pata Negra (p145) across the street.

### DE RUIMTE Map pp286-7
☎ 489 36 19; Eerste Constantijn Huygensstraat 20

The café of the SMART art space is a huge, industrial-style bar with an enormous street-side terrace. Rub shoulders with arty-bohemian types as DJs spin funk and hip-hop.

### JOIA Map pp286-7
☎ 626 67 69; Korte Leidsedwarsstraat 45

The fashionable folks who brought you NOA (the noodle restaurant across the canal; p145) opened this sure-to-impress bar in 2003, and it's been bustling ever since with Dutch trendies and actors. The look? Victorian drawing room on speed, with red velveteen wallpaper and a bamboo garden; a photo of Andy Warhol observes.

### Worth Noting

Near Leidseplein, Marnixstraat has a clutch of funky and busy bars. Join the perpetually clamorous din of 20-something arts students, designers and stylish city workers drinking and dancing:

- **Lux** (Map pp286-7; ☎ 422 14 12; Marnixstraat 403)
- **Kamer 401** (Map pp286-7; ☎ 320 45 80; Marnixstraat 401)
- **Weber** (Map pp286-7; ☎ 627 05 74; Marnixstraat 397)

# SMOKING

First things first: in Amsterdamese, a *coffeeshop* is a place that sells cannabis. A *koffiehuis* (say 'coffee house') is an espresso bar or sandwich shop. If you try to toke up at the latter, you'll receive something between a look of revulsion and a hostile expulsion. The Dutch are nice people; don't push it.

In the former, though, you are free to purchase and smoke away. Many coffeeshops also live up their literal name and serve coffee (as well as beer, other drinks and snacks). There are also a few *hashcafés*.

You'll have no trouble finding a coffeeshop; there are about 200 in total. It's a safe bet that a place showing palm leaves and Rastafarian colours (red, gold and green) will have something to do with marijuana; others are barely distinguishable from pubs.

Ask at the bar for the list of goods on offer, usually packaged in small bags for €4 to €12 (the better the quality, the less the bag will contain). You can also buy ready-made joints in nifty, reusable packaging (a good idea because the stuff can be potent).

'Space' cakes and cookies are sold in a rather low-key fashion, mainly because tourists have problems with them. If you're unused to their effects, or the time they can take to kick in and run their course, you could be in for a rather involved experience. Ask the staff how much you should take and *heed their advice*, even if nothing happens after an hour. Some coffeeshops sell magic mushrooms – quite legal because they're an untreated, natural product – but if you're after serious mushies and other mind-altering products, see Smart Drug Shops in the Shopping chapter.

Most cannabis products used to be imported, but these days the country has top-notch home produce, so-called *nederwiet* (NAY-der-weet) developed by horticulturists and grown in greenhouses with up to five harvests a year. Even the police admit it's a superior product, especially the potent 'superskunk' with up to 13% of THC, the active substance (Nigerian grass has 5% and Colombian 7%). According to a government-sponsored poll of coffeeshop owners, *nederwiet* has captured over half the market and hash is in decline even among tourists.

Price and quality are OK – you won't get ripped off in a coffeeshop like you would on the street. Most shops are open 10am to 1am Sunday to Thursday, and until 3am Friday and Saturday. Note that many coffeeshops don't have phones.

# Medieval Centre

## ABRAXAS Map pp278-9
☎ 625 57 63; Jonge Roelensteeg 12
Hands down the most beautiful coffeeshop in town. Choose from southwest USA, Middle-eastern and other styles of décor spread over three floors. There are live DJs, extra-friendly staff and Internet usage with a drink purchase.

## DAMPKRING Map pp286-7
Handboogstraat 29
Consistently a winner of the Cannabis Cup, Dampkring is dark-ish, young-ish and decorated rather hobbit-ish. Its name means the ring of the Earth's atmosphere where smaller items combust.

## DUTCH FLOWERS Map pp286-7
☎ 624 76 24; Singel 387
Were it not for this shop's main wares, you'd be hard pressed to distinguish it from a brown café, with the game on TV and a lovely view of the Singel. It all means that you needn't slum it with the kids or feel as if you've gone to India in order to enjoy a toke.

## EL GUAPO Map pp278-9
Nieuwe Nieuwstraat 32
Sorta Latin, sorta caveman, this shop is populated by friendly people and is known for some of the best hash in town. You can bring your own music and ask them to play it – just remember to get it back when you leave.

## GREENHOUSE Map pp278-9
☎ 627 17 39; Oudezijds Voorburgwal 191
One of the most popular coffeeshops in town – smokers love the funky music, multicoloured mosaics, psychedelic stained-glass windows and the high-quality weed and hash. The alcohol licence doesn't hurt either.

## GREY AREA Map pp278-9
☎ 420 43 01; Oude Leliestraat 2;
🕒 noon-8pm Tue-Sun
Owned by a couple of laid-back American guys, this tiny shop introduced the extra-sticky, flavoursome 'Double Bubble Gum' weed to the city's smokers. It keeps shorter hours than most coffeeshops.

## HOMEGROWN FANTASY Map pp278-9
☎ 627 56 83; Nieuwezijds Voorburgwal 87A
Quality Dutch-grown product, pleasant staff, good tunes and famous space cakes make this popular with backpackers from nearby hostels. Patrons make use of the three-foot glass bongs to smoke hydroponic weed.

# Western Canal Belt

## BARNEY'S Map pp278-9
☎ 625 97 61; Haarlemmerstraat 102
Ever-popular Barney's is more famous for its enormous all-day breakfasts (the traditional Irish is the most popular) than its quality weed and hash. Go figure. Non-smokers can just go for the food at its new café down the block.

### Gambling

Rounding out the cavalcade of vices that is Amsterdam, the **Holland Casino** (☎ 521 11 00; www.hollandcasino.nl; Max Euweplein 62; admission €3.50, refunded in chips; ☉ 1pm-3am) is prominently located by the Singelgracht, an easy walk from the Leidesplein. More new Amsterdam than old, it's a splashy place with slot machines, poker, touch bet roulette and, our favourite name, Caribbean stud poker. According to the tourist bureau, the casino's one of the top attractions in town.

As with Amsterdam's other vices, an ethic of 'know before you go' prevails. A rack of booklets sits near the entrance in several languages explaining the rules of the games and various strategies for playing. Government-issued photo ID (displaying date of birth) is required for admission.

**LA TERTULIA** Map p277
Prinsengracht 312
A backpackers' favourite, this mother-and-daughter-run coffeeshop has a greenhouse feel. You can either sit outside by the Van Gogh-inspired murals, play some board games, or take in those Jurassic-sized crystals by the counter.

## Southern Canal Belt

**BULLDOG** Map pp286-7
☎ 625 62 78; Leidseplein 13-17
Amsterdam's most famous coffeeshop chain has evolved into its own empire, with multiple locations (some double as cafés), a hotel, bike rental, even its own brand of energy drink. This flagship location on the Leidseplein is in a former police station. How times have changed.

**GLOBAL CHILLAGE** Map pp286-7
☎ 777 97 77; Kerkstraat 51
This relaxed shop with friendly staff looks like a little forest with trippy murals and chilled-out music (African and jazzy beats), populated by happy smokers relaxing on comfortable couches.

## Eastern Islands

**BEST FRIENDS** Map pp274-5
Molukkenstraat 31
Murals of cartoony Dutch boys enjoying smokable pleasures with cartoony African boys make this a worthy symbol of this ethnically mixed neighbourhood south of the Eastern Docklands. Otherwise, it could pass for a Starbuck's. Techno plays in the background.

# CLUBBING

Thursday and Saturday are the most popular club nights, and not much happens before midnight. Most of the venues listed here close at 4am on Thursday and Sunday and 5am on Friday and Saturday. If you're looking for recovery parties, keep an eye out for flyers at record shops, smart-drug and club-wear stores, or ask around the club at closing time. Record shops such as Dance Tracks (p195) and Rush Hour (p198) are known for keeping a bead on the scene.

For a long time, dress at Amsterdam's clubs was decidedly informal, but that's beginning to change. If you end up at a club with a bouncer or hostess, you may well be given the once-over before being allowed to enter. At larger venues, don't be surprised if you have to pass through metal detectors, check your bags and even be frisked before entering.

Some clubs charge exorbitant admission (up to €20); others are free. If there's no entrance fee, it's good etiquette to slip the doorman a couple of euros as you leave. Also, have a bit of change (€0.50) handy for when you visit the toilet.

We're not going to get into listing individual club nights – they'll probably change by the time you read this. But do consult the websites of the venues (they're usually in Dutch but with enough English that you'll get it) or ask around for the hot places – smaller music stores can be great sources.

## Medieval Centre

**BITTERZOET** Map pp278-9
☎ 521 30 01; www.bitterzoet.com; Spuistraat 2
Always full, always changing. This is the freshest, friendliest and best-regarded among the new venues – different nights might see pulse, Latin, Afro-beat, Old School jazz or hip-hop groove.

**DANSEN BIJ JANSEN** Map pp286-7
☎ 620 17 79; www.dansenbijjansen.nl;
Handboogstraat 11

For over a generation, this rambling space has been Amsterdam's most famous student nightclub, and it still thumps nightly. The secret? Cheap drinks, a fun selection of classic disco and house, and a relaxed dress code. Valid student cards are required for entry.

### MEANDER Map pp286-7
☎ 625 84 30; Voetboogstraat 5

In the student club district near the Spui, this venue (capacity up to 350) has a variety of bands, some popular house DJs and, if you're lucky, ridiculously cheap beer.

### ODEON Map pp286-7
☎ 624 97 11; www.odeontheater.nl; Singel 460

This relaxed, friendly venue offers two floors of dancing, five different bars, and is open seven nights a week; choose from dance classics, house or hip-hop. It's a longstanding favourite of students and visitors alike. As stylish as it is, there's no dress code.

### WINSTON Map pp278-9
☎ 623 13 80; www.winston.nl; Warmoesstraat 127

Changing theme nights and a fine line up of local DJs make Winston a popular destination; very hip, very cool and very Amsterdam. It's part of our favourite artist-designed hotel in town.

## Western Canal Belt

### MAZZO Map p277
☎ 626 75 00; www.mazzo.nl; Rozengracht 114

Recently redone but still a firm favourite, this relatively small club programmes a fierce roster of first-rate DJs playing everything from deep house to Latin beats and experimental electro. Check out the plush sofas and cool spotlights on the walls, and check the website for club nights.

### MORE Map p277
☎ 344 64 02; www.expectmore.nl; Rozengracht 133

As if having Nomads supper club (p141) in the building wasn't enough, this downstairs room of many mirror balls has Latin nights, house nights, techno nights and lots of variations. The soundtrack of one club night is recorded for broadcast on Dutch radio.

## Southern Canal Belt

### DE DUIVEL Map pp286-7
☎ 626 61 84; www.deduivel.nl; Reguliersdwarsstraat 87

This small bar, with its spooky, stained-glass portrait of the devil, serves up a menu of hip-hop, rap, ska and drum'n'bass. Famous for its Hell's Kitchen block parties on Queen's Day, it celebrated its 10th anniversary in 2003 and is still going strong.

### ESCAPE Map pp286-7
☎ 622 11 11; www.escape.nl; Rembrandtplein 11

A fixture of Amsterdam nightlife since 1987, it's all lights and video screens. Now it's a venue for special parties: Saturday nights are devoted to the club Chemistry, with house, tech-house and techno. First Friday of each month is Salvation, one of Amsterdam's leading gay clubs.

### K2 Map pp286-7
www.apres-skilounge.nl; Paardenstraat 11-15;
🕑 from 10pm Thu-Sat

*ToNight at Arena (p168)*

Entertainment – Clubbing

For a place that's below sea level, this après-ski lounge works pretty well! Quaff a Red Bull or Smirnoff Ice from a bar beneath mounted deer heads, snowboards and skis; shush on over to the dance floor and groove as DJs play dance or party house. Special event nights have been known to include Mexican, Western and heart-on-your-sleeve Dutch folk.

### MELKWEG Map pp286-7
☎ 531 81 81; www.melkweg.nl; Lijnbaansgracht 234A
Melkweg's a cinema, art gallery, café, multimedia centre, rock and roots concert hall and a superlative club venue, attracting well over 300,000 people per year! Every month offers dozens of club events for virtually every taste, stripe and type.

### MINISTRY Map pp286-7
☎ 623 39 81; www.ministry.nl; Reguliersdwarsstraat 12
This diminutive club calls itself multi-ethnic and multi-sexual. Speed garage, R&B, funk and disco classics play for a crowd ranging from 21 to 35.

### PARADISO Map pp286-7
☎ 626 45 21; www.paradiso.nl; Weteringschans 6

In this former church – a longstanding club – there's something for every young-dancy stripe; the semi-regular night 'Paradiso' is almost always sold out, plus loads of other DJ nights and performances by big-name acts (p180).

### ZEBRA LOUNGE Map pp286-7
☎ 612 61 53; Korte Leidsedwarsstraat 14; ✆ nightly
This one-time strip club (the poles are still there) has received a slick makeover and is now one of the town's most fashionable dance clubs, where folks dressed in the latest club-cool have to pass imposing (but good-natured) bouncers. DJs change frequently, so there are always surprises.

## Other Districts

### ARENA Map p285
☎ 694 74 44; www.hotelarena.nl; Hotel Arena, 's-Gravesandestraat 51
In keeping with the hotel's theme, the club goes by the moniker ToNight, and each night is different – everything from dance classics to salsa. It's worth a visit just for the magnificent interior; the chapel of this one-time orphanage has been given a solid redo. Even the loos are worth checking out.

### Night Mayors Battle Nightmares
Amsterdam has one famous *Nachtwacht* (Night Watch) already (courtesy of a certain Mr Rembrandt), but there's another, newer one you may not have heard of. In response to mounting concern over restrictions on the city's nightlife, in February 2003 a local councilman organised elections for a board of *nachtburgemeesters* (night mayors).

Collectively called the Nachtwacht, this board of eight includes club hosts and promoters, a sociologist, a restaurant owner, a festival programmer and a musical advisor to a rhythm festival. Although they have no government mandate, they view their volunteer job as a matter of the survival of the city's nightlife. Explains *nachtburgemeester* (and club promoter) Maz Weston, Amsterdam's once-unique reputation as a place for outrageous clubs and parties 'has been taken over by the nightlife in cities such as Barcelona, Berlin, and of course Ibiza'.

Part of that may be simple evolution, but the conventional wisdom is that shifting political winds are forcing the change. Political pressure has brought an increase in police raids on clubs, which, Weston says, 'have certainly shaken Amsterdammers up; the discussion over the wrongs or rights of the action has involved everyone from the local greengrocer to the chief of police'.

Either despite the raids, or perhaps because of them, some of the raided clubs have seen an increase in business. 'For clubbers,' Weston says, 'the injustice…has created a *we're-in-this-together* attitude not seen since the beginning of the house-scene in the '80s.'

One unintended consequence of the police actions: club-goers have been moving to parties outside the established system; particularly worrisome is the growth of parties in illegal venues where safety standards may not be enforced.

Not that things are *all* bad here. It's still quite possible for club-goers to spend all night at listening to different DJs in a variety of venues (and never pay a cent in entry fees!); the coffeeshop scene is still going strong; and in summer there are regular festivals along area beaches.

The public is welcome to attend the weekly meetings of the Nachtwacht (upstairs from Club Ines; Amstel 2, ✆ 9-11pm Thu). They're followed by an 'open stage' for anyone who wants to present his or her special talent.

For an update of the activities of the *burgemeesters*, check out www.nachtwachtamsterdam.nl, which has recently added some English text to its website.

## Worth Noting

- **Dance Valley Festival** (www.dancevalley.nl) For one day in August, some 130 of the world's best DJs and bands perform in 15 tents and two outdoor stages to 80,000 enthusiastic dance-music lovers. It's spawned a lot of imitators, all quite popular.
- **Nomads** (p141) This neo-Moroccan place starts as a restaurant serving mezzes (small plates) and ends with DJs spinning very cool tunes.
- **Odessa** (p149) Another restaurant that turns into a cool lounge late at night.
- **Ship of Fools** Part floating theatre troupe, part party boat, you're likely to see this ship at any party near the beach. Look for your host, wearing pointy ears.

### HET PONTHUYS Map pp282-3
☎ 636 33 88; www.ponthuys.nl; Buiksloterweg 3-5
A breezy, city-view café by day and party venue on special nights. Plus, you get the bonus of a free boat trip across the IJ (docks are behind Centraal Station).

### PANAMA Map pp282-3
☎ 311 86 86; Oostelijke Handelskade 4
A brilliant and luxe venue for 25- to 35 somethings, Panama has a salsa-tango dance salon, a restaurant and glam nightclub that programs Cuban big bands, Brazilian circus acts, a soulful selection of DJ talent, and the ladies' night Club Lust.

### POWERZONE Map pp274-5
☎ 0900-POWERZONE; www.thepowerzone.nl; Daniel Goedkoopstraat 1-3
This multilevel dance factory has a capacity of 5000, and sometimes it almost feels full. Different DJs mean that each space seems to have its own vibe. Entry fee includes extras like coat check, and there's no tipping allowed.

### VAKZUID Map pp274-5
☎ 570 84 00; Olympic Stadium 35
A glamorous club-restaurant overlooking the 1928 Olympic Stadium, this has a large dance floor and loads of comfortable lounges to pose on. There's a lot of house, some '80s and disco thrown in for good measure.

### Bloemen Marvellous Beach Gigs

Can't afford Ibiza this year? Don't worry, Amsterdam's club promoters have come up with the next best thing: clubbing at Bloemendaal Beach. Each Sunday from June to October, thousands of flamboyant, party-mad clubbers crowd into, and spill out of, massive and quite sophisticated beach-tents from midday to midnight. Each tent has a different musical style: for example, Republiek attracts hordes of house fans with brilliant local DJs, and Woodstock keeps the party sticky and sexy with soulful house.

To get there from Centraal Station, take the train to Haarlem Station. From there catch bus No 81 and get off at Bloemendaal aan Zee. Whatever you do, don't try to drive out there: traffic is almost certain to be a horror. It's best to check what's on before you set out.

# GAY & LESBIAN

Amsterdam's gay scene is the biggest in Europe, with close to 100 gay and lesbian bars, cafés, clubs, shops and hotels.

The following centres of gay and lesbian culture are good places to start exploring. There are also queer club nights at larger venues, but they don't generally last more than a few years (at least not under the same name). Ask around, pick up the excellent *Bent Guide* (available at bookshops and Pink Point) or contact the **Gay & Lesbian Switchboard** ( ☎ 623 65 65) to find out about the latest 'in' places.

Gay men may also want to note the gay saunas (p180).

## Medieval Centre

Kinky Amsterdam congregates on the Warmoesstraat, next to the Red Light District, at a variety of clubs catering to lovers of leather, rubber, piercings, slings, darkrooms and hard-core porn.

### ARGOS Map pp278-9
☎ 622 65 95; Warmoesstraat 95
Leather boys of all ages head here for the famous darkrooms, cabins and kinky toys. The monthly 'SOS' (Sex On Sunday) is always wild – dress code: nude!

## COCKRING Map pp278-9

☎ 623 96 04; Warmoesstraat 96

This nightclub, playing techno, hard house and trance, has live strip shows and a cruisey, hot darkroom for young leather boys.

## GETTO Map pp278-9

☎ 421 51 51; Warmoesstraat 51; ✇ Tue-Sun

This groovy, long alley of a restaurant and bar is much loved for its fun nightly entertainment (tarot readers, DJs, bingo competitions, cocktail happy hours), people-watching from the streetside and a loungey area in the back where you can chill quite nicely. It's patronised by a hip and up-for-it crowd, and a diverse cross-section of the gay community.

# Southern Canal Belt

Activity here centres on Reguliersdwarsstraat, with some of Amsterdam's longest-running gay favourites. It attracts tanned and beautiful boys who schmooze and cruise their way along the street; follow their lead and meet for happy hour at one of the various bars, eat dinner at a gay-run restaurant and finish the night off in a sweaty, sexy club.

## APRIL Map pp286-7

☎ 625 95 72; Reguliersdwarsstraat 37

April is equally famous for its happy hour (6pm to 7pm Monday to Thursday, 6pm to 8pm Sunday) and the beautiful guys who cram into the space to flirt and drink. The revolving bar in the back can make for a giddy experience after too many cocktails.

## ARC Map pp286-7

☎ 622 99 58; www.bararc.com; Reguliersdwarsstraat 31

ARC's minimalist interior allows the beauty of the fashionable men to shine through as they enjoy fancy flavoured martinis – though bartenders are certainly also happy to pour you a beer. ARC's restaurant serves up some adventurous fusion cuisine.

## BONGOS Map pp286-7

☎ 06-4863 66 84; Reguliersdwarsstraat 45

Bongos thumps regularly with Latin music, Latin men and those who love both. It's small – almost intimate – by comparison to some of its neighbours on the 'straat.

## EXIT Map pp286-7

☎ 625 87 88; Reguliersdwarsstraat 42

This multistorey nightclub plays underground house and has a selection of bars, dance floors and an always busy darkroom. The occasional 'Drag Planet' night is a scream, and 'Male Box' (last Thursday of the month) is a great night for meeting up.

## OTHER SIDE Map pp286-7

☎ 421 10 14; Reguliersdwarsstraat 6

This gay coffeeshop sells hash, grass and energy drinks and plays a mix of disco, funk and soul.

## SOHO Map pp286-7

☎ 616 13 12; Reguliersdwarsstraat 36

Kitschly decorated – imagine an old-world English library on the *Titanic* – this enormous, two-storey bar pumps with a young, ridiculously pretty clientele and an increasing number of straights who drink and flirt on the upstairs Chesterfield sofas.

The following are a short walk away on the Amstel and around Rembrandtplein:

## AMSTEL TAVERNE Map pp286-7

☎ 623 42 54; Amstel 54

On warm nights, 30s-and-up gays spill out onto the street and mix very amicably. On cooler nights, it's perhaps the brownest of the brown cafés in the area, down to the Dutch master reproduction, Delft tiles and mugs hanging over the bar.

## ENTRE NOUS Map pp286-7

☎ 623 17 00; Halvemaansteeg 14

If you need to recover after a visit to Montmartre, this bar across the street with red wallpaper is an understated, friendly choice.

*(Continued on page 179)*

1 *De Bolhoed restaurant, Prinsengracht (p139)* 2 *BBQ meat and duck at Nam Kee restaurant, Zeedijk (p137)* 3 *Wheels of cheese, De Kaaskamer, Runstraat (p201)* 4 *Traditional haring*

1 Reguliersdwarsstraat
2 Live music at Paradiso (p180)
3 Hoppe bruin café (p156)
4 Paradiso clubbing (p168)

1 Chill-out room in Arena (p168)
2 Mulligans Irish bar, (p160)
3 Tuschinskitheater (p183)
4 Theatre poster

1 *Amsterdam ArenA (p180)*
2 *Tropenmuseum (p108)*
3 *Netherlands Media Art Institute (p85)* 4 *Van Gogh Museum (p111)*

1 *A wordy room at the Hotel Winston with message on wall (p214)* 2 *The ornate Hotel Arena (p221)* 3 *Entrance to Seven Bridges hotel (p220)* 4 *A single room at Hotel Brouwer (p213)*

1 Clogs at the Albert Cuypmarkt
(p113) 2 Analik fashion house
(p199) 3 Smoking paraphernalia
(p164) 4 Flower pots at Bloemenmarkt on Singel (p89)

**1** Maps for sale at À La Carte Bookstore on Utrechtsestraat (p203) **2** Womens' underwear in the window of Female & Partners (p195) **3** Old oil paintings at Decorativa (p205) **4** Shoebaloo shoe shop (p206)

1 *Windmills in Wester-Koggen-land, near Alkmaar (p227)*
2 *Cheese market, Alkmaar (p227)*
3 *Rotterdam's Erasmusbrug over the Maas (p237)* 4 *Tulips at Keuke-nhof, near Haarlem (p230)*

*Lounge at Kriterion cinema*

of upcoming films. It was made into a movie theatre after WWII to help student resistance fighters earn an income. It's still student-run, so ticket prices tend to be a hair cheaper here, and the lively and popular café is worth a visit.

### THE MOVIES Map pp274-5
☎ 638 60 16; Haarlemmerdijk 161
Interesting, arty films are mixed in with independent American and Brit pics and big studio releases at this beautiful Art Deco cinema. Its highly regarded separate dining room is lined with publicity stills of famous film food scenes. Go for the three-course 'dinner and a movie' from €27.

### PATHÉ DE MUNT Map pp286-7
☎ 0900-14 58, €0.23 a minute; Vijzelstraat 15
This new, modern multiplex looks kind of like an airport and has 13 screens (seating 120 to 300 people), meaning something for practically any taste.

cutting-edge foreign films (think Iran or Korea) and specials devoted to screen legends and genres such as Bollywood musicals.

### FILMMUSEUM CINERAMA Map pp286-7
aka Calypso; ☎ 623 78 14; Marnixstraat 400-402
At the time of writing, the three halls of 1960s mod cinema screened regular offerings of fare from the Filmmuseum. It's a great venue for this worthy endeavour, but nobody was sure whether it would last. We hope it does.

### HET KETELHUIS Map pp274-5
☎ 684 00 90; Westergasfabriek, Haarlemmerweg 8-10
In the old gas works, soaring ceilings, wooden floors, pegboard walls, comfy chairs and a post-industrial vibe provide a great platform for arthouse films (especially Dutch ones).

### KRITERION Map p285
☎ 623 17 08; Roetersstraat 170
This Amsterdam School/Art Deco building (a one-time diamond workshop) screens cult movies, classics, kids' flicks and 'sneak previews'

### TUSCHINSKITHEATER Map pp286-7
☎ 623 15 10, ☎ 0900-14 58, €0.23 per minute; Reguliersbreestraat 26-34
Extensively refurbished, Amsterdam's most famous cinema is a monument worth visiting for its sumptuous Art Deco/Amsterdam School interior alone, especially its main auditorium. Expect to see mainstream blockbusters, or inquire about 90-minute tours (10am Sunday and Monday in July and August; €7).

## Worth Noting

- **Melkweg** (p168) In addition to all of its other charms, Melkweg has an excellent cinema showing contemporary hits and international films that have made a name for themselves.

# THEATRE & DANCE

There are about 50 theatres in Amsterdam – the ones listed here are merely a selection. Performances are mostly in Dutch, sometimes in English (especially in summer) and sometimes language doesn't matter. Check the *Uitkrant*, the Saturday *PS* magazine in the *Parool* newspaper, the Amsterdam Uitburo or the venues direct for current performances.

## Medieval Centre

### BRAKKE GROND Map pp278-9
☎ 626 68 66; Flemish Cultural Centre, Nes 45
A fantastic array of music, experimental video, modern dance and exciting, young theatre is

performed in Brakke Grond's striking 150-seat theatre.

### CASABLANCA VARIÉTÉ Map pp278-9
☎ 625 56 85; www.casablanca-amsterdam.nl; Zeedijk 24

The other half of Casablanca contains the Netherlands' only theatre devoted to the art of circus performance – sleight of hand, magic, variety shows and singers. The interior is kitsch redefined, but the theatre itself is quite small (meaning there are no large animal acts!). Dinner and a show costs €25 (show alone €5).

### COSMIC Map pp278-9
☎ 626 68 66; www.cosmictheater.nl; Nes 75-87
This theatre originated in Curaçao and has made it all the way to the big city, staging plays representing a variety of cultures. Emphasis is on Surinamese, African, Turkish and Moroccan. There's also a competition for young writers.

### FRASCATI Map pp278-9
☎ 626 68 66; Nes 63
This experimental theatre spotlights young Dutch directors, choreographers and producers. There are multicultural dance and music performances, as well as hip-hop, rap and breakdancing. In May it hosts the urban dance festival.

### MARIONETTEN THEATER Map pp282-3
☎ 620 80 27; www.marionet.demon.nl; Nieuwe Jonkerstraat 8; adult/child €12/4.50; ⏰ ring or check website for showtimes
In a former blacksmith's shop, this intimate theatre presents highbrow culture for little people, with marionettes performing elaborate productions like the *Magic Flute* and *Bastien & Bastienne*. Grownups will appreciate it too, especially the skill of the puppeteers. Lunch and dinnertime performances carry an extra fee. If you can't catch them here, the company also tours to other European countries.

### UNIVERSITEITSTHEATER Map p286-7
☎ 623 01 27; Nieuwe Doelenstraat 16
Home to the Institute for Dramatic Art, this theatre presents occasional performances in English.

## Western Canal Belt
### FELIX MERITIS Map p277
☎ 623 13 11; Keizersgracht 324
The city's former cultural centre now presents innovative, modern theatre, music and dance with lots of co-productions between Eastern and Western European artists. It's also got very cool loos.

## Southern Canal Belt
### BOOM CHICAGO Map pp286-7
☎ 423 01 01; Leidseplein 12
English-language stand-up and improv comedy is performed here year-round; the best way to see it is over dinner and a few drinks – fortunately, the food is decent, as is the café, boomBar. See boxed text.

### DE BALIE Map pp286-7
☎ 553 51 51; Kleine Gartmanplantsoen 10
International productions spotlighting multicultural and political issues are the focus here. De Balie also holds short film festivals and political debates and has new-media facilities and a stylish bar.

### COMEDY CAFÉ AMSTERDAM
Map pp286-7
☎ 638 39 71; www.comedycafé.nl;
Max Euweplein 43-45
If Boom Chicago is improv, the Comedy Café books in Dutch and international stand-up comics. Sundays are regularly reserved for English-speaking acts, but you might catch English speakers other nights as well. Tickets cost €5 to €14, or dinner and a show costs around €20.

### DE KLEINE KOMEDIE Map pp286-7
☎ 624 05 34; Amstel 56
This internationally renowned theatre, founded in 1786, focuses on concerts, dance, comedy and cabaret, sometimes in English.

### When Comedy Hits Amsterdam, What Sound Does it Make?
With legendary improv comedy venues like Second City, Chicago has long been a jumping-off point for some of the world's most famous comedians. But Chicago comedy in Amsterdam? In the early 1990s the idea was about as sexy as a cold croquette.

Yet three Yanks had the vision to set up **Boom Chicago** (above), a comedy nightclub that has evolved into the best (English-language) improvisational and comedy club in the Netherlands. Shows are superfast, musical, political, very funny and, against all odds, really popular with locals as well as visitors. What's more, Boom has begun to join its hometown (and Los Angeles and New York) counterparts on the fast-track to the likes of *Mad TV*, *Saturday Night Live* and even Broadway, and onto international stardom. Catch a show here and who knows? You may catch the next John Belushi, Dan Aykroyd or Mike Myers.

## KONINKLIJK THEATER CARRÉ Map p285

☎ 0900-252 52 55; Amstel 115-125

The largest theatre in town puts on big-budget, international shows, cabaret, circuses and Broadway/West End musicals. Please note this theatre is closed for all of 2004 for renovations. Backstage tours are available 3pm Saturday and Wednesday (€3.50).

## STADSSCHOUWBURG Map pp286-7

☎ 624 23 11; Leidseplein 26

The city's most beautiful theatre, built in 1894 and refurbished in the 1990s, features large-scale productions, operettas, summer English-language productions and performances by the stolid Toneelgroep Amsterdam.

## THEATER BELLEVUE Map pp286-7

☎ 530 53 01; www.theaterbellevue.nl; Leidsekade 90

Come here for experimental theatre, international cabaret and modern dance, mainly in Dutch. Its Club Calotte (second Monday of the month) features live music on a different

theme each time. Its affiliate theatre **Nieuwe de la Mar** ( ☎ 530 53 01; Marnixstraat 404; same box office) presents road shows (sometimes in English), international festivals and occasionally light kids' plays like *Miffy: The Musical*.

# Old South

## AMSTERDAMSE BOS THEATRE Map pp274-5

☎ 643 32 86; Amsterdamse Bos

This large open-air amphitheatre in the park stages plays in Dutch (Brecht, Chekhov, Shakespeare) in summer. We love it when the actors pause as planes pass overhead.

## OPEN AIR THEATRE Map pp286-7

aka Vondelpark Theatre; ☎ 673 14 99; www.openluchttheater.nl, Vondelpark

This cosy open-air amphitheatre in the middle of the Vondelpark presents a wide range of free summer performances. Expect stand-up comedy, musical theatre, dance workshops and pop concerts.

# CLASSICAL

A pleasant fixture on the Amsterdam music scene is the free lunch-time concerts throughout the city. These are usually chamber music and run from 12.30pm to 1.30pm, but concerts are suspended in June, July or August, when everyone goes on holidays. The Muziektheater at the Stopera offers free concerts of 20th-century music on Tuesday in the Boekmanzaal; on Wednesday the Concertgebouw has chamber music or classical concerts (often public rehearsals), sometimes also jazz, but you won't be the only visitor taking advantage of this; and on Friday the Bethaniënklooster puts on anything from medieval to contemporary.

Check the Amsterdam Uitburo for performances in churches (not just organ recitals), including the **Oude Kerk** (p61), **Nieuwe Kerk** (p59), **Engelse Kerk** (p76, English/Scottish Presbyterian church in the Begijnhof) and **Round Lutheran Church** (p77).

# Medieval Centre

## BETHANIËNKLOOSTER Map pp278-9

☎ 625 00 78; www.bethanienklooster.nl; Barndesteeg 6B

A small former monastery near Nieuwmarkt Square with a glorious ballroom, it's the perfect place to take in some Stravinsky or Indian sitar.

## BEURS VAN BERLAGE Map pp278-9

☎ 627 04 66; Damrak 243

This former commodities exchange houses two small concert halls with comfortable seats and underwhelming acoustics. Resident companies the Netherlands Chamber Orchestra and the Netherlands Philharmonic play a varied menu of Mozart, Beethoven, Bach, Mahler and Wagner. However, the building was being

renovated at the time of writing and is due to reopen in summer 2004.

## MUZIEKTHEATER Map pp286-7

☎ 625 54 55; www.hetmuziektheater.nl; Waterlooplein 22

This swanky, large-scale theatre in the Stopera is the official residence of the Netherlands Opera, National Ballet and Netherlands Ballet Orchestra. Renowned international dance companies like Merce Cunningham and Martha Graham perform here too.

# Southern Canal Belt

## KONINKLIJK THEATER CARRÉ Map p285

☎ 622 52 25; www.theatercarre.nl; Amstel 115-125

This large, busy theatre presents a regular

diet of crowd-pleasing opera, operetta, ballet, musicals and cabaret.

## MUZIEKCENTRUM DE IJSBREKER
Map p285

☎ 693 90 93; www.ysbreker.nl; Weesperzijde 23

Itching to hear some avant-garde jazz, a bit of modern Turkish guitar or the latest in atonal works? This centre for contemporary music is the answer, with about 150 concerts per year. In 2005, it's due to open in a spanking new complex in the Eastern Docklands (west of the ship-passenger terminal).

## STADSSCHOUWBURG Map pp286-7
☎ 624 23 11; Leidseplein 26

Home to an eclectic assortment of travelling shows, from dance to opera to theatre, as well as special events like the Julidans (July Dance Festival). An additional, flexible venue is set to open on the site by 2006 – we'll see if it happens.

## Old South

### CONCERTGEBOUW Map pp286-7
☎ 671 83 45; www.concertgebouw.nl;
Concertgebouwplein 2-6

This world-famous concert hall with near-perfect acoustics is home to the Royal Concertgebouw Orchestra led by Riccardo Chailly. Among the 650-or-so performances here per year, the orchestra performs works by Ravel, Stravinsky and Shostakovich. Alternatively, you can catch visiting international soloists and chamber groups in the Recital Hall.

# WATCHING SPORTS

## SOCCER (FOOTBALL)

Local club Ajax usually qualify for the UEFA Champions League, Europe's top competition. Other Dutch leaders are PSV (the Philips Sport Association) from Eindhoven and Feyenoord from Rotterdam, and if any of these clubs play against one another, it's a big event. Dutch soccer is 'cool' and 'technical', characterised by keep-the-ball play and surgical strikes. Local hooligans, however, are every bit as hot-headed as their British counterparts but you should be quite safe if you buy seat tickets (as opposed to standing-room tickets).

ArenA Stadium ( ☎ 311 13 33; www.amsterdamarena.nl; Arena Blvd 1, Bijlmermeer; metro: Bijlmer or Strandvliet/ArenA) is where Ajax plays. Built over a highway, this massive, expensive, high-tech complex with a retractable roof seats 52,000 spectators and has an Ajax museum with cups and other paraphernalia. Soccer games usually take place Saturday evening and Sunday afternoon during the playing season (early September to early June, with a winter break from just before Christmas to the end of January).

Readers have recommended the one-hour guided stadium tour ( ☎ 311 13 36; adult/child €9.70/8.20; ⏰ 11am-4.30pm daily Apr-Sep, noon-4pm Mon-Sat Oct-Mar, except on game days or major events). The tour includes a walk on the hallowed turf and entry to the museum.

## FOOTBALL (AMERICAN)

American football started in Europe from nothing several years ago, but it's developing a moderate following. As of this writing, there were six teams in the NFL (National Football League) Europe: three in Germany, the Scottish Claymores, Barcelona Dragons and Amsterdam's own Admirals. Players are predominately American (many drafted out of college by homeland teams), but there are a number of European and even Japanese players. Home games, complete with cheerleaders, take place at the Amsterdam ArenA ( ☎ 311 13 33; www.amsterdamarena.nl; Arena Blvd 1, Bijlmermeer; metro: Bijlmer or Strandvliet/ArenA). Unlike in the States, European football season is in the spring.

# OUTDOOR ACTIVITIES

Soccer, ice skating, cycling, tennis, swimming and sailing are just a few activities that keep the locals fit – and of course jogging, which is popular in the Vondelpark and other parks.

The Amsterdamse Bos has several walking and jogging trails for serious exercise. Bikes are available for rental in many corners of town. MacBike (p243) is the big agency, but there are many others.

The whole coast of Holland, from the Hook of Holland right up to Den Helder, is one long beach, backed by often extensive dunes that are ideal for walks. The closest seaside resort is Zandvoort, which can get packed in summer (forget about parking then – take the train), but more pleasant resorts can be found farther north, such as Castricum north of IJmuiden, or Egmond and Bergen a bit farther north near Alkmaar.

For information about sport and leisure activities and venues, visit the city hall information centre (Map pp286-7; ☎ 624 11 11, Amstel 1) in the arcade between the Stopera and the city hall. Local community centres (in the phone book under Buurtcentrum) organise fitness courses.

# BUNGY JUMPING

Proof that Amsterdam offers many ways to get high (and hopefully not crash), Bungy Jump Center Amsterdam (Map pp274-5; ☎ 419 60 05; Westerdoksdijk 44; 1st jump/2nd jump/10 jumps €50/40/250; ⏱ Apr-Oct, phone for hours), at the waterfront half a kilometre west of Centraal Station, offers jumps from a crane suspended 75m above the IJ. If you can keep your nerves under control you'll never forget the view.

# GOLF

Golf was long derided as something for the elite but has become increasingly popular in recent years, but don't go expecting a Scottish-style course. The Netherlands space crunch means that land is usually more profitably put to other uses.

## BORCHLAND SPORTCENTRUM

☎ 563 33 33; Borchlandweg 6-12; 9 holes from €10; ⏱ 8am-midnight; metro: Duivendrecht or Strandvliet
Borchland has a nine-hole all par-three course. Call for course hours or to set up a lesson.

## OPENBARE GOLFBAAN SLOTEN

☎ 614 24 02; Sloterweg 1045; round €10-13, club rental per half-set €6; ⏱ 8.30am-8pm Mon-Fri, 8.30am-6pm Sat & Sun May-Aug, 8.30am-8pm Mon-Fri Sep-Apr; bus No 142
Located on the southwest side of town, this course also consists of nine holes.

Look under *Golfbanen* in the pink pages of the phone book for several other options.

# HOCKEY

Dutch (field) hockey teams compete at world-championship level. In contrast to soccer, which is played mainly by boys in school yards, streets and parks, hockey is still a somewhat elitist sport played by either sex on expensive club fields. The season is similar to that for soccer.

## HOCKEY CLUB HURLEY

☎ 645 44 68; Nieuwe Kalfjeslaan 21, Amsterdamse Bos
This is a good contact for information and matches.

# ICE SKATING

When the canals freeze over in winter (which doesn't happen often enough) everyone goes for a skate. Lakes and waterways in the countryside also fill up with colourfully clad skaters making trips tens of kilometres long.

*Bungy Jump Center Amsterdam*

It's a wonderful experience, though painful on the ankles and butt if you're learning. Be aware that people drown under ice every year. Don't take to a patch of ice unless you see large groups of people, and be very careful at the edges and under bridges (such areas often don't freeze properly).

You can only rent skates at a skating rink. A pair of simple hockey skates costs upwards of €50 at department stores (sports shops might have a wider selection but tend to be more expensive). Hockey skates are probably the best choice for learners: figure skates (with short, curved blades) are difficult to master, and speed skates (with long, flat blades) put a lot of strain on the ankles – but are definitely the go if you want to make serious trips. Check for second-hand skates on notice boards at supermarkets or at the **Centrale Bibliotheek** (Central Library; Map pp286-7; ☎ 523 09 00; Prinsengracht 587). Wood-framed skates that you tie under your shoes can be picked up cheaply at antique and bric-a-brac shops. Don't dismiss them: they're among the fastest around if they're sharpened, and make great souvenirs.

The **Ijscomplex Jaap Eden** (Map pp274-5; ☎ 694 9652; Radioweg 64; adult/child under 15 yrs/senior €3.90/2.60; tram No 9) in the eastern suburb of Watergraafsmeer has an indoor and outdoor rink.

In winter you can also skate on the pond on **Museumplein**.

## KORFBALL

This sport (see also p17) elicits giggles from foreigners who don't understand how appealing the game can be. It's a cross between netball, volleyball and basketball, where mixed-sex teams toss a ball around and try to throw it into the opposing team's hoop which is 3.5m off the ground; players can only mark opponents of the same sex. There's a lively local club scene. For information, contact the **Amsterdam Sport Council** ( ☎ 552 24 90).

## SAILING

The Dutch are avid sailors – windsurfing is a national sport, but so is yachting which is curbed only by its expense (the word 'yacht', after all, comes from the Dutch *jachtschip*, 'chase ship'). This includes modern open boats and yachts, but also the more traditional kind, which are revered here like nowhere else. On weekends a fleet of restored flat-bottomed boats, called the 'brown fleet' because of their reddish-brown sails, crisscross the IJsselmeer. Some are privately owned but many are rented, and sailing one is an unforgettable experience.

The cheapest options are *botters* (from about €340 per day), former fishing boats with sleeping space (usually for around eight people) below deck. Larger groups could rent a converted freight barge known as a *tjalk* (from about €570 per day), originally a Frisian design with jib and spritsail rig, though modern designs are made of steel and have diesel motors. Other vessels include anything from ancient pilot boats to massive clippers. Inquire at VVV offices or boat docks for more information.

Costs are quite reasonable if you can muster a group of fellow enthusiasts. Some places only rent boats for day trips, but it's much more fun to go for the full weekend experience. The usual arrangement is that you arrive at the boat Friday at 8pm, sleep on board, sail out early the next morning, and visit several places around the IJsselmeer before returning on Sunday between 4pm and 6pm. Food is not included in the packages, nor is cancellation insurance (trips are cancelled if wind is stronger than 7 Beaufort), but you do get a skipper.

## TENNIS & SQUASH

### BORCHLAND SPORTCENTRUM

☎ 563 33 33; Borchlandweg 8-12; tennis per hr €22.50, squash per hr weekday/weekend €13/18; ☺ 8am-midnight; metro Duivendrecht or Strandvliet

A huge complex next to the ArenA stadium in the Bijlmer, it has tennis, squash and badminton courts, bowling alleys, golf and other facilities including a restaurant.

## TENNISCENTRUM AMSTELPARK
Map pp274-5

☎ 301 07 00; www.amstelpark.nl; Koenenkade 8; court hire per hour summer €20, winter outdoor/indoor €20/25

Amstelpark has 42 open and covered courts and runs the country's biggest tennis school. It's conveniently close to the World Trade Center and RAI exhibition buildings.

## SQUASH CITY Map pp278-9

☎ 626 78 83; www.squashcity.com; Ketelmakerstraat 6; court hire off-peak/peak per person €6.80/9; gym &

sauna off-peak/peak €8/9.50; ☻ 8.30am-midnight Mon-Fri, 8.30am-9pm Sat & Sun

Located across the railway line Haarlemmerplein, at Bickerseiland, west of Centraal Station. Sauna is included with squash court hire. Bonus: go at the right time, and you may catch the Amsterdam Admirals' cheerleading squad in rehearsal.

More courts are listed under *Tennisbanen* and *Squashbanen* in the pink pages of the phone book.

# HEALTH & FITNESS

With the Northern European climate, indoor fitness is quite popular in Amsterdam. In addition to the places listed below, several hotels also have fitness centres available for day use, including the Splash Fitnessclub at the **Renaissance Hotel** ( ☎ 621 22 23; Kattengat 1) and the Okura (p221). More centres are listed in the pink pages of the phone book under *Fitnesscentra*. Amsterdam also has a number of indoor pools and summer outdoor pools, some of them historic and very cool.

## GYMS

### BARRY'S FITNESS CENTRE Map pp286-7

☎ 626 10 36; Lijnbaansgracht 350; day pass €10, month pass €60; ☻ 7am-11pm Mon-Fri, 8am-8pm Sat, 9am-6pm Sun

Visit Barry's to pump iron to a thumping disco beat, or for spinning and yoga classes.

### THE GARDEN GYM Map p285

☎ 626 87 72; Jodenbreestraat 158; day pass €8.50-11.50, month pass €50-59; ☻ 9am-11pm Mon, Wed & Fri, noon-10pm Tue & Thu, 9am-2pm Sat & Sun

The Garden Gym offers aerobics and feel-good activities, including sauna, massage, physiotherapy and dietary advice.

Several hotels also have fitness centres available for day use, including the Splash Fitnessclub at the Renaissance Hotel and the Okura.

## SAUNAS & OTHER BATHS

Saunas are mixed and there's no prudish swimsuit nonsense, though they may cater for people who have a problem with this – ask. Note that gay saunas have another purpose entirely (p180).

### SAUNA DECO Map pp278-9

☎ 623 82 15; www.saunadeco.nl; Herengracht 115; admission noon-3pm Mon-Fri/all other times €12.50/

15.50, children half-price; ☻ noon-11pm Mon-Sat, 1-6pm Sun

Sauna Deco is a respectable, elegant sauna with good facilities including a snack bar. The building itself is an early creation of the architect HP Berlage and its Art Deco furnishings used to grace a Parisian department store. You can also have massages and beauty therapies. Note: mixed facilities only.

### HAMMAM Map pp274-5 ☎ 681 48 18;

www.hammamamsterdam.nl; Zaanstraat 88; admission €11; ☻ noon-10pm Tue-Fri, noon-8pm Sat & Sun, last entry 2½ hours before closing

In the northwest beyond the Haarlemmerpoort, Hammam is an attractive Turkish-style place for women only, offering a range of spa treatments.

### KOAN FLOAT Map pp278-9

☎ 555 00 33; www.koanfloat.nl; Herengracht 321; floating 45/60/90 minutes €29/36/90; ☻ 9.30am-11pm

It's not a sauna, but come here for salt-water floatation tanks – have music piped in if you like – and massages.

## SWIMMING

Amsterdam has a number of indoor pools and summer outdoor pools, some of them historic and very cool. However, we strongly recommend that you phone before you set out – English is almost always spoken. In recent years, some public pools have been shut down, and hours can vary from day to day or season to season. Few are open past 7pm.

Also, note that there are often restricted sessions – nude, Muslim, children, women, seniors, clubs, lap swimming etc. Of course that might just be what you're after.

### BIJLMERSPORTCENTRUM Map pp274-5
☎ 697 25 01; Bijlmerpark 76, Bijlmer; adult/child €2.70/2.50; ⏲ Wed, Sat & Sun
This place has a sports centre with indoor and outdoor pools, a small kids' pool and snack bars.

### DE MIRANDABAD Map pp274-5
☎ 536 44 44; De Mirandalaan 9; adult/concession €3.15/2.50, Sun €3.50/2.80; ⏲ 7am-7pm Mon-Fri, 9.30am-5pm Sat-Sun May-Sep
A tropical 'aquatic centre', complete with beach and wave machine, indoor and outdoor pools, and waterslide, Mirandabad is south of the city centre. It also has squash courts.

### FLEVOPARKBAD Map pp274-5
☎ 692 50 30; Zeeburgerdijk 630; adult/child 3-15/senior €2.40/2.20/1.80; ⏲ 10am-5.30pm May–early Sep (until 7pm in hot weather)

Located east of the city centre, there's only an outdoor pool here.

### FLORAPARKBAD Map pp274-5
☎ 632 90 30; Sneeuwbalweg 5, Amsterdam North; adult/child €3.40/2.90; ⏲ daily
Florapark has indoor and outdoor pools, a kids' play area and a good sunbathing section.

### SLOTERPARKBAD Map pp274-5
☎ 506 35 06; Slotermeerlaan 2-4; adult or child €3.50, child under 2yrs free; ⏲ Tue-Sun
Set in an attractive recreational area with a yacht harbour in the western suburbs next to the terminus of tram No 14, this place has indoor and outdoor pools. In summer, on cold, rainy days the indoor pool will be open. The outdoor pools can get overcrowded, but this bath is known for a less frequented nudist island, past the pools and across a causeway.

### ZUIDERBAD Map pp286-7
☎ 678 13 90; Hobbemastraat 26; adult/child €2.80/2.50; ⏲ daily
This 1912 edifice behind the Rijksmuseum has been restored to its original glory. Now it's unique and full of character.

# Shopping

# Shopping

During the 17th century, Amsterdam was the warehouse of the world, stuffed with imperial riches from far-off colonies and nearby neighbours. The Dutch empire has since crumbled but its capital remains a shopper's paradise. In particular, Amsterdam's speciality shops and markets truly stand out. Sure, you can probably find glowing Mexican shrines or banana-flavoured condoms back home, but Amsterdam has whole shops devoted to such items and, of course, dope, flower bulbs, clogs, wheels of cheese and obscure types of *genever* (Dutch gin). Fantastic bargains are rare here but it may be worth chasing pictorial art, music, vintage clothes, diamonds and collectors' books.

The most-popular shopping streets are downmarket Nieuwendijk and slightly less lowbrow Kalverstraat, with department stores and clothing boutiques serving large crowds, especially on Saturday and Sunday. Leidsestraat is more upmarket. Well-heeled shoppers head for the expensive shops along PC Hooftstraat, and antique and art buffs visit Nieuwe Spiegelstraat. The Jordaan is full of quirky shops and galleries, as are the radial streets in the canal belt, especially in the western section.

Souvenir shops have sprung up on Damrak like tulips in the flower market, and also around Leidseplein. Most, however, are pretty cheap (in the 'poor quality' sense) and sometimes unpleasant. For a souvenir of quality, try elsewhere for a Delft-blue tulip vase or bulbs to plant back home (home legislation permitting).

Most stores are open seven days a week

## Top Five Shopping Strips

- Soak up the local atmosphere at the **Albert Cuypmarkt** (p113), buy clothing and food, and break at the neighbourhood's ethnic restaurants (pp151).
- If you've got dubloons to spare, **PC Hooftstraat** (p110) has the city's most high-end fashions.
- Swing, sway, rock and roll alongside DJs at the tiny music shops of **Nieuwe Nieuwstraat** (p195) and surrounds.
- Lose yourself in the **Negen Straatjes** (Nine Streets; p84), where boutiques specialise in everything from clothing to art to tempting chocolates.
- Hunt for antiques in the **Nieuwe Spiegelstraat** (p91).

(at least in the city centre) but many start late on Monday. Opening hours are typically noon to 6pm on Monday; 10am to 6pm on Tuesday, Wednesday, Friday and Saturday; 10am to 9pm on Thursday; and, in the city centre, noon to 6pm on Sunday, but there are many variations.

# MEDIEVAL CENTRE

### 3-D HOLOGRAMMEN
Map pp278-9         *Speciality Shop*
☎ 624 72 25; Grimburgwal 2
This fascinating (and trippy) collection of holographic pictures, jewellery and stickers will delight even the most jaded peepers.

### AFRICAN HERITAGE
Map pp278-9         *Ethnic Culture*
☎ 627 27 65; Zeedijk 59; ☼ daily
Breathtakingly cramped, this store is chock-full of African curios, colourful clothing, wooden toys, musical instruments and a ceiling full of masks.

### AMERICA TODAY Map pp278-9    *Clothing*
☎ 638 84 47; Magna Plaza, Nieuwezijds Voorburgwal
Try this one-stop shop for Levi's-engineered jeans, Calvin Klein underwear, Triple 5 Soul hoodies and Carhartt pants, for men and women. Stock up on imported snacks like root beer, cookies and chocolate bars too.

### ANTIQUARIAAT KOK Map pp278-9    *Books*
☎ 623 11 91; Oude Hoogstraat 14-18
A wide and engaging range of used and antiquarian stock (literature, coffee-table books, old prints etc) is sold here, including biology, art and architecture titles.

### ATHENAEUM Map pp286-7       *Books*
☎ 622 62 48; Spui 14-16

This enormous, multilevel store on the square has a vast assortment of both usual and unusual books and cheerful, helpful staff. The separate news agency on the corner has the city's largest selection of international newspapers and magazines.

### AU BOUT DU MONDE Map pp278-9   *Books*
☎ 625 13 97; Singel 313; 🕑 Mon-Sat

From angels to Zen, this tranquil two-storey shop stocks books on Eastern and Western philosophy, Tibet, Freud, alternative medicine and pretty much anything else you'll need for your religious, psychological or spiritual needs.

### AUSTRALIAN HOMEMADE
Map pp286-7   *food*
☎ 428 75 33; Singel 437, & other locations all over the city centre

There's nothing particularly Australian about these chocolates, but they're delicious, as is the freshly made ice-cream. This chain has become a local phenomenon.

### BAMBAM Map pp278-9   *Children*
☎ 624 52 15; Magna Plaza, Nieuwezijds Voorburgwal 182

Luxurious clothes and handmade furniture, for pampered little princes and princesses, are sold here.

### BEAUFORT Map pp278-9   *Jewellery*
☎ 625 91 31; Grimburgwal 11; 🕑 Tue-Sat

Exquisite handcrafted contemporary jewellery is created on site; many of the pieces combine silver and gold. The necklaces and rings are particularly beautiful.

### BIG RED MACHINE Map p285 *Speciality Shop*
☎ 622 68 77; Waterlooplein 123; 🕑 noon-5pm Tue-Sat

---

## Top Five Food & Drink Shops

- **Unlimited Delicious** (p203) For gorgeous cakes and adventurous chocolates.
- **De Kaaskamer** (p201) For choice cheeses.
- **'t Zonnetje** (p203) For tea and smiley service in a centuries-old setting.
- **De Bierkoning** (p194) 950 varieties of beer. 'Nuff said.
- **Meeuwig & Zn** (p202) Amsterdam winter got you down? Escape to the Mediterranean with olive oils, vinegars and condiments.

---

## Clothing Sizes
**Measurements approximate only, try before you buy**

**Women's Clothing**

| | | | | | | |
|---|---|---|---|---|---|---|
| Aust/UK | 8 | 10 | 12 | 14 | 16 | 18 |
| Europe | 36 | 38 | 40 | 42 | 44 | 46 |
| Japan | 5 | 7 | 9 | 11 | 13 | 15 |
| USA | 6 | 8 | 10 | 12 | 14 | 16 |

**Women's Shoes**

| | | | | | | |
|---|---|---|---|---|---|---|
| Aust/USA | 5 | 6 | 7 | 8 | 9 | 10 |
| Europe | 35 | 36 | 37 | 38 | 39 | 40 |
| France only | 35 | 36 | 38 | 39 | 40 | 42 |
| Japan | 22 | 23 | 24 | 25 | 26 | 27 |
| UK | $3\frac{1}{2}$ | $4\frac{1}{2}$ | $5\frac{1}{2}$ | $6\frac{1}{2}$ | $7\frac{1}{2}$ | $8\frac{1}{2}$ |

**Men's Clothing**

| | | | | | | |
|---|---|---|---|---|---|---|
| Aust | 92 | 96 | 100 | 104 | 108 | 112 |
| Europe | 46 | 48 | 50 | 52 | 54 | 56 |
| Japan | S | | M | M | | L |
| UK/USA | 35 | 36 | 37 | 38 | 39 | 40 |

**Men's Shirts (Collar Sizes)**

| | | | | | | |
|---|---|---|---|---|---|---|
| Aust/Japan | 38 | 39 | 40 | 41 | 42 | 43 |
| Europe | 38 | 39 | 40 | 41 | 42 | 43 |
| UK/USA | 15 | $15\frac{1}{2}$ | 16 | $16\frac{1}{2}$ | 17 | $17\frac{1}{2}$ |

**Men's Shoes**

| | | | | | | |
|---|---|---|---|---|---|---|
| Aust/ UK | 7 | 8 | 9 | 10 | 11 | 12 |
| Europe | 41 | 42 | 43 | $44\frac{1}{2}$ | 46 | 47 |
| Japan | 26 | 27 | $27\frac{1}{2}$ | 28 | 29 | 30 |
| USA | $7\frac{1}{2}$ | $8\frac{1}{2}$ | $9\frac{1}{2}$ | $10\frac{1}{2}$ | $11\frac{1}{2}$ | $12\frac{1}{2}$ |

This shop, operated by the local chapter of the Hell's Angels, offers one-stop shopping for all your biking needs: leather jackets (naturally), t-shirts, camisoles, even kiddie clothes. If you've got a problem with that, we know some people who can give you an attitude adjustment.

### BIJENKORF Map pp278-9   *Department Store*
☎ 621 80 80; Dam 1

The city's most-fashionable department store, it has a small restaurant or snack bar on each floor. The design-conscious will enjoy the well-chosen clothing, toys, household accessories and books. Head to the 'Chill Out' section for club and street wear.

### BLOND Map pp278-9   *Speciality Shop*
☎ 06-2468 40 86; Spuistraat 257; 🕑 Tue-Sat

Femque and Janneke, who are both blonde, glaze plates and dishes in designs that are hilarious, adorable and very colourful: ladies lunching, beach scenes, chocolates, cheeses, etc. You can custom order as well, but note that there's no shipping.

## Top Five Speciality Shops

We love these small shops because they really, really specialise. Some are quirky, some are serious and some...we're not sure.

- **Big Red Machine** (p193) If the Hell's Angels opened up a shop...oops, they did.
- **De Witte Tanden Winkel** (p201) Becasue it's the only shop we know that specialises in toothbrushes.
- **Condomerie Het Gulden Vlies** (p194) Buy creative condoms here, at the edge of the Red Light District.
- **Vlieger** (p207) Two floors of adventurous paper from around the world.
- **De Klompenboer** (this page) You've come all the way to Holland. Don't you need a pair of wooden shoes?

### BLUE NOTE Map pp278-9 *Music*
☎ 428 10 29; Gravenstraat 12

This is *the* place for jazz (Dutch, European and American), Japanese pressings, lounge music, jazz and a few listening decks.

### C&A Map pp278-9 *Clothing*
☎ 530 71 50; Beurspassage 12A

There's little fancy about this Euro-chain (what's a designer brand?), but if you need cheap knockabout clothes, it's a fine choice. Choose carefully, and you may even find some wares with style.

### CHILLS & THRILLS
Map pp278-9 *Smart Drugs*
☎ 638 00 15; Nieuwendijk 17

Always packed with tourists straining to hear each other over thumping techno music, this busy shop sells herbal trips, mushrooms, psychoactive cacti, amino-acid/vitamin drinks, novelty bongs and life-size alien sculptures. Check out the minivaporiser, a smoke-free way to consume grass.

### CONDOMERIE HET GULDEN VLIES
Map pp278-9 *Speciality Shop*
☎ 627 41 74; www.condomerie.nl; Warmoesstraat 141

Where the well-dressed Johnson shops. Perfectly positioned for the Red Light District, this boutique stocks hundreds of types of condoms, lubricants and saucy gifts. Some of the condoms are decorated like mini-tropical scenes, or may remind you of your favourite cartoon character.

### DE BAKKERSWINKEL Map pp278-9 *Food*
☎ 330 94 83; Warmoesstraat 69

Part of a trend that's sweeping the city: the techno-gorgeous bakery. This long shop has seating in the back for enjoying rather expensive breads, plus *broodjes* (sandwiches) and salads (lunch, noon to 4pm). There's also a comforting apple tart.

### DE BEESTENWINKEL Map pp286-7 *Children*
☎ 623 18 05; Staalstraat 11; ☯ Tue-Sun

From teeny tiny teddy bears to plastic pig snouts, this pleasantly crowded shop sells *de best* (best) of *de beesten* (animals). Other bests: plush toys from great makers, lamps in animal shapes, and lots of plastic reptiles.

### DE BIERKONING Map pp278-9 *Drinks*
☎ 625 23 36; Paleisstraat 125

Beer. Just beer. Some 950 varieties including hundreds from Belgium, Germany, Britain and, of course, Holland – plus glasses, mugs and books on home brewing.

### DE KLOMPENBOER
Map pp278-9 *Traditional Souvenirs*
☎ 623 06 32; Sint Antoniesbreestraat 39-51

Bruno, the eccentric owner of this cute clog shop, works downstairs from Knuffels toy shop. Come at the right time, and you can see shoes being made and painted (the cow print ones are pretty funky). There are also samples of miniature wooden shoes and a 700-year-old pair.

### DEPT Map pp286-7 *Clothing*
☎ 528 79 07; Heiligeweg 49

Good-quality, stylish men's and women's pieces (eg, cotton t-shirts, woollen sweaters, well-cut suits) in the latest colours make this the perfect pit stop for savvy, elegant shoppers.

### FAIR TRADE SHOP
Map pp286-7 *Ethnic Culture*
☎ 625 22 45; Heiligeweg 45

This charitable shop features quality, stylish products from developing countries including clothes, comestibles, toys, CDs and interesting ceramics. The company works directly with producers and provides ongoing business training.

### FAME MUSIC Map pp278-9 *Music*
☎ 638 25 25; Kalverstraat 2-4, at Dam

This megastore has an enormous number of titles with broad (and mainstream) collections of pop, jazz, classical, CD-ROMs and videos. It also sells tickets to big concerts. Sale prices can be quite reasonable.

### FEMALE & PARTNERS
Map pp278-9 *Speciality Shop*
☎ 620 91 52; Spuistraat 100

Everything you need for your inner dominatrix…or the one who's waiting for you at home. Female & Partners is filled with clothing, undies, leather and toys for women and those who love them. Thank goodness men aren't the only ones who get to have fun

### FUN FASHION Map pp278-9 *Clothing*
☎ 420 50 96; Nieuwendijk 200

Proof positive that California has taken over the world. Even though there's no surfing in Amsterdam, this busy surf- and skatewear shop bustles with cool clothes for guys and girls. Brands include Carhartt, Quiksilver, Lonsdale, gsus and our favourite, Pornstar.

### GEELS & CO Map pp278-9 *Food & Drinks*
☎ 624 06 83; Warmoesstraat 67; ☟ Mon-Sat

Operating from this glorious, aromatic store for over 140 years, the distinguished tea-and-coffee merchant also sells chocolate, teapots and coffee plungers. Be sure to visit the interesting little museum upstairs (museum hours 2pm to 4.30pm, Tuesday and Saturday).

### GROOVE CONNECTION
Map pp278-9 *Music*
☎ 624 72 34; home.planet.nl/~riches/ilh/; Sint Nicolaasstraat 41

Shop here during the day, and you may brush elbows with the DJ who'll be spinning for you that night. Techno, trance and harder beats are the speciality. It's also a nice place to hang out and find club info.

### Top Five Bookshops
- **Boekie Woekie** (p200)
- **The English Bookshop** (p203)
- **Galerie Lambiek** (p205)
- **International Theatre & Film Books** (p205)
- **Athenaeum** (p192)

### Worth Noting
If you're after club music, or info on the club scene, consider:
- **Dance Tracks** (Map pp278-9; ☎ 639 08 53; Nieuwe Nieuwstraat 69)
- **Killa Cutz** (Map p278-9; ☎ 428 40 40; Nieuwe Nieuwstraat 19D)
- **Rhythm Imports** (Map p278-9; ☎ 622 28 67; Nieuwendijk 159)

### H&M Map pp286-7 *Clothing*
☎ 624 06 24; Kalverstraat 125

This fashion chain store has up-to-the-minute clothes for all ages and several locations. You may find higher quality elsewhere, but prices are remarkably low.

### HANS APPENZELLER
Map pp278-9 *Jewellery*
☎ 626 82 18; Grimburgwal 1; ☟ Tue-Sat

Appenzeller is one of Amsterdam's leading designers in gold and stone, known for the simplicity and strength of his designs. If his sparse work is not to your taste, all along the same street is a row of jewellery shops of all kinds.

### HEMA Map pp278-9 *Department Store*
☎ 638 99 63; Nieuwendijk 174

What used to be the nation's equivalent of Woolworths or K-Mart has undergone a facelift and now attracts as many design aficionados as bargain hunters. Expect low prices, reliable quality and a wide range of products including good-value wines and delicatessen goods.

### HERMAN BROOD GALERIE
Map pp286-7 *Art & Antiques*
☎ 623 37 66; Spuistraat 320

This gallery is dedicated to Herman Brood, Amsterdam's legendary club promoter (1946–2001) who shone briefly but brightly before being undone by drugs and alcohol. Fittingly, his oil paintings are displayed upstairs from the busy Café Dante.

### HIMALAYA Map pp278-9 *New Age*
☎ 626 08 99; Warmoesstraat 56; ☟ Mon-Sat

What a surprise: a peaceful, New Age oasis amid the Red Light District. Stock up on crystals, incense and oils, ambient CDs and books on the healing arts, then visit the lovely tearoom.

Shopping – Medieval Centre

## HOUSEWIVES ON FIRE

Map pp278-9 *Clothing*
☎ 422 10 67; Spuistraat 102; ☺ Mon-Sat

One-stop shopping for all your club needs: deck yourself out in techno-style clothes, get yourself a wild 'do' at the in-house hairdressing salon, *and* purchase tickets to one-off club nights. Plus, we love the homage-to-Charlie's-Angels logo.

### INNERSPACE Map pp278-9 *Smart Drugs*
☎ 624 33 38; Spuistraat 108

Known for good service and information, this large shop started as a supplier to large parties, and now the shop sells herbal ecstasy, mushrooms, psychoactive plants and cactus. True to its origins, it's also a good place for party info and tickets.

### INTERMALE Map pp278-9 *Books*
☎ 625 00 09; www.intermale.nl; Spuistraat 251

One of Amsterdam's leading gay bookstores, it has 1½ floors of photo books, sexy magazines, videos and pornographic postcards. As the name suggests, it's intended for men only.

## JACOB HOOY & CO

Map pp278-9 *Alternative Medicine*
☎ 624 30 41; Kloveniersburgwal 12; ☺ Mon-Sat

This charming chemist's shop – with its walls of massive, wooden drawers – has been selling medicinal herbs, homeopathic remedies and natural cosmetics since 1743. You can also get teas and seasonings for chicken or fish.

## KALVERTOREN

Map pp286-7 *Shopping Centre*
Singel 457

This popular, modern shopping centre contains a small Hema, Vroom & Dreesmann and big-brand fashion stores like Replay, Quiksilver, Levi's, Timberland and DKNY.

### KNUFFELS Map pp278-9 *Children*
☎ 623 06 32; Sint Antoniesbreestraat 39-51

This entrancing shop delights adults and kids alike with soft toys, puppets, beautiful mobiles, teddies and jigsaw puzzles. Downstairs is the city centre's sole (pun intended) maker of wooden shoes.

### KOKOPELLI Map pp278-9 *Smart Drugs*
☎ 421 70 00; Warmoesstraat 12

Were it not for its main trade, you might swear this large, beautiful space was a fashionable clothing or housewares store. In addition to mushrooms and smart drugs, there's an art gallery, Internet facilities, books and a chilled-out lounge area overlooking Damrak.

## LAUNDRY INDUSTRY

Map pp286-7 *Clothing*
☎ 420 25 54; Spui 1

*Laundry Industry fashion shop on Spui.*

Hip, urban types head here for well-cut, well-designed clothes by this Dutch design house (the Spui location is the main store). Watch glam couples coveting soft leather coats and perfectly fitted suits. There's also a branch at **Magna Plaza** (Map pp278-9; ☎ 625 39 60; Nieuwezijds Voorburgwal 182).

### LE CELLIER Map pp278-9 *Drinks*
☎ 638 65 73; Spuistraat 116

This large store sells liqueurs, a great selection of genevers and New World wines, and over 75 types of beer.

### MAGIC MUSHROOM GALLERY
Map pp278-9 *Smart Drugs*
☎ 427 57 65; Spuistraat 249

There are fresh and dried magic mushrooms on sale (it's recommended that first-timers try the Mexican ones for a relaxed, happy trip) as well as mushroom-growing kits, herbal ecstasy and smart drinks.

### MAGNA PLAZA
Map pp278-9 *Shopping Centre*
☎ 626 91 99; Nieuwezijds Voorburgwal 182

This grand 19th-century building, once the main post office, has over 40 upmarket fashion, gift and jewellery stores. Our faves include Ordning & Reda (swanky, colourful stationery) and Shu Uemura (stylish makeup).

### MAISON DE BONNETERIE
Map pp286-7 *Department Store*
☎ 531 34 00; Rokin 140

Exclusive and classic clothes for the whole family are featured here. Men are particularly well catered for with labels like Ralph Lauren

## Markets

No visit to Amsterdam is complete if you haven't experienced one or more of its lively markets. The following is merely a selection. Oh, and watch out for pickpockets.

- **Albert Cuypmarkt** (Map pp286-7; Albert Cuypstraat; ⏱ 9am-5pm Mon-Sat) This general market has food, clothing, hardware and household goods at cheap prices. It's a great place to watch Amsterdam's melting pot in action.
- **Antiques market** (Map pp278-9; Nieuwmarkt; ⏱ 9am-5pm Sun May-Sep) There are many genuine articles here and lots of books and bric-a-brac.
- **Art markets** (Maps pp286-7; Thorbeckeplein & Spui Square; ⏱ 10.30am-6pm Sun Mar-Oct) These quiet markets, dealing in mostly modern pictorial art, are a bit too modest in scope to yield real finds.
- **Bloemenmarkt** (Map pp286-7; Along Singel near Muntplein; ⏱ 9am-5pm daily summer, 9am-5pm Mon-Sat winter) Colourful in the extreme, but photographers take note: it's almost always in the shade.
- **Boerenmarkt** (Farmer's Markets; Map pp278-9; Noordermarkt & Nieuwmarkt Square; ⏱ 10am-3pm Sat) Pick up home-grown produce, organic foods and picnic provisions.
- **Book market** (Map pp278-9; Oudemanhuispoort; ⏱ 11am-4pm Mon-Fri) In the old arcade between Oudezijds Achterburgwal and Kloveniersburgwal (blink and you'll miss either entrance), this is the place to find that 19th-century copy of *Das Kapital* or a semantic analysis of Icelandic sagas, and some newer books and art prints.
- **De Looier antiques market** (Map pp286-7; ☎ 624 90 38; Elandsgracht 109, Jordaan; ⏱ 11am-5pm Sat-Thu) The indoor stalls in the De Looier complex sell jewellery, furniture, art and collectibles.
- **Lindengracht** (Map p277; Lindengracht, Jordaan; ⏱ 11am-4pm Sat) General market, very much a local affair.
- **Noordermarkt** (Map pp278-9; Noorderstraat, Jordaan; ⏱ 9am-1pm Mon, 10am-3pm Sat) This Jordaan market is good for antiques, fabrics and second-hand bric-a-brac.
- **Mosveldmarkt** (Map pp274-5; Mosveld, Amsterdam North; ⏱ Tue-Sat) This (untouristy) typical Dutch market sells mostly food and clothing. Take bus No 34/35 from Centraal Station thorough the IJ-Tunnel.
- **Plant market** (Map pp286-7; Amstelveld; ⏱ 3-6pm Mon Easter-Christmas) All sorts of plants, pots and vases are sold here.
- **Stamp & coin market** (Map pp278-9; Nieuwezijds Voorburgwal 276; ⏱ 10am-4pm Wed & Sat) This little street-side market, just south of Wijdesteeg, sells stamps, coins and medals.
- **Waterlooplein flea market** (Map pp286-7; Waterlooplein; ⏱ 9am-5pm Mon-Fri, 8.30am-5.30pm Sat) Amsterdam's most-famous flea market is full of curios, second-hand clothing, inexpensive Doc Martens, music, electronic stuff slightly on the blink, hardware and cheap New Age gifts.
- **Westermarkt** (Map p277; Westerstraat, Jordaan; ⏱ 9am-1pm Mon) Cheapish clothes and textiles, some real bargains.

## Smart-drug shops

Generally funky but sometimes quite swanky, 'smart-drug' shops began popping up all over the city in the mid-1990s and are now an established addition to the coffeeshop scene. They sell legal, organic hallucinogens like magic mushrooms, herbal joints, seeds (poppy, marijuana, psychoactive), mood enhancers and aphrodisiacs. Note that while it's legal to buy these items over the counter in Amsterdam, the same products are probably illegal to take back home.

In addition to mood- and mind-enhancing products, these shops sell books (on shamanism, psychedelia, spiritualism), jewellery, trancey videos and bongs.

One thing we beg you: before you buy, ask the staff to explain exactly what dosage to consume and what to expect from your trip. The shops we've listed here all do that, but if you happen on one that doesn't, take your business elsewhere.

and Armani, best purchased during the brilliant 50%-off sales. Note the amazing chandeliers and beautiful glass cupola.

### MASSIVE SOUL FOOD Map pp278-9 *Music*
☎ 428 61 30; Nieuwe Nieuwstraat 27C
Fuel your funky appetite with imported rap, R&B, house, two-step and garage titles while listening to budding DJs honing their skills on the turntables. You can also stock up on DJ gear here.

### NIJHOF & LEE Map pp286-7 *Books*
☎ 620 39 80; www.nijhoflee.nl; Staalstraat 13a; ☺ Tue-Sat
Design fans will want to head here for a swell selection of international architecture, art and typography books and posters in an intimate but contemporary setting. One wall boasts an substantial selection of well-priced remainders.

### PIED À TERRE Map pp286-7 *Books*
☎ 627 44 55; Singel 393
This shop specialises in pretty much anything you'll need for outdoor pursuits: hiking and cycling books, topographical maps and travel guidebooks.

### PINOKKIO Map pp278-9 *Children*
☎ 622 89 14; Magna Plaza, Nieuwezijds Voorburgwal 182
This pleasant shop stocks wooden and educational toys, rocking horses, replica canal houses, mobiles and of course, lots of Pinocchio dolls.

### PO CHAI TONG
Map pp286-7 *Alternative Medicine*
☎ 428 49 56; Waterlooplein 13; ☺ Mon-Sat
If nothing seems to take away your stress, fatigue or jet lag, pay a visit to Dr Kai Zhang's kindly Chinese herbal-medicine and acupuncture shop. It's far from fancy, but clients have included opera singers and conductors from the nearby Stopera. There are also numerous other shops in the Chinese area near Nieuwmarkt.

### PUCCINI BOMBONI Map pp278-9 *Food*
☎ 427 83 41; Singel 184; ☎ 626 54 74; Staalstraat 17
We're not the only ones who go gaga over Puccini's large, handmade chocolate bonbons with rich fillings. Unforgettable chocolates include plum, marzipan or the calvados cup. Note: shops have been known to close in warm weather.

### ROOTS Map pp278-9 *Music*
☎ 620 44 70; Jonge Roelensteeg 6; ☺ Tue-Sun
Small as a stamp, Roots stocks an impressive array of reggae and dance-hall vinyl and CDs. It also sells concert videos and knows about reggae club nights. The shop publishes the Amsterdam reggae guide, with clubs and calendar listings.

### RUSH HOUR RECORDS Map pp278-9 *Music*
☎ 427 45 05; Spuistraat 98
Join Amsterdam's best DJs scouring the racks of just-released, imported dance music (deep house, electro, hip-hop, soul-jazz, techno and broken beat) and listening at a few decks. A knowledgeable staff gives great tips on the best nightclubs.

### SCHILDERHUIS PAULUS VAN
### PAUWVLIET Map pp278-9 *Art & Antiques*
☎ 310 74 12; Singel 87
It's hardly high art, but if you've fallen in love with Amsterdam's streetscapes and need to take one home, this simple shop specialises in oils and watercolours.

### SEVENTYFIVE Map pp278-9 *Clothing*
☎ 626 46 11; Nieuwe Hoogstraat 24
At this true temple to trainers, stimulate your sports-shoe obsession with brands like Gola, Diesel, Everlast and, of course, Nike and Adidas, all at prices lower than in the UK.

### THE BOOK EXCHANGE Map pp278-9 *Books*
☎ 626 62 66; Kloveniersburgwal 58

This rabbit warren features four rooms of second-hand books, with temptingly priced occult, sci-fi and detective novels.

### TRIX & REES Map pp278-9 *Clothing*
☎ 420 25 30; St Antoniniesbreestraat 30
Teeny-tiny, well-fitting women's clothing is sold here, beneath a giant chandelier that marries Adam and Eve with the Addams Family.

### UNIVERSITY SHOP
Map pp286-7 *Clothing*
☎ 525 36 55; Spui 23
The University of Amsterdam has a lovely logo, and you can wear it on your lovely person with T-shirts, sweatshirts and the like, not to mention book bags and even bottle openers.

### VAN PARIDON
Map pp278-9 *Speciality Shop*
☎ 623 59 11; Nieuwzijds Voorburgwal 361
Should you become inspired by your visit to the Begijnhof, this 100-plus-year-old shop around the back has a selection of religious figurines, both ancient and very modern.

### VROLIJK Map pp278-9 *Books*
☎ 623 51 42; www.vrolijk.nu; Paleisstraat 135; ◷ daily, closed Sun Oct-Dec
Said to be the Netherlands' largest gay and lesbian bookstore, it carries most of the world's major gay and lesbian magazines, as well as novels, guidebooks and postcards. Climb the stairs for art, travel, poetry and DVDs/videos.

### VROOM & DREESMANN
Map pp286-7 *Department Store*
☎ 622 01 71; Kalverstraat 201
Slightly more upmarket than Hema (p195), this national chain is popular for its clothing and cosmetics. Its fabulous cafeteria, La Place, serves well-priced, freshly prepared salads, hot dishes and pastries.

### WATERSTONE'S Map pp286-7 *Books*
☎ 638 38 21; Kalverstraat 152
Library-style shelving, four storeys and a central location near Spui Square make Waterstone's a great resource for English-language books. There's an emphasis on travel guidebooks, magazines, newspapers and novels, and if you need a book on tape for that trip out of town, head here. English language titles are often discounted.

# WESTERN CANAL BELT

### AFFAIRE D'EAU
Map pp278-9 *Specialty Shop*
☎ 422 04 11; Haarlemmerdijk 148-150; ◷ Mon-Sat
Nobody seriously expects tourists to buy an antique French bathtub, but these claw feet beauties sure are cool to look at, along with commodes and showers of bygone days. If you get inspired, you can pick up fixtures like faucet handles and towel racks – some old, some new.

### ANALIK Map pp278-9 *Clothing*
☎ 422 05 61; Hartenstraat 34-36; ◷ Mon-Sat

Shopping – Western Canal Belt

## Diamonds
Amsterdam has been a major diamond centre since Sephardic Jews introduced the cutting industry in the 1580s (one of a limited number of occupations open to them at the time). The 'Cullinan', the largest diamond ever found (3106 carats), was split into more than 100 stones here in 1908, after which the master cutter spent three months recovering from stress. The Kohinoor (Mountain of Light) – a very large, oval diamond (108.8 carats), acquired by Queen Victoria that now forms part of the British crown jewels – was cut here too.

There are about a dozen diamond factories in the city, five of which offer guided tours – the Gassan tour is probably the most interesting, but Coster is centrally located and has a great history. The tours are free and are usually conducted 9am to 5pm seven days a week, but ring ahead for details.

Diamonds aren't necessarily cheaper in Amsterdam than elsewhere, but prices are fairly competitive. At least you will have seen how they're worked, and when you buy from a factory you get an extensive description of the purchase so you know exactly what you're buying.

The factories are **Amsterdam Diamond Center** (Map pp278-9; ☎ 624 57 87; Rokin 1); **Coster Diamonds** (Map pp282-3; ☎ 305 55 55; Paulus Potterstraat 2-6); **Gassan Diamonds** (Map pp282-3; ☎ 622 53 33; Nieuwe Uilenburgerstraat 173-175); **Stoeltie Diamonds** (Map pp286-7; ☎ 623 76 01; Wagenstraat 13-17) and; **Van Moppes & Zoon** (Map pp286-7; ☎ 676 12 42; Albert Cuypstraat 2-6).

Analik, one of Amsterdam's pre-eminent fashion designers, creates stylish pieces for smart young things.

## ANTONIA BY YVETTE

Map pp278-9 *Clothing*
☎ 627 24 33; Gasthuismolensteeg 12

If 'Sex in the City' were shot in Amsterdam, we bet that the girls would spend half their time in this shop. Shoes, boots, sandals and espadrilles run from supremely classy to just plain fun. There's also a small guys' section.

## AQUA DIVING

Map pp278-9 *Camping, Outdoor & Sports*
☎ 623 35 03; Haarlemmerstraat 165

Imagine a cone of soft-serve ice-cream visited a coffeeshop and then made itself comfy indoors – now you've got an idea of this shop's trippy displays. Even if you have no intention of buying diving equipment, a bike or inline skates, it's worth a visit to gawk.

## ARCHITECTURA & NATURA

Map pp278-9 *Books*
☎ 623 61 86; www.architectura.nl; Leliegracht 22;
☺ Mon-Sat

This charming canalside shop has art, architecture, design, landscape and coffee-table books on the ground floor. Upstairs, **Architectuurantiquariat Opbouw** (Upstairs Architecture Antique Shop; ☎ 638 70 18) has a swell selection of its namesake.

## BAKKERIJ PAUL ANNÉ ENTREES

Map pp286-7 *Food*
☎ 623 53 22; Runstraat 25; ☺ Mon-Sat

This healthy organic bakery has delicious breads (eg, the tofu bread), sandwiches, scrumptious apple turnovers and date tarts.

## BOEKIE WOEKIE Map p277 *Books*
☎ 639 05 07; Berenstraat 16; ☺ noon-6pm Tue-Fri, noon-5pm Sat, 1-5pm Sun

It's one of our favourite shops: an art gallery cleverly masquerading as a bookstore. While other shops handle art books, here they sell books *as* art, created by artists specifically for this medium. Some tell stories (elegantly illustrated, naturally), others are riffs on graphic motifs; you may want to browse for a long time.

## BRILMUSEUM Map pp278-9 *Speciality Shop*
☎ 421 24 14; Gasthuismolensteeg 7; ☺ Wed-Sat

Here you can take in the 700-year history of eyeglasses, as well as a very 21st-century collection, some of them pretty outlandish.

## BROER & ZUS Map p277 *Children*
☎ 422 90 02; Eerste Bloemdwarsstraat 19;
☺ Mon-Sat

Cosy little 'bro and sis' specialises in Dutch makers and fabrics for kids from birth to six years. You can get brands like Kidscase, tiny tops emblazoned with slogans like 'macho' and 'ladykiller', and wild prints (think Hawaiian shirts).

## CHRISTODOULOU & LAMÉ

Map p277 *Speciality Shop*
☎ 320 22 69; Rozengracht 42

Handwoven Tibetan silk pillows, velvet throws and hand-beaded saris from this treasure-trove of sumptuous soft furnishings will transform your home into a plush sanctuary. It's a real festival of colours.

## COMPUTER COLLECTIEF

Map p285 *Books*
☎ 638 90 03; Amstel 312; ☺ Mon-Sat

Come here for computer books, magazines, software and friendly service. Prices are higher than in the USA, but if you need it, you need it.

## DE BELLY Map p277 *Food*
☎ 330 94 83; Nieuwe Leliestraat 174

This organic supermarket, with 30-plus years in the Jordaan, has a great bakery and a small but smart selection of prepared foods, even organic tarts and chocolates.

### DE KAASKAMER Map pp286-7 *Food*
☎ 623 34 83; Runstraat 7
A small shop full of hundreds of cheeses from around Europe and Holland and deli items like pate, cured meats and baguettes, this does a roaring sandwich trade at lunch.

### DE LACH Map p277 *Speciality Shop*
☎ 626 66 25; Eerste Bloemdwarsstraat 14; ☺ Tue, Thu-Sat
This eccentric corner shop sells vintage movie posters from all over the world (eg the Italian version of *Some Like it Hot*) at prices from €12 to €1000. There's even a mini Walk of Fame, signed by Dutch stars, on the sidewalk outside.

### DEMMENIE SPORT
Map p277 *Camping, Outdoor & Sports*
☎ 624 36 52; Marnixstraat 2; ☺ Mon-Sat
For professional outdoor gear for the serious enthusiast, this shop specialises in mountaineering tents, shoes and clothes.

### DE NIEUWE KLEREN VAN DE KEIZER
Map pp286-7 *Clothing*
☎ 422 68 95; Runstraat 29

*Large cheeses at De Kaaskamer*

'The Emperor's New Clothes' sells clingy clubwear and tight-fitting shirts that seem to fit gay men to a T (and any other men who are reasonably fit). You'll need a little money to shop here, but you may catch a sale.

### DE WITTE TANDEN WINKEL
Map pp286-7 *Speciality Shop*
☎ 623 34 43; Runstraat 5
We love shops that are obsessed, and the 'white-teeth shop' certainly is – with dental hygiene. There's a huge selection of toothbrushes, toothpastes from around the world, brushing accessories you never knew you needed (eg, a tiny hourglass so that you can make sure you've brushed long enough) and friendly advice.

### DUO SPORTS
Map pp278-9 *Camping, Outdoor & Sports*
☎ 530 41 70; Radhuisstraat 30-40
Ajax, Amsterdam's football club, has only one official shop in the city centre, on the top floor of this multilevel sporting goods store. Don't expect bargains – jerseys sell for €60-plus and almost never go on sale. The only other official store is at the stadium.

### EXOTA Map pp278-9 *Clothing*
☎ 620 91 02; Hartenstraat 10; 420 68 84; Nieuwe Leliestraat 32
This funky clothes emporium for men, women and kids mixes well-known labels like Lee, Kookai and French Connection with more-alternative brands and cutesy Japanese giftware. The Nieuwe Leliestraat location features women's and children's clothing. Its own kids' label, Petit Louie, is decidedly groovy.

### FRONTIER Map p277 *Books*
☎ 330 91 51; Eerste Bloemdwarsstraat 15
For anything to do with conspiracies, aliens, UFOs, lost civilisations, crop circles and the like, this is the flagship bookshop of the Dutch magazine of the same name. It specialises in both common and hard-to-find books – some overseas bookshops use it as a supplier!

### GALLERIA D'ARTE RINASCIMENTO
Map p277 *Traditional Souvenirs*
☎ 622 75 09; Prinsengracht 170
This pretty shop sells Royal Delftware ceramics (both antique and new), all manner of vases, platters, brooches, Christmas ornaments and interesting 19th-century wall tiles and plaques.

## GOLDSTRASSE Map pp286-7 _Jewellery_

☎ 420 20 95; Elandsgracht 89; ☻ Wed-Sat

Marina Alexandre is an Amsterdam-based jewellery designer and teacher, with students at the Rietveld Academie among others. You'll see her rings (in gold, silver and silicone) on display at this new gallery, although they're more like wearable art.

## INTERNATIONAAL DESIGN CENTRUM (WONEN 2000) Map p277 _Speciality Shop_

☎ 521 87 10; Rozengracht 215-217; ☻ Tue-Sat

Begun over a century ago, this shop has repped the forefront of Dutch design ever since. The main gallery has handsome displays of Dutch modern (and Italian – that's the 'international' part) from names like Gispen, Edra and Artifoort. There's even a cool café. Its affiliate, De Kasstoor (across the street) applies the same design concept to kitchens and lighting (the towel hooks manage to be both slick and cute).

## JOSINE BOKHOVEN

Map p277 _Art & Antiques_

☎ 623 65 98; Prinsengracht 154

Across the canal from the Anne Frankhuis, this friendly gallery features contemporary art and the work of emerging young artists, including German artist, Ralph Fleck.

## KITSCH KITCHEN Map p277 _Speciality Shop_

☎ 622 82 61; Rozengracht 8-12

You want it flowered, frilly, colourful, over the top or just made from plastic? Chances are you'll find it here – everything from handbags to housewares to kiddie toys and doll gowns. Plus lamps, Mexican tablecloths, pink plastic chandeliers from India and, of course, bouquets of plastic flowers.

## KUNSTHAAR Map p277 _Art & Antiques_

☎ 625 99 12; Berenstraat 21

The only gallery we know that's also a hair salon, it stages exhibitions of abstract and realistic contemporary Dutch and European art.

## LADY DAY Map pp278-9 _Clothing_

☎ 623 58 20; Hartenstraat 9

This is the premier location for unearthing spotless vintage clothes from Holland and elsewhere. The leather jackets, swingin' 1960s and '70s wear, and woollen sailors' coats are well-priced winners. There are also some men's suits and new shoes.

## LAURA DOLS Map pp278-9 _Clothing_

☎ 624 90 66; Wolvenstraat 7

Compulsive style-watchers head to this vintage clothing store for fur coats, 1920s beaded dresses, lace blouses and '40s movie-star accessories like hand-stitched leather gloves.

## LOCAL SERVICE Map pp286-7 _Clothing_

☎ 620 86 38; Keizersgracht 400-2

Media types (both male and female) hunt here for the latest Paul Smith (Amsterdam's exclusive dealer for his main line), Ghost and Stone Island collections.

## MECHANISCH SPEELGOED

Map p277 _Children_

☎ 638 16 80; Westerstraat 67; ☻ Mon, Tue, Thu-Sat

This fun shop is crammed full of nostalgic and wind-up toys like snowdomes, glow-lamps, masks and finger puppets. And who doesn't need a good rubber chicken every once in a while?

## MEEUWIG & ZN Map pp278-9 _Food_

☎ 626 52 86; Haarlemmerstraat 70; ☻ Mon-Sat

Fill your own bottle from metal crocks containing over 50 types of olive oil from around the world. You'll also find bottles of gourmet vinegar, mustard and chutney, and fresh olives.

## MENDO Map p277 _Art & Antiques_

☎ 612 12 15; Berenstraat 11; ☻ Wed-Sun

The Mendo ad agency has opened this smart, black-walled gallery specialising in young Dutch painters, from the bright to the disturbing but alluring. They also sell an intriguing selection of art, design, architecture and photography books.

## PAUL ANDRIESSE Map p277 _Art & Antiques_

☎ 623 62 37; Prinsengracht 116

Contemporary art's the go here – think video installations, avant-garde sculpture and works by international and Dutch artists like painter

---

## Top Five Shops for Dutch Design

- **Hans Appenzeller** (p195) Jewellery
- **Internationaal Design Centrum** (this page) Furniture and housewares
- **Mendo** (this page) Art, books and design
- **Reflex Modern Art Gallery** (p206) Painting
- **Wonderwood** (p207) Furniture

Marlene Dumas, photographer Thomas Struth and Keith Edmier, who works in several media.

## PINK POINT OF PRESENCE
Map p277 *Books*
www.pinkpoint.org; Westermarkt; ☿ vary seasonally
Next to the Homomonument, this volunteer-staffed kiosk (also known as Pink Point or PPP) is Amsterdam's unofficial gay and lesbian welcome wagon. In addition to books and souvenirs, it dispenses free information, from listings magazines to inside advice.

### RAZZMATAZZ Map pp278-9 *Clothing*
☎ 420 04 83; Wolvenstraat 19
These flamboyant and expensive designer outfits and avant-garde club clothes for women and men include the Westwood, Frankie Morello and Andrew Mackenzie labels.

### SANTA JET Map pp278-9 *Speciality Shop*
☎ 427 20 70; Prinsenstraat 7
The interior's vivid colours are worth a visit alone, as are the Mexican shrines, religious icons, *Day of the Dead* paraphernalia, candles and love potions.

## THE ENGLISH BOOKSHOP
Map p277 *Books*
☎ 626 42 30; Lauriergracht 71; ☿ Tue-Sun
This attractive, canalside shop has a well-chosen selection of English-language biographies, novels and translations of the works of Dutch writers.

## UNLIMITED DELICIOUS
Map pp278-9 *Food*
☎ 622 48 29; Haarlemmerstraat 122
Is it ever! It's tempting to dive into the gorgeous, sculptural cakes and tarts, but – if you can – you can walk past them to the dozens of varieties of chocolates made in-house. Some of the more-outlandish combinations (that somehow work!) are tomato balsamic allspice, caramel cayenne and Laphroaig whisky. More standard choices include coffee, nougat and our favourite: Ceylon cinnamon.

### VAN RAVENSTEIN Map pp286-7 *Clothing*
☎ 639 00 67; Keizersgracht 359
Chic men and women shop here for upmarket Dutch and Belgian designers like Dries Van Noten, Ann Demeulemeester and Dirk Bikkembergs. For men: Martin Margiela and Viktor & Rolf.

## WEGEWIJS KAAS & DELICATESSEN
Map p277 *Food*
☎ 624 40 93; Rozengracht 32
Don't be surprised to see a line out the door of this high-end shop specialising in Dutch meats and cheeses. It's so tempting that you may want to succumb to a *broodje* (sandwich) – we say 'go for it!'

### WIJNKOPERIJ OTTERMAN Map p277 *Food*
☎ 625 50 88; Keizersgracht 300
Come here for French wines selected for the character of their *terroir* (soil), plus a few selections from Belgium, the Netherlands, even Lebanon, and organic wines that have been made without preservatives.

### 'T ZONNETJE Map pp278-9 *Food*
☎ 623 00 58; Haarlemmerdijk 45; ☿ Tue-Sat
In a space that's been a teashop since 1642, you can find teas from all over the world, coffees and implements, and be waited on by a commendably cheerful owner. High tea is served upstairs (reserve for large groups).

# SOUTHERN CANAL BELT

## À LA CARTE Map pp286-7 *Books*
☎ 625 06 79; Utrechtsestraat 110
Travellers head here for guidebooks, maps, globes and beautiful photography books.

## ART MULTIPLES
Map pp286-7 *Art & Antiques*
☎ 624 84 19; Keizersgracht 510; ☿ Mon-Sat
You could spend hours here flipping through thousands of postcards with unusual subject matter; take a peek at the raunchy ones in 3-D viewers. It also sells beautiful art posters and museum-shop gifts.

## ASTAMANGALA
Map pp286-7 *Art & Antiques*
☎ 623 44 02; Kerkstraat 168; ☿ Tue-Sat
This gallery has ancient art and ethnographical objects from the Himalayan region.

## AURORA KONTAKT
Map pp286-7 *Electronics*
☎ 623 40 62; Vijzelstraat 27-35
If your favourite electronic or computer gizmo has stopped working, this place can sell you a replacement at competitive prices.

## BEVER ZWERFSPORT

Map pp286-7                    *Camping, Outdoor & Sport*

☎ 689 46 39; Stadhouderskade 4; ☻ Mon-Sat & first Sun of each month

Everything you need for a local hike or a Himalayan expedition: camping equipment, mountaineering gear, clothes and shoes.

## BLOEMENMARKT

Map pp286-7                    *Traditional Souvenirs*

Singel, near Muntplein; ☻ closed Sun winter

The traders at the floating flower market should be able to tell you if you can take the flower bulbs back home: Ireland and the UK allow an unlimited number of bulbs to be brought back in, as do Canada and the USA (accompanied by a certificate, which will be provided). Japan permits up to 100 certified bulbs, while Australia and New Zealand have banned the importation of bulbs altogether.

## BROEKMANS & VAN POPPEL

Map pp286-7                    *Music*

☎ 679 65 75; Van Baerlestraat 92-4; ☻ Mon-Sat

Head to the 1st floor for a comprehensive selection from the Middle Ages through classical to today. It's also the city's top choice for classical and popular sheet music, as well as music books.

## CARL DENIG

Map pp286-7                    *Camping, Outdoor & Sport*

☎ 626 24 36; Weteringschans 113-15; ☻ closed Sun & most Mon

Opened in 1912, this is Amsterdam's oldest and best outdoor retailer, though you pay for the quality. There are five floors of packs, tents, hiking and camping accessories, snowboards and skis.

## CITYBOEK Map pp286-7                    *Art & Antiques*

☎ 627 03 49; www.cityboek.nl; Kerkstraat 199; ☻ Tue-Fri or by appointment

We normally don't recommend shops selling souvenir posters, but this small publishing house is an exception, with precisely drawn, multicoloured, architecturally faithful prints, books and postcards of Amsterdam's canalscapes (eg, images of the entire Herengracht or Singel).

## CONCERTO Map pp286-7                    *Music*

☎ 623 52 28; Utrechtsestraat 52-60

This excellent, rambling shop, spread over several buildings, has Amsterdam's best selection of new and second-hand CDs and records; you could spend hours browsing in here. It's often cheap, always interesting and has good listening facilities.

*Getting advice on flowers at Bloemenmarkt*

### CORA KEMPERMAN Map pp286-7 *Clothing*
☎ 625 12 84; Leidsestraat 72

This successful Dutch designer specialises in floaty, layered separates and dresses in linen, cotton and wool.

### DECORATIVA Map pp286-7 *Art & Antiques*
☎ 320 10 93; Nieuwe Spiegelstraat 9a; ☺ daily

An amazing and massive jumble of European antiques, collectables and weird vintage gifts fills this large space. Look up and you'll even see paintings on the ceilings.

### DREAM LOUNGE Map pp286-7 *Smart Drugs*
☎ 626 69 07; Kerkstraat 93

Enhance whatever might need enhancing at Amsterdam's original smart shop; the enthusiastic staff can explain everything about the stock, which includes magic mushrooms, trippy herbs and cacti. There are books, club flyers advertising upcoming trance/ambient nights, and Internet facilities.

### EDUARD KRAMER
Map pp286-7 *Art & Antiques*
☎ 623 08 32; Nieuwe Spiegelstraat 64

Specialising in antique Dutch wall and floor tiles, glass and silver, Eduard Kramer is bursting with vintage homewares.

### EH ARIËNS KAPPERS
Map pp286-7 *Art & Antiques*
☎ 623 53 56; Nieuwe Spiegelstraat 32

This pretty gallery stocks original prints, etchings, engravings, lithographs, maps from the 15th to 20th centuries, and Japanese woodblock prints.

### EICHHOLTZ Map pp286-7 *Food & Drink*
☎ 622 03 05; Leidsestraat 48

This small deli is bursting with everything homesick Brits and Americans yearn for, like Oreo cookies, Betty Crocker cake mix, Heinz baked beans, peanut butter (Skippy, Jif *or* Peter Pan!), HP sauce and Bird's custard.

### GALERIE LAMBIEK Map pp286-7 *Books*
☎ 626 75 43; www.lambiek.nl; Kerkstraat 78; ☺ daily

Serious collectors of comics will lose themselves amid tens of thousands of titles of Dutch and worldwide comic-book art. Crumb, Avril and Herriman are just the tip of the 4000-author-plus iceberg. Note: it may have moved to a new location by the time you read this – check the website or phone for an update.

### GALERIE ZWIEP
Map pp286-7 *Art & Antiques*
☎ 320 87 59; Kerkstraat 149

This sparse space is filled with primitive and oceanic sculpture, masks and statues. The Amazonian feather masks are especially alluring.

### GET RECORDS Map pp286-7 *Music*
☎ 622 34 41; Utrechtsestraat 105

This deceptively large store has an eclectic and wide range of rock, folk, country and blues CDs. It's a decent break from the club music scene.

### HART'S WIJNHANDEL Map pp286-7 *Food*
☎ 623 83 50; Vijzelgracht 27; ☺ Tue-Sat

Listen to classical music as you peruse the large selection of genevers and French and Italian wines at this peaceful shop. It's been around since 1880.

### HEINEN Map pp286-7 *Traditional Souvenirs*
☎ 627 82 99; Prinsengracht 440

With four floors of delftware, all the major factories are represented and all budgets catered for (spend about €4 for a spoon, €2600-plus for a replica 17th-century tulip vase).

### INTERNATIONAL THEATRE & FILM BOOKS Mapp286-7 *Books*
☎ 622 64 89; Leidseplein 26; ☺ Mon-Sat

In the Stadsschouwburg building, this excellent shop is crammed with books on its namesake subjects, as well as speciality sections on, for example, musicals and famous directors. A majority of titles are in English.

### JASKI Map pp286-7 *Art & Antiques*
☎ 620 39 39; Nieuwe Spiegelstraat 27-29

This large, commercial gallery sells paintings, prints, ceramics and sculptures by the most famous members of the CoBrA movement (p28).

### LIEVE HEMEL Map pp286-7 *Art & Antiques*
☎ 623 00 60; Nieuwe Spiegelstraat 3

You'll find exemplary contemporary Dutch realist painting and sculpture at this smart gallery. It handles painting Dutchmen, Ben Snijders and Theo Voorzaat, and astounding, lifelike representations of clothing – hewn from wood! – by Italian Livio de Marchi.

## MARAÑON HANGMATTEN
Map pp286-7 *Speciality Shop*
☎ 420 71 21; Singel 488
Those who love hanging around should explore Europe's largest selection of hammocks. The colourful creations, made of everything from cotton to pineapple fibres, are for everyone from adults to babies, made by everyone from indigenous weavers to larger manufacturers.

## MARE Map pp286-7 *Clothing*
☎ 620 15 64; Leidsestraat 79
This sleek, modern shop has friendly staff and sexy labels for men and women (eg, Voyage, Day, Betsey Johnson, rare, Antonio Marras and Chloé).

## MARTYRIUM Map pp274-5 *Books*
☎ 673 20 92; Van Baerlestraat 170-172; ☺ daily
There's a good English section, but even better, almost half of this large, quiet store is devoted to discounted stock. Categories include art books, literature, biographies and cooking titles.

## NANKY DE VREEZE
Map pp286-7 *Art & Antiques*
☎ 627 38 08; Lange Leidsedwarsstraat 198-200; ☺ Wed-Sat
This large, impressive gallery displays modern, representative art by European and Asian artists.

## PERRY SPORT
Map pp286-7 *Camping, Outdoor & Sport*
☎ 618 91 11; Overtoom 2-8; ☎ 624 71 31; Kalverstraat 99
Camping goods are perhaps cheaper here than elsewhere, but the quality may not be as good.

## PRESTIGE ART GALLERY
Map pp286-7 *Art & Antiques*
☎ 624 01 04; www.prestige-art-amsterdam.com; Reguliersbreestraat 46; ☺ Tue-Thu or by appointment
This gallery, located just off Rembrandtplein, specialises in 17th- to 20th-century oil paintings and bronzes. A large percentage of the artists displaying here have been in museum exhibitions or art books, and there are a number of works once in the Jewish Historical Museum.

## REFLECTIONS Map pp286-7 *clothing*
☎ 664 00 40; Pieter Cornelisz Hooftstraat 66-8; ☺ daily
This surprisingly unintimidating store attracts the haute-couture crowd with its men's and women's collections by Issey Miyake, Dolce e Gabbana, Comme des Garçons, Junya Watanabe and John Galliano.

## REFLEX MODERN ART
Map pp286-7 *Art & Antiques*
☎ 627 28 32; Weteringschans 79A; ☺ Tue-Sat
This prominent gallery, opposite the Rijksmuseum, is filled with contemporary art and photography, including works by CoBrA members and members of the Nouveau Réaliste movement.

## SCHELTEMA Map pp286-7 *Books*
☎ 523 14 11; Koningsplein 20; ☺ daily
The largest bookshop in town is a true department store with many foreign titles, New Age and multimedia sections. It can be dizzying, but if you need it you should be able to find it here.

## SHOEBALOO Map pp286-7 *Clothing*
☎ 626 79 93; Leidsestraat 10
We like the chic shoes here: imports like Fendi, Helmut Lang, Miu Miu and Prada Sport, and the less-expensive, but just-as-wearable house label. The **PC Hooftstraat branch** (☎ 671 33 10; Pieter Cornelisz Hooftstraat 80) has one of our favourite interiors in town: imagine a giant spaceship-green tanning bed lined with shoe shelves and eggs for you to sit on.

## THE AMERICAN BOOK CENTER
Map pp286-7 *Books*
☎ 25 55 37; www.abc.nl; Kalverstraat 185
Always jam-packed, this large store specialises in English-language books, holds interesting sales, has a good travel-guidebook section and stocks many US periodicals (eg, the Sunday edition of the *New York Times*). It's often cheaper than its competitors and offers 10% student discount.

## THE SHIRT SHOP
Map pp286-7 *Clothing*
☎ 423 20 88; Reguliersdwarsstraat 64
At the edge of gay Amsterdam's main street, this funky, two-storey shop sells tight-fitting men's shirts to make you look fabulous. Some go on sale from about €25.

*Kindermuseum at the Tropenmuseum (p108)*

### TINKERBELL Map pp286-7      *Children*
☎ 625 88 30; Spiegelgracht 10; ☺ Mon-Sat
The mechanical bear blowing bubbles outside this shop fascinates kids, as do the intriguing technical and scientific toys inside. You'll also find historical costumes, plush toys and an entire section for babies.

### VLIEGER Map pp286-7      *Speciality Shop*
☎ 623 58 34; Amstel 34
Since 1869 this two-storey shop has been supplying paper to Amsterdam. You've seen paper, you say? How about Egyptian papyrus; lush handmade papers from Japan, India, Nepal and Guatemala; papers inlaid with flower petals or bamboo, textured to look like snakeskin; or just made from hemp? And that's just a teensy percentage.

### VROUWEN IN DRUK
Map p277      *Books*
Women in Print; ☎ 624 50 03; Westermarkt 5;
☺ Tue-Sat
Across from the Homomonument and Pink Point, this second-hand bookshop specialises in women's titles (with a reasonable English section): history, lesbian, biographies and fiction.

### WALLS Map pp286-7      *Art & Antiques*
☎ 616 95 97; Prinsengracht 737; ☺ Tue-Sat

If you're looking for paintings by the next generation, this long, cheerful warehouse-y space leases its walls to some 20 artists working in abstract, realism, photography, oils, and more. Shows change about every two months. Who knows? The name you buy today may be on the walls of a museum later.

### WONDERWOOD
Map pp286-7      *Art & Antiques*
☎ 625 37 38; www.wonderwood.nl; Weteringstraat 48; ☺ noon-6pm Wed-Sat or by appointment
Head here for originals or reproductions of '40s and '50s Dutch furniture design. Classics include the T46 coffee table by Hein Stolle, works by Gijs Bakker and Han Pieck, and the box chair, which folds up into its own box – you can actually ship it with your luggage! There are also smaller furnishings and toys.

# OTHER DISTRICTS

### DE ODE Map p284      *Speciality Shop*
☎ 419 08 82; Levantkade 51, KNSM Island;
☺ by appointment
Looking for a coffin or funeral with a difference? You can purchase a bookcase that converts to a coffin when you join the library in the sky, or a coffin on wheels with bicycle towbar – perfect for pedalling friends to their last bike rack.

### DE WATERWINKEL Map pp274-5 *Drinks*
☎ 675 59 32; Roelof Hartstraat 10

Thirsty? With over 100 types of bottled water (mineral, sparkling, still and flavoured), this calm & pretty store will quench your thirst.

### DE WINKEL VAN NIJNTJE
Map pp274-5 *Children*
Miffy Shop; ☎ 671 97 07; Beethovenstraat 71;
⚒ Mon-Sat

Dutch illustrator Dick Bruna's most-famous character, Miffy (Nijntje in Dutch), is celebrated in toys and kids' merchandise. Items range from pencils and soap bubbles (€0.50) through note pads, mouse pads, books, plush toys, clothing and playhouses, to Royal Delft kiddie plates (€130).

### STADSBOEKWINKEL Map pp274-5 *Books*
☎ 572 02 29; Amsteldijk 67

Run by the city printer, this is the best source for books about Amsterdam's history, urban development, ecology, politics etc. Most titles are in Dutch (but you can always look at the pictures) – you'll also find some in English. It's in the City Archives building.

### TROPENMUSEUM
Map pp274-5 *Speciality Shop*
☎ 568 82 15; Linnaeusstraat 2

This museum gift shop has an intriguing, well-picked selection of books, fabrics, clothing and accessories from exotic locales around the world, plus a great variety of ethnic music CDs.

# Sleeping

# Sleeping

In its typically charming way, Amsterdam has loads of hotels in creative spaces: old buildings have been repurposed, and canal houses have been joined together to create wholes much greater than the sum of their parts. Some of these lodgings overlook gorgeous canals or courtyards, others are filled with art that's historic or modern, still others are triumphs of design.

However, charm doesn't come cheap. There are some 33,000 hotel rooms in town, and given Amsterdam's status as a top short-break holiday destination, it sometimes seems as if all 33,000 are full. If you're looking to 'do' Amsterdam on the cheap, you might find yourself in a tiny, threadbare room and pay more for it than you thought possible. Leave the budget options to the college kids, take a deep breath, swipe that card and sally forth.

There is a ray of hope: with the spread of the Internet, careful shoppers can often find substantial discounts on published rates at some of the city's finest hotels.

A locational note: it's worth paying extra to be somewhere central just so you don't have to deal with Europe's most-expensive taxis or rely on night buses, but this does not mean having to stay in a flophouse on the Damrak (we certainly wouldn't) or even the canal belts. There are some excellent, reasonably priced lodgings in the Old South, just minutes' walk from busy Leidseplein and its convenient tram connections.

## PARKING
Ask about parking if travelling by car. In almost all cases parking is a major problem and the most you'll get is a (payable) parking permit out on the street – with all the attendant headaches and security risks – or a referral to the nearest parking garage (up to €35 a day), which may be a fair distance away. The top-end hotels have their own expensive parking arrangements but prefer to be notified in advance.

## SECURITY
Theft is rare in normal hotel rooms, although it's always wise to deposit valuables for safekeeping at the reception desk. Some hotels have in-room safes (sometimes for a fee). Theft is more common at hostels; bring your own lock for your locker.

## Styles of Accommodation
Amsterdam's lodgings run the gamut from large multinational hotel chains and splendid boutique properties, to little 'mum and dad' guesthouses, youth hostels and sprawling budget hotels. By and large, the hotels in town are small compared to those in other world capitals, even European capitals – any hotel with more than 20 rooms is considered 'large'. This is because a lot of hotels have their origins as houses lining the canals. One unique and very agreeable type of hotel in town strings two or more such homes together; the Sheraton Hotel Pulitzer (p217) is composed of 25 houses!

You'll see a 'star' plaque on the front of every hotel in town, indicating its rating according to the Benelux Hotel Classification. The stars (from one to five) have more to do with the existence of certain types of facilities than their quality.

This means that a two-star hotel, for example, may be in better condition than a hotel of higher rank – we've tried to pick out the good ones for you. Accommodation that rates less than one star can call

### The Stars Have It...Or Do They?
- One star: rooms have table, chair and sink but no private bath or toilet.
- Three stars: every room has private toilet and bath or shower, bedside lamps, full-length mirror and central heating. There is an elevator for hotels of more than two storeys.
- Five stars: single/double rooms must be at least 18/24 sq m.

itself a pension or guesthouse but not a hotel. Rooms with private showers usually include a toilet but not always, so ask when booking. If a room has both shower and toilet we've used the term 'private facilities'; if they're in the corridor we've used 'shared facilities'.

The 💻 symbol means that the hotel has some sort of Internet access available. It may be as elaborate as a full-on business centre or as simple as a computer that guests are permitted to use to briefly check email. Prices for Internet access vary widely. As always, inquire if this matters to you. If your room has a telephone, you can usually hook up your computer to the in-room telephone line.

Please note: space limitations do not allow us to list every type of room for every hotel. If you have a special need (wheelchair access, elevator, bathtub as opposed to shower, triple or family size room), be sure to inquire.

*Canal House Hotel (p216)*

## GAY & LESBIAN HOTELS
Hotels are pretty relaxed about same-sex couples (and would be breaking the law if they refused them) but some cater specifically for them. We've noted them where appropriate.

## 'STONER' HOTELS
This being Amsterdam, there are a number of hotels in the budget category where pot smoking is welcome. By and large they're pretty shabby affairs, but we've included a few.

If in doubt whether smoking is permitted, be sure to ask when you book your reservation. At many hotels, smoking of any kind is prohibited in rooms, and in others lighting a joint anywhere on site will get you kicked out so fast that you'll lose your buzz. Don't be embarrassed about asking ahead of time – Amsterdam hoteliers are pretty matter-of-fact.

## YOUTH HOSTELS
The Netherlands youth hostel association is now going by the new name **Stay Okay** ( ☎ 010-264 60 64; www.stayokay.com) and uses the Hostelling International (HI) logo for the benefit of foreigners. The head office is in Rotterdam; there are two official hostels in Amsterdam.

A youth hostel card entitles you to receive €2.50 a night discount. Prices include breakfast and clean linen upon arrival. Be sure to book well ahead, especially in busy periods (spring, summer and autumn holidays).

There are also a number of non-Stay Okay/HI hostels in town, some with loads of character.

# Price Ranges
It may sound contradictory but, once you get used to the idea of cramped rooms at high rates, in general you'll find that you get what you pay for. Hotels in the lowest price bracket (below €70 for a double) can be run-down and poorly maintained and invariably seem to suffer from mouldy smells due to the damp climate and the Dutch aversion to decent ventilation. But the more you spend, the grander you get.

We list rates for single/double rooms where available; where no distinction is made, we give the price per room. For a triple room, figure on a third to a half again above the double-room price. Hotels that accept children (many don't) often have family rates.

### MID-RANGE (DOUBLES €70 TO €140)

Most hotels in this category are big on comfort, low on formality and small enough to offer personal attention. All rooms have a toilet and shower (and/or bath) and, unless stated, come with TV, phone and breakfast.

### TOP END (DOUBLES €140 TO €270)

If you're looking for a bit of luxury, loads of privacy and lashings of personal service, these boutique hotels will put a smile on your dial. Expect extras like nonsmoking rooms, lifts, in-room dataports, minibars and room service. Note that substantial discounts may be available in low season or through the hotel websites or travel agents. Unless stated, rates include breakfast.

### DELUXE (DOUBLES OVER €270)

Facilities like nonsmoking rooms, air-conditioning, fitness centres (some with pocket-sized swimming pools), conference and banquet rooms, and business centres (or at least 'desks') are par for the course at these hotels. Breakfast is rarely included (and can cost €20 and up). However, competitively priced weekend, summer and low-season packages offer substantial discounts – check websites.

The rates we list here are the basic, nondiscounted 'rack' rates; treat them as a guide and not an absolute. Prices at many hotels drop in the low season (roughly October to April excluding Christmas/New Year and Easter). Even in high season it's always worth asking for 'special' rates, especially if you're staying a few nights. Top-end hotels often rely on business travellers and tend to be markedly cheaper in the summer months and on weekends. Many hotels also offer discounts via their websites, especially for last-minute bookings.

Most of the quoted rates include a 5% city hotel tax; at the most expensive hotels, however, this is added separately to the bill. Also, if you're paying by credit card, some hotels have taken to adding a surcharge of up to 5% – be sure to inquire.

> ## Top Five Mid-Range Hotels
>
> - **Hotel Arena** (p221)
> - **Hotel Brouwer** (p213)
> - **Hotel de Filosoof** (p223)
> - **'t Hotel** (p217)
> - **Seven Bridges** (p220)

> ## Top Five Deluxe Hotels
>
> - **Amstel Intercontinental Hotel** (p218)
> - **Blakes** (p216)
> - **Hilton Amsterdam** (p221)
> - **Hotel Okura** (p221)
> - **Seven One Seven** (p220)

## Reservations

The VVV (Vereniging voor Vreemdelingen Verkeer; nationwide tourist bureau) offices at Schiphol Airport, in front of and inside Centraal Station, or the GWK (grens wissel kantoor; money-exchange office) inside Centraal Station, have last-minute hotel-booking services that can save you a lot of hunting around during busy periods. The VVV offices charge €13 commission per booking; the GWK office charges €9.75 per reservation.

Travellers arriving at Centraal Station may be accosted by touts offering accommodation. Some readers have reported good results this way, others have been ripped off. Maintain a healthy suspicion; if you have any doubts, walk away and use a reputable booking agent.

If you're targeting a particular hotel, check its website or phone directly to inquire. Otherwise, you might try through a travel agent, or there are some websites that specialise in discounted room rates, especially last-minute bookings, even at some of the city's tippity-top hotels.

Note that when booking with the hotel directly via phone or fax, some smaller hotels won't accept credit-card details over the

> ## Accommodation Online
>
> - www.amsterdam-hotels-guide.com
> - www.bookings.nl
> - www.hotelres.nl
> - www.lastminute.com
> - http://amsterdam.ratestogo.com

phone (if they accept cards at all – check) and may insist on a deposit by cheque or money order before they'll confirm the booking.

When booking for two people, make it clear whether you want a twin (two single beds) or double (a bed for two). It should make no difference to the price, but the wrong bed configuration could be impossible to fix on the spot if the hotel is fully booked.

Always get a confirmation in writing.

## Long-term Stays

If you're planning on being in town for a while, it may make sense to rent a flat. Certainly, you may feel more at home this way – get yourself a bike and you'll practically be a local. Prices for furnished apartments start at about €1000 per month but can easily be twice that, getting more expensive as the lodgings get grander or more central. More romantic options include houseboats. Typically, there is a minimum rental period (eg six months), but if you specify a shorter stay you may get lucky. You may also be able to find a home stay or share with roommates.

# MEDIEVAL CENTRE

### BLACK TULIP HOTEL Map pp278-9
☎ 427 09 33; www.blacktulip.nl; Geldersekade 16; d €110-200; 💻
The nine rooms of this (exclusively gay male) hotel are fitted out with a mind-boggling array of bondage equipment: cages, slings, bondage chairs, hooks, masses of black leather and latex etc. Other than that, it's actually quite clean and fashionable. Rates include buffet breakfast, all rooms have private facilities, and nonsmoking rooms are available.

### GRAND SOFITEL DEMEURE
Map pp278-9
☎ 555 31 11; www.thegrand.nl; Oudezijds Voorburgwal 197; s/d €380/420; 💱 💻 📺
…and grand it is. Amsterdam's former city hall (1808–1987) was the scene of Queen Beatrix's civil wedding in 1966. You may feel a bit royal yourself as you wander through the cavernous lobby, grandiose stairwells and spacious inner courtyard. All rooms are meticulously kept in Old World style, and there's an indoor pool with fitness and steam rooms.

### HOTEL AGORA Map pp286-7
☎ 627 22 00; www.hotelagora.nl; Singel 462; s/d €98/115; 💻
In the centre of everything, the well-run Agora offers smallish rooms, up-to-date bathrooms, and a cheerful garden off the breakfast room. All rooms have phone, TV and computer hookups (there's also Internet access in the lobby). Rooms without private facilities cost about one-third less; a four-bed room costs €175.

### Flat Chat

- **All-Inn Apartment Service** ( ☎ 428 23 00; www.apartment.nl; Singel 315)
- **Amsterdam Apartment** ( ☎ 668 26 54; www.amsterdamapartment.nl; Oude Nieuwstraat 1)
- **Apartment Services** ( ☎ 672 18 40; www.apartmentservices.nl; Waalstraat 58 )
- **Citymundo** ( ☎ 676 52 70; www.citymundo.com; Schinkelkade 47)
- **Goudsmit Estate Agents** ( ☎ 644 19 71; www.goudsmit.com; AJ Ernststraat 735)
- **IDA Housing Services** ( ☎ 624 83 01; ida@ida-housing.demon.nl; Den Texstraat 30)
- **Intercity Room Service** ( ☎ 675 00 64; Van Ostadestraat 348)

Some visitors (and this author) have achieved excellent results by reading or posting a notice on local message boards. Among them:
- **www.expatica.com** An excellent resource for the expat community.
- **www.viavia.nl** But for this one you'll need to read Dutch.

### HOTEL BROUWER Map pp278-9
☎ 624 63 58; www.hotelbrouwer.nl; Singel 83; s/d €50/85; 🍴
Our favourite hotel in this price range, just eight rooms in a house dating back to 1652. Rooms, is furnished with Dutch simplicity, all have canal views and private bath. There's a mix of Delft-blue tiles and early 20th–century furniture, and, get this, a tiny elevator. Staff dispense friendly advice. Reserve well in advance.

*Hotel Brouwer (p213)*

## HOTEL DE L'EUROPE Map pp286-7
☎ 531 17 77; www.leurope.nl; Nieuwe Doelenstraat 2-8; s/d €295/335;
Oozing Victorian elegance, l'Europe welcomes you with a glam chandelier, marble lobby and gloriously large rooms (some have terraces and all have handsome marble bathrooms). Plus, the hotel maintains its own boats for canal cruises. The attached Excelsior restaurant and chichi gym (said to be admired by no less than Governor Schwarzenegger) with small swimming pool are equally impressive.

## HOTEL DE MARTELAAR Map pp278-9
☎ 623 92 08; Martelaarsgracht 18; s/d €55/75;
A spanking new renovation makes this the best budget option near the station. Rooms with en suite are cheerful, bright, smallish and irregularly shaped; rates include breakfast.

## HOTEL HOKSBERGEN Map pp278-9
☎ 626 60 43; www.hotelhoksbergen.nl; Singel 301; s/d €76/90, apartments €150
You sure can't beat Hoksbergen's fantastic canalside location, but be warned: even sardines would have trouble squishing into the microscopically small rooms (with TV, phone and clean but plain furnishings). If you get

claustrophobic, the six-bed, self-contained apartments may be a better option.

## HOTEL LE COIN Map pp286-7
☎ 524 68 00; www.lecoin.nl; Nieuwe Doelenstraat 5; s/d €110/130
This shiny new hotel owned by the University of Amsterdam offers high-class apartments spread over seven historical buildings, all equipped with designer furniture and kitchenettes – and all reachable by lift. Staff are pleasant, and larger family rooms are available. Breakfast (€8) is served in a nearby café.

## HOTEL NOVA Map pp278-9
☎ 623 00 66, www.novahotel.nl; Nieuwezijds Voorburgwal 276; s €76-107, d €95-147.50
Across five houses near the city centre, the rooms here are warm, crisp and modern, even if not particularly distinctive, and have small refrigerators.

## HOTEL THE CROWN Map pp278-9
☎ 626 96 64; www.hotelthecrown.com; Oudezijds Voorburgwal 21; s €45/50, d with shared/private shower €90/100
Rooms at this Brit-run, Red Light District hotel have shared toilets and no TV or phone – and don't even bother asking for breakfast. Prices just make it into our upper-middle price bracket, but quality is firmly in the lower-middle. So what's the draw? Fun. The downstairs bar – with Sky TV, pool table, dart board and hordes of celebrating stag-nighters – and spliff smoking is allowed in the tidy rooms.

## HOTEL WINSTON Map pp278-9
☎ 623 13 80; www.winston.nl; Warmoesstraat 123; s/d from €67/89
Party central for touring bands and up-for-anything tourists, with rock'n'roll rooms and a rockin' bar scene. About half of the rooms are 'art' rooms: local artists were given free rein, with results from super-edgy (all stainless steel) to playful to colour-drenched and questionably raunchy. All rooms have showers, but only about half have en suite toilets (small discount for rooms without).

## NH BARBIZON PALACE Map pp278-9
☎ 556 45 64; www.nh-hotels.com; Prins Hendrikkade 59-72; standard d €125-280;
Stretching over 19 houses (some 17th-century) and incorporating the 15th-century St Olof Chapel, Barbizon Palace seamlessly blends Old

World charm with modern amenities. Both traditionally and contemporarily decorated rooms are decent size for the price, and the health club (with Turkish bath) is large for a hotel gym. Plus, it's just across the canal from Centraal Station.

## NH GRAND HOTEL KRASNAPOLSKY
Map pp278-9

☎ 554 91 11; www.nh-hotels.com; Dam 9;
d from €160; 💻

This gargantuan, 450-room edifice across from the Royal Palace was one of the city's first grand hotels (1866). It has elegant if compact rooms and spectacular public spaces. The 19th-century 'winter garden' breakfast and lunch room, with its soaring steel-and-glass roof, is a national monument (elaborate breakfast buffet not included), and there are fitness and business centres. Note: rates can vary widely.

## RADISSON SAS Map pp278-9

☎ 623 12 31; www.radissonsas.com; Rusland 17;
d €218; 💻

The Radisson's row-home facade looks very much in keeping with its old-city surrounds, yet once you enter the skylit, soaring, post-industrial cool lobby you know you're somewhere else. Rooms are not huge but were recently redesigned in themes from maritime to old Dutch. There's a fitness centre, sauna and friendly, professional staff. Breakfast is €19.

## SWISSÔTEL AMSTERDAM Map pp278-9

☎ 522 30 00; www.raffles.com; Damrak 96; d €295;
✕ 🐾 💻

An understated escape from the madness that is Damrak. Standard rooms are Amsterdam-cramped (bigger rooms available), but they make up for it with a smart remodel of hardwood, very comfy beds, contemporary design, Internet hookups and complimentary espresso machines. Good-deal discounts often available.

## ZOSA HOTEL Map pp278-9

☎ 330 62 41; www.zosa-online.com;
Kloveniersburgwal 20; s/d €120/140; 💻

What Zosa's six rooms lack in size, they make up for in visuals: each is ineffably fashionable and individually designed. Feeling romantic? Book the 'baroque' room with soothing lamps and lollypop-pink walls. Stressed out? The minimal, modern 'zen' room is a tranquil balm. Our favourite, the 'room of wonders', is a modern Middle Eastern escapade with delicate murals and Moroccan lanterns.

# CHEAP SLEEPS

## ANNA YOUTH HOSTEL Map pp278-9

☎ 620 11 55; Spuistraat 6; dm weekday/weekend €18/20; 💻

Funky Anna's, with two co-ed rooms (18 and 19 beds respectively), is a real winner. Much better than it needs to be, it's got a caring proprietor, a quiet, respectful vibe and wonderful, cheery, modern–Middle Eastern interior. Rates include clean bed linen, towels and safety deposit box, but no breakfast. There's also a huge private double apartment (the bad news: it's five storeys up!). Note: there's a 3am curfew, or you pay €2.50 each time someone has to open the door.

## CHRISTIAN YOUTH HOSTEL
## 'THE SHELTER CITY' Map pp278-9

☎ 625 32 30; www.shelter.nl; Barndesteeg 21;
dm €16.50, Jul-Aug €18.50 incl breakfast; ✕

The price is right at this rambling hostel just off the Red Light District, but only if you can handle Christian rock music piped through the PA system and enormous 'Jesus loves you' signs everywhere. The pros of staying here include large, airy, single-sex dorms (and bathrooms), filling breakfasts, free Internet facilities, a quiet garden courtyard, eternal salvation and a tough no-drugs or alcohol policy. The cons include a midnight curfew (1am Friday and Saturday) – and the tough no-drugs or alcohol policy. Its partner hostel in the Jordaan has somewhat less missionary zeal.

## FLYING PIG DOWNTOWN HOSTEL
Map pp278-9

☎ 420 68 22; www.flyingpig.nl; Nieuwendijk 100;
dm €21-27; 💻

Hang out with hundreds of dope-smoking, young backpackers at this very relaxed, very central, 30-room hostel. It's pretty grungy, but no-one seems to mind, especially when there's so much fun to be had in the throbbing lobby bar, with pool table, DJs some nights and a chilled-out, cushion-lined basement nicknamed the 'happy room'.

## HOTEL BRIAN Map pp278-9

☎ 624 46 61; www.hotelbrian.com; Singel 69;
s/d with shared facilities €37/54; 💻

This ardently shabby and relaxed joint ('joint' being the operative word) was recently renovated, but to be honest it's hard to tell. Anyway, it's churlish to quibble when the rates include a good breakfast buffet, advice from fun, knowledgeable staff, and the odd chance of scoring a room with skylights and canal views. Kitchen facilities available, but no phones or TVs in rooms.

### HOTEL GROENENDAEL Map pp278-9

☎ /fax 624 48 22; Nieuwendijk 15; d with private facilities €52.15

Groenendael's small rooms are pretty clean, the clientele not too wild and the big breakfast sufficient for a day of sightseeing. It's close to Centraal Station and is one of the better-kept places in this smoky, bargain-basement category.

### STADSDOELEN YOUTH HOSTEL

Map pp278-9 & Map pp286-7

☎ 624 68 32; www.stayokay.com; Kloveniersburgwal 97; dm/d €21.65/53.30

Efficient Stadsdoelen is always bustling with backpackers and we can understand why. The staff is friendly and the eight, nonsmoking, ultra-clean rooms (each with 20 beds and free lockers) offer a modicum of privacy. There's a mix of single-sex and co-ed dorms and bathrooms, a big TV room, bar, pool table, laundry, Internet facilities and a pretty lenient 2am curfew. Hostel cardholders get a €2.50 discount per night.

# WESTERN CANAL BELT

### AMBASSADE HOTEL Map pp278-9

☎ 555 02 22; www.ambassade-hotel.nl; Herengracht 341; s/d €165/195

Flick through the books in Ambassade's spiffy little library and you'll spy signed copies by Salman Rushdie and Umberto Eco. Literary luminaries and well-heeled tourists alike love this tastefully appointed hotel, spread over 10 canal houses. The beautiful antique furniture and fixtures are traditional without being cloying, service is kind, and the sparkling lounge (with fresh flowers and chandeliers) is ideal for business meetings or afternoon tea. Breakfast is €16 per person.

### BLAKES Map p277

☎ 530 20 10; www.blakesamsterdam.com; Keizersgracht 384; s/d from €240-370

London hotelier Anouska Hempel's creation is a true temple of style. Slink through the 17th-century canal house's courtyard entrance, past the gorgeous staff, to ensconce yourself

## Top Five Hotels for Design

- **Sheraton Hotel Pulitzer** (p217) It's quite an amazing thing to string together 25 canal houses so seamlessly.
- **Anna Youth Hostel** (p215) Proof that a cheap stay doesn't need to mean poor aesthetics.
- **Hotel de l'Europe** (p214) If you define good design as opulence, look no further.
- **Radisson SAS** (p215) Canal house exterior belies a sprawling, post-industrial cool interior.
- **Hotel Winston** (p214) Snag a room individually decorated by an artist at Amsterdam's most rocking lodging.

And don't forget: hotels have made our other Top Five lists because we think they've got great design too.

in the restaurant or black-and-white lobby where world beats don't so much play as fizz. Its 41 sophisticated, individually decorated rooms might have Japanese or Indonesian motifs; fluffy towels, silk pillows piled high and spacious bathrooms make them serene and sumptuous. Plus, there's a free health club and overnight guests get seating preference in the excellent lounge.

### BUDGET HOTEL CLEMENS AMSTERDAM Map pp278-9

☎ 624 60 89; www.clemenshotel.nl; Raadhuisstraat 39; d/tr €110/150, s/d/tr with shared facilities €55/70/75; 🖳

Tidy, renovated, steep-staired Clemens gears itself to all budgets. Take your pick of the chic, themed rooms (one with a sexy red-gold interior, another with delicate French antiques) all with TV, phone, safe and fridge. Your gregarious hostess will lend PCs for in-house wireless Internetting (€8/night). Breakfast is €7 extra.

### CANAL HOUSE HOTEL Map pp278-9

☎ 622 51 82; www.canalhouse.nl; Keizersgracht 148; rooms €140-190

Where to spend your time in this splendid boutique hotel? In the ornately furnished, 17th-century dining room resplendent with chandeliers, grand piano and garden views? The cosy, plush, burgundy-hued bar? Or the small but inviting, antique-filled guest rooms? Rooms have phones and computer connections but no TV.

## HAMPSHIRE CLASSIC HOTEL TOREN

Map pp278-9

☎ 622 60 33; www.toren.nl; Keizersgracht 164; s/d from €110-125; 🖳

Exquisitely renovated Toren – its public areas all 17th-century with gilded mirrors, fireplaces and chandeliers, its guest rooms all elegantly furnished with modern facilities – is this category's title-holder for price, room size and personal service. Go all out and book the room with the two-person Jacuzzi and garden patio. Breakfast is not included.

## HOTEL AMSTERDAM WIECHMANN

Map pp286-7

☎ 626 33 21; www.hotelwiechmann.nl; Prinsengracht 328; s/tw/d €75/120/130

This family-run hotel has a marvellous canalside location, smallish rooms furnished like an antique shop with country quilts and chintz, and lobby *tchotchkes* (knick-knacks) that have been there for some 50 years (eg Russian samovar, potbellied stove). It's very *Ghost & Mrs Muir*, and very friendly.

## HOTEL RAMENAS Map pp278-9

☎ 624 60 30; www.amsterdamhotels.com; Haarlemmerdijk 61; d with shared/private facilities €70/80

Ramenas, on increasingly hip Haarlemmerdijk, has been operating for over a hundred years, so it knows what it's doing. The 11 rooms – so sparsely decorated they make monasteries look ostentatious – are reasonably big and scrupulously clean. The staff serves up friendly advice and satisfying Dutch breakfasts (included).

## HOTEL VAN ONNA Map p277

☎ 626 58 01; Bloemgracht 102-108; d per person €80; ✂

Rooms here are cheery and clean even if they won't win any design awards, but you're in a gorgeous section of the Jordaan, within earshot of the bells of the Westerkerk (get a room in the back if you're sensitive to noise). Try to book the attic room with its old wooden roof beams and panoramic views over the Jordaan. No phone, TV or credit cards.

## SHERATON HOTEL PULITZER Map p277

☎ 523 52 35; www.luxurycollection.com/pulitzer; Prinsengracht 315-331; d €250; ✂ 🖳

Spread over 25 17th-century canal houses, Pulitzer manages to combine big-hotel efficiency with boutique-hotel charm. Beautifully restored rooms vary from house to house, but all have mod-cons galore, including sweet and cosy bathrooms. There are loads of extras too: choose from a cigar bar, art gallery, private 75-minute canal cruises, garden courtyards and a wonderful restaurant, all high on elegance and low on pomposity.

## 'T HOTEL Map pp278-9

☎ 422 27 41; www.thotel.nl; Leliegracht 18; d €134-148; 🖳

Dutch Modern furnishing meets 17th-century canal house setting at this quiet and understated spot. Its eight comfortable, individual rooms all have canal or (upscale) neighbourhood views, and top-floor rooms have loads of light. The staff is very accommodating. Significant off-season discounts are available.

# CHEAP SLEEPS

## CHRISTIAN YOUTH HOSTEL 'THE SHELTER JORDAN Map p277

☎ 624 47 17; www .shelter.nl; Bloemstraat 179; dm €15-18

OK, we'll put up with the 'no-everything' (smokin', drinkin', spliffin') policy and 2am curfew at this small hostel because it's such a gem. Single-sex dorms are quiet and clean, breakfasts – especially the fluffy pancakes – are beaut and the garden patio is a relaxing retreat.

## HOTEL PAX Map pp278-9

☎ 624 97 35; Raadhuisstraat 37; s with shared facilities €25-40, d €35-60, with private facilities from €55

This budget choice in hotel-lined Raadhuisstraat – run by two friendly, funky brothers – has an artsy-student vibe. All eight rooms have a TV and each is individually decorated. The larger rooms face the street, which has noisy trams, so bring earplugs. Rates include breakfast.

# SOUTHERN CANAL BELT

## AMISTAD HOTEL Map pp286-7

☎ 624 80 74; www.amistad.nl; Kerkstraat 42; s/d €63/77, with private facilities €99/128

Rooms at this bijou hotel in the middle of the gay action are dotted with hip designer flourishes like Philippe Starck chairs, CD players, chic soft furnishings (and TV, phone, safe and fridge). Highlights include breakfasting in the kitchen/dining room – with ruby red walls and make-a-friend communal table – while chatting with the two super-spunky owners. In the afternoon, the breakfast room becomes an Internet café for the gay community.

### AMSTEL INTERCONTINENTAL HOTEL
Map p285

☎ 622 60 60; www.amsterdam.intercontinental.com; Professor Tulpplein 1; d from €490; ❌ 🖵

Everything about this five-star edifice is spectacular, from its imposing location overlooking the Amstel, to its magnificent colonnaded lobby and, of course, its wallet-walloping room prices. Lavishly decorated rooms, reverential service and luxe extras such as La Rive restaurant (two Michelin stars), chauffeured limousines, heated indoor pool and fitness centre with all sorts of steam options delight even the fussiest trans-Atlantic celebrities and Euro-royalty.

### BRIDGE HOTEL Map p285
☎ 623 70 68; www.thebridgehotel.nl; Amstel 107-111; d €98

At this family-run hotel near the namesake skinny bridge, rooms are large, spotless, updated frequently and, despite industrial-style flooring, rather warm. Plus, the lobby is marble and the bathrooms are nice for the price. The four-person 'Skinny Bridge Room' has a kitchen and handsome views (though no lift to get you way up there).

### CITY HOTEL Map pp286-7
☎ 627 23 23; www.city-hotel.nl; Utrechtsestraat 2; d with shared/private facilities €60/80

Above the Old Bell pub is this unexpectedly fabulous choice: it's clean, neat, well-run and

## Top Five Gay & Lesbian Lodgings

While most hotels in town are lesbian- and gay-friendly (by law as well as by nature), there are some hotels that cater specificially to a lesbian or gay clientele.

- Hotel Aero (p219)
- Amistad Hotel (p217)
- Black Tulip Hotel (p213)
- Liliane's Home (p221)
- Orfeo Hotel (p220)

## Hotel Dining Worth the Trip

- **Blakes** (Blakes Hotel; p216)
- **Yamazato** (Hotel Okura; p221)
- **La Rive** (Amstel Intercontinental Hotel; p218)
- **To Dine** (Hotel Arena; p221)
- **Winter Garden** (NH Grand Hotel Krasnapolsky; p215)

good value. The rooms are decorated with crisp blue-and-white linens and each comes with TV. We enjoyed staying in the six-bed room (€45 per person) complete with skylights and curved girders overlooking Utrechtsestraat.

### CROWNE PLAZA AMERICAN HOTEL
Map pp286-7

☎ 556 30 00; www.amsterdam-american.crowneplaza .com; Leidsekade 97; r €320-355; ❌ 🖵

You can't get much closer to the action than the Crowne Plaza American Hotel. Its grand Art Deco shell is filled with a mixture of deco and '90s contemporary furnishings, though it's somehow less than entrancing; there's bold, colourful art hanging in the lobby. Rooms are decent-sized. You don't need to be a guest to breakfast in the stunning Café Americain.

### EUPHEMIA HOTEL Map pp286-7
☎ 622 90 45; www.euphemiahotel.com; Fokke Simonszstraat 1; s €40-75, d €65-100, dm €25-40; 🖵

Euphemia's institutional layout falls short of glamorous, but the rooms are neat and many are quite large. Other pluses? It's gay-friendly, on a quiet block, and there's a sharp, funny manager (though maybe too sharp for some). Buffet breakfast is €5. Check the website for specials.

### HEMP HOTEL Map pp286-7
☎ 625 44 25; www.hemp-hotel.com; Frederiksplein 15; s with shared facilities €50, d with shared/private facilities €65/70; 🖵

Proof positive that Amsterdam is the capital of the northern 'hempisphere', this chilled-out hotel serves hemp-flour rolls (tetrahydrocannabinol or THC-free) with your breakfast, the café sells hemp teas and beers, and all five colourful and individually decorated rooms exude a 'just-back-from-Goa' vibe. Dope smokers apply now.

## HOTEL ADOLESCE Map p285

☎ 626 39 59; www.adolesce.nl; Nieuwe Keizersgracht 26; s/d €60/80

This neat 10-room hotel, located in a quiet spot just off the Amstel, has steep stairs, large rooms with TV, industrial carpeting, paint and linoleum that surprisingly don't make it too drab, and sme very helpful service. Try for a canal-view room. Breakfast foods are available all day.

## HOTEL AERO Map pp286-7

☎ 622 77 28; www.aerohotel.nl; Kerkstraat 45-9; d €70, with private facilities €85-100

Mere steps from some of gay Amsterdam's favourite places, the Aero has been nicely renovated with cosy, if typically small rooms. Newer quarters are much cleaner, roomier and have modern bathrooms. All rooms come with TV and VCR, phone and breakfast. Rooms facing the back are quiet. Guests (and others) can greet the world at Camp Café downstairs.

## HOTEL DE ADMIRAAL Map pp286-7

☎ 626 21 50; fax 623 46 25; Herengracht 563; d with shared/private facilities €70/98

Located near the bustling Rembrandtplein, the nine-room Admiraal is sweet and homely if a wee bit tattered. Clean and bright canal-side rooms (which all come with safes and TV, no phone) are furnished in an unpretentious, mix'n'match fashion. There's a large 'family room' available and a mammoth, Persian-style lamp sitting in the breakfast room. The hotel attic is said to have been used as a hideout for Jews during WWII, while Nazi soldiers lodged and dined below. Breakfast is €5 per person.

## HOTEL DE MUNCK Map pp286-7

☎ 623 62 83; www.hoteldemunck.com; Achtergracht 3; s/d €70/85

De Munck's breakfast room is a slice of rock'n'roll heaven, like a 1950s diner with a working jukebox and record covers lining the walls. Add in a flower-filled courtyard and whip-smart, witty staff. All 14 rooms are bright and well kept and come with TV and phone. Subtract €10 for rooms with shared facilities.

## HOTEL FANTASIA Map p285

☎ 623 82 59; www.fantasia-hotel.com; Nieuwe Keizersgracht 16; s €55-63, d €80

Situated down the block from the Adolesce, the Fantasia is filled with cow portraits. Even if its modular furniture could stand updating, rooms all have private facilities, and many have radio, phone and coffee maker, but no TV.

## HOTEL ORLANDO Map pp286-7

☎ 638 69 15; fax 625 21 23; Prinsengracht 1099; s/d from €70/80

Oh Orlando, how do we love thee? Let us count the ways. One: biggish, high-ceilinged, canalside rooms at smallish rates. Two: an hospitable, gay-friendly host. Three: breakfast in bed. Four: impeccably chic, boutique style.

## HOTEL PRINSENHOF Map pp286-7

☎ 623 17 72; www.hotelprinsenhof.com; Prinsengracht 810; s/d €40/60, with shower €75/80

A sure-fire winner, this beautiful 18th-century house has ahh-lovely canal views and 'Captain Hook', an electric luggage hoist in the central stairwell. Staff are affable and the rooms spacious with natty antique furnishings. The attic quarters with diagonal beams are most popular.

## HOTEL QUENTIN Map pp286-7

☎ 626 21 87; www.quentinhotels.com; Leidsekade 89; s with shared facilities €40; d with/without private facilities €90/65

Hotel Quentin, decorated with colourful murals, rock-star art and contemporary handmade furniture, offers a variety of rooms for the weary traveller from cramped to well-sized, some with balconies, canal views, phone and TV. It's popular with lesbians and international actors and musicians performing at nearby Theatre Bellevue, Melkweg and Paradiso. There's an elevator available and breakfast costs €5.

## NH SCHILLER HOTEL Map pp286-7

☎ 554 07 00, toll-free 00800 0115 0116; nhschiller@nh-hotels.nl; Rembrandtplein 26-36; s/d €190/230; 🖳

Although it's been restored to its original (1912) Art Deco splendour, with paintings by the artist-hotelier Frits Schiller adorning the walls, this hotel has blandly corporate rooms. You'd best lap up the atmosphere in the attached Brasserie Schiller (the stained-glass windows are magnificent) or out on bustling Rembrandtplein. Breakfast is not included in the room rate.

*Seven Bridges*

### SEVEN BRIDGES Map pp286-7
☎ 623 13 29; Reguliersgracht 31;
s €80-170, d €100-190
Private, sophisticated Seven Bridges – one of the city's loveliest little hotels on one of its loveliest canals – has nine tastefully decorated rooms (all incorporating lush oriental rugs and elegant antiques). Morning sightseeing will seem superfluous once breakfast, served on fine china, is delivered to your room.

### SEVEN ONE SEVEN Map pp286-7
☎ 427 07 17; www.717hotel.nl; Prinsengracht 717; rooms €375-625; ✂ 🖳
Without doubt, this is the most wonderful hotel in Amsterdam – designed, boutiqued and simply breathtaking. Its eight hyperplush, deliciously appointed rooms come with that rare luxury: space. Step into the splashy Picasso suite – with its soaring ceiling, prodigiously long sofa, gorgeous contemporary and antique decorations, and bathroom as big as some European principalities – and you may never, *ever* want to leave. Rates include breakfast, afternoon tea, house wine and oodles of one-on-one service.

## CHEAP SLEEPS
### HANS BRINKER BUDGET HOTEL
Map pp286-7
☎ 622 06 87; www.hans-brinker.com; Kerkstraat 136; dm €21, tw/tr/q per person €35/30/24; 🖳
When a hotel promotes itself with the slogan 'It can't get any worse', you're bound to be pleasantly surprised. The lobby is always in a state of mayhem, spartan rooms have all the ambience of a public hospital, and its 538 beds are almost always filled to capacity with schoolgroups and boisterous backpackers. The good news: the bar is bright and happy, the disco pulsates, the restaurant serves cheap meals, rooms have shower and toilet, and rates include breakfast and bed linen. Drug use equals automatic expulsion.

### INTERNATIONAL BUDGET HOSTEL
Map pp286-7
☎ 624 27 84; www.internationalbudgethostel.com; Leidsegracht 76; dm €27-28, tw €72; 🖳
Reasons to stay: canalside location in a former warehouse; really close to nightlife; cool mix of backpackers from around the world smoking in the lounge (though smoking is strictly prohibited in rooms, as are hard drugs); Mondrianesque murals; clean rooms with lockers; a staff that's more pleasant than it needs to be. Reasons not: your money will stretch further elsewhere; a little hectic; can be cramped and dark; breakfast costs extra.

### ORFEO HOTEL Map pp286-7
☎ 623 13 47; www.hotelorfeo.com; Leidsekruisstraat 14; d with shared/private facilities €67/105
A cheap option for gay fellas, opened in 1969, central Orfeo has simple, small, wood-panelled rooms (with TV, phone, minibar) and the flirtiest breakfast room in town. The breakfast room turns into a reasonably priced bar/restaurant for lunch and dinner.

## THE PLANTAGE & EASTERN ISLANDS
### AMSTEL BOTEL Map pp282-3
☎ 626 42 47; www.amstelbotel.com; Oosterdokskade 2-4; d with land/water view €84/89; 🖳
This floating hotel is packed with dazed, Europe-in-four-days bus groups and packs of Brit boys/girls celebrating bucks'/hens'

## Worth the Trip

**Hotel Van Bonga** (Map pp274-5; ☎ 662 52 18; fax 679 08 43; Holbeinstraat 1; d €75), southwest of the city centre, is worth a stay if you need to be near the RAI exhibition centre. Its 10 home-style rooms are quite large, and the street is quiet and residential.

Although it's an old-school hotel with lots of business guests, the **Hilton Amsterdam** (Map pp274-5; ☎ 710 60 00; www.hilton.com; Apollolaan 138-140; rooms €200-406; 🖳 🗶 ) grabs the spotlight every once in a while. It was 'flower-power' central in 1969 when John Lennon and Yoko Ono staged their 'bed-in' for world peace (you can rent the room), and Herman Brood, Holland's most famous junkie-artist-musician, committed suicide here in 2001 by jumping off the roof – he used to frequent the hotel's popular bar (carrying a parrot on his head). This tower fronts a grassy park with a marina out back; rooms are international business standard; the health club features sauna and Turkish bath; and service is crisp and professional. The upper floors have sweeping city views.

The **Hotel Okura** (Map pp274-5; ☎ 678 71 11; www.okura.nl; Ferdinand Bolstraat 333; s/d from €240/275; 🗶 🖳 🗶 🗶 ) is the business traveller's choice, with close proximity to the RAI exhibition centre, private in-room fax lines, WiFi for computers, and professional staff. Plus, it's got Holland's largest hotel pool, an amazing health club, several fine restaurants (including a Michelin-rated Japanese choice) and delicious, panoramic views of Amsterdam.

---

nights. Rooms are sterile (in both senses) and have TV, phone and itty-bitty bathrooms. Breakfast is €9 per person. And no, it was never a cruise ship.

### HOTEL ARENA Map p285
☎ 850 24 00; www.hotelarena.nl;
's Gravesandestraat 51; s/d from €100-150; 🖳
With more facelifts than a Hollywood star, this building, bordering lush Oosterpark, has morphed from chapel to orphanage to backpackers hostel and, now, a slick, modern, 121-room hotel with fashionable restaurant, café and nightclub. Minimalist rooms – 'designer-industrial-hospital' chic – are more IKEA than *Wallpaper** magazine, but the large, split-level double rooms are a sun-drenched delight. Rooms in sections A, B, E and F tend to be quieter.

### HOTEL EDEN LANCASTER Map p285
☎ 535 68 88; www.edenhotelgroup.com;
Plantage Middenlaan 48; s/d from €95/120; 🖳
A tip-to-toe renovation in 2003 has made the Eden Lancaster one of the smartest lodgings in the Plantage. Rooms all have a TV, phone, modem hookup and motifs of blondwood, red, tan, and the stylised St. Andrew's crosses of the city seal.

### HOTEL PARKLANE Map p285
☎ 622 48 04; www.hotel-parklane.nl;
Plantage Parklaan 16; s/d €75/105; 🖳
This 12-room, one-time dressmaker's shop was taken over by new management in 2003

and is slowly being renovated. Quad rooms are available.

### HOTEL REMBRANDT Map p285
☎ 627 27 14; www.hotelrembrandt.nl;
Plantage Middenlaan 17; s/d €65/75-100; 🖳
Although the hallways could stand a touch-up, the Rembrandt shines where it matters: rooms are spotless and have TV, phone, coffee maker and some hardwood floors and bathtubs. A feature is the wood-panelled breakfast room (with chandeliers and 17th-century paintings on linen-covered walls). Rooms 2 (large double with a balcony overlooking a small garden) and 21 (four-person, split-level, sunny and modern) offer plenty of bang for your buck.

### LILIANE'S HOME Map p285
☎ 627 40 06; Sarphatistraat 119; d with private facilities €100
This nine-bedroom private home, the sole women-only establishment in town, has loads of personality. Rooms with huge windows (some with balconies) include TV (no phone), fridge, books to read and a basket of breakfast goodies delivered to your door each morning.

## CHEAP SLEEPS

### HOTEL HORTUS Map p285
☎ 625 99 96; www.hotelhortus.com; Plantage Parklaan 8; d with shared or private facilities €50
Facing the Botanical Garden, this old-shoe comfy, 20-room hotel has small doubles

Sleeping – The Plantage & Eastern Islands

*Bar at Hotel Arena (p221)*

with or without showers (luck of the draw) – all have safe and sink. It's run by the same crew as hotel Brian, so it's no surprise that the lounge is chock-full of young, happy stoners transfixed by the large-screen TV. Rates include a cooked breakfast.

### HOTEL PENSION KITTY Map p285
☎ 622 68 19; Plantage Middenlaan 40;
s/d with shared facilities €45/55
We love Kitty, and how could you not? She's 80-something and speaks halting English, and a stay in her creaky, antique-filled, ruby-red-carpeted mansion is like a stay at grandma's. Its 10 rooms are big, comfortable and very lived-in. No wonder she has so many loyal guests. Breakfast is not included and there are no phones in rooms.

# OLD SOUTH

### HESTIA HOTEL Map pp286-7
☎ 618 08 01; www.hotel-hestia.nl,
Roemer Visscherstraat 7; s €70-84, d €93-133
Friendly, family-run Hestia, with 18 rooms decorated in fresh blue and white, offers a quiet retreat after a day of sightseeing. Scrupulously neat rooms vary in size and height – some have balconies overlooking the Vondelpark.

### HOTEL AALDERS Map pp286-7
☎ 662 01 16; www.hotelaalders.nl;
Jan Luykenstraat 13-15; s/tw from €75/87
There are fancier hotels in town, but the family-owned Aalders is quite homey and well-situated on a quiet street near Museumplein. Each room in its two row homes is different (the old-style room has wood panelling and leaded windows), but all have TV, phone and shower. The breakfast room has a Venetian glass chandelier. Huge rooms are available for large parties.

### HOTEL ACRO Map pp286-7
☎ 662 55 38; www.acrohotel.nl; Jan Luykenstraat 44;
s €60-80, d €70-115; 🖳
So it's a bit austere and its '80s-decor rooms could use an update, but it's reasonably priced for the quiet location (near Museumplein), there's a bar, and the staff is welcoming. Maybe that's why so many British guests return year after year.

## HOTEL BELLINGTON Map pp286-7

☎ 671 64 78; www.hotel-bellington.com; PC Hooft-straat 78-80; d with shared/private facilities €60/80

What a difference new paint, carpet and owners can make. This formerly (and incongruously) shabby lodging on Amsterdam's ritziest shopping street was recently redone and has a lovely garden that you can contemplate from the breakfast room. It's still short of luxury, but it's good value for the location.

## HOTEL BEMA Map pp286-7

☎ 679 13 96; www.bemahotel.com; Concertgebouwplein 19B; s from €45, d with shared/private facilities €65/75; 🖳

This seven-room hotel in a higgledy-piggledy mansion house is filled with African art. Expect extra-big doubles and breakfast in bed but no phone in the room.

## HOTEL DE FILOSOOF Map pp286-7

☎ 683 30 13; www.hotelfilosoof.nl; Anna van den Vondelstraat 6; s/d from €97.50/111

Sounds quaint, no? A hotel owned by two sisters, with 38 rooms themed after philosophers (eg Aristotle, Wittgenstein and Spinoza). But it's also a professional, warm and well-run operation near the Vondelpark. There are larger rooms in town, but few more thoughtfully decorated: from lush furniture and over-the-top wallpaper to minimalist paeans to serenity. The variety of breakfast rooms may remind you of museums you've visited.

## HOTEL FITA Map pp286-7

☎ 679 09 76; www.fita.nl; Jan Luykenstraat 37; s/d €90/115; ✂

This tiny, family owned hotel on a quiet street off Museumplein and PC Hooftstraat was just renovated. Now it's got handsome rooms, nicely appointed bathrooms and an English-style breakfast buffet. Rates include free telephone calls to Europe and the USA.

## HOTEL JAN LUYKEN Map pp286-7

☎ 573 07 30; www.janluyken.nl; Jan Luykenstraat 58; s/d from €195/210; 🖳

After a much-needed renovation, this Art Nouveau delight is in top form, with a crisp white and caramel colour scheme and sleek designer furniture. Other pleasures: solarium, sauna and whirlpool, alluring bar with garden views and staff who take their time with you. Buffet breakfast is €16 per person.

## HOTEL KAP Map pp286-7

☎ 624 59 08; www.kaphotel.nl; Den Texstraat 5B; s/d/tw €55/91/75; 🖳

Even if it could use a touch-up around the edges, we like the bright rooms with French windows, wicker furniture and up-to-date bathrooms. There's a big breakfast buffet in an attractive breakfast room and courtyard garden, and courteous, gay-friendly owners round out the experience. Most rooms have private showers but shared toilets.

## HOTEL NICOLAAS WITSEN Map pp286-7

☎ 626 65 46; www.hotelnicolaaswitsen.nl; Nicolaas Witsenstraat 4-8; s/d from €65/80; 🖳

Style-aficionados may squirm at the plain décor and odd brickwork of this family run place, but the staff is kindly and, unlike most other hotels in this price range, there's a lift and some rooms have baths. All 29 rooms are spotless, recently renovated and come with TV, phone and safe.

## MARRIOTT HOTEL Map pp286-7

☎ 607 55 55; www.marriotthotels.com; Stadhouderskade 12; d from €169

American visitors will feel right at home in the Marriott's spacious rooms with decor that could be in the Midwest. 'Executive' suites (from €219) allow access to the private lounges and are especially nice for business travellers. Extras include a fitness centre, shops and even a Pizza Hut. Breakfast is from €14.50.

## NH AMSTERDAM CENTRE Map pp286-7

☎ 685 13 51; www.nh-hotels.com; Stadhouderskade 7; r from €145; ✂ 🔲 🖳

In an Amsterdam School building that dates back to around the Amsterdam Olympics, this hotel was being renovated as we went to press, with striking results. Rooms have all mod-cons and a pale tan-and-white colour palette (and your choice of pillow), plus there's a fitness centre with a spa and sauna.

## OWL HOTEL Map pp286-7

☎ 618 94 84; www.owl-hotel.nl; Roemer Visscherstraat 1; s €75-92, d €98-115

The staff here is warm and welcoming, and even if the common areas appear a bit drab, the dapper, bright and quiet rooms come with lots of facilities (hairdryers, laptop plug-ins and so on). Best of all, buffet breakfast (included in the price) is served in a serene, light-filled room overlooking a gorgeous garden.

# CHEAP SLEEPS

## STAY OKAY VONDELPARK Map pp286-7

☎ 589 89 96; www.stayokay.com; Zandpad 5; dm low season €20.50-26, high season €23-28, tw low/high season €65/77; 🖳

Sitting just a blink away from the Vondelpark, this bustling, 475-bed hostel attracts over 300,000 guests a year – no wonder the lobby feels like a mini-UN. All bedrooms here are nonsmoking, have lockers, a shower, toilet and well-spaced bunks. There are lifts, a café, two restaurants and bike-hire facilities. There's no curfew but the no-visitors-at-night, no-drugs policy is strictly enforced. From March to October and during public holidays the maximum stay at the hostel is three nights.

# Excursions

# Excursions

You may not want to leave Amsterdam, but there are sights of tremendous history, beauty and tradition around the Randstad (rim-city), the circular urban agglomeration formed by Amsterdam, Den Haag (The Hague), Rotterdam, Utrecht and smaller towns such as Haarlem, Leiden and Delft. It's all within an hour of Amsterdam Centraal, easily accessible by train or bus. Thank goodness the Netherlands is a small country.

## CITIES

Lovely **Haarlem** (p229) and its central Grote Markt are within easy reach. **Leiden** (p230) is a legendary university town, while **Den Haag** (p233) is known for its stately atmosphere. For cutting-edge architecture, don't miss **Rotterdam** (p237).

## WINDMILLS

They're atmospheric, they're beautiful, they're Holland. See them in **Zaanse Schans** (p228) and **Leiden** (p230).

## CHEESE & FLOWERS

Only in the Netherlands will you see events such as the **Alkmaar cheese market** (see following), and the world's biggest flower auction in **Alsmeer** (p230). 'Amazing' is the only way to describe the bulb fields of the 32-hectare **Keukenhof** (p230), the world's largest flower garden, when it explodes in colour between March and May.

Leiden (p230)

## ART

Explore Dutch art, from the masters to modern, at museums in Den Haag, Haarlem and Rotterdam. East of the city, the **Kröller-Müller Museum** (p240) gets special mention for a fantastic collection of Van Goghs in a gorgeous national park.

# ALKMAAR

Most visitors come to this picturesque ringed town for the traditional **cheese market**, dating back to the 17th century.

On Friday mornings, waxed rounds of *kaas* (cheese) are ceremoniously stacked on the square. Soon, porters appear in colourful hats (denoting the cheese guild), and dealers (in white smocks) insert a hollow rod to extract a cheese sample, and sniff and crumble to check fat and moisture content. Once deals are struck, the porters whisk the cheeses on wooden sledges to the old cheese scale, accompanied by a zillion camera clicks. It's primarily for show – nowadays the dairy combines have a lock on the cheese trade. Still, as living relics go it's quite a spectacle.

The **Waaggebouw** (weighhouse, 14th century) houses the **Hollands Kaasmuseum**, a reverential display of cheese-making utensils, photos and a curious stock of paintings by 16th-century female artists. The building's mechanical tower **carillon** with jousting knights still springs to life.

Across the square, the **Nationaal Biermuseum** has a decent collection of beer-making equipment and wax dummies showing how the suds were made. The rare video of Dutch beer commercials since the 1950s is a howler. Cool off in the friendly bar.

## Sights & Information

**Carillon** ( 6.30pm & 7.30pm Thu, noon & 1pm Sat, 11am & noon Fri mid-Apr–mid-Sep)

**Cheese Market** (Waagplein; 10am-noon Fri Apr-Sep)

**Hollands Kaasmuseum** (Dutch Cheese Museum; 072-511 42 84; adult/child €3/2; 10am-4pm Mon-Sat)

**Nationaal Biermuseum** ( 072-511 38 01; Houttil 1; adult/child €3/1.50; 10am-4pm Tue-Fri, 1-4pm Sat & Sun)

**Tourist office** ( 072-511 42 84; www.vvvalkmaar.nl; Waagplein 2; 10am-5.30pm)

## Eating

**De Tromp Kaaswinkel** ( 072-511 34 22; Magdalenenstraat 11) If you're looking to grab some cheese after seeing

so much of it, check out this quality certified shop with Dutch and French cheeses stacked everywhere you look.

**Het Hof van Alkmaar** ( 072-512 12 12; Hof van Sonoy 1; mains €15-20; lunch & Dinner Tue-Sun) Contemporary-creative cooking in a former 15th-century monastery.

# ZAANSE SCHANS

Zaanse Schans is a good stab at recreating a local village from the 17th and 18th centuries. The most-striking structures are the six working **windmills** along the riverbanks. One mill sells its freshly ground mustard; others turn out pigments, oils, meal and timber. All are open for inspection and it's a treat to clamber about the creaking works while the mills shake in the North Sea breeze.

This open-air museum also stands out because its 'residents' actually live here, in historic structures brought from around the country. Workshops, shops and raised wooden homes sit on a sweet little tract complete with canals and tulip gardens. In sunny weather, it's a grand day out despite the inevitable crowds. The **visitors centre** hands out the free maps you'll need. Admission is free, but there are shops where you can spend: a colonial supermarket, a **cheesemaker** and a popular **clog factory**. The clogmaker will demonstrate a device that grinds out wooden shoes in tandem. The engaging **pewter smith** will explain the story behind dozens of tiny figures in several languages while the soft metal sets in the moulds.

When you're finished poking round the village, a **tour boat** does 50-minute spins on the river Zaan several times a day.

On the adjacent lot, the shiny new **Zaans Museum** runs temporary exhibitions featuring historical objects relating to the Zaan river communities.

## Sights & Information

**Boat Tours** (adult/child €5/2.50, Tue-Sun Apr-Sep)

**Visitors Centre** ( 075-616 82 18; Schansend 1; 10am-5pm Tue-Sun Mar-Oct, Sat & Sun only Nov-Feb)

**Zaans Museum** ( 075-616 28 62; adult/child €4.50/2.70; 10am-5pm Tue-Sat, noon-5pm Sun)

# HAARLEM

It's hard not to be enthusiastic about Haarlem, which has retained more of its 17th-century layout than any other Randstad city. Its wealth of historic buildings, courtyards and posh antique shops lends a refined elegance.

The main square of the old town is **Grote Markt**, flanked with restaurants and cafés and a clutch of historical buildings. Its florid, 14th-century **Stadhuis** (Town Hall) has many extensions including a balcony where judgments from the high court were pronounced. The counts' hall contains 15th-century panel paintings and is normally open during office hours, for a discreet peek.

Across from the Stadhuis looms the **Grotekerk van St Bavo**, the Gothic cathedral, with a 50m-high steeple. It contains some fine Renaissance artworks, but the star attraction is its **Müller organ** – one of the most magnificent in the world, standing 30m high with about 5000 pipes; try to catch a recital. It was played by Handel and Mozart.

In the centre of Grote Markt stand the 17th-century **Vleeshal**, a former meat market, and the **Verweyhal**, an old fish market. Today they are modern art annexes of the Frans Hals Museum, known collectively as **De Hallen** – the latter contains the museum's collection of modern art, including Dutch impressionists and CoBrA artists. On the square north of the Grotekerk is a statue of Laurens Coster, whom Haarlemmers claim, along with Gutenberg, as the inventor of moveable type.

The **Frans Hals Museum** is a must for anyone interested in the Dutch masters. In an almshouse where Hals spent his final, impoverished years, the collection focuses on the 17th-century Haarlem School, the pinnacle of Dutch mannerist art. The museum's pride and joy, eight group portraits by Hals detailing the companies of the Civic Guard, reveal the painter's exceptional attention to mood and psychological tone.

The **Teylers Museum** is the oldest museum in the country (1778), named after the philanthropist-merchant Pieter Teyler van der Hulst. It houses an array of whizz-bang inventions, drawings by Michelangelo and Raphael, and paintings from the Dutch and French schools. The interiors are as good as the displays. **Canal boat tours** depart from opposite the Museum.

Haarlem has a number of lovely **hofjes** (courtyards and gardens) – most are open on weekends only. The tourist office has walking guide brochure, *Hofjeswandeling*, and conducts *hofje* tours.

## Transport

**Distance from Amsterdam** 24km

**Direction** West

**Travel time** 15-20 minutes

**Train** Services to Haarlem are frequent (€3.10, four to five per hour). Haarlem's train station is an Art Deco masterpiece. Grote Markt is a 500m walk to the south.

**Car** From the ring road west of the city, take the N200 which becomes the A200.

## Detour: Zandvoort

If you think of the beach as an oasis of peace and quiet, think again. In the nation that gave the world *gezellig* (see boxed text, p12), even going to the beach is a party.

The beach at Zandvoort is lined with pavilion after pavilion, some 25 in all, serving food, spinning tunes and, just by the way, offering beach access. Choices run from sedate to wild, gay, straight and nudist, and the season runs from late March through to late September, although some venues remain open in winter. Bloemendaal aan Zee is a quieter beach community about 1km north of Zandvoort station.

On the weekends, don't even think about driving! There's frequent train service from Amsterdam via Haarlem.

# Sights & Information

**Canal boat tours** (leaves from opposite the Frans Hals Museum; adults/seniors/children under 12 yrs €7/5/3.50; first tour 10.30am, 5 times daily Apr-Oct) Tours are available in English.

**De Hallen** ( ☎ 023-511 57 75; adult/child €7/3.50; 11am-5pm Mon-Sat, noon-5pm Sun)

**Frans Hals Museum** ( ☎ 023-511 57 75; www.frans halsmuseum.nl; Groot Heiligland 62; adult/child €4/2; 11am-5pm Mon-Sat, noon-5pm Sun)

**Grotekerk van St Bavo** (adult/child €5.50/3.50; ⏰ 10am-4pm Mon-Sat; organ recitals 3pm Sat & 8.15pm Tue Apr-Sep)

**Teylers Museum** ( ☎ 023-531 90 10; Spaarne 16; adult/child €5/1.50; ⏰ 10am-5pm Tue-Sat, noon-5pm Sun)

**Tourist Office** ( ☎ 0900-616 16 00; www.vvvzk.nl; Stationsplein 1; ⏰ 9.30am-5.30pm Mon-Fri, 10am-2pm Sat)

**VVV hofje tours** (adult/child €5/3.50; ⏰ 10am Sat, also 10am Wed Jul-Aug; commentary is in Dutch but most guides will take questions in English)

## Eating

**Café Applause** ( ☎ 023 531 14 25; Grote Markt 3; mains €6-20; ⏰ lunch & dinner) This café provides elegant atmosphere, lunchtime pastas and salads and seriously upmarket dinners.

**De Haerlemsche Vlaamse** (Spekstraat 3; regular French fries €1.70) Frites house and local institution.

## Sleeping

**Joops Hotel** ( ☎ 023-532 20 08; joops@easynet.nl; Oude Groenmarkt 20; s/d €65/85) Located near the Grote Kerk, Joops offers 60 very individual rooms which are spread over an entire block.

**Hotel Amadeus** ( ☎ 023-532 45 30; Grote Markt 10; s/d incl breakfast €53/74; 🖳 ) Nestled in a row of old gabled houses on the main square.

# AALSMEER

This town hosts the world's biggest **flower auction** ( ☎ 0297-39 21 85; adult/child €4/2; ⏰ 7.30-11am Mon-Fri) in Europe's largest commercial complex, one million square metres. The experience may blow you away: about 90 million flowers and plants worth €6 million change hands here every single day. Arrive by 9am to catch the spectacle from the viewing gallery. Selling is conducted – surprise! – by Dutch auction, with a huge clock showing the starting price dropping until someone takes up the offer. There's a self-guided tour of the site with audio boxes at strategic points.

Mondays are quietest, Thursdays very, very busy.

# LEIDEN

Home to the country's oldest **university**, Leiden's effervescent, intellectual aura is partly generated by the 20,000 students that make up one-sixth of the population. The university was a gift from William the Silent for withstanding two Spanish sieges in 1574; a third of the residents starved before the Spaniards retreated on 3 October (the town's big festival day).

Wealth from the linen industry buttressed Leiden's growing prosperity, and during the 17th century the town produced several brilliant artists, most-famously Rembrandt van Rijn – he was born here in 1606 and remained in Leiden for 26 years before achieving greater fame

# LEIDEN

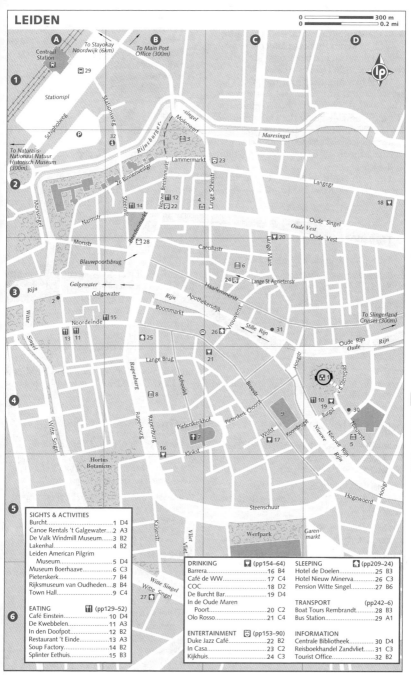

| 0 | | 300 m |
| 0 | | 0.2 mi |

**SIGHTS & ACTIVITIES**
| | |
|---|---|
| Burcht.................................1 | D4 |
| Canoe Rentals 't Galgewater....2 | A3 |
| De Valk Windmill Museum......3 | B2 |
| Lakenhal............................4 | B2 |
| Leiden American Pilgrim | |
| Museum...........................5 | D4 |
| Museum Boerhaave................6 | C3 |
| Pieterskerk.........................7 | B4 |
| Rijksmuseum van Oudheden....8 | B4 |
| Town Hall...........................9 | C4 |

**EATING** 🍴 (pp129–52)
| | |
|---|---|
| Café Einstein......................10 | D4 |
| De Kwebbelen....................11 | A3 |
| In den Doofpot....................12 | B2 |
| Restaurant 't Einde..............13 | A3 |
| Soup Factory......................14 | B2 |
| Splinter Eethuis..................15 | B3 |

**DRINKING** 🍷 (pp154–64)
| | |
|---|---|
| Barrera...............................16 | B4 |
| Café de WW........................17 | C4 |
| COC..................................18 | D2 |
| De Burcht Bar......................19 | D4 |
| In de Oude Maren | |
| Poort...............................20 | C2 |
| Olo Rosso..........................21 | C4 |

**ENTERTAINMENT** 🎭 (pp153–90)
| | |
|---|---|
| Duke Jazz Café....................22 | B2 |
| In Casa..............................23 | C2 |
| Kijkhuis.............................24 | C3 |

**SLEEPING** 🛏 (pp209–24)
| | |
|---|---|
| Hotel de Doelen..................25 | B3 |
| Hotel Nieuw Minerva............26 | C3 |
| Pension Witte Singel.............27 | B6 |

**TRANSPORT** (pp242–6)
| | |
|---|---|
| Boat Tours Rembrandt..........28 | B3 |
| Bus Station........................29 | A1 |

**INFORMATION**
| | |
|---|---|
| Centrale Bibliotheek.............30 | D4 |
| Reisboekhandel Zandvliet......31 | C3 |
| Tourist Office......................32 | B2 |

in Amsterdam. The tourist office has printed guides to painter-related sights.

Today Leiden is a typical old Dutch town with a refreshing overlay of student vibrancy. Look for literary quotes painted on many walls in their original languages – everything from Russian to Hebrew to Spanish.

Walk five minutes from the grim Centraal Station area to the old city centre. The town is divided by many waterways, the most notable being the Oude Rijn and also the Nieuwe Rijn, which meet at Hoogstraat to form a canal called simply the Rijn.

**Rijksmuseum van Oudheden** (National Museum of Antiquities) has a world-class collection, particularly from Egypt, including human and animal mummies and the Temple of Taffeh.

The 17th-century **Lakenhal** (Cloth Hall) houses the Municipal Museum, with an assortment of works by old masters, as well as period rooms and temporary exhibits. The 1st floor has been restored to the way it would have looked when Leiden was at the peak of its prosperity.

Leiden's landmark windmill-museum, **De Valk** (The Falcon), has been carefully restored.

Leiden University was an early centre for Dutch medical research, and you can see the often grisly results (five centuries of pickled organs, surgical tools and skeletons) at the **Museum Boerhaave**.

A stuffed elephant greets you at **Naturalis – Nationaal Natuurhistorisch Museum** (National Museum of Natural History), a large, well-funded collection of all the usual dead critters and, notably, the one million-year-old Java Man discovered by Dutch anthropologist Eugene Dubois in 1891.

### Did you know?

According to lore, when the retreating Spanish fled Leiden in 1574, they abandoned a kettle of hotpot (stew) on the fire. Nowadays hotpot's a staple of Dutch cooking, in the form of *hutspot* (p132). It's washed down, along with herring, with lots of beer at Leiden's biggest festival each 3 October.

### Transport

**Distance from Amsterdam** 45km southwest

**Distance from Amsterdam** Southwest

**Travel time** 35 minutes

**Train** NS runs services from Amsterdam six times per hour (€5.80).

**Car** From the southwest point of the A10 ring road, take the A4, Leiden will be clearly signposted.

## Sights & Information

**De Valk** (The Falcon; ☎ 071-516 53 53; Tweede Binnenvestgracht 1; adult/child €2.50/1.50; ☺ 10am-5pm Tue-Sat, 1-5pm Sun)

**Lakenhal** (Cloth Hall; ☎ 071-516 53 60; Oude Singel 28-32; adult/child €2/1; ☺ 10am-5pm Tue-Fri, 12-5pm Sat & Sun)

**Museum Boerhaave** ( ☎ 071-521 42 24; Lange St Agnietenstraat 10; €2/1; ☺ 10am-5pm Tue-Sat, 12-5pm Sun)

**Naturalis – Nationaal Natuurhistorisch Museum** ( ☎ 071-568 76 00; Darwinweg 2; adult/child €8/4.50; ☺ 10am-6pm Tue-Sun).

**Rijksmuseum van Oudheden** (National Museum of Antiquities; ☎ 071-516 31 63; Rapenburg 28; adult/child under 18 €6/5.50; ☺ 10am-5pm Tue-Fri, 12-5pm Sat & Sun)

**Tourist information office** ( ☎ 0900-222 23 33, €1 per min; www.leiden.nl; Stationsweg 2D; ☺ 10am-6.30pm Mon-Fri, to 2pm Sat)

## Eating

**De Kwebbelen** ( ☎ 071-512 61 90; Nordeinde 19; 3-course menu €17.50; ☺ dinner) The most fun restaurant in Leiden, with kitschy menu names ('Joe Formaggio' cheese fondue) but fantastic cooking.

**Restaurant 't Einde** ( ☎ 071-512 21 15; Rembrandtstraat 2; mains from €15; ☺ dinner Tue-Sun) Small, classy place with mildly progressive, always delicious food.

## Sleeping

**Hotel de Doelen** ( ☎ 071-512 05 27; www.dedoelen.com; Rapenburg 2; s/d €70/90) Stately and classic; some canalside rooms border on palatial opulence.

**Hotel Nieuwe Minerva** ( ☎ 071-512 63 58; www .nieuwminerva.nl; Boommarkt 23; s/d €75/100) Located in six 16th-century canalside houses, this central hotel has themed rooms, including a room with a bed that king Lodewijk Bonaparte slept in.

# DEN HAAG (THE HAGUE)

The Netherlands' third-largest city has a refined air, thanks to the stately mansions and palatial embassies lining its green boulevards. It's known for its prestigious art galleries and one of the world's best jazz festivals (North Sea Jazz), held annually near the seaside suburb of Scheveningen.

Confusingly, although the **parliament** and royal family are based here, Den Haag is not the national capital. It *was* the capital until 1806, when Louis-Napoleon installed his government in Amsterdam. Eight years later, the French were ousted and the government returned to Den Haag, but Amsterdam retained the title of capital.

In the 20th century, Den Haag became the home of several international legal entities including the UN's International Court of Justice and the Academy of International Law. These genteel organisations and their attendant legions of diplomats give the town its rather sedate and urbane air today.

The **Mauritshuis** is a small but grand museum, housing some of the world's best-loved Dutch and Flemish works. Almost every piece is a masterpiece, including Rembrandt's *Anatomy Lesson of Dr Tulp*, Vermeer's *Girl with a Pearl Earring* and a touch of the contemporary with Andy Warhol's portrait of Queen Beatrix.

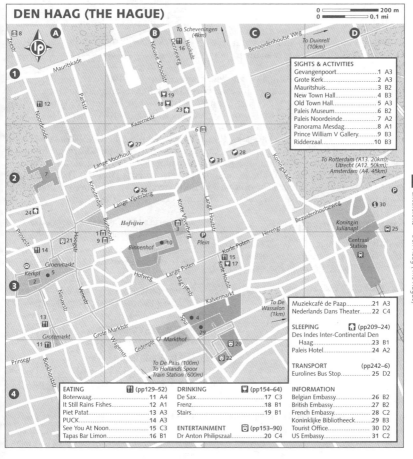

**DEN HAAG (THE HAGUE)**

0 — 200 m
0 — 0.1 mi

SIGHTS & ACTIVITIES
Gevangenpoort.........................1 A3
Grote Kerk..............................2 A3
Mauritshuis.............................3 B2
New Town Hall.......................4 B3
Old Town Hall........................5 A3
Paleis Museum........................6 B2
Paleis Noordeinde...................7 A2
Panorama Mesdag...................8 A1
Prince William V Gallery..........9 B3
Ridderzaal.............................10 B3

To Rotterdam (A13. 20km);
Utrecht (A12. 50km);
Amsterdam (A4. 45km)

EATING                    (pp129–52)
Boterwaag...............................11 A4
It Still Rains Fishes..................12 A1
Piet Patat...............................13 A3
PUCK....................................14 A3
See You At Noon....................15 C3
Tapas Bar Limon.....................16 B1

DRINKING                    (pp154–64)
De Sax..................................17 C3
Frenz....................................18 B1
Stairs....................................19 B1

ENTERTAINMENT                    (pp153–90)
Dr Anton Philipszaal...............20 C4

Muziekcafé de Paap................21 A3
Nederlands Dans Theater........22 C4

SLEEPING                    (pp209–24)
Des Indes Inter-Continental Den
  Haag...................................23 B1
Paleis Hotel............................24 A2

TRANSPORT                    (pp242–6)
Eurolines Bus Stop.................25 D2

INFORMATION
Belgian Embassy.....................26 B2
British Embassy.......................27 B2
French Embassy.......................28 C2
Koninklijke Bibliotheeck..........29 B3
Tourist Office.........................30 D2
US Embassy............................31 C2

Excursions – Den Haag (The Hague)

233

The parliamentary buildings around the adjoining **Binnenhof** (Inner Court) have long been the heart of Dutch politics, though parliament now meets in a modern building (1992) on the south side. The buildings are best seen on a tour.

Admirers of De Stijl, and in particular of Piet Mondriaan, mustn't miss the HP Berlage-designed **Gemeentemuseum**. Mondriaan's unfinished *Victory Boogie Woogie* takes pride of place (it should; the museum paid €30 million for it), and there are also a few Picassos and other works by some famous 20th-century names. It's also home to a fabulous **Photography Museum.**

The **Gevangenpoort** (prison gate) is a surviving remnant of the 13th-century city fortifications. It has hourly tours showing how justice was dispensed back then (painfully). Next door, the **Prince William V Gallery** was the first public museum in the Netherlands (1773). It's been restored to its original appearance, and the paintings are hung in the 18th-century manner; not a bit of wall is left bare.

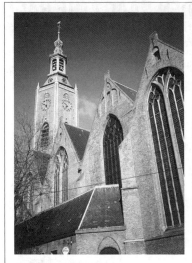

*Grotekerk, Den Haag*

The **Grotekerk** (1450) has a fine pulpit, which was constructed 100 years later. The neighbouring 1565 **old town hall** is a splendid example of Dutch Renaissance architecture.

The huge **new town hall** at the corner of Grote Marktstraat, is the hotly debated work by US architect Richard Meier (who also designed Los Angeles' Getty Center). The 'official' nickname of the building is the 'white swan', but locals prefer the 'ice palace'.

It stands in contrast to the **Vredespaleis** (Peace Palace), housing the UN's **International Court of Justice**. The grand building was donated by American steel maker Andrew Carnegie for use by the International Court of Arbitration, an early international body whose goal was the prevention of war. Sadly, though, WWI broke out one year after it opened in 1913. There are hourly guided tours, though these may be cancelled if courts are in session. You need to book ahead (security is strict). Take tram No 7 or bus No 4 from CS.

## Sights & Information

**Tourist information office** ( ☎ 0900-340 35 05; €0.45/min; info@vvvdenhaag.nl; Koningin Julianaplein 30; ❂ 8.30am-5.30pm Mon-Sat, 10am-2pm Sun Jul/Aug)

**Mauritshuis** ( ☎ 070-302 34 56; Korte Vijverberg 8; adult/child €7/3.50; ❂ 10am-5pm Tue-Sat, 11am-5pm Sun)

---

### Transport

**Distance from Amsterdam** 56km

**Travel time** 40 minutes

**Trains** Run from Amsterdam Centraal Station four times per hour, take about 40 minutes and cost €8.

**Car** From the southwest point of the A10 ring road, take the A4 from where Den Haag will be clearly signposted.

---

**Binnenhof tour** ( ☎ 070-364 61 44; adult/child €3.50/1.50; ❂ 10am-3.45 Mon-Sat) One-hour tours.

**Gemeentemuseum** ( ☎ 070-338 11 20; Stadhouderslaan 41; adult/concession/child under 18 €7.50/5/free; ❂ 11am-5pm Tue-Sat)

**Gevangenpoort** ('Prison Gate'; ☎ 070-346 08 61; Buitenhof 33; tour adult/child €3/2; ❂ 11am-4pm Tue-Fri, from noon Sat & Sun)

**Prince William V Gallery** ( ☎ 070-362 44 44; Buitenhof 35; adult/child €1.50/1; ❂ 11am-4pm Tue-Sun)

**New Town Hall** (Spui 170)

**Vredespalais** ( ☎ 070-302 41 37; Carnegieplein 2; adult/child €2.50/1.50; tours ❂ 10am-4pm Mon-Fri) Hour tours.

## Eating

**It Still Rains Fishes** ( ☎ 070-365 25 98; Nordeinde 123; mains from €20-27; ❂ dinner) Top seafood place with a delightfully bizarre name.

PUCK (Pure Unique Californian Kitchen; ☎ 070-427 76 49; www.puckfoodandwines.nl; Prinsestraat 33; mains from €20; ☉ lunch & dinner Tue-Sat) Perhaps the most innovative menu in the Netherlands (grilled orange dusted lollypop scallops); its menu also includes small and large 'bites'.

## Sleeping

Des Indes Inter-Continental Den Haag ( ☎ 070-363 29 32; Lange Voorhout 54-6; r from €145; ⓟ ☒ ⬛ ) Visiting heads-of-state: fire your assistant if you're not booked into this sumptuous hotel.

# DELFT

Had the potters who lived in Delft long ago not been so accomplished, today's townsfolk would probably live in relative peace. But the distinctive blue-and-white pottery, which the 17th-century artisans duplicated from Chinese porcelain, became famous worldwide as 'delftware'. Delft has a strong association with the Dutch royal family and was the home of Vermeer.

In summer, the number of day-tripping tourists can be overwhelming; in winter, however, its old-world charm and narrow, canal-lined streets make a pleasant day trip.

Delft was founded around 1100 and grew rich off weaving and trade in the 13th and 14th centuries. In the 15th century a canal was dug to the Maas River; the small port there, Delfshaven, was eventually absorbed by Rotterdam.

There are three places where you can see the artists working; the most central and modest is the Aardewerkatelier de Candelaer, just off the Markt. When it's quiet you can usually get a detailed tour of the manufacturing process.

The other two locations are factories outside the town centre. De Delftse Pauw is the smaller, employing 35 painters who work mainly from home – you won't see them on weekends. De Porceleyne Fles is the only original factory operating since the 1650s; it's slick and pricey.

The Museum Lambert van Meerten has a fine collection of porcelain tiles and delftware dating back to the 16th century.

One of the greatest Dutch masters, Johannes Vermeer (1632–75), lived his entire life in Delft, fathering 11 children and dying at age 43, leaving behind a mere 35 incredible paintings. His works have rich and meticulous colouring and he captures light as few other painters have ever managed. His scenes come from everyday life in Delft. You can visit the location of his most-famous exterior work, *View of Delft*, at Hooikade.

Unfortunately, none of Vermeer's works remain in Delft. The work above can be seen at the Mauritshuis in Den Haag.

The 14th-century Nieuwekerk houses the crypt of the Dutch royal family and the mausoleum of William the Silent. The same ticket admits you to the Gothic Oude Kerk; it looks every one of its 800 years, with its leaning tower 2m from the vertical. Among the tombs inside is Vermeer's.

Opposite the Oude Kerk is the Prinsenhof. This collection of buildings is a former convent and is where William the Silent held court until he was assassinated in 1584. The bullet hole in the wall has been enlarged by visitors' fingers and is now covered. The buildings host displays of historical and contemporary art.

In old Delft, the Beestenmarkt is a large open space surrounded by fine buildings where much of Tracy Chevalier's novel *Girl with a Pearl Earring* was set. Further east, Oostpoort is the sole surviving piece of the town's walls. Koornmarkt, leading south from the Waag, is a quiet and tree-lined canal.

Excursions – Delft

# Sights & Information

**Tourist Information** ( ☎ 015-215 40 51, www.delft.nl;
Hippolytusbuurt 4; 🕙 11am-4pm Mon, 10am-4pm Tue-Sat, 10am-3pm Sun)

**Aardewerkatelier de Candelaer** ( ☎ 015-213 18 48; Kerkstraat 14; 🕙 9am-5pm Mon-Sat, Sun 9am-5pm Mar-Oct)

**De Delftse Pauw** ( ☎ 015-212 49 20; Delftweg 133;
🕙 9am-4.30pm Mon-Fri, 11am-1pm Sat & Sun Nov-Mar)

Tram No 1 to Pasgeld, walk up Broekmolenweg to the canal, turn left.

**De Porceleyne Fles** ( ☎ 015-251 20 30; Rotterdamseweg 196; tour €3; 🕙 9.30am-5pm, closed Sun Nov-Mar) Bus No 63 from the train station stops nearby at Jaffalaan.

**Money** The number of ATMs in Delft is infinitesimal. It's best to use the two ATMs just outside the train station by the GWK (grens wissel kantoor, money-exchange office; 🕙 8am-7pm Mon-Fri, 8am-6pm Sat & Sun)

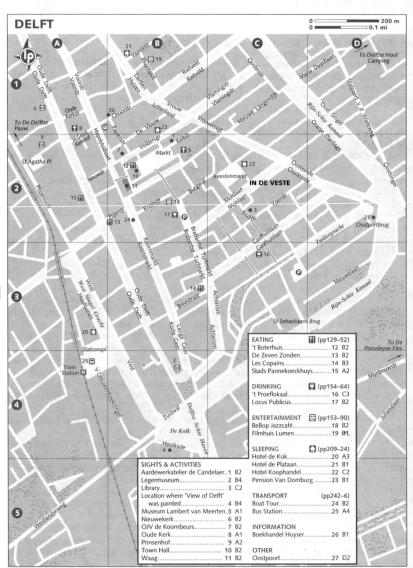

DELFT

| EATING | 🍴 (pp129–52) |
| --- | --- |
| 't Boterhuis | 12 B2 |
| De Zeven Zonden | 13 B2 |
| Les Copains | 14 B3 |
| Stads Pannekoeckhuys | 15 A2 |

| DRINKING | 🍺 (pp154–64) |
| --- | --- |
| 't Proeflokaal | 16 C3 |
| Locus Publicus | 17 B2 |

| ENTERTAINMENT | 🎭 (pp153–90) |
| --- | --- |
| BeBop Jazzcafé | 18 B2 |
| Filmhuis Lumen | 19 B1 |

| SLEEPING | 🛏 (pp209–24) |
| --- | --- |
| Hotel de Kok | 20 A3 |
| Hotel de Plataan | 21 B1 |
| Hotel Koophandel | 22 C2 |
| Pension Van Domburg | 23 B1 |

| TRANSPORT | (pp242–6) |
| --- | --- |
| Boat Tour | 24 B2 |
| Bus Station | 25 A4 |

| INFORMATION | |
| --- | --- |
| Boekhandel Huyser | 26 B1 |

| OTHER | |
| --- | --- |
| Oostpoort | 27 D2 |

| SIGHTS & ACTIVITIES | |
| --- | --- |
| Aardewerkatelier de Candelaer | 1 B2 |
| Legermuseum | 2 B4 |
| Library | 3 C2 |
| Location where 'View of Delft' was painted | 4 B4 |
| Museum Lambert van Meerten | 5 A1 |
| Nieuwekerk | 6 B2 |
| OJV de Koornbeurs | 7 B2 |
| Oude Kerk | 8 A1 |
| Prinsenhof | 9 A2 |
| Town Hall | 10 B2 |
| Waag | 11 B2 |

**Museum Lambert van Meerten** (☎ 015-260 23 58; Oude Delft 199; adult/child €2/1; ☻ 10am-5pm Tue-Sat, 1-5pm Sun)

**Nieuwekerk** (☎ 015-212 30 25; adult/child €2/1; ☻ 9am-6pm Mon-Sat, to 4pm Nov-Mar)

**Prinsenhof** (☎ 015-260 23 58; St Agathaplein 1; adult/child €2.20/1; ☻ 10am-5pm Tue-Sat, 1-5pm Sun)

---

## Transport

**Distance from Amsterdam** 62km
**Duration** southwest
**Travel Time** 50 minutes
**Train** Two trains per hour run from Amsterdam CS (€8.50), and take the best part of an hour.
**Car** From the Amsterdam ring road, take the A4 to Den Haag and turn onto the A13, from which Delft will be clearly signposted.

---

## Eating

**Les Copains** (☎ 015-214 40 83; Breestraat 8; seafood mains around €20-25; ☻ dinner) Clean, quiet dining room belies a hint of Gallic flamboyance.

**Stads Pannekoekhuys** (☎ 015-213 01 93; Oude Delft 113; mains €3-10; ☻ lunch & dinner) 90 kinds of pancakes and classic Dutch pea soup.

## Sleeping

**Hotel de Koophandel** (☎ 015-214 23 02; www.hotelde koophandel.nl; Beestenmarkt 30; s/d from €75/90) A little bland, readers of *Girl With a Pearl Earring* may be able to look out their window and see locations from the book.

**Hotel de Plataan** (☎ 015-212 60 46; www.hoteldeplataan .nl; Doelenplein 10; s/d €82.50/92.50) Delft's nicest accommodation is on a delightful square, with hospitality to match.

# ROTTERDAM

Europe's busiest port, Rotterdam's history as a shipping nexus dates back to the 16th century. However, modern Rotterdam's genesis began on 14 May 1940, when the invading Germans issued an ultimatum to the Dutch: surrender, or Rotterdam would be destroyed. The government capitulated, but the raid was carried out anyway (Amsterdam was spared).

As a result, Rotterdam spent most of the 20th century rebuilding. The results are unique in Europe: by turns vibrant, ugly, impressive and astonishing. Today's Rotterdam (the Netherlands' second-largest city) has a dynamic, Berlin-like postmodern-metropolis aesthetic and a crackling energy that seems to feed off the 'anything goes' attitude for reconstruction.

Rotterdam is split by the Nieuwe Maas, a vast shipping channel crossed by a series of tunnels and bridges. The mostly reconstructed centre is north of the water. From Centraal Station (CS), a 15-minute walk along the canal-like ponds leads to the waterfront. The commercial centre is to the east, with most of the museums to the west.

The recently expanded **Museum Boijmans van Beuningen** is one of the best in the Netherlands, if not Europe. The collection includes superb Old Masters, works from Renaissance Italy, French impressionists, and 'the other surrealists': Dali, Duchamp, Magritte and Man Ray.

At the south end of Museum Park, the **Kunsthal** hosts temporary exhibitions. The building is a sight itself.

In nearby De Heuvel park on the Nieuwe Maas is the needle-like (185m) **Euromast**. It's one of the less successful – yet most recognisable – examples of modern architecture in the city. If the sky is clear, you can go to the top and see great views of the city that *don't* include it.

Highlights of maritime Rotterdam include the **Maritiem Museum Rotterdam**, right near the landmark Erasmus bridge, with the usual array of models that any youngster would love to take into the tub. The **Oude Haven** area preserves bits of the oldest part of the harbour, some of which date from the 14th century. It's a decent place for a stroll, especially for the large collection of historic boats.

The city's history is preserved at one of the few surviving 17th-century buildings in the centre at the **Historisch Museum Het Schielandhuis**. Exhibits focus on items from everyday life through the ages, such as the (purportedly) oldest-surviving wooden shoe.

The **Nederlands Fotomuseum** has recently amalgamated with other photographic institutions, and offers interesting exhibits, as well as a shop and a library.

# ROTTERDAM

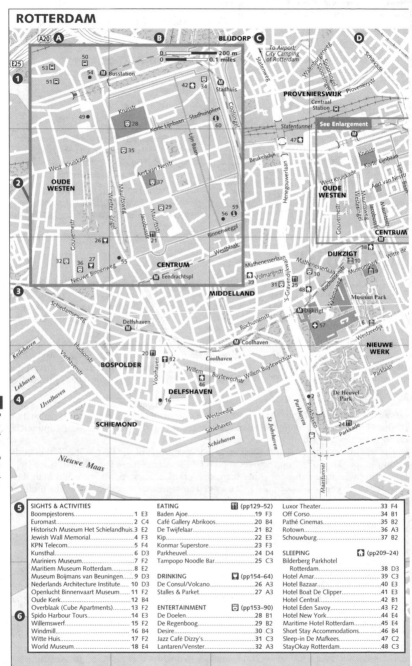

Excursions – Rotterdam

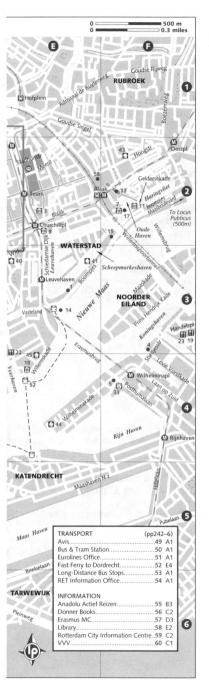

## Transport

**Distance from Amsterdam** 77km
**Direction** Southwest
**Travel time** 60 to 70 minutes
**Train** NS runs four services per hour (€11, 70 minutes); look for the intercity service to save a lot of time.
**Bus** Rotterdam is a hub for Eurolines bus services ( ☎ 412 44 44; Conradstraat 20; ☯ 9.30am-5.30pm Mon-Fri, 9.30am-3pm Sat). Long-distance bus stops are immediately west of CS.
**Car** From the Amsterdam ringroad, take the A4, and then the A13 from Den Haag with Rotterdam clearly signposted from here.

## Sights & Information

**Caution!** The area about 1km west of Centraal Station and the immediate surrounds of the station are the scene of many hard drug deals. Try not to be alone or look scared around CS late at night.

**Euromast** ( ☎ 010-436 48 11; Parkhaven 20; adult/child €7.75/5; ☯ 10am-5pm Oct-Mar, 10am-7pm Apr-Sep, to 10.30pm Jul-Aug)

**Historisch Museum Het Schielandhuis** ( ☎ 010-217 67 67; Korte Hoogstraat 31; adult/child €3/1.50; ☯ 10am-5pm Tue-Sat, 11am-5pm Sun)

**Kunsthal** ( ☎ 010-440 03 00; Westzeedijk 341; adults/child 13-18/under 12/under 6 €7.50/4.50/1/free; ☯ 10am-5pm Tue-Sat, 11am-5pm Sun)

**Maritiem Museum Rotterdam** ( ☎ 010-413 26 80; Leuvehaven 1; adult/child 4-15 €3.40/1.80; ☯ 10am-5pm Tue-Sat, 11am-5pm Sun, open Mon Jul & Aug)

**Money** GWK money exchange in Centraal Station ( ☯ 7am-9pm) and ATMs just outside Centraal Station.

**Museum Boijmans van Beuningen** ( ☎ 010-441 94 00; www.boijmans.rotterdam.nl; Museumpark 18-20; adult/child under18 €7/free; ☯ 10am-5pm Tue-Sat, 11am-5pm Sun)

**Nederlands Fotomuseum** ( ☎ 010-213 2011; Witte de Withstraat 63; adult/child €2.30/1.60; ☯ 11am-5pm Tue-Sun)

**Netherlands Architecture Institute** ( ☎ 010-440 12 00; Museumpark 25; adult/child 4-16 €5/3; ☯ 10am-5pm Tue-Sat, 11am-5pm Sun)

**Tourist Information Office** ( ☎ 010-413 31 24; www.vvv.rotterdam.nl; Coolsingel 67; ☯ 9am-6pm Mon-Fri, to 5pm Sat & Sun)

## Rotterdam Architecture

A brief tour of Rotterdam's stunning architecture can begin at the north end of Ben van Berkel's 800m-long **Erasmusbrug** (Erasmus Bridge, 1996), spanning the Nieuwe Maas near the Leuvehaven metro station. Walk part of the way across and you'll see the **KPN Telecom** building (2000) – the Renzo Piano–designed building looks like it's about to fall over but for a long pole giving it support.

Retrace your steps and walk northeast alongside the water, past the three **Boompjestoren** (1988) apartment blocks, and continue on until you see the striking **Willemswerf** (1988), headquarters of the huge Nedlloyd shipping company. Note the dramatic lines casting shadows on its sleek, white surface.

Another 100m will bring you to Rotterdam's other signature bridge, the **Willemsbrug** (1981), with its red pylons. Turn north at Oude Haven on Geldersekade. The regal 11-storey building on the corner is the **Witte Huis** (White House, 1897), a rare survivor of the prewar period.

Walk north for about three minutes to Blaak and the metro station of the same name. The surprising **Overblaak** (1978–84) is to your right, marked by the cube-shaped apartments and pencil-shaped tower. Designed by Piet Blom, the project has graced a thousand postcards.

The **Netherlands Architecture Institute** is in a fittingly stunning building on Museum Park. The institute stages ambitious special exhibitions through the year, and building tours are available.

Ask at the VVV and architecture institute about architectural tours of the city.

## Eating

**Baden Ajoe** ( ☎ 010-290 01 56; in the Vlif Werelddelen building; rijsttafel around €20; ☺ 5pm til late) Up-market Indonesian in the huge Vrij Entrepot complex of shops and restaurants.

**Kip Restaurant** ( ☎ 010-436 9923; van Vollenhovenstraat 25; mains €25; ☺ dinner Tue-Sun) Despite its name (the Chicken), this is a very classy dining establishment with white tablecloths.

## Sleeping

**Hotel Bazar** ( ☎ 010-206 51 51; www.hotelbazar.nl; Witte de Withstraat 16; s/d €60/75) What Rotterdam's all about: polyethnic vibe, air of tolerance and fantastic ground-floor bar and restaurant.

**Hotel New York** ( ☎ 010-439 05 00; www.hotelnewyork.nl; Koninginnenhoofd 1; r from €91-208; ☒ ☒ ☐ ☐ ) The city's favourite hotel, in the former headquarters of the Holland-America passenger ship line.

# KRÖLLER-MÜLLER MUSEUM

**De Hoge Veluwe National Park** ( ☎ 0318 59 16 27; www.hogeveluwe.nl; park adult/child €5/2.50, park & museum adult €10, car surcharge €5; ☺ 9am-5.30pm Nov-Mar, 8am-8pm Apr, 8am-9pm May & Aug, 8am-10pm Jun & Jul, 9am-8pm Sep, 9am-7pm Oct), the Netherlands' largest, would be a fantastic place to visit for its marshlands, forests and sand dunes alone, but its brilliant museum makes it unmissable.

It was once owned by Anton and Helene Kröller-Müller, a wealthy German-Dutch couple. He wanted hunting grounds, she wanted a museum site – they got both. Ticket booths at each of the three entrances (Hoenderloo, Otterlo and Rijzenburg) have basic information and useful park maps (€2.50). In the heart of the park, the main **visitors centre** has displays on the flora and fauna within.

The **Kröller-Müller** has works by **Picasso**, **Gris**, **Renoir**, **Sisley** and **Manet**, but it's the **Van Gogh** collection that makes it world-class. It's about 10km into the park, but well worth the hour's cycling to witness a stunning collection of Van Gogh's work (and other modern masterpieces) rivalling Amsterdam's own Van Gogh Museum. There's an evocative **sculpture garden** behind the museum. The museum is 1km from the visitors centre.

# Directory

# Directory

## TRANSPORT

Amsterdam's Schiphol Airport has copious air links worldwide, including many on low-cost European airlines, train links are especially good from France, Belgium and Germany, and most journeys within the Netherlands are so short that you can reach most regional destinations before your next meal.

## AIR
### Airlines

Airline offices in Amsterdam are listed under 'Luchtvaartmaatschappijen' in the pink pages of the phone book. Some airlines are best contacted via the Web.

**Aer Lingus** ( ☎ 517 47 47; www.aerlingus.com; Heiligeweg 14)

**Aeroflot** ( ☎ 627 05 61; www.euro-transit.nl; Weteringschans 26)

**Air France** ( ☎ 654 57 20; www.airfrance.nl; Evert van der Beekstraat 7; Schiphol)

**Air India** ( ☎ 624 81 09; www.airindia.com; Papenbroeksteeg 2)

**Alitalia** ( ☎ 676 44 79; www.alitalia.com; van Baerlestraat 70)

**British Airways** ( ☎ 346 95 59; www.britishairways.com; Neptunusstraat 33; Hoofddorp)

**British Midland** ( ☎ 346 92 11; www.flybmi.com)

**Cathay Pacific** ( ☎ 653 20 10, 653 20 10; www.cathaypacific.nl; Evert van der Beekstraat 18; Schiphol)

**China Airlines** ( ☎ 646 10 01; www.china-airlines.com; De Boelelaan 7)

**Delta Air Lines** ( ☎ 201 35 36, www.delta.com; Evert van der Beekstraat 7; Schiphol)

**El Al** ( ☎ 644 01 01; www.elal.com; Prof Bavincklaan 5; Amstelveen)

**EasyJet** ( ☎ 023-568 48 80; www.easyjet.com)

**Garuda Indonesia** ( ☎ 550 26 40, www.garuda-indonesia.nl; Singel 540)

**Japan Airlines** ( ☎ 305 00 60; www.jal-europe.com; Jozef Israelskade 48E)

**KLM** ( ☎ 474 77 47; www.klm.nl; Amsterdamseweg 55; Amstelveen)

**Lufthansa** ( ☎ 582 94 56; www.lufthansa.nl; Wibautstraat 129)

**Malaysia Airlines** ( ☎ 521 62 62; www.malaysiaairlines.com.my; Weteringschans 24A)

**Northwest Airlines** ( ☎ 474 77 47; www.nwa.com; Amsterdamseweg 55; Amstelveen)

**Qantas** ( ☎ 569 82 83; www.qantas.com.au; Neptunsstraat 33; Hoofddorp)

**Ryanair** ( ☎ 0900 202 21 84, €0.45 per minute; www.ryanair.com)

**Singapore Airlines** ( ☎ 548 88 88; www.singapore.nl; De Boelelaan1067)

**South African Airways** ( ☎ 554 22 88; www.flysaa.com; Polarisavenue 49; Hoofddorp)

**Thai Airways** ( ☎ 596 13 01; www.thaiairways.com; Wibautstraat 3)

**Transavia** ( ☎ 406 04 06; www.transavia.nl; Westelijke Randweg 3)

**United Airlines** ( ☎ 201 37 08; www.unitedairlines.nl; Strawinskylaan 831)

### Airport

A mere 18km from central Amsterdam, Schiphol Airport is the Netherlands' main international airport and the third busiest in Europe. It's the hub of Dutch passenger carrier KLM, and over 100 airlines have direct flights and connections to all continents. Its shopping arcades, both in public areas and the See Buy Fly duty free inside the gate areas, are renowned throughout the world. We also love it because its name is unpronounceable (say 'S-*khip*-hol' fast).

Arrivals can be met in the large lobby known as Schiphol Plaza. For **airport and flight information** call ☎ 0900-01 41 (€0.10 per minute) or see www.schiphol.nl.

If you're phoning into Amsterdam from the airport, note that they are in the same area code ( ☎ 020).

#### TRAIN

Trains run on the **Nederlandse Spoorwegen** (NS, national railway) to Centraal Station (one-way/return €3.10/5.50; 15 to 20 minutes; every 10 to 15 minutes) from right beneath Schiphol Plaza. Train-ticket counters are in Schiphol Plaza's central court; buy your ticket before taking the escalator down to the platforms. Ticket windows at the airport also sell the *strippenkaart* (see Local Transport, p245), not normally available at NS windows. There are also ticket vending machines which do not sell the *strippenkaart*.

Tip: if you're flying with KLM and you bought your ticket in the Netherlands, your ticket gives free train transport within the country to/from the airport on your day of departure/arrival.

### TAXI
A taxi into Amsterdam from Schiphol airport takes 20 to 45 minutes (maybe longer in rush hour) and costs about €30.

### BUS/SHUTTLE
Some of the international hotel chains have free shuttle services for their guests. Public services such as Connexxion bus 197 or Interliner 370 also run regular services to/from central Amsterdam. Connexxion also runs a paid hotel shuttle – when making your hotel reservation, ask whether yours is on the route. To most hotels the cost is €10.50.

Another way to get to the airport is by the minivan service **Schiphol Travel Taxi** (☎ 0900-8876, €0.10 per minute; ☎ 31 38 339 47 68 from outside The Netherlands; www.schiphol .nl). This minivan service can transport up to eight people from anywhere in the country to the departure terminal. From central Amsterdam the fare is fixed at €22 per person, one way.

### CAR
By car, take the A4 freeway to/from the A10 ring road around Amsterdam. A short stretch of A9 connects the A4 close to Schiphol. Car-rental offices at the airport are in the right corner near the central exits of Schiphol Plaza.

### AIRPORT PARKING
The airport's P1 and P2 short-term parking garages (under cover) charge €1.70 per half-hour for the first three hours, then €2.50 per hour. The charge is €22.50 a day for the first three days, €11.50 a day thereafter. The P3 long-term parking area (open air) is a fair distance from the terminal but is linked by a 24-hour shuttle bus. The charge is €45 for up to three days (minimum charge) and €5 for each day thereafter – a good alternative to parking in the city (see also Car & Motorcycle, p244).

### LEFT LUGGAGE
Luggage may be deposited at the **left luggage office** (☎ 601 24 43) in the basement between arrival areas 1 and 2. Costs are €4.65 for the first

24 hours, €3.30 for each subsequent 24 hours (days two to five), and €2.80 per day thereafter.

## Travel Agents
One of the more conveniently located travel agents in the city is **Kilroy Travels** (Map pp278-9; ☎ 524 51 00; www.kilroytravels.com; Singel 413-15; ⏰ 10am-6pm Tue-Fri, noon-6pm Mon, 11.30am-4.30pm Sat). For more listings, look in the telephone book under 'Reisbureaus'.

Also try **lastminute.com** (☎ 0900 405 06 07, €0.15 per minute; www.nl.lastminute.com).

Gay & lesbian travellers might want to try **De Gay Krant** (Map pp278-9; ☎ 620 62 17; Kloveniersburgwal 40). It specialises in gay resort and tour travel.

## BICYCLE
With 750,000 Amsterdammers and an estimated 600,000 bikes, you *know* how most of the population gets around. Many visitors rent a bike towards the end of their stay and wish they had done so sooner, although the chaotic traffic can be challenging.

## Bicycle Rental
All the companies listed below require ID plus a credit-card imprint or a cash deposit with a passport. Amstel Stalling is the cheapest, but it's a little remote and their bicycles can be a bit run-down towards the end of the tourist season. Prices are for basic 'coaster-brake' bikes; gears and handbrakes, and especially insurance, usually cost more.

**Amstel Stalling** (Map pp274-5; ☎ 692 35 84; Amstelstation; day/week incl insurance €6/26.20, plus €100 deposit but no credit-card imprints)

**Bike City** (Map p277; ☎ 626 37 21; Bloemgracht 68-70; day/week €6.75/38.50, deposit €22.75). There's no advertising on the bikes, so you can pretend you're a local.

**Damstraat Rent-a-Bike** (Map pp278-9; ☎ 625 50 29; Damstraat 20-2; day/week, €7/31, deposit with passport €25)

**Holland Rent-a-Bike** (Map pp278-9; ☎ 622 32 07; Damrak 247 (Beurs van Berlage); day/week €6.25/32.50, deposit with passport €30)

**MacBike** (Map pp278-9; ☎ 624 83 91; Centraal Station; Map p285; ☎ 620 09 85; Mr Visserplein 2; Map pp285; ☎ 528 76 88, Weteringschans 2; www.macbike.nl; day/week €6.50/19.75, plus deposit €50)

If you're taking a bike aboard a train, you'll need to purchase a bike day pass (€6), valid throughout the country. There are no fees for collapsible bikes as long as they can be considered hand luggage.

An alternative to renting a bike is to buy one – worth considering depending on your timing. Figure on about €80 for a used bike and at least that for the locks.

# BOAT
## Ferries
There are free ferries from behind Centraal Station to destinations around the IJ, notably Amsterdam Noord and the Eastern Docklands.

## Canal Boat, Bus & Bike
For information about regular canal tours, see Canal Tours (p163).

**Lovers Museum Boat** (Map pp278-9; ☎ 622 21 81; day pass adult/child €14.25/9.50) leaves every 30 or 45 minutes from the Lovers terminal in front of Centraal Station.

**Canal Bus** (Map pp278-9; ☎ 623 98 86; day pass adult/child €15/10.50) does several circuits between Centraal Station and the Rijksmuseum between 9.50am and 8pm. The day pass is valid until noon the next day.

Quaintly named **canal bikes** (really paddleboats) can be hired from kiosks at Leidseplein, Keizersgracht/Leidsestraat, the Anne Frankhuis and the Rijksmuseum; two/four seaters cost €8/7 per person per hour.

# CAR & MOTORCYCLE
We absolutely don't recommend having a car in Amsterdam, unless you're considering a trip out of town.

## Parking
Parking in the city hits you where it hurts. Pay-and-display applies in the central zone from 9am to midnight Monday to Saturday, and noon to midnight on Sunday, and costs €3/18/12 per hour/daytime/evening; prices ease as you move away from the centre. Day passes are available from the ticket machines.

Parking police are merciless. Nonpayers in the Centrum district will find a bright yellow *wielklem* (wheel clamp) attached to their car and have to pay €69 to get it removed. Then you'll have to visit the closest *Stadstoezicht* (City Surveillance) office to pay the fine. Otherwise, within 24 hours the vehicle will be towed and the fine skyrockets to €245.

Parking garages in the city centre include ones at Damrak, near Leidseplein and under the Stopera, but they're often full and cost more than a parking permit. Here are some other options for parking:

**Transferium parking garage** ( ☎ 400 17 21; under the Amsterdam Arena; Bijlmer; per day incl 2 free return tickets for public transport to Centraal Station €5.50).

**Stadionplein** Park & Ride in the southwestern outskirts.

**Amsterdam North** Park for free and take the ferry across.

## Rental
Local companies are usually cheaper than the big multinationals like Avis, Budget, Hertz, and Europcar, but don't offer as much backup or flexibility (eg one-way rentals). Rates change almost weekly, so it pays to call around. Rentals at Schiphol airport incur a €40 surcharge.

Look for local car-rental firms in telephone directories under the heading *Autoverhuur*. This is a list of some of the better-known car-rental companies:

**Avis Autoverhuur** (Map pp286-7; ☎ 0800-235 28 47; www.avis.nl; ☎ 683 60 61; Nassaukade 380) International reservations weekdays only.

**Budget Rent a Car** (Map pp286-7; ☎ 0900-15 76; www.budget.nl; Overtoom 121; ☽ 8am-8pm Mon-Fri, 8am-5pm Sat)

**easyCar** (Map pp274-5; www.easycar.nl; Stephensonstraat 16, near Amstelstation) This is the place for bargain-basement deals.

**Europcar Autoverhuur** ( ☎ 070 381 18 91; www.europcar.nl; ☎ 683 21 23; Overtoom 197) International reservations weekdays only.

**Hertz** (Map pp274-5; ☎ 0900-235 54 37 89, 612 24 41; www.hertz.nl; Overtoom 333; ☽ 8am-8pm)

**Kuperus Autoverhuur** (Map pp274-5; ☎ 693 87 90; www.autoverhuur-kuperus.nl; Middenweg 175)

**Sixt** ( ☎ 023 569 86 56; www.sixt.nl; Smaragdlaan 3, Hoofddorp)

## Road Rules
Traffic in Amsterdam travels on the right and is generally quite busy. The minimum driving age is 18 for cars and 16 for motorcycles. Seat belts are required for everyone in a vehicle. Children under 12 must ride in the back if there's room.

Be very alert for bicycles, and if you are trying to turn right, bikes have priority. Trams always have the right of way. In traffic circles (roundabouts), approaching vehicles technically have right of way, but in practice they yield to vehicles already travelling on the circle.

The blood-alcohol limit when driving is 0.05%, and the speed limits are 50km/h in built-up areas, 80km/h in the country, 100km/h on major rural through-roads and 120km/h on freeways (sometimes this is reduced to 100km/h, but is generally clearly indicated).

## LOCAL TRANSPORT

Most public transport within the city is by tram; buses and Amsterdam's metro (subway) serve some outer reaches. Services are run by the local transit authority, the GVB; NS tickets are not valid on local transport.

The GVB has an **info office** (Map pp278-9; ☎ 0900 92 92, €0.50 per min; www.gvb.nl; Stationsplein 10; ☺ 7am-9pm Mon-Fri, 8am-9pm Sat & Sun) across the tram tracks from the Centraal Station entrance. Here you can get tickets, maps and the like. If you can't make it there, their website has lots of useful information including details of how to reach key sights in town.

At the time of writing, the GVB was in the process of changing the boarding system for trams. Under the old system, passengers could board through any door and validate their tickets by stamping them as they boarded via little yellow machines. However, to combat fare-beating, the GVB reintroduced conductors on trams. Under the new system, you must enter through doors near the rear of the tram and purchase or validate your ticket with the conductor (see GVB fares and Strippenkaart following). If you are transferring from another line, show your ticket to the conductor. You may exit through any door. Buses are more conventional, with drivers stamping the strips as you board.

There are also a few *sneltram* ('fast tram', or light rail) lines in the southern and southeastern suburbs. Tickets are validated in the same way as ordinary trams except where the *sneltram* shares the metro line, in which case you use the yellow machines at the stairways to the platforms.

Always assume that pickpockets are active on busy trams.

## GVB fares

Tickets on GVB trams and buses are calculated by zone and are valid for one hour from the time they're stamped. Within the centre of Amsterdam (virtually anywhere on our maps on pages 278-9 and 286-7) you are in Zone 1.

When in doubt, consult the transport maps at bus and tram stops, or ask the driver or conductor. Single trip fares for one/two/three/four zones are €1.60/2.40/3.20/4.

GVB passes are valid in all zones, and fares for one/two/three/seven days are €5.50/8.80/11.30/21.30. Children (aged four to 11) and seniors can obtain a day pass for €3.80 per day, but do not have the option to purchase multiple day passes.

## Strippenkaart

Depending on how much you plan to travel, consider a *strippenkaart* ('strip card'; 15-/45-strip cards €6.20/18.30) available at train and bus stations, post offices, many VVV offices, supermarkets and tobacconists. Each strip is numbered, beginning at one and up to the highest number on the card. These are stamped when you board, but there's a trick; you need to stamp for the number of zones you're travelling *plus one*, and you stamp one strip only. In other words, if you're travelling in Zone 1, stamp the second available strip but not the first (this would invalidate the second stamp). Note that you should begin stamping from the lowest number available. You can also use a strip card if you're travelling with a companion, so if both of you are traveling within Zone 1, you stamp only the fourth strip (two strips plus two strips).

If you're boarding transport with a conductor, simply state the number of zones you're travelling and the conductor will stamp your card for you. If you need to validate it yourself, fold the card so that the strip you want to stamp is first on the top, and insert it into the machine.

Note that if you get caught without a ticket or properly stamped strip, playing the ignorant foreigner (the 'dufus' strategy) will guarantee that you get fined €30.

Bonus: *strippenkaart* are valid on local public transit throughout the country.

## TAXI

Amsterdam taxis are among Europe's most expensive. You're not supposed to hail taxis on the street, but many will stop if you do. You can also usually find them at hotels and, especially at night, on Leidseplein.

The most reliable bet for calling a cab is probably **Taxicentrale Amsterdam** (☎ 677 77 77).

Taxis cost the same day or night – flag fall is €2.90 and €1.80 per kilometre, plus a 5% to 10%

tip. Some independent cabs charge lower fares; many will charge more – best play it safe.

There's also the informal strategy of setting a price with the driver before you get in – figure about two thirds of the metered price. Some haggling is usually involved. If a driver's waiting in a long-enough queue he may agree.

Note that taxi-drivers are among the few people you'll encounter in Amsterdam who may not speak great English.

# TRAIN

Trains are frequent and serve domestic destinations at regular intervals, sometimes five or six times an hour. However, the network has been plagued by poor punctuality in recent years, particularly at rush hour. The situation may be improving if only because the profitability of the Nederlandse Spoorwegen (NS) is linked to its on-time rates.

Domestic trains have 1st-class sections but these are often little different from the 2nd-class areas.

Trains can be a stopping-all-stations *Stoptrein*, a faster *Sneltrein* (Fast Train, indicated with an 'S'), or an even faster Intercity (IC). EuroCity (EC) trains travel between Amsterdam and Cologne making only two stops en route.

The high-speed *Thalys* train only stops at Schiphol, Den Haag and Rotterdam before going on to Antwerp, Brussels and Paris (or Luxembourg). It requires a special ticket, available at international ticket counters.

## Centraal Station

Amsterdam's main train station is Centraal Station (CS). For tickets within the Netherlands, you can purchase tickets from machines.

For international train information and reservations, visit the **NS international office** (Centraal Station; www.ns.nl; ☺ 6.30am-10.30pm) facing Track 2, to see Dutch inefficiency at its worst. At peak times (eg summer) the queues can be up to two hours. To save time, you may also purchase tickets in advance by phone ( ☎ 0900-92 92, €0.50 per min; ☺ 6am-midnight Mon-Fri, 7am-midnight Sat, Sun & holidays) and pick them up at the international ticket office.

Before you enter, you'll need to stop at the counter and specify the type of ticket you want: advance ticket, pickup of reserved ticket, or departing within an hour – you'll be given a coded number ticket and sent into the waiting room. Pickups and immediate

departures get highest priority. Don't take a number for other than what you're planning to buy, smartypants – you'll be dismissed and sent back to start all over.

There's a left-luggage desk downstairs from Track 2, ground floor near the southeastern corner of the station.

# Schedules

In stations, schedules are posted by route. Trip duration and arrival time information aren't included on the station schedules, so you'll have to ask staff.

For train and ticketing information, ring the national public-transport number, ☎ 0900-92 92 (€0.50 per min; ☺ 6am-midnight Mon-Fri, 7am-midnight Sat, Sun & holidays). The **NS Website** (www.ns.nl) has complete schedules (English info available).

# Domestic Tickets

Tickets can be bought at the window or ticketing machines. Buying a ticket on board means you'll pay almost double the normal fare.

To use ticketing machines, generally in Dutch only, check your destination on the alphabetical list of place names, enter the relevant code into the machine, then choose 1st/2nd class: *zonder/met korting* (without/with discount – discount card required) and *vandaag geldig/zonder datum* (valid today/without date). For the latter you can travel on another day but you'll have to stamp the ticket in a yellow punch gadget near the platforms. The machine will then indicate how much it wants to be fed – coins or PIN cards only, though change is given.

With a valid ticket you can break your journey along the direct route. Day return tickets are 10% to 15% cheaper than two one-ways.

If you plan to do a lot of travelling, the €49 Voordeel-Urenkaart is valid for one year and gives 40% discount on train travel weekdays after 9am, as well as weekends, public holidays and the whole months of July and August. The discount also applies to up to three people travelling with you on the same trip. As well, the card gives access to evening returns valid from 6pm (but not on Fridays) that are up to 65% cheaper than normal returns. A similar version for those aged 60 and over gives an additional seven days free travel a year. The card is available at train station counters (passport photo required, plus driving licence or passport for the 60-plus version).

# PRACTICALITIES
## ACCOMMODATION

This book breaks accommodation ('Sleeping' chapter) down by district, and within that we list mid-range lodgings and up, with a separate category for cheap sleeps. Refer to the chapter (p000) for a rundown of types of accommodation, and a list of websites that you can use for bookings.

## BUSINESS
### Business Hours

Business hours are similar to most European countries, with banks open from 9am to 4pm Monday to Friday. General office hours are 8.30am to 5pm Monday to Friday. Shops are open from 9am to 5.30pm Monday to Friday, although some shops will only open from noon on Mondays. *Koopavond* (late-night shopping) is on Thursday nights, with shops staying open until 8pm or 9pm. Within the canal belt of Amsterdam, shops are allowed to open from noon until 5pm on Sunday, although not all choose to do so. Supermarkets near the city centre stay open until 8pm.

The opening hours for government offices and museums vary considerably, but the most common day for museums to be closed is Monday.

### Business Services

Luxury hotels – and of course Schiphol airport – all offer business services; some have full-blown business centres. A cheaper option might be the first European branch of the Kinko's chain (Map pp286-7; ☎ 589 09 10; fax 589 09 20; Overtoom 62), near Leidseplein. See also Internet Cafés (p251).

For complex translations, contact **Berlitz Globalnet** (Map pp278-9; ☎ 639 14 06; fax 620 39 59; Rokin 87), though they're not cheap.

### Exhibitions & Conferences

Amsterdam is a popular place for trade fairs and conferences – it hosts more than 100 international and many hundreds of national conventions each year.

The major luxury hotels, such as NH Grand Hotel Krasnapolsky on Dam Square, the NH Barbizon Palace opposite Centraal Station or the Okura Hotel in the southern suburbs, often host modest meetings and shows, and

have facilities to handle groups of 25 to 2000 people.

Amsterdam RAI (p115) is the largest exhibition centre in the country. It's also a conference centre with 21 conference rooms. Nearby is the **World Trade Center** (Map pp274-5; ☎ 575 91 11; fax 662 72 55; Strawinskylaan 1), with conference rooms for four to 200 people, and a full range of facilities and support services

## CHILDREN

There is much to keep kids occupied in Amsterdam, but be careful of all the open water (Dutch kids all learn to swim at school). Lonely Planet's *Travel with Children* is worth reading.

In general attitudes to children are very positive, apart from some hotels with a no-children policy – check when you book. Most restaurants have high chairs and children's menus. Facilities for changing nappies, however, are limited to the big department stores, major museums and train stations and you'll pay to use them. Breast feeding is generally OK in public if done discreetly. Kids are allowed in pubs but aren't supposed to drink until they're 16.

When you take the train, children under four travel free if they don't take up a seat. Ages four to 11 pay a 'Railrunner' fare of €1 as long as an adult comes along.

Many special events and activities aimed at children take place throughout the year. Check the *Uitkrant* street paper (under 'Agenda Jeugd') or contact the Amsterdam Uitburo.

Some great places to go with the kids are the Vondelpark (p112) for picnics, a children's playground, ducks and the like or, for something a bit more wild, the Amsterdamse Bos (p115) has a huge recreational area with an animal enclosure and a children's farm. While you're in that area, the Tram Museum Amsterdam (p113) has a historic tram that goes past the Bos.

The Tropenmuseum (p108) has a separate children's section with activities focusing on exotic locations (although shows tend to be in Dutch only), while more exotica can be seen at the Artis Zoo (p102).

Being a city situated on the water, there are numerous aquatic options for little 'uns, including the hi-tech Mirandabad (p190) public pool, or a unique canal bike (p244) or cruise (p244).

Some of the more unusual things for kids to experience include Koninginnedag (Queen's

Day; p9) on 30 April – a wonderful party for kids as much as grown-ups, the NEMO science and technology centre (p105), or some *ijsschaatsen* (ice skating) at the Jaap Edenbaan (p187), in Amsterdam's southeast.

Further out of town, the family can explore the windmills at Zaanse Schans (p228).

## Babysitting

Babysitters charge between €4.50 and €6 an hour depending on the time of day, sometimes with weekend and/or hotel supplements, and you might have to pay for their taxi home if it gets late. Agencies use male and female students and you may not always be able to specify which gender. Agencies may be booked out on weekends, so book ahead. Some hotels offer a babysitting service and others may be able to advise.

Otherwise, the following agencies receive good reports:

**Oppascentrale Kriterion** (Map p285; ☎ 624 58 48; Valckenierstraat 45hs; ⏱ 4.30-8pm daily, 9am-11am Mon-Wed)

**Oppascentrale De Peuterette** (Map pp274-5; ☎ 679 67 93; Roelof Hartplein 2A; ⏱ 9am-5pm)

## CLIMATE

Amsterdam has a temperate maritime climate with cool winters and mild summers. Precipitation is spread evenly over the year, often in the form of endless drizzle, though between March and May it tends to fall in short, sharp bursts. May is a pleasant time to visit; the elms along the canals are in bloom, and everything is nice and fresh.

The sunniest months are May to August and the warmest are June to September. Summer can be humid and uncomfortable for some people, exacerbated by swarms of annoying mosquitoes; very few hotels have air conditioning. Indian summers are common in September and even into early October, which is usually an excellent time to visit. Blustery autumn storms occur in October and November.

December to February are the coldest months, with occasional slushy snow and temperatures around freezing point. Frosts usually aren't severe enough to allow skating on the canals, but when they are, the city comes alive with colourfully clad skaters. And you couldn't wish for better photo material than Amsterdam after a snowfall.

## CUSTOMS

Each person may bring up to the following quantities of each item tax free into the Netherlands:

200 cigarettes or 250g of tobacco (shag or pipe tobacco) or 100 cigarillos or 50 cigars.

1L of strong liqueur or 2L of sparkling wine or fortified wine such as sherry or port.

2L of non-sparkling wine.

50g of perfume and 0.25L of eau de toilette.

500g of coffee or 200gr of coffee extracts or coffee essences.

100g of tea or 40g tea extracts or tea essences.

## DISABLED TRAVELLERS

Travellers with a mobility problem will find Amsterdam only moderately well equipped to meet their needs. A large number of government offices and museums have lifts (elevators) and/or ramps. Many hotels, however, are in old buildings with steep stairs and no lifts; restaurants tend to be on ground floors, though 'ground' sometimes includes a few steps. The metro stations have lifts, many trains have wheelchair access, and most train stations and public buildings have toilets for the disabled.

People with a disability get discounts on public transport and, with some limitations, can park in the city free of charge. Train timetables are published in Braille.

Residents can make use of the *stadsmobiel* (citymobile), which is a fabulous taxi service for people with limited mobility, but foreigners have to use one of the commercial wheelchair-taxi services; **Garskamp** ( ☎ 633 39 43; ⏱ 7am-midnight) or **Connexxion Jonkars** ( ☎ 606 22 00; ⏱ 6am-6pm). Ring a couple of days in advance to ensure a booking at a time that suits you. One-way trips within Amsterdam cost €16 to €50 depending on the destination.

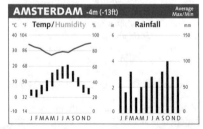

AMSTERDAM  -4m (-13ft)

| | | Temp/Humidity | | | Rainfall | |
| Average Max/Min |

# Organisations

While many Dutch organisations work with and for people with disabilities, there's no central information service. But the helpful Utrecht-based **Nederlands Instituut voor Zorg & Welzijn** (NIZW; ☎ 030-230 66 03; www.nizw.nl) has extensive information and can refer you to other organisations for more specific requests.

The Amsterdam Uitburo (see Tourist Offices, p255) provides information regarding accessible entertainment venues and museums, as does the VVV. There are also the following British and US organisations and websites:

**Royal Association for Disability & Rehabilitation** (RADAR; ☎ 020-7250 3222; www.radar.org.uk; 12 City Forum, 250 City Rd, London EC1V 8AF)

**Holiday Care** ( ☎ 01293 774 535; www.holidaycare .org.uk; 2nd fl, Imperial Buildings, Victoria Rd, Horley, Surrey RH6 7PZ)

**Society for Accessible Travel and Hospitality** (SATH; ☎ 212 447 7284; www.sath.org; 347 Fifth Ave, Suite 610, New York, NY 10016)

**Mobility International** ( ☎ 541 343 1284; www.miusa .org; PO Box 10767, Eugene, OR 97440)

**Global Access Disabled travel Network** (www.geocities .com/Paris/1502)

**Access Able** (www.access-able.com)

# DISCOUNT CARDS

Artists, journalists and museum conservators should bring some sort of professional accreditation for discounts at (some) venues. There are also other options for discounts:

**Amsterdam Pass** (24/36/72 hours €26/36/46; available at VVV offices and some hotels) Admission to most museums in town, discounts and freebies at shops, attractions and restaurants around town. Also includes a GVB transit pass.

**Museumkaart** (aka *Museumjaarkaart*; Museum Card; over/ under 26 €25/€12.50, plus €4.50 for first-time registrants) Free entry to some 400 museums all over the country for one year. Photo required.

**Hostelling International Card** Provides €2.50 per night discounts at associated youth hostels.

**International Teacher Identity Card (ITIC)** Free or discounted admission to selected museums.

**Cultureel Jongeren Paspoort** (Cultural Youth Passport; €11) Big discounts to museums and cultural events nationwide for people under 27.

**International Student Identity Card** (ISIC; www.isic.org) Some discounts on admissions, air and ferry tickets.

**Senior discounts** For people over 65 (60 for partner) covering public transport, museum entry fees, concerts and more. You could try flashing your home-country senior card but you might have to show your passport too.

# DRIVER'S LICENCE

Visitors are entitled to drive in the Netherlands on their foreign licenses for a period of up to 185 days. However, some travellers prefer the instant legitimacy of the International Drivers Licence.

If you stay in the Netherlands over 185 days per calendar year, under Dutch law you must get a Dutch licence (with some exceptions).

For all queries, ring the **National Transport Authority** ( ☎ 0900-0739, €0.10 per min).

# ELECTRICITY

The standard voltage throughout the Netherlands is 220V, 50Hz. Plugs are of the Continental two-round-pin variety. If you need an adapter, get it before you leave home because most of the ones available in the Netherlands are for locals going abroad.

# EMBASSIES & CONSULATES

## Dutch Embassies & Consulates

The following offices form part of Dutch diplomatic representation abroad:

**Australia** ( ☎ 06-273 3111) 120 Empire Circuit, Yarralumla, Canberra, ACT 2600

**Belgium** ( ☎ 02-679 17 11) ave Herrmann-Debroux 48, 1160 Brussels

**Canada** ( ☎ 613-237 50 30) Suite 2020, 350 Albert St, Ottawa, Ont K1R 1A4

**France** ( ☎ 01 40 62 33 00) 7-9 Rue Eblé, 75007 Paris

**Germany** ( ☎ 030-20 95 60) Friedrichstrasse 95, 10117 Berlin

**Ireland** ( ☎ 01 269 34 44) 160 Merrion Road, Dublin 4

**Italy** ( ☎ 06 321 58 27) Via Michele Mercati 8, 00197 Rome

**Japan** ( ☎ 03 5401 0411) Shiba-koen, 3-6-3 Minato-ku, 105 0011 Tokyo

**New Zealand** ( ☎ 04 473 8652) Investment House, cnr Ballance & Featherston Sts, Wellington

**United Kingdom** ( ☎ 020-7590 3200) 38 Hyde Park Gate, London SW7 5DP

**USA** ( ☎ 202-244 5300) 4200 Linnean Ave NW, Washington, DC 20008

Directory – Practicalities

## Embassies & Consulates in The Netherlands

Amsterdam is the country's capital, but confusingly Den Haag is the seat of government – so that's where all the embassies are:

**Australia** ( ☎ 070-310 82 00) Carnegielaan 4

**Belgium** ( ☎ 070-312 34 56) Lange Vijverberg 12

**Canada** ( ☎ 070-311 16 00) Sophialaan 7

**France** ( ☎ 070-312 58 00) Smidsplein 1

**Finland** ( ☎ 070-363 85 75) Groot Hertoginnelaan 16

**Germany** ( ☎ 070-346 97 54) Groot Hertoginnelaan 18-20

**Ireland** ( ☎ 070-363 09 93) Dr Kuijperstraat 9

**Italy** ( ☎ 070-302 10 30) Alexanderstraat 12

**Japan** ( ☎ 070-346 95 44) Tobias Asserlaan 2

**New Zealand** ( ☎ 070-346 93 24) Carnegielaan10-IV

**South Africa** ( ☎ 070-392 45 01) Wassenaarseweg 40

**Sweden** ( ☎ 070-412 02 00) Van Karnebeeklaan 6A

**United Kingdom** ( ☎ 070-427 04 27) Lange Voorhout 10

**USA** ( ☎ 070-310 92 09) Lange Voorhout 102

Consulates in Amsterdam include:

**Denmark** (Map pp274-5; ☎ 682 99 91) Radarweg 503

**France** (Map pp286-7; ☎ 530 69 69) Vijzelgracht 2

**Germany** (Map pp286-7; ☎ 673 62 45) Honthorststraat 36-8

**Italy** (Map pp286-7; ☎ 550 20 50) Vijzelstraat 79

**Norway** (Map pp286-7; ☎ 624 23 31) Keizersgracht 534-I

**Spain** (Map pp286-7; ☎ 620 38 11) Frederiksplein 34

**United Kingdom** (Map pp274-5; ☎ 676 43 43) Koningslaan 44 near the Vondelpark

**USA** (Map pp286-7; ☎ 575 53 09) Museumplein 19 near the Concertgebouw

## EMERGENCIES

In a life-threatening emergency, the national telephone number for ambulance, police and fire brigade is ☎ 112.

## GAY & LESBIAN TRAVELLERS

Without a doubt, Amsterdam is one of the gay capitals of Europe. Lesbians and gays here arguably have the greatest freedom of any city on earth, including same-sex marriage (legalised in 2001; Belgium and Canada now grant the same right).

In general, gay and lesbian venues are open and welcoming to anyone who wants to come in (and 'out'). There are more than 100 bars and nightclubs, gay hotels, bookshops, sport clubs, choirs, archives etc, and a wide range of support organisations. Important events in the gay social calendar are the gay pride festival (featuring the world's only floating gay pride parade, down the Prinsengracht, p15) and Queen's Day (p9; celebrating Dutch Queens, not Dutch queens).

See p169 for more information.

## Information
### GUIDES AND MAPS

As you would expect, there is no shortage of printed information for the gay traveller in Amsterdam:

**Bent Guide (Pink Point)** Published in English, updated at least annually, full of insider info on all facets of gay life.

**Dykes below Sealevel (Xantippe)** In-the-know guide to lesbian life (Dutch with English translation).

**Gaymap Amsterdam** and **Gay News Amsterdam** Both available for free around town.

### INTERNET SITES

Some relevant internet sites:

**www.cocamsterdam.nl**

**www.gayamsterdamlinks.nl**

**www.gay.nl** Directory to pretty much anything in town. It's in Dutch only but you can figure it out.

**www.wild4women.nl** Lesbian dance and club nights.

### BOOKSTORES & INFO POINTS

**Intermale** (p196)

**Pink Point** (aka Pink Point of Presence or PPP, p203)

**Vrolijk** (p199)

**Vrouwen in Druk** (p207)

The local gay radio station MVS broadcasts 6pm to 8pm Monday to Thursday, 6pm to 9pm Friday and 6pm to 7pm Saturday and Sunday on 106.8 FM (cable 88.1 FM), with an English programme on Sunday.

## Organisations

Always a solid source of information are the local organisations:

**COC Amsterdam** (Map p277; ☎ 623 40 79, www cocamsterdam.nl; Rozenstraat 14). Amsterdam branch of the national gay and lesbian organisation. It also offers club nights and other events.

**Gay & Lesbian Switchboard** ( ☎ 623 65 65; www .switchboard.nl) The best first source for gay and lesbian

Directory – Practicalities

information, addresses, what's on etc, 10am to 10pm daily. Also provides advice on an anonymous basis.

**IHLIA** (Internationaal Homo/Lesbisch Informatiecentrum & Archief; Map pp274-5; ☎ 606 07 12; www.ihlia.nl; Nieuwpoortkade 2A; ☺ 10am-4pm Mon-Fri, telephone inquiries 9am-5pm) The largest international gay/lesbian library collection in the Netherlands.

For HIV/AIDS Information, see Medical Services, p252.

## Safe Sex
The Dutch government and organisations such as the COC, Schorer Foundation and HIV Vereniging all do their bit to prevent the spread of STDs and HIV. Virtually all bars, bookshops and saunas that cater for gays provide safe-sex leaflets; many also sell condoms.

# HOLIDAYS
## Public Holidays
People take public holidays seriously and you won't get much done. Most museums adopt Sunday hours on the days below (except Christmas and New Year) even if they fall on a day when the place would otherwise be closed.

**Nieuwjaarsdag** (New Year's Day) Parties and fireworks galore.

**Pasen** (Easter) Goede Vrijdag (Good Friday); Eerste and Tweede Paasdag (Easter Sunday and Easter Monday).

**Koninginnedag** Queen's Day, 30 April.

**Bevrijdingsdag** Liberation Day, 5 May. This isn't a universal holiday; government workers have the day off but almost everyone else has to work.

**Hemelvaartsdag** Ascension Day.

**Eerste and Tweede Pinksterdag** Whit Sunday (Pentecost) and Whit Monday. Depending on Easter, Ascension Day and the Whit holidays usually fall between mid-May and mid-June.

**Eerste and Tweede Kerstdag** Christmas Day and Boxing Day.

Many people also treat **Remembrance Day** (4 May) as a day off.

# INTERNET ACCESS
Amsterdam led the digital revolution in Europe, so the city is as wired as many of its visitors are.

Many hotels offer Internet access, from business centres and in-room WiFi to a simple computer behind the front desk. In virtually any hotel room with a phone you will be able to hook up your laptop.

There are Web cafés dotted all over town; costs are roughly €1.50 to €2 per hour, via snappy high-speed lines.

**easyInternetCafé** (Map pp286-7; ☎ 320 62 94; Reguliersbreestraat 22; ☺ 9am-10pm) 275 flat screens and Web cams, Net phone and Microsoft applications. There are smaller outlets at Damrak 33 (Map pp278-9; same hours) and at Leidsestraat 24 (Map pp286-7; ☺ 11am-7pm Mon, 9.30am-7pm Tue-Sat, 11am-6pm Sun).

**Internet Café** (Map pp278-9; ☎ 627 10 52; Martelaarsgracht 11; ☺ 9am-1am Sun-Thu, 8am-3am Fri-Sat) 20-odd PCs a stone's throw from Centraal Station. You can surf 20 minutes for free with a drink, or just read the papers under the huge cartoon murals.

**Internet City** (Map pp278-9; ☎ 620 12 92; Nieuwendijk 76; ☺ 10am-midnight) 100-plus terminals in a bland office not far from the main coffee-shop drag. Draws backpackers and bleary-eyed party animals.

Many coffeeshops double as Web cafés. You can also surf the Web for free in the Centrale Bibliotheek (Map pp286-7; ☎ 523 09 00; Prinsengracht 587).

# LEGAL MATTERS
The Amsterdam *politie* (police) are pretty relaxed and helpful unless you do something instinctively wrong like chucking litter or smoking a joint right under their noses. They can hold offenders up to six hours for questioning (another six hours if they can't establish your identity, or 24 hours if they consider the matter serious) and do not have to grant a phone call, though they'll ring your consulate. You're presumed innocent until proven guilty.

In principle there's a 'limited' requirement for anyone over 12 years of age to carry ID. Roughly speaking this means on public transport, at soccer games, in the workplace or when opening a bank account. Foreigners should carry their passport or a photocopy of the relevant data pages; a driving licence isn't sufficient.

The **Bureau voor Rechtshulp** (Office for Legal Aid; Map pp278-9; ☎ 520 51 00; Spuistraat 10) with numerous branches, is a nonprofit organisation of law students and lawyers who give free legal advice during business hours to those who can't afford it. They deal with a wide range of issues, including immigration and residency, but will refer you if they can't deal with the matter themselves or if they think you're wealthy enough. It's best to phone first.

# MAPS

The maps in this book will probably suffice for casual touring. Lonely Planet's handy *Amsterdam City Map* is plastic-coated for the elements, and has a street index that covers the most-popular parts of the city.

Otherwise you'll find a wide variety of maps for sale at any VVV office, as well as at bookstores and newsstands.

# MEDICAL SERVICES

The Netherlands has reciprocal health arrangements with other EU countries and Australia – check with your public health insurer which form to include in your luggage (E111 for British and Irish residents, available at post offices). You still might have to pay on the spot but you'll be able to claim back home. Citizens of other countries are advised to take out travel insurance; medical or dental treatment is less expensive than in North America but still costs enough.

There are no compulsory vaccinations, but if you've just travelled through a yellow fever area you could be asked for proof that you're covered. Up-to-date tetanus, polio and diphtheria immunisations are always recommended whether you're travelling or not.

For minor health concerns, see a local *drogist* (chemist) or *apotheek* (pharmacy, to fill prescriptions). For more serious problems, go to the casualty ward of a *ziekenhuis* (hospital) or try the **Centrale Doktersdienst** (☎ 0900-503 20 42), the 24-hour central medical service that will refer you to an appropriate doctor, dentist or pharmacy.

In a life-threatening emergency, the national telephone number for ambulance, police and fire brigade is ☎ 112.

Forget about buying flu tablets and antacids at supermarkets; for anything more medicinal than toothpaste you'll have to go to a *drogist* or *apotheek*.

There are a number of hospitals that have 24-hour emergency facilities:

**Onze Lieve Vrouwe Gasthuis** (Map p285; ☎ 599 91 11) Eerste Oosterparkstraat 1 at Oosterpark near the Tropenmuseum. The closest public hospital to the centre of town.

**Sint Lucas Ziekenhuis** (Map pp274-5; ☎ 510 89 11) Jan Tooropstraat 164, in the western suburbs

**Slotervaart Ziekenhuis** (Map pp274-5; ☎ 512 41 13) Louwesweg 6, in the southwestern suburbs

**Academisch Ziekenhuis der VU** (Map pp274-5; ☎ 444 36 36) De Boelelaan 1117, Amsterdam Buitenveldert. Hospital of the VU (Vrije Universiteit, Free University).

**Academisch Medisch Centrum** (☎ 566 91 11) Meibergdreef 9, Bijlmer. Hospital of the Universiteit van Amsterdam.

**Boven-IJ Ziekenhuis** (☎ 634 63 46) Statenjachtstraat 1, Amsterdam North; bus No 34 from Centraal Station.

# STDs & HIV/AIDS

HIV/AIDS is a problem in the Netherlands but it has been contained to some extent by practical education campaigns and free needle-exchange programmes.

Free testing for sexually transmitted diseases is available at the **Municipal Medical & Health Service** (GG&GD; Map pp286-7; ☎ 555 58 22; Groenburgwal 44; ☼ 8.30am-11.30am & 1.30-4.30pm Mon-Fri, 7-9pm Tue & Thu). You must arrive early in the morning for same-day testing. If a problem is diagnosed they'll provide free treatment immediately, but blood test results take a week (they'll give you the results over the phone if you aren't returning to Amsterdam). This excellent service is available to all and it's not necessary to give an address or show identification (English is spoken). The HIV Vereiniging (see below) offers HIV testing on Friday nights (€15; ring for appointment), with results in 15 minutes.

There are bilingual telephone help lines for those seeking infomation or a friendly ear:

**AIDS Information Line** (☎ 0800-022 22 20, free call; ☼ 2-10pm Mon-Fri) Discretion guaranteed.

**HIV Vereiniging** (Map pp286-7; ☎ 616 01 60, help line ☎ 689 25 77; Eerste Helmersstraat 17; ☼ 2-10pm Mon-Fri) National organisation for the HIV positive; provides personal assistance.

**Schorer Foundation** (Map pp286-7; helpdesk ☎ 662 42 06; www.schorer.nl; PC Hooftstraat 5; ☼ 10am-4pm Mon-Fri) NGO offering lesbian and gay health-care services; HIV prevention, buddy care.

# MONEY

The Netherlands is one of the European nations to use the Euro. There are €5, €10, €20, €50, €100, €200 and €500 notes, and €0.01, €0.02, €0.05, €0.10, €0.20, €0.50, €1 and €2 coins (amounts under €1 are called cents). Euro notes are the same in all participating countries: coins have a 'European' side and a 'national' side (in the Netherlands, with an image of Queen Beatrix). All are legal tender throughout the euro area. Note that many businesses won't accept the larger notes.

To check the latest exchange rates with your home country, visit www.oanda.com.

## ATMs

Automatic teller machines can be found outside most banks, at the airport and Centraal station. Most accept credit cards like Visa and MasterCard/Eurocard, as well as cash cards that access the Cirrus and Plus networks. Logos on ATMs show what they accept; if in doubt, shove the card in and see what happens. Beware that if you're limited to a maximum withdrawal per day, the 'day' will coincide with that in your home country. Also note that using an ATM can be the cheapest way to exchange your money from home – but check with your home bank for service charges before leaving.

## Cash

Cash is still common and nothing beats it for convenience – or risk of theft/loss. Plan to pay cash for most daily expenses, but big-name hotels and car-rental companies generally insist on plastic. Keep around €50 in a safe place as an emergency stash.

## Credit Cards

All the major international cards are recognised, and most hotels, restaurants and major stores accept them – but always check first to avoid disappointment. Some hotels and shops levy a 5% surcharge (or more) on credit cards to offset the commissions charged by card providers.

To withdraw money at a bank counter instead of through an ATM, go to a GWK branch (see the following Changing Money section). You'll need to show your passport.

Report lost or stolen cards to the appropriate 24-hour number:

**American Express** ( ☎ 504 80 00 9am- 6pm Mon-Fri, ☎ 504 86 66 at other times)

**Diners Club** ( ☎ 654 55 11)

**Eurocard** and **MasterCard** have a number in Utrecht ( ☎ 030-283 55 55) but foreigners are advised to ring the emergency number in their home country to speed things up.

**Visa** ( ☎ 660 06 11)

## PIN Cards

While in Amsterdam you'll notice folks gleefully using 'PIN' cards everywhere from shops to public telephones and cigarette vending machines. The cards look like credit or bank cards with little gold-printed circuit chips on them, and they link directly to the owner's bank account. However, they won't be of much use to visitors without a Dutch bank account. Note that places that accept PIN cards don't always accept credit cards.

## Changing Money

Avoid the private exchange booths dotted around tourist areas. They're convenient and open late, but rates or commissions tend to be lousy. Banks and the Postbank (at post offices) stick to official exchange rates and charge a sensible commission, as does the **GWK** (Grenswissel-kantoren; ☎ 0900-566, €0.25 per min).

## Travellers Cheques

Banks charge a commission to cash travellers cheques (with ID such as a passport). American Express and Thomas Cook don't charge commission on their own cheques but their rates might be less favourable. Shops, restaurants and hotels always prefer cash; a few might accept travellers cheques but their rates will be anybody's guess.

The use of Eurocheques is on the decline, although you can still cash them at banks and GWKs with a guarantee card. Few shops accept them.

## NEWSPAPERS & MAGAZINES

Leading newspapers are the right-wing *De Telegraaf*, the populist *Volkskrant*, the highly regarded *NRC Handelsblad* and *Het Parool* for culture and politics. See p17 for details.

European editions of *The Economist*, *Newsweek* and *Time*, as well as most of the major international newspapers are available.

## POST

Post offices are generally open 9am to 5pm weekdays. The main **post office** (Map pp278-9; Singel 250; ☺ 9am-7pm Mon-Fri, 9am-noon Sat) is large and well equipped, but there's also a branch in the **Stopera complex** (Map pp286-7; Waterlooplein 10; ☺ 9am-6pm Mon-Fri, 10am-1.30pm Sat). For queries about postal services ring ☎ 058-233 33 33.

The standard rate for letters under 20g is €0.39 within the Netherlands, €0.55 within Europe, and €0.70 outside Europe. Unless you're sending mail within the Amsterdam region, use the slot marked Overige Postcodes (Other Postal Codes) on the red letterboxes.

## SAFETY

Although violent crime is rare (especially involving foreigners) petty theft is not unheard of. Watch out for pickpockets in crowded markets and trams, and use hotel safes where available.

Cars with foreign registration are popular targets for smash-and-grab theft. Don't leave valuable items in the car; remove registration and ID papers and the radio/stereo if possible.

If something is stolen, get a police report for insurance purposes, but don't expect the police to retrieve your property or apprehend the thief.

Bicycles are numerous and can be quite dangerous for pedestrians. When crossing the street look for speeding bikes as well as cars; *please* don't stray into a bike lane without looking both ways. Cyclists, meanwhile, should take care to lock their bikes.

### Scams

Take special care in the train stations; someone might want to help you put your bags into a luggage locker, lock the door and hand you the key. When you return you find the key fits a different locker and your stuff is gone.

Readers have written in about thieves masquerading as police in plain clothes. Usually these fraudsters address tourists in English, flash a false ID and demand to see money and credit cards for 'verification' or some other nonsense. They might also go through the victim's pockets and pretend to look for drugs. Dutch police rarely conduct this kind of search. To foil the crooks, ask to see their police identity card (note that Dutch police don't have badges as ID). Then call the real cops at ☎ 0900-88 44.

### Senior Travellers

Take heart; people up to 24 years of age are six times more likely to become a victim of crime here than those aged over 65.

### Dog Dirt

Watch your step!

## TELEPHONE

The Dutch phone network, KPN, is efficient, and prices are reasonable by European standards. Most public phones accept credit cards as well as various phonecards. Phone booths are scattered around towns and you can always call from a post office.

**National directory inquiries** ( ☎ 118 €0.60 per number, voice-activated; ☎ 0900-8008, €1.15 per number, human operator).

**International directory inquiries** ( ☎ 0900-84 18 €1.15 per number).

**Collect call** *(collect gesprek;* free call, domestic ☎ 0800-01 01, free call, international ☎ 0800-04 10).

**Operator assistance** ( ☎ 0800-04 10 free call, though you'll be charged €3.50 if you could have rung the country direct).

## Costs

All calls are time-based. The official, KPN-Telecom public phone boxes charge €0.30 per minute for all national calls, around the clock. The minimum charge from a public phone is €0.20. Phones in cafés, supermarkets and hotel lobbies often charge more.

Calling from private phones is considerably cheaper. Typically, calls within the metropolitan area cost €0.028 a minute from 8am to 7pm weekdays, €0.015 a minute in the evenings, and €0.01 a minute from midnight to 8am and from 7pm Friday to 8am Monday. There's a €0.04 connection charge. Calls outside the metropolitan area cost €0.0425 a minute between 8am and 7pm weekdays, and half that at other times.

The cost of international calls varies with the destination and changes frequently due to competition. At the time of writing, calls to Britain and the USA cost €0.05 to €0.07 a minute, and Australia €0.19. These rates jump to between €0.30 and €0.40 when ringing from a KPN phone box.

Ringing a mobile number costs €0.50 per minute from a public phone and around €0.30 from a private line.

Many public phones also accept credit cards, although cards issued in North America may not work or may require extra steps during dialling.

## Mobile Phones

The Netherlands uses GSM 900/1800, which is compatible with the rest of Europe and Australia but not with the North American

GSM 1900 (some convertible phones work in both places).

Prepaid mobile phones, which run on chips that store call credits, should be available at mobile shops for under €100. Packages with prepaid SIM cards have spread like wildfire – look out for KPN, Telfort, Orange, T-Mobile and Vodaphone with deals between €15 and €30.

## Phone Codes

To ring abroad, dial ☎ 00 followed by the country code for your target country, the area code (you usually drop the leading 0 if there is one) and the subscriber number. The country code for calling the Netherlands is ☎ 31 and the area code for Amsterdam is 020. You don't have to dial this code if you are in the area covered by it.

☎ 06 Mobile or pager numbers

☎ 0800 Free information calls

☎ 0900 Paid information calls (cost varies between €0.10 and €0.70 per minute)

## Phonecards

Most public telephones are cardphones. Cards are available at post offices, train station counters, VVV and GWK offices and tobacco shops for €5, €10 and €20. KPN's Hi card is the most common but other brands are muscling in – T-Mobile, Orange, Vodaphone, Belnet and others – with rates superior to KPN's. Note that railway stations have Telfort phone booths that require a Telfort card (available at GWK offices or ticket counters), although there should be KPN booths nearby.

Lonely Planet's eKno Communication Card is aimed specifically at independent travellers. It provides budget international calls from public as well as private phones, a range of messaging services, free email and travel information. Join online at www.ekno.lonelyplanet.com, or by phone from the Netherlands by dialling ☎ 0800 023 3971 (free call). For local calls, however, you're better off with a KPN card.

## TIPPING

Restaurant bills usually include a service charge and taxes, but a little extra is always welcome as tip. It could be something as simple as rounding up to the next euro – or up to 10% (considered quite generous).

For porters, figure €1 per bag. Figure also €1 for taxi drivers unless it's a long trip (then add more). The standard for toilet attendants is €0.50.

## TV & RADIO

Leading TV channels are the national broadcaster **NOS** (Nederlandse Omroep Stichting; www.nos.nl), RTL4 and RTL5, as well as Dutch-language MTV. Foreign channels – BBC, CNN, Germany's ARD and Belgium's Canvas are widely available. Foreign programmes are traditionally broadcast in their original version with subtitles.

Radio stations include Noordzee FM (100.7 FM), Radio 538 (102 FM) and Sky Radio (101.2 FM), plus offerings from RTL and NOS.

See p17 for details.

## TIME ZONE

Central European time zone (same as Berlin and Paris). It is one hour ahead of the UK, six hours ahead of New York, nine hours ahead of Los Angeles and eight hours behind Sydney. For Daylight Savings Time, clocks are put forward one hour at 2am on the last Sunday in March and back again at 3am on the last Sunday in October.

When telling the time, be aware that Dutch uses 'half' to indicate 'half before' the hour. If you say 'half eight' (8.30 in many forms of English), a Dutch person will take this to mean 7.30.

## TOURIST OFFICES

Tourist information is supplied by the **VVV** (Vereniging voor Vreemdelingenverkeer, Netherlands Tourism Board; www.vvv.nl), which has offices throughout the country. They all have a huge amount of information on not just their area but the rest of the country as well. However, most VVV publications cost money and there are commissions for services (eg €2 to €3 on theatre tickets).

The **VVV information number** (☎ 0900-400 4040; 🕙 9am-5pm Mon-Fri) costs €0.55 a minute; from abroad ☎ 020-551 25 25 (no extra charge). They have offices at numerous locations around the city, although the most obvious ones are by **Centraal Station** (Map pp278-9; Stationsplein 10) and **Leidseplein** (Map pp286-7; Leidseplein 1)

**Amsterdams Uitburo** (Map pp286-7; ☎ 621 13 11; www.aub.nl in Dutch; Kleine-Gartmanplantsoen 21) is a useful organisation which can provide information on anything entertainment related.

# VISAS

Tourists from nearly 60 countries – including Australia, Canada, Israel, Japan, South Korea, New Zealand, Singapore, the USA and most of Europe – need only a valid passport to visit the Netherlands for up to three months. EU nationals can enter for three months with just their national identity card.

Nationals of most other countries need a so-called Schengen visa, named after the Schengen Agreement that abolished passport controls between the EU member states (except the UK and Ireland) plus Norway and Iceland. A visa for any of these countries is valid for 90 days within a six-month period. Some countries may impose restrictions on some nationalities.

Schengen visas are issued by Dutch embassies or consulates and can take a while to process (expect up to two months). You'll need a passport valid until at least three months after your visit, and be able to prove sufficient funds for your stay. Fees vary depending on your nationality – the embassy or consulate can tell you more. Tourist visas can be extended for another three months maximum, but you'll need a good reason and the extension will only be valid for the Netherlands, not the Schengen area.

Visa extensions are handled by the **Vreemdelingenpolitie** (Aliens' Police; ☎ 559 63 00; Johan Huizingalaan 757; 🕙 8am-5pm Mon-Fri) out in the southwestern suburbs. Study visas must be applied for via your college or university in the Netherlands. For working visas, see the Work section later in this chapter. Also check www.lonelyplanet.com /destinations/europe/netherlands for up-to-date visa information.

# WOMEN TRAVELLERS

Equality has long been taken for granted, although far fewer women than men are employed full-time, and fewer still hold positions in senior management (see p14).

In terms of safety, Amsterdam is probably as secure as it gets in the major cities of Europe. There's little street harassment, even in the Red Light District, although it's best to walk with a friend to minimise unwelcome attention.

Organisations include:

**De Eerste Lijn** (The First Line; ☎ 613 02 45) Hotline for victims of sexual violence.

**Rutgershuis Amsterdam** (Map pp274-5; ☎ 616 62 22; Sarphatistraat 618) Clinic offering information and help with sexual problems and birth control, including morning-after pills.

**Het Vrouwenhuis** (Women's House; Map p285; ☎ 625 20 66; Nieuwe Herengracht 95) Centre for several women's organisations that holds workshops, exhibitions and parties. There's also a bar and a library.

# WORK

Work permits must be applied for by your employer in the Netherlands; in general, the employer must prove that the position cannot be filled by someone from within the EU before offering it to a non-EU citizen. Nationals from many countries must apply for a Temporary Entry Permit (MVV, or *Machtiging tot Voorlopig Verblijf*). Citizens of EU countries as well as Australia, Canada, Iceland, Japan, Monaco, New Zealand, Norway, Switzerland and the USA are exempt.

You'll need to apply for temporary residence before an employer can ask for your work permit. The process should take five weeks and cost €430; contact the Dutch embassy or consulate in your home country.

In the Netherlands, residence permits are issued by the **Immigratie en Naturalisatiedienst** ( ☎ 070-370 35 55; www.ind.nl; Postbus 30125, 2500 GC Den Haag). For details of work permits, contact the **CWI** (Employment Services Authority; ☎ 079-371 29 03; www.cwinet.nl; Box 195, 2700 AD Zoetermeer). The CWI also runs a bilingual website with up-to-date job offers (www.werk.nl).

The minimum adult wage is about €1250 a month after tax.

# Language

# Language

It's true – anyone can speak another language. Don't worry if you haven't studied languages before or that you studied a language at school for years and can't remember any of it. It doesn't even matter if you failed English grammar. After all, that's never affected your ability to speak English! And this is the key to picking up a language in another country. You just need to start speaking.

Learn a few key phrases before you go. Write them on pieces of paper and stick them on the fridge, by the bed or even on the computer – anywhere that you'll see them often.

You'll find that locals appreciate travellers trying their language, no matter how muddled you may think you sound. So don't just stand there, say something! If you want to learn more Dutch than we've included here, pick up a copy of Lonely Planet's user-friendly *Europe phrasebook*, which also includes many of Europe's other languages.

## SOCIAL
## Meeting People
Hello.
Dag/Hallo.
Goodbye.
Dag.
Please.
Alstublieft/Alsjeblieft. (pol/inf)
Thank you.
Dank u/je (wel). (pol/inf)
Thank you very much.
Hartelijk bedankt.
Yes/No.
Ja/Nee.
Do you speak English?
Spreekt u/Spreek je Engels? (pol/inf)
Do you understand (me)?
Begrijpt u/Begrijp je (me)? (pol/inf)
Yes, I understand.
Ja, ik begrijp het.
No, I don't understand.
Nee, ik begrijp het niet.

Could you please ...?
Kunt u ... alstublieft?
  repeat that     dat herhalen
  speak more slowly  trager spreken
    slowly
  write it down    dat opschrijven

## Going Out
What's on ...?
Wat is er ... te doen?
  locally        hier
  this weekend    dit weekend

| | |
|---|---|
| today | vandaag |
| tonight | vanavond |

Where are the ...?
Waar zijn de ...
| | |
|---|---|
|   clubs | (nacht)clubs |
|   gay venues | gay clubs en cafés |
|   places to eat | eetgelegenheden/ |
| |   restaurants |
|   pubs | cafés/kroegen |

Is there a local entertainment guide?
Heeft u een plaatselijke uitgaansgids?

## PRACTICAL
## Question Words
| | |
|---|---|
| Who? | Wie? |
| What? | Wat? |
| When? | Wanneer? |
| Where? | Waar? |
| How? | Hoe? |

## Numbers & Amounts
| | |
|---|---|
| 1 | één |
| 2 | twee |
| 3 | drie |
| 4 | vier |
| 5 | vijf |
| 6 | zes |
| 7 | zeven |
| 8 | acht |
| 9 | negen |
| 10 | tien |
| 11 | elf |
| 12 | twaalf |

| 13 | dertien |
| 14 | veertien |
| 15 | vijftien |
| 16 | zestien |
| 17 | zeventien |
| 18 | achttien |
| 19 | negentien |
| 20 | twintig |
| 21 | eenentwintig |
| 22 | tweeëntwintig |
| 30 | dertig |
| 40 | veertig |
| 50 | vijftig |
| 60 | zestig |
| 70 | zeventig |
| 80 | tachtig |
| 90 | negentig |
| 100 | honderd |
| 1000 | duizend |
| 2000 | tweeduizend |

## Days

| Monday | maandag |
| Tuesday | dinsdag |
| Wednesday | woensdag |
| Thursday | donderdag |
| Friday | vrijdag |
| Saturday | zaterdag |
| Sunday | zondag |

## Banking

I'd like to ...
Ik wil graag ...

| cash a cheque | een cheque wisselen |
| change money | geld/cash wisselen |
| change some travellers cheques | (een paar) reischeques wisselen |

Where's the nearest ...?
Waar is ...?

| automatic teller machine | de dichtsbijzijnde geldautomaat |
| foreign exchange office | het dichtsbijzijnde wisselkantoor |

## Post

Where is the post office?
Waar is het postkantoor?

I want to send a ...
Ik wil een ... versturen.

| fax | fax |
| parcel | pakket |
| postcard | briefkaart |

I want to buy ...
Ik wil een ... kopen.

| an aerogram | luchtpostblad/ aerogram |
| an envelope | envelop |
| a stamp | postzegel |

## Phone & Mobile Phones

I want to buy a phone card.
Ik wil een telefoonkaart kopen.

I want to make ...
Ik wil ...

| a call (to ... ) | telefoneren (naar ... ) |
| reverse-charge/ collect call | voor rekening van de opgeroepene telefoneren |

Where can I find a/an ...?
Waar vind ik een ...?
I'd like a/an ...
Ik wil graag een ...

| adaptor plug | adaptor plug |
| charger for my phone | lader voor mijn telefoon |
| (rechargeable) battery for my phone | (herlaadbare) batterij voor mijn telefoon |
| mobile/cell phone for hire | GSM (telefoon) huren |
| prepaid mobile/ cell phone | voorafbetaalde GSM (telefoon) |
| SIM card for your network | SIM-kaart voor uw netwerk |

## Internet

Where's the local Internet café?
Waar is het plaatselijke internetcafé?

I'd like to ...
Ik wil graag ...

| check my email | mijn email checken |
| get online | op het net gaan |

## Transport

What time does the ... leave?
Hoe laat vertrekt ...?

| bus | de bus |
| ferry | de veerboot/ferry |
| plane | het vliegtuig |
| train | de trein |

What time's the ... bus?
Hoe laat is de ... bus?

| first | eerste |

| last | laatste |
| next | volgende |

Are you free? (taxi)
Bent u vrij?
Please put the meter on.
Gebruik de meter alstublieft.
How much is it to ...?
Hoeveel kost het naar ...?
Please take me to (this address).
Breng mij alstublieft naar (dit address).

## FOOD

*For more detailed information on food and dining out, see the Eating chapter, pp129-52.*

| breakfast | ontbijt |
| lunch | lunch/middageten |
| dinner | diner/avondeten |
| snack | snack |
| eat | eten |
| drink | drinken |

Can you recommend a ...
Kunt u een ... aanbevelen? (pol)
Kan je een ... aanbevelen? (inf)

| bar/pub | bar/café |
| café | café/koffiehuis |
| coffee shop | koffieshop (note: a café where legal soft drugs are also sold) |
| restaurant | restaurant |

## EMERGENCIES

It's an emergency!
Dit is een noodgeval!
Could you please help me/us?
Kunt u me/ons alstublieft helpen?
Call the police/a doctor/an ambulance!
Haal de politie/een dokter/een ziekenwagen!
Where's the police station?
Waar is het politiebureau?

## HEALTH

Where's the nearest ...?
Waar is de dichtsbijzijnde ...?

| chemist (night) | apotheek (met nacht-dienst) |
| dentist | tandarts |
| doctor | dokter |
| hospital | ziekenhuis |

I need a doctor (who speaks English).
Ik heb een dokter nodig (die Engels spreekt).

## Symptoms

I have (a) ...
Ik heb ...

| diarrhoea | diarree |
| fever | koorts |
| headache | hoofdpijn |
| pain | pijn |

## Glossary

**amsterdammertje** – phallic-shaped posts, about knee-high, lining streets of inner Amsterdam
**ansichtkaart** – postcard
**apotheek** – chemist/pharmacy
**benzine** – petrol/gasoline
**bevrijding** – liberation
**bezet** – occupied
**bezoeker** – visitor
**bibliotheek** – library
**borrel(tje)** – general term for a strong alcoholic drink, spirit
**bos** – woods, forest
**boterham** – sandwich
**botter** – type of 19th-century fishing boat
**brandweer** – fire brigade/department
**broodje** – breadroll (with filling)
**bruin café** – brown café; traditional Dutch pub
**buurt** – neighbourhood
**café** – pub, bar; also known as *kroeg*

**coffeeshop** (also spelt *koffieshop* in Dutch) – café authorised to sell cannabis
**CS** – Centraal Station
**dagschotel** – daily special in restaurants
**douche** – shower
**drop** – salted or sweet liquorice
**eetcafé** – cafés serving meals
**fiets** – bicycle
**fietsenstalling** – secure bicycle storage
**fietspad** – bicycle path
**gasthuis** – hospice, hospital (old)
**gemeente** – municipal, municipality
**gevel** – gable, façade
**gezellig** – convivial, cosy
**GG&GD** – Municipal Medical & Health Service
**GVB** – Gemeentevervoerbedrijf (Amsterdam municipal transport authority)
**GWK** – Grenswisselkantoor; official money exchange offices
**hal** – hall, entrance hall

Language

**haven** – port
**herberg** – hostel
**hervormd** – reformed (as in church)
**hof** – courtyard
**hofje** – almshouse or series of buildings around a small courtyard, also known as Begijnhof
**hoofd** – main

**jacht** – yacht
**jenever** – Dutch gin; also spelled g*enever*

**kaas** – cheese
**kantoor** – office
**kassa** – cashier, check-out
**koffiehuis** – espresso bar (as distinct from a *coffeeshop*)
**klompen** – clogs
**klooster** – cloister, religious house
**koningin** – queen
**koninklijk** – royal
**korfbal** – a cross between netball, volleyball and basketball
**krakers** – squatters
**kunst** – art
**kwartier** – quarter

**loodvrij** – unleaded petrol/gasoline
**luchthaven** – airport

**markt** – town square
**meer** – lake
**molen** – windmill

**NS** – Nederlandse Spoorwegen; national railway company

**paleis** – palace
**polder** – area of drained land
**postbus** – post office box
**postzegel** – postage stamp

**raam** – window
**Randstad** – literally 'rim-city'; the urban agglomeration including Amsterdam, Utrecht, Rotterdam and Den Haag
**regen** – rain
**Rijk, het** – State, the

**rondleiding** – guided tour

**schaap** – sheep
**scheepvaart** – shipping
**schilder** – artist, painter
**schouwburg** – theatre
**schuilkerk** – clandestine church
**sluis** – lock (for boats/ships)
**spionnetje** – outside mirror allowing a house occupant to see who's at the door downstairs
**spoor** – platform (in train station)
**stadhouder** – stadholder, or chief magistrate
**stadhuis** – town hall
**stedelijk** – civic, municipal
**stichting** – foundation, institute
**strand** – beach
**strippenkaart** – punchable multi-ticket used on public transport

**treintaxi** – taxi especially for train passengers
**tuin** – garden
**tulp** – tulip

**veer/veerboot** – ferry
**verzet** – resistance
**Vlaams** – Flemish
**voorlichting** – information
**VVV** – tourist office

**waag** – old weigh house
**wadlopen** – mud-walking
**wasserette/wassalon** – laundrette
**weeshuis** – orphanage
**werf** – wharf, shipyard
**wielklem** – wheel clamp attached to illegally parked vehicles
**windmolen** – windmill
**winkel** – shop

**zaal** – hall
**zee** – sea
**ziekenhuis** – hospital

# Behind the Scenes

## THE LONELY PLANET STORY

The story begins with a classic travel adventure: Tony and Maureen Wheeler's 1972 journey across Europe and Asia to Australia. There was no useful information about the overland trail then, so Tony and Maureen published the first Lonely Planet guidebook to meet a growing need.

From a kitchen table, Lonely Planet has grown to become the largest independent travel publisher in the world, with offices in Melbourne (Australia), Oakland (USA), London (UK) and Paris (France).

Today Lonely Planet guidebooks cover the globe. There is an ever-growing list of books and information in a variety of media. Some things haven't changed. The main aim is still to make it possible for adventurous travellers to get out there – to explore and better understand the world.

At Lonely Planet we believe travellers can make a positive contribution to the countries they visit – if they respect their host communities and spend their money wisely.

## THIS BOOK

This edition was written by Andrew Bender. The previous (3rd) and 2nd editions were written by Rob van Driesum and Nikki Hall. The 1st edition was written by Rob van Driesum. The guide was commissioned in Lonely Planet's London office, and produced by:

**Commissioning Editors** Judith Bambe, Heather Dickson & Tim Ryder
**Coordinating Editor** Craig Kilburn
**Coordinating Cartographer** Chris Thomas
**Coordinating Layout Designer** Indra Kilfoyle
**Editors** Melanie Dankel, Cherry Prior, Victoria Harrison, Stephanie Pearson, Pete Cruttenden
**Cartographers** Csanad Csutoros
**Layout Designers** Laura Jane, Andrew Ostroff, Tamsin Wilson, Sally Darmody
**Cover Designer** Annika Roojun
**Series Designer** Nic Lehman
**Series Design Concept** Nic Lehman & Andrew Weatherill
**Layout Manager** Adriana Mammarella
**Managing Cartographer** Mark Griffiths
**Mapping Development** Paul Piaia
**Managing Editor** Bruce Evans
**Project Manager** Andrew Weatherill
**Language Editors** Quentin Frayne & Annelies Mertens
**Regional Publishing Manager** Katrina Browning
**Series Publishing Manager** Gabrielle Green
**Series Development Team** Jenny Blake, Anna Bolger, Fiona Christie, Kate Cody, Erin Corrigan, Janine Eberle, Simone Egger, James Ellis, Nadine Fogale, Roz Hopkins, Dave McClymont, Leonie Mugavin, Rachel Peart, Ed Pickard, Michele Posner, Howard Ralley & Dani Valent
**Thanks to** Danielle North, Eoin Dunlevy & Darren O'Connell

**Cover photographs** by Lonely Planet Images: Treated and untreated clogs, Jon Davison (top); cyclist in action, Martin Moos (bottom); residential architecture, Richard Nebeský (back).

**Internal photographs** by Lonely Planet Images and Richard Nebeský except for the following: p74 (#2) Christian Aslund; p71 (#1) Mark Daffey; p178 (#4) Leanne Logan; p234 Chris Mellor; p2 (#2 & 4), p27, p39, p40, p50, p59, p67 (#2 & 4), p68 (#1), p69 (#1), p70 (#2 & 3), p 71 (#2), p73 (#2 & 3), p74 (#1), p95, p98, p102, p116, p171 (#3), p173 (#1), p174 (#1 & 4), p176 (#2 & 3), p177 (#1, 2 & 3), p201, p207 Martin Moos; p178 (#3) Glenn van der Knijff; p2 (#3) Wayne Walton; p227 Zaw Yu. All images are the copyright of the photographers unless otherwise indicated. Many of the images in this guide are available for licensing from Lonely Planet Images: www.lonelyplanetimages.com.

## THANKS
### ANDREW BENDER

I was treated with *gezelligheid* even before I left the States. Jelte Bekker opened the door in Los Angeles, Barbara Veldkamp at the Netherlands Tourist Office in New York held it open, and Els Wamsteeker, Constant Broeren and Rob Gerritsen at the Amsterdam Tourist Board ushered me in after I arrived. Old friends (Alexandra and Piet-Hein Heemskerk, Andreas Teyema, Kevin Ingersent, Greg Pettigrew, Nicholas Caron and Rob Nicholson) blended with new friends (Erik Kouwenhoven, Gary Feingold, Dennis May, Steve Schneider, Jasper Jansen, Neil Finaughty and Nathalie Bloemkolk) to offer opinions and help me get my mind off my 14-hour days. Nienke Trap and Gavin Arm provided the home (and the Gazelle) – both indispensible.

In house, thanks to Tim Ryder, Judith Bamber, Heather Dickson, Craig Kilburn, Mark Griffiths and Andrew Weatherill for all their help and understanding.

Finally, a bottomless thank you to Jeremy Gray, inveterate travelling companion, international man of mystery and all-round great guy.

## OUR READERS

Many thanks to the travellers who used the last edition and wrote to us with helpful hints, useful advice and interesting anecdotes. Your names follow:

Marlies Aanhaanen, Nick Adlam, Amie Albrecht, Cynthia Ang, Elizabeth Arnstein, Renee Banky, Heidi Bardsley, Kate Barfield, Ivan Bartal, Wes Beard, Rogier Beekman, Tony Bellette, Barb Bellinger, Walt Bilofsky, Andy Blackett, Trinka Brine, George Aaron Broadwell, Carol Brown, Hanna Bruin, Craig Bryant, Jeroen Buter, Natasha Cabrera, Robert Caden, Maurice Carboeux, Carolyn Castiglia, Yau-Man Cheng, Penelope Collins, Paul Conway, Brenda Cooke, Erwin Coombs, Nathan Coombs,

Anne M. Core, Nicole Coulom, Martin Croker, Ricardo Cuan, Frans & Mei-lan de Lange-Wang, Shane de Malmanche, Dan De Voogd, Shane Demalmanche, Steve Dougherty, Sam Durkin, Jutta Eberlin, Bronwyn Edwards, Johnathan Farley, Amanda Feeney, Tyler Flood, Fayette Fox, Agnes Frank, Peter Franzese, Angel Gambrel, Eveline Gebhardt, John & Betty Geddes, Periklis Georgiadis, Bart Giepmans, John Goss, John Graven, Beth Gray, Joe Green, Dan Greenberg, Marilena Hadjilogiou, Mariska Hansen, Donald Hatch, Edward Haughney, Linda Hendry, Lisa Herb, Henk Hiddinga, Helen Hols, Peter Hopcroft, Amy & Birger Horst, R Jackson, Marco Jacobs, Milla Jansen, Tushar Jiwarajka, Eric Johnson, Steven Johnson, Miles Johnston, Oliver Johnston, Martin Jonsson, Sandra Kastermans, Kim King, Dorothy Koenig, Mark Kohler, Minette Korterink, Kurt Kron, Nicole Kroon, Klaas & Lysette Lebbing, Ankie Lenders, Michael Lin, Barbara Lopes-Cardozo, Stephanie Ludmer, Nick Lux, Marsha Maarschalkerweerd, Antti Maattanen, Diana Maestre, Paul McKnight, Lucas Meijknecht, Kees Meijll, Constance Messer, Bartlett Miller, Ming Ming Teh, Heather Monell, Rebekah Moore, Jim Moss, Marcus Muhlethaler, Samantha Nelson, Henrik Skov Nielsen, William Noble, Ricardo Olaeta, Min Tzy Ong, Aaron Osterby, Jill Pearson, Valentina M Pennazio, Peter J Perkins, Brian Perrett, Gemma Phillips, John Pilgrim, Tony & Jill Porco, Tony & Jill at Gallandet University Press Porco, Adrian Pritchard, Jan Propper, Francesco Randisi, Neil Rawlings, Jonathan Rebholz, Kurt Rebry, Maurits Renes, Mary Richards, Paul Roos, Jeffrey Ian Ross, Theo Ruigrok, Niels Sadler, Monique Samsen, Christopher Schrader, Brett Shackelford, Mary Sheargold, Kim Shrosbree, Susan Shweisky, Don Simpson, Anneke Sips, Hazel Smith, K Smith-Jones, Don & Phyllis Snyder, Jaime Stein, Annie Stolk, Christina Strauch, Chris Sturdy, Brigitte Sucre, Victoria Svahn, Terence Tam, Anouchka-Virginie Thouvenot, Janneke T Tinga, Robert Tissing, Jens Tobiska, Erwin van Dam, Marlies van den Nieuwendijk, Arthur van der Mast, Chris van der Starre, Erwin van Engelen, Sofie van Hapert, Han van Kasteren, Jacqueline van Klaveren, Irene Van Seggelen, Nathalie van Spaendonck, Frank van Wagtendonk, Ron Vermeulen, Thomas Von Hahn, R Vos, Fons Vrouenraths, Vera Wellner, Astrid Wevers, Rob Wheaton, Vincent Wiers, Jan Williamson, Steve & Judith Willis, Fiona Wilson, Andrew Woolf, Maryam Yahyavi

# SEND US YOUR FEEDBACK

We love to hear from travellers – your comments keep us on our toes and help make our books better. Our well-travelled team reads every word on what you loved or loathed about this book. Although we cannot reply individually to postal submissions, we always guarantee that your feedback goes straight to the appropriate authors, in time for the next edition. Each person who sends us information is thanked in the next edition – and the most useful submissions are rewarded with a free book.

To send us your updates – and find out about LP events, newsletters and travel news – visit our award-winning website: www.lonelyplanet.com.

Note: We may edit, reproduce and incorporate your comments in Lonely Planet products such as guidebooks, websites and digital products, so let us know if you don't want your comments reproduced or your name acknowledged. For a copy of our privacy policy visit www.lonelyplanet.com/privacy.

# Notes

# Notes

# Index

See also separate indexes for Eating (p269), Entertainment (p270), Shopping (p271) and Sleeping (p272).

Index

271

**000** map pages
**000** photographs

## LEGEND

### ROUTES

| | |
|---|---|
| Tollway | One Way Street |
| Freeway | Unsealed Road |
| Primary Road | Mall/Steps |
| Secondary Road | Tunnel |
| Tertiary Road | Walking Tour |
| Lane | Walking Path |

### TRANSPORT

| | |
|---|---|
| Ferry | Rail |
| Monorail | Rail (Underground) |
| Bus Route | Light Rail |

### HYDROGRAPHY

| | |
|---|---|
| River, Creek | Canal |
| Intermittent River | Water |

### AREA FEATURES

| | |
|---|---|
| Airport | Cemetery, Christian |
| Area of Interest | Land |
| Beach | Mall |
| Building, Featured | Market |
| Building, Information | Park |
| Building, Other | Sports |
| Building, Transport | Urban |

### SYMBOLS

| SIGHTS/ACTIVITIES | EATING | INFORMATION |
|---|---|---|
| Beach | Eating | Bank, ATM |
| Buddhist | **DRINKING** | Embassy/Consulate |
| Castle, Fortress | Drinking | Hospital, Medical |
| Christian | Café | Information |
| Hindu | **ENTERTAINMENT** | Internet Facilities |
| Islamic | Entertainment | Parking Area |
| Jewish | **SHOPPING** | Petrol Station |
| Monument | Shopping | Police Station |
| Museum, Gallery | **SLEEPING** | Post Office, GPO |
| Picnic Area | Sleeping | Telephone |
| Point of Interest | Camping | Toilets |
| Ruin | **TRANSPORT** | **GEOGRAPHIC** |
| Shinto | Airport, Airfield | Lighthouse |
| Sikh | Bus Station | Lookout |
| Skiing | Cycling, Bicycle Path | Mountain |
| Winery, Vineyard | General Transport | National Park |
| Zoo, Bird Sanctuary | Taxi Rank | Waterfall |

*NOTE: Not all symbols displayed above appear in this guide.*

# Map Section

**A** · **B** · **C** · **D**

**WESTPOORT**

**1**

Noordzeeweg
To IJmuiden
Australiëhavenweg

Basisweg

Einsteinweg

Nieuwe Hemweg

Isolatorweg

Transformatorweg

Spaarndammerstraat
5

Tasma

**2**

Haarlemmerweg
To Haarlem

Abram Kuyperlaan

Haarlemmerweg

Sloterdijk
Station Sloterdijk
Volkstuinenpark Sloterdijkermeer

**WESTERGASFABRIEK**

21 18
Westerpark
46

**SLOTERDIJK**
74
Haarlemmerweg

59
55
Westerg

**GEUZENVELD**

Eendrachtspark

Burgemeester de Vlugtlaan
Gerbrandy Park

Burgemeester Roëlistr

Burgemeester Roëlistraat

Jan van Galenstr
Station De Vlugtlaan
Bos En Lommer Weg

Erasmuspark

**BOS EN LOMMER**

41
45

Bos en Lommerweg

See Jordaan Map (p

**STAATSLIEDEN/
FREDERIK HENDRIKBUUR**

Jan van Galenstr

**JORD**

**SLOTERMEER**

Jan van Galenstr

Jachthaven Sloterplas
34

Jan van Galenstr
25

78

Hoofdweg

De Clercqstr

**OUD WEST**

Rozen

**DE BAARSJES**

**3**

Sloterpark

Sloterplas

Sloterpark

President Allendelaan

Rembrandtpark

**OVERTOOMSE VELD**

Postjesweg

See Southern Canal & Old South Map (pp286–7)

**OUD WEST**

Overtoom
50
71
1

Vondelpark

**OUD**

**OSDORP**

Osdorperban

Baden Powellweg

Meer en Vaart

Louis Davidsstr

Cornelis Lelylaan
Station Lelylaan
Lelylaan

**SLOTERVAART**

Rembrandtpark

Hoofdweg

Einsteinweg

Overtoom
10

79

Vondelpark

Cornelis Krusemanstraat
75

De Lairessestraat
63
82

66

**NIEUW ZUID**

**4**

Plesmanlaan
77

39

Plesmanlaan

Johan Huizingalaan

Heemstedestraat

**OVERTOOMSE VELD**

Aalsmeerweg

Amstelveenseweg

Haarlemmermeer Station
37

Stadionweg

Parnassusweg

67

**SLOTEN**

**BADHOEVENDORP**

Langsom

Openbare Golfbaan Sloten

Henk Sneevlietweg

Sportpark

29
81

Beatrix

**5**

Nieuwe Haagseweg

Oude Haagseweg

To Haarlem

Ringweg Zuid

Museum Tram Line

80

42

**A'dam Zuid/WT**

**NIEUWEMEER**

**BADHOEVEDORP**

HET NIEUWE MEER

Amstelveenseweg

Buitenveldertselaan

VU
40

A.J. Ernststr

Van Nijenrode

**BUITENVELDE**

**6**

To Leiden & The Hague

Schiphol Airport

Bosmuseum

Openlucht Theater
53

Amsterdamse Bos

35

2

22 To Camping Het Amsterdamse Bos

To CoBrA Museum

van Boshuizenstr
Uilenstede

31
Wagenaarstadion

**AMSTELVEEN**

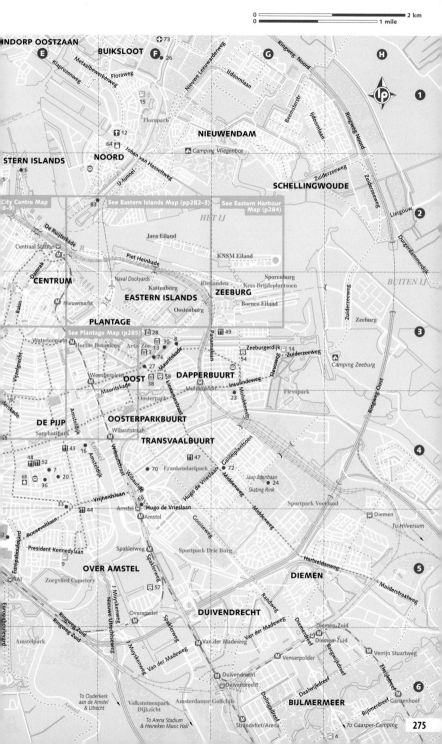

# GREATER AMSTERDAM (pp274–5)

| 0 | | | 200 m |
|---|---|---|---|
| 0 | | | 0.1 miles |

JORDAAN

OUD WEST

See City Centre Map (pp278–9)

HET IJ

JORDAAN

See Eastern Islands Map (pp282-3)

See Jordaan Map (p27

Prins Hendri

Prins Hendrikkade

Central Station

Centraal Station

Stationsplein

Open Havenfront

De Ruijterkade

Prins Hendrikkade

Multi-Jewel
Bicycle Garage

Nieuwendijk

Martelaarsg

Haarlemmerdijk

De Ruijterkade

Westerdokskade

Nieuwe Westerdokstraat

Droogbak

Haarlemmer Houttuinen

Buiten Brouwerstr

Haarlemmerstraat

Binnen Wieringerstraat

Binnen Wieringerstraat

Haarlemmerstraat

Herenmarkt

Binnen Brouwerstr

Herengracht

Roomolenstr

Singel

Langestraat

Herengracht

Keizersgracht

Keizersgracht

Herenstraat

Herenstraat

Kattengat

Spuistraat

Brouwersgracht

Kore Prinsengracht

Korte Prinsengracht

Prinsengracht

Prinsengracht

Brouwersgracht

Haarlemmerplein

Ketelmakerstr

H Jonkerplein

Haarlemmerdijk

Binnen Oranjestraat

Vinkenstraat

Willemstraat

Lindengracht

Lindenstraat

Lindengracht

Noordermarkt

Noorderkerkstraat

Prinsenstraat

Brouwersgracht

Goudsbloemstraat

Binnen Brouwersstraat

Nieuwstraat

Antilliesstraat

Tuinstraat

Westerstraat

278

0       200 m
0       0.1 mi

See Southern Canal Belt & Old South Map (pp286–7)

279

# CITY CENTRE (pp278–9)

A    B    C    D

1

17

See City Centre Map (pp278–9)

Bulksloterweg

Adelaarsweg

Meeuwenlaan

Gedempte Insteekhaven

Ferry to Centraal Station
Adelaarswegveer

32.39

IJ-Tunnel

8
7

2

6

5

4

3

De Ruijterkade

Future home of IJsbreker
and Bimhuis (est'd early 2005).
This building hasn't opened yet.
24

23

Centraal
Station

22

3

De Ruijterkade

Piet Heinkade

39.43

Prins Hendrikkade

Oosterdokskade

22

Oosterdokskade

Stedelijk located
here temporarily
8

Dijksgracht

IJ-Tunnel

4

Kromme Waal

20

15

Oosterdok

eldersst

Waalt

P

GVB Head Office

7

Prins Hendrikkade

5

Naval Dockyards

18

Lastageweg

Binnenkant

22.32.39

Waalseilandsgracht

25

Nieuwe Jonkerstr

10

Nieuwe Riddentr

Oude Waal

5

Montelbaanstr

Oude Schans

Rechtboomssloot

Oude Schans

3

Korte Koningsstraat

Oude Schans

Peperstraat

1

4

Korte Keizerstraat

14

Rapenburg

Kattenburgergracht

Nieuwe Vaart

Oude Schans

2

Jodenbreestraat

Nieuwe Uilenburgerstraat

19

Uilenburgergracht

12

Kadijksplein

9

Nieuwe Vaart

11

Hoogte Kadijk

Laagte Kadijk

Mattrozenhof

Buitenkadijken

P

Jodenbreestraat

Houttuinen

Valkenburgerstraat

Anne Frankstr

See Plantage Map (p285)

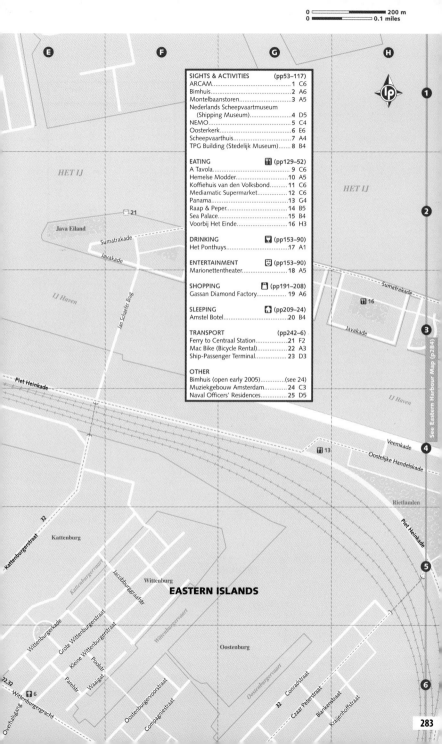

**SIGHTS & ACTIVITIES** (pp53–117)
ARCAM.................................................1 C6
Bimhuis...............................................2 A6
Montelbaanstoren................................3 A5
Nederlands Scheepvaartmuseum
  (Shipping Museum).........................4 D5
NEMO..................................................5 C4
Oosterkerk..........................................6 E6
Scheepvaarthuis..................................7 A4
TPG Building (Stedelijk Museum)......8 B4

**EATING** 🍴 (pp129–52)
A Tavola..............................................9 C6
Hemelse Modder................................10 A5
Koffiehuis van den Volksbond...........11 C6
Mediamatic Supermarket....................12 C6
Panama...............................................13 G4
Raap & Peper......................................14 B5
Sea Palace..........................................15 B4
Voorbij Het Einde...............................16 H3

**DRINKING** 🍷 (pp153–90)
Het Ponthuys......................................17 A1

**ENTERTAINMENT** 🎭 (pp153–90)
Marionettentheater.............................18 A5

**SHOPPING** 🛍 (pp191–208)
Gassan Diamond Factory....................19 A6

**SLEEPING** 🛏 (pp209–24)
Amstel Botel.......................................20 B4

**TRANSPORT** (pp242–6)
Ferry to Centraal Station.....................21 F2
Mac Bike (Bicycle Rental)...................22 A3
Ship-Passenger Terminal.....................23 D3

**OTHER**
Bimhuis (open early 2005)............(see 24)
Muziekgebouw Amsterdam................24 C3
Naval Officers' Residences................25 D5

0 ——————— 200
0 ——————— 0.1 miles

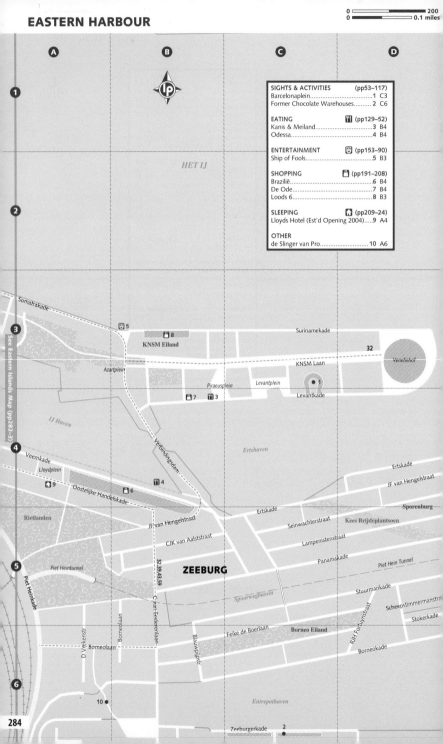

SIGHTS & ACTIVITIES (pp53–117)
Barcelonaplein.................................1 C3
Former Chocolate Warehouses..........2 C6

EATING 🍴 (pp129–52)
Kanis & Meiland.............................3 B4
Odessa.........................................4 B4

ENTERTAINMENT 🎭 (pp153–90)
Ship of Fools.................................5 B3

SHOPPING 🛍 (pp191–208)
Brazilië.........................................6 B4
De Ode.........................................7 B4
Loods 6.........................................8 B3

SLEEPING 🛏 (pp209–24)
Lloyds Hotel (Est'd Opening 2004).....9 A4

OTHER
de Slinger van Pro............................10 A6

HET IJ

Sumatrakade

Surinamekade

KNSM Eiland

Azartplein

32

Venetiëhof

KNSM Laan

Piraeusplein

Levantplein

Levantkade

See Eastern Islands Map (pp282–3)

IJ Haven

Ertshaven

Verbindingsdam

Veemkade

Lloydplein

Oostelijke Handelskade

Ertskade

Ertskade

JF van Hengelstraat

Sporenburg

Rietlanden

JF van Hengelstraat

CJK van Aalststraat

Seinwachterstraat

Kees Brijdeplantsoen

Lampenistenstraat

Panamakade

Piet Hein Tunnel

Piet Heintunnel

ZEEBURG

32,39,43,59

C Kern Eesterenlaan

Spoorwegbassin

Stuurmankade

Scheepstimmermanstr

Stokerkade

Piet Heinkade

D Vlekenstr

Borneolaan

Borneolaan

Blauwpijlstr

Feike de Boerlaan

Borneo Eiland

RJH Fortuynstraat

Borneokade

Entrepothaven

10

Zeeburgerkade

2

# PLANTAGE

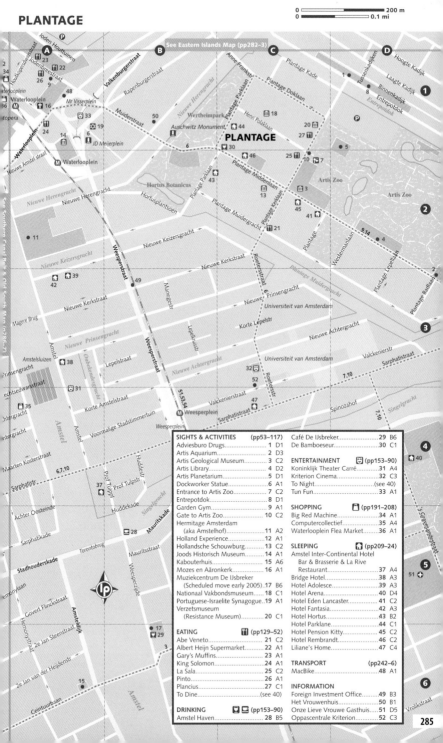

| SIGHTS & ACTIVITIES | (pp53–117) |
|---|---|
| Adviesburo Drugs | 1 D1 |
| Artis Aquarium | 2 D3 |
| Artis Geological Museum | 3 C2 |
| Artis Library | 4 D2 |
| Artis Planetarium | 5 D1 |
| Dockworker Statue | 6 A1 |
| Entrance to Artis Zoo | 7 D1 |
| Entrepotdok | 8 D1 |
| Garden Gym | 9 A1 |
| Gate to Artis Zoo | 10 C2 |
| Hermitage Amsterdam (aka Amstelhof) | 11 A2 |
| Holland Experience | 12 A1 |
| Hollandsche Schouwburg | 13 C1 |
| Joods Historisch Museum | 14 A1 |
| Kabouterhuis | 15 A6 |
| Mozes en Aäronkerk | 16 A1 |
| Muziekcentrum De IJsbreker (Scheduled move early 2005) | 17 B6 |
| Nationaal Vakbondsmuseum | 18 C1 |
| Portuguese-Israelite Synagogue | 19 A1 |
| Verzetsmuseum (Resistance Museum) | 20 C1 |

| EATING | (pp129–52) |
|---|---|
| Abe Veneto | 21 C2 |
| Albert Heijn Supermarket | 22 A1 |
| Gary's Muffins | 23 A1 |
| King Solomon | 24 A1 |
| La Sala | 25 C2 |
| Pinto | 26 A1 |
| Plancius | 27 C1 |
| To Dine | (see 40) |

| DRINKING | (pp153–90) |
|---|---|
| Amstel Haven | 28 B5 |

| Café De IJsbreker | 29 B6 |
|---|---|
| De Bamboeseur | 30 C1 |

| ENTERTAINMENT | (pp153–90) |
|---|---|
| Koninklijk Theater Carré | 31 A4 |
| Kriterion Cinema | 32 C3 |
| To Night | (see 40) |
| Tun Fun | 33 A1 |

| SHOPPING | (pp191–208) |
|---|---|
| Big Red Machine | 34 A1 |
| Computercollectief | 35 A4 |
| Waterlooplein Flea Market | 36 A1 |

| SLEEPING | (pp209–24) |
|---|---|
| Amstel Inter-Continental Hotel Bar & Brasserie & La Rive Restaurant | 37 A4 |
| Bridge Hotel | 38 A3 |
| Hotel Adolesce | 39 A3 |
| Hotel Arena | 40 D4 |
| Hotel Eden Lancaster | 41 C2 |
| Hotel Fantasia | 42 A3 |
| Hotel Hortus | 43 B2 |
| Hotel Parklane | 44 C1 |
| Hotel Pension Kitty | 45 C2 |
| Hotel Rembrandt | 46 C2 |
| Liliane's Home | 47 C4 |

| TRANSPORT | (pp242–6) |
|---|---|
| MacBike | 48 A1 |

| INFORMATION | |
|---|---|
| Foreign Investment Office | 49 B3 |
| Het Vrouwenhuis | 50 B1 |
| Onze Lieve Vrouwe Gasthuis | 51 D5 |
| Oppascentrale Kriterion | 52 C3 |

OUD WEST

A

B

See Jordaan Map (p277)

C

D

Johnny Jordaanplein

Elandsgracht

56

280

332

228

3e Looiersdwarsstraat

Zd Looiersdwarsstraat

Oude Looiersstraat

Looiersgracht

124

69

204

216 70 214

238

217

Huidens

263

215

Looiersgracht

Looiersgracht

Slingergracht

Nassaukade

Marnixstraat

Lijnbaansgracht

Runstraat

1

198

171

Kinkerstraat

J v Lennepstr

Passeerdersstraat

Circus Elleboog

Passeerdersgracht

Passeerdersgracht

119

313

224

Prinsengracht

Keizersgracht

Keizersgr

Kinkerstr

Molenpad

Leidsegracht

81

2

Jacob van Lennepstr

Bilderdijkgracht

Bilderdijkstraat

Jacob van Lennepkade

Jacob van Lennepkade

De Genestetstr

Nwe Passeerdersstr

Raamplein

Raamstraat

295

130

133

3,12

128

334

78

66

270

Jacob van Lennepkanaal

Bosboom Toussaintstr

Albedingk Thijmstraat

3e Helmersstraat

Leidsekade

Leidsegracht

Lange Leidsedwarsstraat

Korte Leidsedwarsstraat

141

31

139

231

61

1,2,5

24

157

143

164

Leidsegracht

Leidsestraat

302

2e Helmersstraat

305

Nassaukade

Marnixstraat

Lijnbaansgracht

145

193

160

154

172

62

294

159

178

331

50

OUD WEST

131

Eerste Constantijn Huygensstr

Eerste Helmersstraat

318

186

180

190

271

115

Leidseplein

188

163

299

3

322

Overtoom

42

247

205

Stadhouderskade

Singelgracht

310

128

Kleine Gartmanplantsoen

327

330

177

Lijnbaansgr

Leidsekruisstraat

Hirschpassage

123

297

296

Vondelstraat

Tesselschadestr

308

25

104

166

184

Max Euweplein

232

306

Overtoom

307

300

275

304

Zandpad

7

176

Weteringsc

Ziesenisskade

Visscherstraat

Vondelkerk

38

18

11

284

Anna v/d Vondelstr

86

Vondelpark

Vossiusstraat

Vondelpark

79

325

Stadhouder

255

251

281

Pieter Cornelisz Hooftstraat

54

288

277

van de Veldestraat

Jan Luijkenstraat

276

211

287

OUD ZUID

57

5

182

Conservatorium

Eerste Constantijn Huygensstr

van Baerlestraat

2,5

Paulus Potterstraat

37

34

Willem Sandberghplein

Honthorststraat

31

Gerard Doustraat

40

48

Albert Cuypstraat

49

77

55

60

107

Oudestraat

Museumplein

206

311

Museumplein

45

Johannes Vermeerstraat

256

Same Scale as Main Map

Inset

8

329

Jacob Obrechtstraat

van Eeghenstraat

Willemsparkweg

3,5,12

6

100

van Breestraat

Cornelis Schuytstraat

Bartstraat

106

323

Concertgebouwplein

282

Deridas Pup

Theatre

De Lairessestraat

Nicolaas Maesstraat

van Baerlestraat

0 — 200 m
0 — 0.1 miles

**E**  **F**  **G**  **H**

Roskamsteeg
Rozenboomst. Begijnenst. Waterst.
Herengracht
Wijde Heist
Heist
Spui
Spuist.
Takst.
UvA
UvA
Waterlooplein
Stopera
Turfdraagsterpad
Binnen Gasthuisst.
Binnengasthuis UvA
Staalstraat
Zwanenburgwal
Zwanenburgwal
Muntenvesburgwal
Koventecsburgwal
Geesengeest
Verversstraat
Handboogstr.
Voetboogstr.
Oude Turfmarkt
Nieuwe Doelenst.
's Gravelandse Veer
Staalkade
Spui
Ohetgeest
Kalverstraat
Klosterst.
Rokin
Nieuwe Doelenst.
Binnen Amstel
Heiligeweg
Koningsplein
Kalvertoren
Muntplein
Singel
Amstel
Amstel
Amstel
Amstel
Leidsestraat
Reguliersdwarsstraat
Vijzelstraat
Reguliersbreestraat
Bakkerstraat
Halvemaan
Balk in 't 009t
Paardenstraat
Wagenstraat
Blauwbrug
Rembrandtplein
Amstelstraat
Utrechtsestraat
Herengracht
Golden Bend
Thorbeckeplein
Herengracht
Herengracht
Keizersgracht
Kerkstraat
Keizersgracht
Keizersgracht
Kerkstraat
Prinsengracht
Nieuwe Spiegelstraat
Nieuwe Spiegelstraat
Spiegelgracht
Prinsengracht
Prinsengracht
Utrechtsedwarsstraat
Achtergracht
Amstelveld
Eerste Weteringdwarsstraat
Tweede Weteringdwarsstraat
Derde Weteringdwarsstraat
Vijzelgracht
Prinsengracht
Noorderstraat
Nieuwe Looiersstraat
Falckstraat
Frederiksplein
Reguliersgracht
Nieuwe Weteringstraat
Fokke Simonszstraat
Lijnbaansgracht
Canal Bike
Weteringschans
Weteringschans
Weteringschans
Oosteinde
Westeinde
Weteringcircuit
Den Textstraat
Nicolaas Witsenstraat
Nicolaas Witsenkade
Singelgracht
Stadhouderskade
Stadhouderskade
Hemonylaan
Nic. Berchemstr.
2e Jacob van Campenstraat
Govert Flinckstraat
Frans Halsstraat
Marie Heinekenplein
Quellijnstraat
Ferdinand Bolstraat
1e van der Helststraat
1e van der Helststraat
2e Jan van der Heydenstraat
Ruysdaelkade
Saenredamstraat
Albert Cuypmarkt
1e Sweelinckstraat
2e Steenstraat
2e Jan van der Heydenstraat
Boerenwetering
See Inset
Gerard Doustraat
Albert Cuypstraat
Govert Flinckstraat
Sarphatipark
Baerlestraat
Twarsstraat
See Plantage Map (p285)

**DE PIJP**

**1** **2** **3** **4** **5** **6**

# PUBLIC TRANSPORT